How Open is the Futu

Marleen Wynants & Jan Cornelis (Eds)

How Open is the Future?

Economic, Social & Cultural Scenarios
inspired by Free & Open-Source Software

The contents of this book do not reflect the views of the VUB, VUBPRESS or the editors, and are entirely the responsibility of the authors alone.

Cover design: Dani Elskens
Book design: Boudewijn Bardyn
Printed in Belgium by Schaubroeck, Nazareth

2005 VUB Brussels University Press
Waversesteenweg 1077, 1160 Brussels, Belgium
Fax + 32 2 6292694
e-mail: vubpress@vub.ac.be
www.vubpress.be

ISBN 90-5487-378-7
NUR 740
D / 2005 / 1885 / 01

This work is licensed under the Creative Commons Attribution-NonCommercial-NoDerivs License. To view a copy of this license, visit http://creativecommons.org/licenses/by-nc-nd/2.0/be/ or send a letter to Creative Commons, 559 Nathan Abbott Way, Stanford, California 94305, USA. There is a human-readable summary of the Legal Code (the full license) available at http://creativecommons.org/licenses/by-nc-nd/2.0/be/legalcode.nl.

Foreword & Acknowledgements

This volume offers a series of articles ranging from the origins of free and open-source software to future social, economic and cultural perspectives inspired by the free and open-source spirit. A complete version of *How Open is the Future?* is available under a Creative Commons licence at *http://crosstalks.vub.ac.be*.

How Open is the Future? is also available as printed matter, as you can experience at this moment.

The topic of free and open-source software emerged from the initiative by Professor Dirk Vermeir of the Computer Science Department of the VUB – Vrije Universiteit Brussel – to award Richard Stallman an honorary doctorate from the VUB. From then on we set out to create a neutral platform where the voices of artists, journalists, key social and economic players, policymakers and scientific researchers could mingle and reflect on a possible future and the preservation of our digital and intellectual commons.

First of all, we want to thank all the participants and speakers at the first CROSSTALKS workshop, *Windows by Day, Linux by Night*, on 11 December 2003 and all the participants at our first *Science and Industry Dinner* on 20 February 2004, in particular, guest speaker Tim O'Reilly for his talk and Richard Stallman for popping in and increasing the complexity of the discussions.

We are grateful to all who contributed to this publication and spent a considerable part of their time clearing the trajectory from the free and open-source software issue towards a future agenda for a new kind of commons in an open-minded knowledge and communication society.

Special thanks go to people who engaged in fruitful debates with us on the issue, who gave tips and comments and reviewed the texts: Jean-Claude Burgelman, Marc Nyssen, Bruno De Vuyst, Serge Gutwirth, Mirko Tobias Schäfer, Marianne Van den Boomen, Séverine Dusollier, Peter Hanappe, Bernard Rieder, Marc Nyssen, Leo Van Audenhove, Leo Van Hove, Caroline Pauwels, Bram Lievens, Jo Pierson, Jacques Vilrokx, Ilse Laurijssen, Jan Belgrado, Jean Vereecken, Frank Gielen and Frederik Questier. Many thanks go to the people who supported the CROSSTALKS events and refined their concept: Dirk Tombeur, Luc De Vuyst, Michel Flamée, Theo D'Hondt, Viviane Jonckers, Dirk Vermeir, Olga De Troyer, Koen Smets, Nadine Rons, Christ'l Vereecken, Sandra Baeyens, Mieke Gijsemans, Kris van Scharen, and Monique Peeters. Particular thanks go to Marnix Housen for his inspiring support in the end phase of the book.

We owe a lot of gratitude to Sara Engelen for her indispensable and creative dynamism.

Luc Steels was the backstage motivator and caterer of critical comments.

Furthermore we thank Veronica Kelly for enhancing this book with her wonderful and meticulous English editing, Boudewijn Bardyn for the art direction and layout, Kris van Scharen for the production and Dani Elskens for the cover design.

CROSSTALKS owes a great deal to the stimulation of the Head of the VUB Interface Cell, Sonja Haesen. Last but not least, we thank Rector Benjamin Van Camp for his continuous support and his encouraging engagement in the CROSSTALKS activities.

The Editors

Table of Contents

Foreword & Acknowledgements   5

Preface   11
    Marleen Wynants & Jan Cornelis

PART I – DRIVING FORCES: KEY PLAYERS & PROJECTS   29

Will the revolution be open-sourced?   31
    How open source travels through society
    Marianne van den Boomen & Mirko Tobias Schäfer
Free as in Freedom, *not* Gratis!   69
    An interview with Richard Stallman,
    the embodiment of the dilemma of our digital commons
    Marleen Wynants
The Open Source Paradigm Shift   85
    Tim O'Reilly
Open Courseware and Open Scientific Publications   111
    Frederik Questier & Wim Schreurs
Roots Culture - Free Software Vibrations Inna Babylon   135
    by Armin Medosch

Table of Contents

PART II – MAKING IT HAPPEN: CASE STUDIES FROM BRUSSELS, BELGIUM, EUROPE & BEYOND   165

Extremadura and the Revolution of Free Software   167
    Achieving digital literacy and modernizing the economy of one
    of the European Union's poorest regions
    Angel Vaca
Building Open Ecosystems for Collaborative Creativity   199
    Peter Hanappe
A Walk through the Music Bazaar & the Future of Music   231
    Sara Engelen
Open Source, Science and Education   275
    Marc Nyssen & Frederik Cheeseman
Open Standards Policy in Belgium   285
    Peter Strickx & Jean Jochmans

PART III - ETHICS & BOTTLENECKS   293

The Patenting of Life   295
    An interview with VUB scientist Lode Wyns about the dangers of patents in
    biotechnology and the pressing need for ethics in law
    Lode Wyns
Fostering Research, Innovation and Networking   309
    Jan Cornelis
Is Open-Sourced Biotechnology possible?   357
    Daniel de Beer
Legal Aspects of Software Protection through Patents,   375
    and the Future of Reverse Engineering
    Bruno de Vuyst & Liv Steuts

PART IV – THE FUTURE IS OPEN   393

Advancing Economic Research on the Free and Open Source Software   395
   Mode of Production
   J.-M. Dalle, P. A. David, Rishab A. Ghosh, and W.E. Steinmueller
The Future of Open Source   429
   Ilkka Tuomi
The Future of Software: Enabling the Marketplace to Decide   461
   Bradford L. Smith
Dual Licensing – A Business Model from the Second Generation of   479
   Open-Source Companies
   Kaj Arnö
Towards a EU Policy for Open-Source Software   489
   Simon Forge

ANNEXES   505

I. The GNU General Public License (GPL)- Version 2, June 1991   507
II. Building Innovation through Integration   517
   A Microsoft White Paper – July 2000

Index   527
List of Pictures   533

Preface

Marleen Wynants & Jan Cornelis

"What if Leonardo da Vinci had patented his ideas?" At first sight, the question seems a perfect metaphor for what might happen to our knowledge-based and commercially driven society if fundamental ideas are no longer a public good. Given the growing skepticism about the intrinsic value of patented technologies and copyrighted content descriptions, it could indeed seem that patents on da Vinci's ideas might have obstructed the engineering industry and most of the innovations and developments that make our society what it is today. But let's concentrate on facts, not myths: da Vinci's ideas were not public! The artist Leonardo da Vinci worked on commission throughout his life and did not publish or distribute the contents of the technological innovations in his mirror-written *codici*. The fact is that most of the notebooks remained obscure until the 19th century, and were not directly of value to the explosive development of science and technology that occurred in the 17th and 18th centuries. If some of Leonardo's ideas had been patented, they might have changed history and the engineering landscape of society in a fundamental way, just as Galileo's patent on the telescope led to enormous breakthroughs in astronomical research and its instruments. But why then did Leonardo never allow his anatomical studies to be examined during his life? Maybe the answer lies in his explicit comment on intellectual property: *"Do not teach your knowledge, and you alone will excel"*. So maybe it's not so strange after all that da Vinci's best preserved notebook, the Codex Leicester, was bought by Bill Gates in 1994 and has found a home in Seattle.

Bowling Alone?

The da Vinci case proves that the issues of creativity, invention and ownership and their potential social, economic and cultural relevance are not simple. And especially in a time of increased networking and digital collaboration, the traditional notions of property and ownership are challenged in many ways. One of the possible incentives to start reflecting on the opposing social and economic forces in our society is the Free and Open-Source Software (FOSS) movement. Most of the initial discussions were restricted to free and open versus proprietary software. Yet the interdependence of innovation and society calls for an interdisciplinary and constructive approach when exploring the processes of creating, validating and distributing. Where are the limits to owning and sharing? Where does *using* end and *abusing* start? How about ethics in politics and law? What about sharing what is yours? What about sharing what is not yours? How can we move to a more open culture and economy and yet preserve the quality and efficiency a thriving society needs? Can we learn from the perspectives and models of the open-source software industry? The following pages offer an affirmative answer to this last question.

There are different perspectives to be taken into account, in which facts and history play a fundamental role. That's why we begin our book with the driving forces, the key players and projects associated with the Free and Open-Source movement (Part I). What follows are innovative scientific experiments and some current and colorful educational, cultural and political cases (Part II). Then the focus shifts to legal and policymaking ethics and bottlenecks: where are the ethics in law-making? How to preserve the freedom of academic research (Part III)? The perspectives on the future proposed in the last part of this book go from the new challenges in the social sciences to extended outlooks and pitfalls for the open-source and the proprietary software industries (Part IV).

Leading Edges

There are two reasons why today the free and open-source software issue has become such an inspirational and powerful force: the rise of the Internet and the excesses of intellectual property. Internet technology made massive, decentralized projects possible for the first time in human history. It's a unique tool that has irreversibly changed our personal and professional communication and information research. Intellectual property, on the other hand, is a legal instrument that has become a symbol of the exact opposite of what it was developed for: the protection of the creative process. As a result, thousands of free-thinking programmers, scientists, artists, designers, engineers and scholars are daily trying to come up with new ways of creating and sharing knowledge.

The Free and Open-Source movement pushes the paradigms of ownership, copyrights and patenting around. At present there are dozens of licenses, from Stallman's General Public License to the Creative Commons ShareAlike agreement, that allow open products to exist in a proprietary world. Under these licenses, knowledge-based property becomes something to be distributed in order to create new ideas rather than protected in order to make (more) money.

Of course, the concept of free and open source is not new, and with a little effort one could go back to the ideals of the Greek philosophers and their agora where knowledge was shared and openly discussed, at least by those who were not slaves. Closer to our times, in 1905, the scientist and philosopher Rudolf Steiner formulated what he called the "Fundamental Social Law":

> The well-being of a community of people working together will be the greater, the less the individual claims for himself the proceeds of his work, i.e., the more of these proceeds he makes over to his fellow-workers, the more his own needs are satisfied, not out of his own work but out of the work done by others. (Rudolf Steiner, 1905)

In 1968 the biologist and ecologist Garrett Hardin raised the issue again in a probing way in his famous article in *Science*, "The Tragedy of the Commons":

> However, selfish households accumulate wealth from the commons by acquiring more than their fair share of the resources and paying less than their fair share of the total costs. Ultimately, as population grows and greed runs rampant, the commons collapses and ends in "the tragedy of the commons". (Garrett Hardin, Science 162:1243, 1968)

Most of the dilemmas associated with Hardin's "tragedy of the commons" can be associated with the difficulties the free and open-source software movement is facing today: balancing well-being versus wealth, fast innovation versus quality, and developing a sustainable business model versus sociability.

Maximum Openness

The creativity and enthusiasm of information technologists have changed the way in which millions of people work and communicate. Since the 1990s we have grown familiar with personal computers, software, mobile phones, global networking, the Internet, downloading games and music and lots more. The idea that software developers in many different locations and organizations were sharing code to develop and refine the software programs that enable us to use all these tools has never been headline news. Except that these whiz kids – as that's how we prefer to think of them – were in tune with a revolutionary movement called "copyleft" which was to change our views on intellectual ownership and organizing creativity more profoundly than we could ever have imagined. In this context it should not be forgotten that the movement was initiated by a small group of computer scientists who engaged in a collaborative project driven by personal motivation, a clear focus and hard concentration. The impact of and interplay with ongoing sociological, economic and cultural movements were not predictable, in the sense that the real importance of the free and open-source software movement is not only the opening up of new perspectives in information technology, but – even more – the fact that it is inextricably bound up with cultural and economic innovation and social and ethical restoration.

The story of the Free Software Movement started in the 1970s with the release of software that was NOT free. Before that time, software was not seen by the computer industry as a product that could be profitable. The industry was focused on producing and selling hardware, and the software was delivered with it, including the source code. When UNIX, the mother of all computer programs, became partly commercialized, Richard Stallman started working on GNU – a free, gratis version of UNIX accessible to everybody. Stallman initiated a great deal that was crucial for the development and breakthrough of the Internet – like Sendmail, Apache, and PERL. But for a GPL-licensed or free UNIX version, we had to wait until 1991, when a student from the university of Helsinki who didn't have enough money for an official UNIX version decided to make one himself – with a little help from the world out there...

```
Message-ID:
1991Aug25.205708.9541@klaava.helsinki.fi
From: torvalds@klaava.helsinki.fi (Linus Benedict Torvalds)
To: Newsgroups: comp.os.inix

Subject: What would you like to see most in minix?

Summary: small poll for my new operating system
Hello everybody out there using minix-I'm doing a (free)
operating system (just a hobby, won't be big and professional
like gnu) for 386 (486) AT clones. This has been brewing since
april, and is starting to get ready. I'd like any feedback on
things people like/dislike in minix, as my OS resembles it
somewhat
Any suggestions are welcome, but I won't promise I'll implement
them :-)

Linus
```

Linus Torvalds launched his project on the web and called on the international hacker community to develop the system together with him. They succeeded, and it became known by the name LINUX – or more correctly, GNU/Linux, as from the outset it was released under the GPL license. What's so amazing and inspiring about GNU/Linux is not only its success in the market but also that the true revolution is in the method.

In 1998 some people in the free-software community began using the term "open-source software – OSS" instead of "free software". The issue of whether software should be open-source is a practical question, it's about a methodology. Hence, OSS is the collective noun for all software with available source code, adaptable by all, under the limitation that the adaptations should be made available to others. Free software, on the other hand, stands for a social movement, for an ethical issue. For the open-source movement, non-free software is simply not such a good solution, while for the free-software movement, non-free software is a real social problem. In the following pages, we will use the term *open source* to indicate a collaborative methodology for producing OSS, not limited to programming only, and *free software* when referring to the societal concept of Richard Stallman.

The architecture of participation

The greatest success of open source was in fact the Internet. Software development in the 60s and 70s took place in academic, governmental (read: military) and industrial laboratories, and it was an inherent part of the research culture that people built on each other's software, modifying and exchanging it. Then came ARPAnet – the first transcontinental, high-speed computer network, launched by the U.S. Defense Advanced Research Projects Agency (DARPA). This network allowed scientists and engineers to exchange information easily and cheaply. The rise of the Internet has to be situated in the 1960s, in both the "closed" world of the Cold War and the open, decentralized world of the antiwar movement and the rise of the counterculture.

Keeping this dual heritage in mind, it is easier to understand the current controversies on whether the Internet should be "open" or "closed" and on whether the Net will foster a truly democratic dialogue or a centralized hierarchy, a new kind of "commons" or reinforced capitalism, or a mixture of both.

The collaborative spirit of the Internet has spread and reinforced open communication and community behaviour in other disciplines, from the hard sciences to the liberal arts.

The Human Genome project, for example, uses open-source methods to advance the state of knowledge in genomics and bioinformatics. In the US, NASA has adopted open-source principles as part of its Mars mission, there is open-source publishing with library efforts like Gutenberg Project, and there are open-source projects in law and religion. There are Open-Source P (calculating Pi), Open-Source Movies, Open-Source Recipes, Open-Source Propaganda, Open-Source Crime Solving, Open-Source Curriculum... There is WOWEM or Women's Open World Empowerment Movement, a project focusing on gender and open source. Last summer, the gratis and open-content online encyclopedia Wikipedia – www.wikipedia.org – surpassed Britannica.com in daily hits, according to Web traffic monitor Alexa.com. Wikipedia's popularity is all the more extraordinary because, like Linux, it started as a small-scale experiment, challenging Britannica, until then an unrivalled 235-year-old institution.

In a world where making a profit and commercial thinking are in the driver's seat, it remains a challenge to feel happy while giving away your best ideas, although precisely therein may lie the ultimate solution for the future happiness of our society.

Crosstalking

In 2003 the Vrije Universiteit Brussel launched its university and industry network, called CROSSTALKS, aimed at developing a new interdisciplinary exchange dynamic for key players in society. This first CROSSTALKS book offers an open and constructive platform to a large scope of researchers, lawyers, artists, journalists and activists and their analyses, complementary and contradictory views and their direct or ambiguous relations with the forces of our present times.

The following collection of articles will contribute further insights into novel social and economic and cultural commitments, but will not bring new answers to old problems. Instead, new problems will arise within a framework enabling non-obvious questions to be raised and possible answers to be cross-examined.

PART I – DRIVING FORCES

The first part of this book is dedicated to the key players and projects that are the driving forces of the so-called copyleft culture.

1. Will the revolution be open-sourced? How open source travels through society, by Marianne van den Boomen & Mirko Tobias Schäfer

"There seems to be more at stake than just a vague metaphor for some transparent, democratic, non-private constitution. Of course, notions of 'freedom' and 'openness' appeal strongly to the social imagination, and this can easily result in utopian day-

dreaming. But imagination is a necessary part of any innovation, and metaphorical associations can certainly be productive." From the breakthrough of the Internet, the Dutch sociologist Marianne van den Boomen engaged herself as webmaster and investigative witness to the effects of digital networking. For this book she teamed up with Mirko Tobias Schäfer, and together they have written an essay about the people who set the scene for the Free and Open-Source Software movement and its potential social and cultural innovative power.

2. *"Free as in Freedom, not Gratis!"* Interview with Richard Stallman, the embodiment of the dilemma of our digital commons, by Marleen Wynants

Richard Stallman is the legendary programmer and founding father of the Free Software Movement who made it all possible. In 2003 he received an honorary doctorate from the VUB, and from then on CROSSTALKS decided to take the free and open-source software issue as its first theme to work on. The interview presented here is the result of some personal encounters and an extensive email correspondence with Richard Stallman who wraps up the major challenges in the following quote: *"What can be done? Trying to avoid using algorithms that are patented, and organizing a severe countermovement to convince governments all over the world that the manipulation of information is not something that should be patented. And trying to convince business leaders that the patenting of software is comparable to the patenting of business methods, so that there comes a solidarity from that side too".*

3. The Open-Source Paradigm Shift, by Tim O'Reilly

We must give Tim O'Reilly the credit for the title of our first workshop and for the pragmatic but challenging insights into the future of the open-source movement. O'Reilly's premise is *"(...) that free and open-source developers are in much the same position today that IBM was in 1981 when it changed the rules of the computer industry, but failed to understand the consequences of the change, allowing others to reap the benefits. Most existing proprietary software vendors are no better off, playing by the old rules while the new rules are reshaping the industry around them".*

4. Open Courseware and Open Scientific Publications, by Frederik Questier & Wim Schreurs

The authors report on their work and their vision of what open source and particularly open science and courseware can mean for education and research in a university context. *"... in the old, analogue system, the copyright exemptions were used by the users as a defence mechanism in litigation for copyright infringements. The user could only be stopped after infringement. In the digital world, the function of the exemptions is completely different: it is the rights-holder now, not the user, who defines, by DRM systems and technological measures, whether the use of a work is exempted or not."*

5. Roots Culture – Free Software Vibrations Inna Babylon, by Armin Medosch

Armin Medosch is a European artist and journalist who is constantly crossing disciplinary borders. From inside the digital counterculture, he provides us with inspiring insights, fitting links and metaphors to extend our knowledge about the cultural cross-fertilizing mechanisms of our society. *"The conventional view of software development therefore denies the link between software and culture as something that exists before the result. Software is understood as facilitating the production of cultural representations and influencing culture by the tools that it makes available, but is usually not also regarded a product of' social imaginary signification'."*

Part II – Making it happen: Case-Studies from Brussels, Belgium, Europe & Beyond

One of the challenges of the open-source spirit is to come up with a sustainable business model, with a next economy of ideas, and to enhance the motivation of the people engaged in the process. This part offers a range of inspiring cases and experiments.

An interesting additional metaphor came from communication scientist Jean-Claude Burgelman who pointed out that the olive cooperatives in Spain have developed an innovative and fruitful alternative collaboration model to the existing ones. *"Let's suppose software becomes a public good,"* he said. *"The only way you can motivate people to write good code, is through paying them back in the sense* that usage of more of their code leads to more gain for them. That makes it interesting or a challenge to work independently. In the olive cooperative, all the farmers of a specific valley go to a bank together. The bank buys the installations and everybody brings in his/her olives and according to what you bring in, oil is being made and sold. What's in it for the individual farmer? The more he brings in, the smaller his dept to the bank becomes. At the same time, he gains parts in the cooperative, so he wins twice. I think we should state somewhere very clear that the challenges for open source are the sustainability of any underlying business model and the dynamics to keep the creativity and motivation for producing quality. These are elements that apart from the industrial policy issue, the open-source community does care too little about. The motive for the people of Extremadura was: we want to guarantee the participation and keep entrance thresholds to the knowledge society of the second poorest region of Spain as low as possible, and that's a valuable motive of course, but that is not enough as a valid statement on a European level." Dixit Jean-Claude Burgelman.

6. Extremadura and the Revolution of Free Software, by Angel Vaca

"It is up to humans to get the most out of these computer tools, to use them as a way of achieving higher goals. This is why the FOSS model was so important to us: it focuses more on what can be done with computers than on the path one must follow in order to make them work. Some other models can end up regarding computers in classrooms as an end in themselves. Our idea was exactly the opposite." The open-source initiative of the Region of Extremadura is just one of the recent projects by regional authorities who opt for open-source software with an eye to enabling all levels of the population to participate and to share open access to the region's administrative, technological, economic and educational resources.

7. Building Open Ecosystems for Collaborative Creativity, by Peter Hanappe

Peter Hanappe from the Sony Science Lab in Paris came up with an inspiring contribution about some recent experiments on open ecosystems in a cultural context and reflections on the stimulation of collaborative creativity. Apart from the novel technologies and communication concepts, the paper sheds an alternative light on the personal motivation of the members of creative communities: *"Instead of concentrating on financial awards, I find it interesting to consider other forms of reward, such as human capital and social capital. For many people, the social and learning aspects may be a sufficient reason to participate. Can these forms of reward be made more tangible? Can they become more important than financial rewards?"*

8. A Walk through the Music Bazaar & the Future of Music, by Sara Engelen

Travel to the Internet… and experience one of the most striking revolutions that has taken place, namely the way we – and especially the younger generations – deal with the creation and distribution of music. Sara Engelen takes us on a kaleidoscopic tour through the legal, commercial and alternative culture of music creation and distribution of recent decades. *"File-swapping and new forms of broadcasting applications – over the net and over the airwaves – open up a wide horizon of possibilities for production, distribution and consumption in the music industry. As these technologies are still in transition, the legal framework they operate in needs to be balanced fairly, to serve the interests of both the givers and the receivers of the goods this industry produces, in a flexible interpretation of the notion of "fair use"."*

9. Open Source, Science and Education, by Marc Nyssen & Frederik Cheeseman

"Recent history has shown that changes in management, or a company take-over, can lead to legal harassment concerning the use of file formats that have been tolerated for a long time but then suddenly, without warning, are no longer – as illustrated by the Unisys company's threat to charge for the use of the "gif" image format." The authors are a winning team of the backstage open-source activists that every university fosters and they provide a case-study and technological account of what it means to set up a collaborative network of educators and students in a particular environment, in this case, that of biomedical image-processing.

10. Open Standards Policy in Belgium, by Peter Strickx & Jean Jochmans

Peter Strickx is the Chief Technology Officer of FEDICT, the organization whose task is the initiation, implementation and assistance of e-government projects for the federal government of Belgium. Despite the fact that the existing e-gov building blocks from FEDICT were all built with open standards, there was a persistent need for a more formal agreement between the different Federal Administrations. This document presents an information model based on open standards: *"In order to benefit from new technologies like PDAs and digital home platforms, in bringing government information and applications to citizens, enterprises and civil servants, we wanted an information model that was not tied to any platform or product but based on open specifications/open standards".*

PART III – ETHICS & BOTTLENECKS

What constraints and bottlenecks do the laws of competition entail at the moment, and what can be done about them? These are questions that are asked in various fields and disciplines, but the risks at stake are highest when our own lives are involved. This part contains two contributions from the field of biotechnology and some perspectives from the legal and research-management points of view.

11. "The Patenting of Life" – Interview with VUB scientist Lode Wyns, by Marleen Wynants

From the patenting of a staircase to the patenting of a gene is a small step for most lawyers, but voices from academic research in biotechnology seek to challenge the privatization, the monopoly, that controls organisms, and are determined to build sustainable, healthy and creative societies. Lode Wyns is such a voice, and makes a crucial contribution to the discussion on the openness of our future. *"You cannot just map the context and conditions of one patent bluntly onto anything else. You cannot just extend that in a linear way, and there is an enormous contradiction emerging between these lawyers and their tremendous legal knowledge on the one hand, and their absolute ignorance about science and biology on the other."*

12. Fostering Research, Innovation & Networking, by Jan Cornelis

For VUB vice-rector for research Jan Cornelis, one of the key objectives for a university is to preserve long-term thinking processes and foster the discovery of new knowledge. "*The profile of the VUB is based on free inquiry – 'free as in freedom, not gratis' – which manifests itself in an open attitude towards research, one that is unlimited (except financially). There is a research-driven academic machinery for pursuing this goal. But there are also the increasing short-term demands for results, made by a fast evolving and economics-driven society.*"

To capture the knowledge emerging from fundamental research, and to build a bridge leading towards its exploitation in innovative inventions, an appropriate support for what he calls *strategic research* is needed. "*With regard to strategic research, we deliberately have to define specific areas and themes for development (building on existing strengths and creating new niches) and create a critical mass for tackling the multidisciplinary problems associated with growing complexity in our society. Sustainable management of these large, excelling research groups working on a program basis should preserve creativity and should continue to provide support to research bodies whose members can still sit all together around the same table at lunch-time, in a nice restaurant and talk about fabulous new discoveries and ideas.*"

13. Is Open-Sourced Biotechnology Possible? by Daniel de Beer

Daniel de Beer analyses the transposition of the open-source model into fields other than that of information technology. He states that the model could work, but only under certain conditions: "...*communal development of a technology, complete transparency in how it works, and the ability to use and improve it freely, provided improvements are shared openly*". In biotechnology, the distinction between invention and discovery has become fuzzy, so that the restrictions imposed on patentable inventions, for example that they should be man made, are difficult to put in practice and few things "*escape the patent trap*".

14. *Legal Aspects of Software Protection through Patents, and the Future of Reverse Engineering,* by Bruno de Vuyst & Liv Steuts

"This chapter will show U.S. and emerging European law complementing copyright with patent protection in an attempt to protect valuable investments by innovators, including through the attempted exclusion of certain forms of unfair reverse engineering. Failure to evolve in this direction, the authors argue, would be a disincentive to innovators, particularly those just starting out as entrepreneurs." The authors cite a series of crucial and decisive court-cases in the dispute over the economic justification for protecting software. Yet patent protection should not be a disincentive to bringing innovation into the world. The authors therefore insist that certain forms of re-engineering should be allowed, and this should be made explicit in the TRIPS agreement (trade-related aspects of intellectual property rights).

PART IV – THE FUTURE IS OPEN

How can you maintain the urge to be creative when there is no competition? How can we maintain the innovative and creative drive, the rights and the plights typical of our lives in our society while constantly balancing the constraints and possibilities?

15. *Advancing Economic Research on the Free and Open-Source Software Mode of Production,* by J.-M. Dalle, Paul A. David, Rishab A. Ghosh & W.E. Steinmueller

"To develop the means of assessing how, where, and why this and other related frameworks succeed in supporting other specific objectives – and where they are likely to fail – is both a challenge and an opportunity to contribute significantly to the advancement of the social sciences, but even more significantly to effective human social organization." The authors are outstanding researchers who once more try to take all the research on FOSS a step further, from the development of simulation models, designed to reveal the properties of self-organized community-mode software production, to the dissection of parameters for advancing economic and social-science studies on FOSS.

16. The Future of Open Source, by Ilkka Tuomi

The open-source movement is not just hype or a temporary fad, and several stiff challenges need to be tackled if it is to remain viable and thrive. Ilkka Tuomi carefully discusses the factors the movement needs for growth and those that could lead to its downfall. *"The sustainability of the open-source model depends on several factors. Some of these are internal to the model itself, including its economic viability, the availability of competent contributors, and the extensibility and flexibility of the model. Other factors are external, including the potential reactions of proprietary software developers and policymakers, or technological developments leading down evolutionary paths that are fundamentally incompatible with the model."*

17. The Future of Software: Enabling the Marketplace to Decide, by Bradford L. Smith

The article by Bradford L. Smith is a crucial contribution to the discussion on the economics of software development and gives us an insight into its evolution and future prospects as seen from the leading proprietary side of the matter. *"The open-source and commercial software models have been critical elements of the software ecosystem for decades, and both are likely to continue to play important roles in the years ahead. Recent events suggest that firms across the industry are now working to incorporate what they perceive to be the best elements of both models in their broader strategies. While predicting the final result of this process is difficult, much easier to predict is that the principal beneficiaries of this process will be consumers, who will enjoy benefits in the form of more choices and lower prices."*

18. Dual Licensing – A Business model from the Second Generation of Open Source Companies, by Kaj Arnö

The vice-president of training, certification and documentation at MySQL sketches the challenges of the open-source software industry in a very transparent way. He takes the reader on a short trip from the first generation of OSS companies to the second generation, to which MySQL belongs. He unhesitatingly draws a comparison with the proprietary software industry, and points out possible pitfalls and major challenges for the open industry. *"Hijacking existing open-source software projects and making them 'dual licensing' will not work, unless every single contributor to the project agrees to set up a joint company to sign the copyright over to."*

19. Towards a EU policy for Open-Source Software, by Simon Forge

The book ends with an introduction to a report by the Institute for Prospective Technological Studies in Seville (capital of Andalucia), a Joint Research Institute of the European Commission. *"Some economists have tried to show that government subsidies are at best an inefficient use of public funds. But do these calculations take into account the benefits of giving access to OSS as a result of subsidies, rather than leaving the initiative to chance in the hands of a commercial concern? These benefits are particularly marked given the unique character of OSS development – which can lead to products that may never be produced in a purely commercial software model."*

January 2005

Preface

Biographies

Jan Cornelis (MD 1973, Ph.D. 1980) is Professor in electronics, medical imaging and digital image processing at the Vrije Universiteit Brussel – VUB, and head of the department of Electronics and Information Processing – ETRO at the Faculty of Applied Sciences. He is also Consultant Professor at Northwestern Polytechnic University, Xi'an, China. He coordinates the research group on image processing and machine vision - IRIS. His current research interest is primarily focused on image and video compression.

Since 1 January 2001, he got involved in management of research and innovation as Vice-rector for research of VUB. He is member of the board of directors of the Interuniversity MicroElectronics Centre – IMEC in Leuven, vice-president of the DISC - the ICT knowledge centre of the Brussels Capital Region, and Chairman of the board of directors BI^3 – the incubation fund of VUB.

Marleen Wynants graduated in linguistics and literature, with a Masters in audio-visual communication sciences (KULeuven). She is an independent content producer and journalist. She worked for the official Belgian radio and television in its pre-commercial stage and was the editor of the post-punk magazine *Fabiola*, leaving the scene in 1988, the year that Hillel Slovak, Chet Baker, Divine and Roy Orbison died.

Since the birth of her two daughters and the breakthrough of the Internet, she has reoriented her focus towards learning processes and the emergence of creativity, the social impact of ICT technologies and the communication of fundamental science and the people behind it. At present she writes for the interdisciplinary magazine *JANUS* and is the operational manager of CROSSTALKS, the university and industry network of the VUB – Vrije Universiteit Brussel.

PART I

Driving Forces: Key Players & Projects

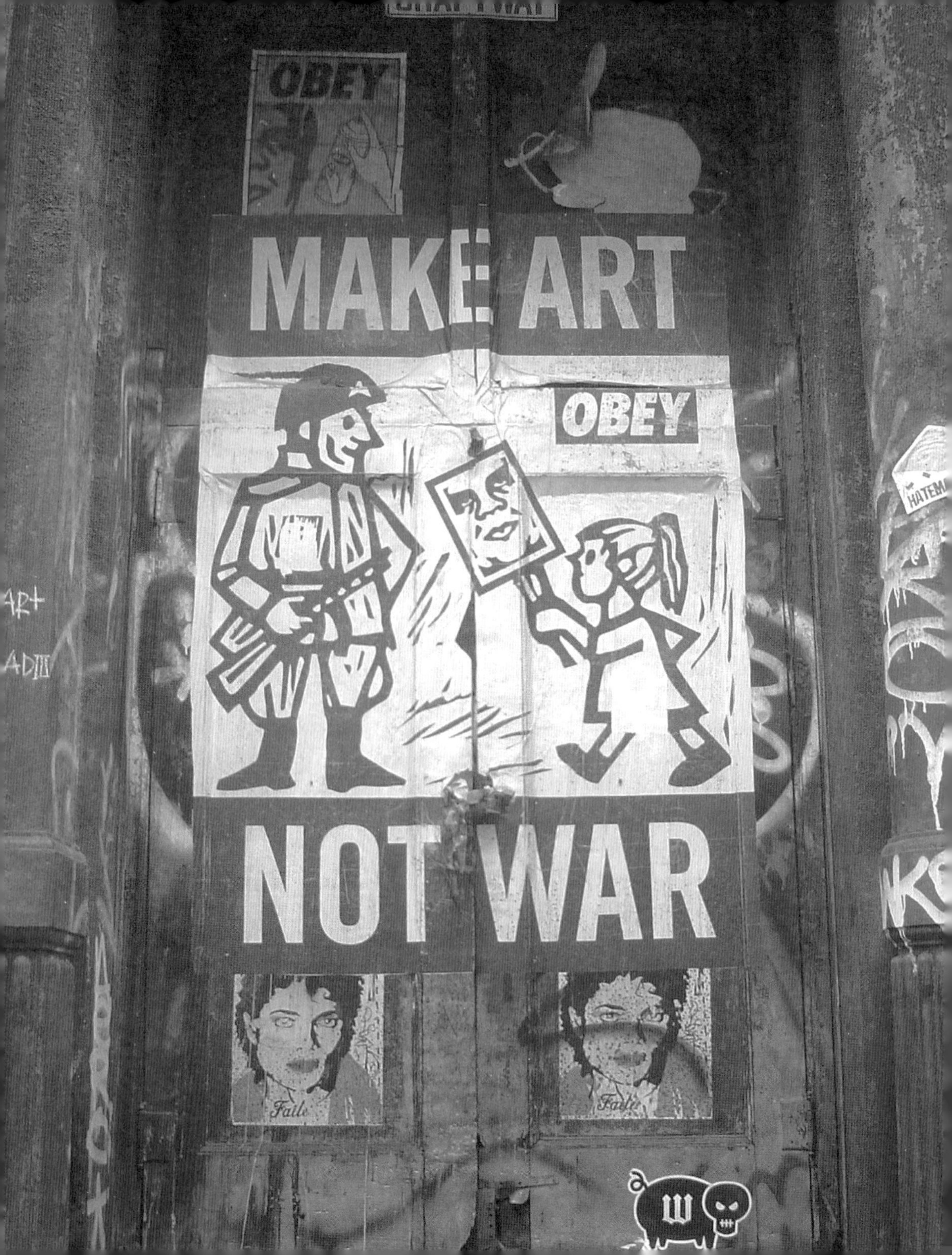
OBEY
MAKE ART
OBEY
NOT WAR
Faile
Faile

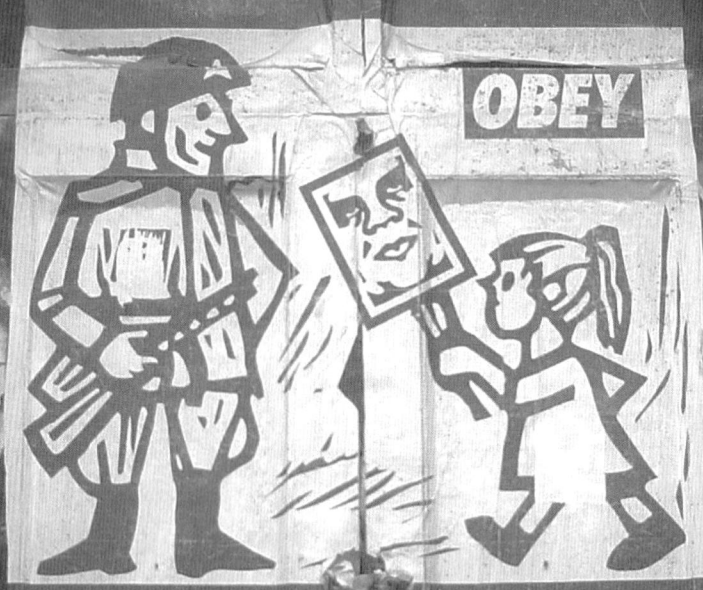

Will the revolution be open-sourced?
How open source travels through society

Marianne van den Boomen & Mirko Tobias Schäfer

Introduction

For a long time, open source was an issue only for hackers and other passionate programmers. Since the late 1990s, however, the idea of open source has emerged from underground. Though it can not yet be called mainstream, the discourse on open source is infiltrating society at several levels, and in several different domains. While the concept of 'open source' once meant providing the source code of software together with executable code, nowadays it covers far more than just a mode of software distribution. Today, it connects old and new social, political and cultural practices, constructing a heterogeneous field.

In this article we will provide an explorative cartography of this expanding open-source discourse. We will sketch the constitutive nodes in the open-source network: the spokesmen who represent it, the claims, the products, and the discursive strategies involved. We will argue that 'open source' functions as a generative and transformative concept, so that the term 'open source' can itself be described as an open concept, capable of formulating and transforming several different claims. The concept will be analysed as travelling into different spheres of society, mobilised by agenda-setting, political/semiotic strategies and metaphorical translations. We will conclude with some evaluative remarks on the political aspects of open source.

Marianne van den Boomen & Mirko Tobias Schäfer

How open source hit the headlines

How did open source became a public issue – when and where did it all begin? To answer these questions, most authors dive deep into the history of the Internet and hacker culture,[1] but here we take a different starting point: the moment the established ICT press began to cover open-source issues. The professional ICT press is aimed at software developers, system builders, hardware vendors, IT consultants, marketing managers and chief executives in the ICT economy. As such it represents a permeable boundary between the hacker subculture and the software establishment.

Checking the archives of the Dutch weekly magazine *Automatisering Gids*, for example, we can clearly see how from 1998 on there has been a sharp increase in the number of news reports and features on the issue of open source.[2] Its very first news report containing the term 'open source', dated 3 November 1998, is significant:

> **Microsoft sees threat in Linux** – Microsoft regards Linux and other open-source operating systems as a serious threat to its own product, Windows NT. This can be concluded from an internal Microsoft memo that was spread throughout the World Wide Web last Monday...
>
> *(Automatisering Gids 03-11-1998)*

This article is about the so-called *Halloween Documents,* an internal Microsoft memoranda that was leaked to the press. The memo dealt with how the company could confront the potential threat posed by the Linux operating system.[3] The memo swept open source immediately onto the agenda of ICT professionals. When a big player like Microsoft was rethinking its position and strategies, something was at stake, so its allies, rivals and customers had to rethink their positions too. From then on the ICT press began to keep an eye on what was happening around Linux.

Since then, thousands of articles have been published about open source, showing how Linux and open source have become hot issues in the world of ICT, and how many players have become involved. Sample headlines from the last six months illustrate this:[4]

'Open source' in US less open than in Europe – The American magazine *Wired* praised Linus Torvalds recently as 'the leader or the free world'. No wonder. By now, the Linux community has 140,000 registered users and some 18 million unregistered... (12-12-2003)

Asia breaks power Microsoft with Linux – Asian resistance to Microsoft is becoming epidemic. Several countries want to ban Windows from government offices. Thailand threatened with Linux to force Microsoft to lower its prices, and Japan, Korea and China... (12-12-2003)

SCO now attacks GPL – SCO[5] continues its crusade against the world of Linux. In an open letter, CEO Darl McBride attacks the open-source movement, in particular the General Public License (GPL)... (5-12-2003)

Linux sales growing sneakily – Europe has far more points of sale for Linux than generally assumed. More than 30% of computer retailers are selling Linux distributions... (10-12-2003)

SCO under cyber-attack – The SCO Group's systems today suffered a denial of service-attack... (12-12-2003)

Red Hat shows rising profits – Over the third quarter of its fiscal year, Red Hat recorded a profit of 4.1 million dollars. The sales volume of the supplier of Linux distributions rose from... (19-12-2003)

Public sector still shy about open source – Open-source software provides good opportunities for public administration, health care and education, but decision-makers are still hesitant. This is the main conclusion of a survey by the Multiscope bureau... (19-12-2003)

SCO brings politics into fight against Linux – SCO tries to mobilise the members of the American Congress in its fight against Linux... (22-01-2004)

Torvalds counters SCO claims – Linus Torvalds has today systematically countered SCO claims about the Linux copyright… (23-12-2003)

EU stimulates open source with website – The European Commission has launched a website to promote the achievements of open-source software. The website 'Free and Open-Source Software' (F/OSS) is… (23-12-2003)

'Linux users need not worry' – Law professor Eben Moglen states in a 'white paper' that companies who use Linux need not worry about possible claims by SCO… (11-02-2004)

Sun should release Java code – Open-source ambassador Eric Raymond stated that Sun should release control over Java code so the computer language can be used in open-source programs… (16-02-2004)

French government desktops with open source (17-02-2004)

Microsoft promises to make some programs open-source (30-03-2004)

Demonstration in Brussels against software patents – Opponents of software patents are today protesting against plans by the European Union. They fear that a lobby of big companies… (14-04-2004)

Insurance against Linux copyright claims (19-04-2004)

Computer Associates goes for open source (06-05-2004)

Microsoft feels Linux price pressure (14-06-2004)

Munich opts definitively for Linux (17-06-2004)

Munich freezes Linux project – Today the German city of Munich announced a freeze on the so-called LiMux project. This has been reported by the ICT news agency Heise Online. Uncertainty about software patents was the main reason... (04-08-2004)

In fact, this sample of news reports shows the whole open-source discourse in a nutshell. When we take a closer look at what is happening we encounter several kinds of players: software companies like Microsoft, SCO, Sun, Red Hat and Computer Associates, but also insurance companies, lawyers, countries, continents and political institutions. There are numbers at stake – numbers of users, of sales, of prices, of profits. The overall image is one of commotion and action – growing, attacking, countering, claiming, promising, stimulating and doubting – but we can discern at least three patterns in all this turmoil.

The first is the story of the world-wide rise of Linux. Some articles report that the number of users is still rising, that more retailers than expected are selling Linux, and that some Linux distribution companies are making huge profits. In absolute numbers, especially on desktops, Linux is still negligible compared with Windows,[6] but the symbolic power of Linux is apparently capable of provoking several players. Microsoft, and companies like SCO who have vested interests in the software market, fight back with all the economic, symbolic and discursive strategies at their command. They lower prices, claim ownership of Linux code, and promise to make some of their own code available. These activities provoke all kinds of counter-actions: white papers, insurance policies, counter-claims and 'hacktivist' attacks on websites, to name but a few.

Secondly, although Linux is the main issue in the headlines, open source involves more than just the domain of operating systems. The numerous requests, decisions or refusals to open up source code, as featured daily in the ICT press, concern all kinds of software: not just operating systems, but also desktop applications, databases, security programs, Java code, and so on. The idea that open-sourcing can be done with any kind of software is spreading into the professional ICT world.

Thirdly, we can see how the open-source discourse is gradually extending to other domains besides the software industry, drawing new players into the discourse such as public authorities, research institutes, lawyers, insurance companies, governments and the European Commission. All these players are exploring, propagating or contesting the possibilities of open-source software. Clearly, open source is no longer merely a technological issue, but has become widely discussed among the general public. The floor is now open to all kinds of participants and players, who contribute to the open-source discourse with their own concepts and expectations.

It may be even more relevant to speak in terms of a *battle* for the open-source discourse. Indeed, we can easily identify protagonists and antagonists in these news reports. On one side we see the hacker programmers and their spokesmen, creating and advocating open source. On the other we witness the established 'powers that be', who are fighting against open source. On closer inspection, however, the battle appears to be more complicated, especially when we dive deeper into the culture of open-source developers. There, for instance, we come across two opposing definitions of open source, one in terms of 'free software' and the other 'open-source software'. Several initiatives try to evade or transcend this ideological debate by using the reconciling term 'Free/Open Source' (FOSS),[7] as the European Commission does on its website. Regardless of these types of moves, the battle on political/technical correctness rages on, and we will explore some of these dynamics shortly. First, however, we will look at how and where open source began to travel outside the ICT headlines.

How open source became more than software

It is clear that this commotion all started with Linux. In 1991 the Finnish student Linus Torvalds placed a modest proposal online, encouraging fellow hackers to improve and extend his rudimentary free operating system. In 1994 the first working version of Linux was distributed; in 1998 Microsoft's anxiety leaked out, and from then on it was on the agenda of the ICT industry. Linux appeared to be more than just a toy for hackers. Propelled by Linux, the open-source hacker culture surfaced from its underground location. Amateur hacker programmers began to create coalitions with more established parts of the software production and distribution sector. New companies and organisations were founded, new products, licences and communities were created.

While there has been a hacker subculture developing open-source applications and Internet protocols for more than thirty years – without explicitly using the label 'open source' – it is only in the last few years that this practice has become visible to a broader public. The process started with publications in the professional ICT press, but it soon spread to other media.

The media domain is an extremely important factor in propelling the open-source discourse. In the mid 1990s, when Linux became a market and business opportunity, special-interest magazines emerged all over the world, such as the US *Linux Journal*, the German *Linux Magazin* and the French *LinuxMag*. A few years later, open-source issues entered the pages of established ICT magazines and also general magazines, daily newspapers and other mainstream media. The interview became a popular discursive genre, whether with open-source protagonists or antagonists. An example can be found on the November 2003 cover of the popular technophile magazine *Wired*, which features: 'Linus Torvalds: leader of the free world. His open-source software is making Bill Gates sweat. What's next: open-source science, law, and design'[8]

Though the general media domain is an important vehicle for extending the open-source discourse, the latter's main habitat remains the Internet. Most of the *production* of open-source software takes place on the Internet. This happens mostly on mailing lists, but also on platforms such as Sourceforge, an open-source developers' website which hosts thousands of projects.[9] In addition, the Internet provides the main platform for the *distribution* of open-source software. Almost every distribution can be downloaded free online, and the same goes for numerous open-source applications.

The Internet of course also plays a role in stimulating the discourse about open source as it unfolds on websites, weblogs, web forums, in news groups and mailing lists. Surveys and books on open source are often published online, such as the German *Open Source Jahrbuch 2004,* or Lawrence Lessig's *Free Culture*. O'Reilly Media, one of the best-known publishing houses specialising in ICT, offers a wide range of free books on open-source issues on its website. Other important discursive nodes online are the interactive user forums of mainstream newspapers and weekly magazines. Here the discussions on open source continue, and they are often quite heated. One example is the extremely critical IT forum of the Austrian newspaper *Der Standard*. The users, mostly IT professionals, continually criticise the newspaper. They verify facts, add information, correct mistakes and, of course, fight battles with one another. The German publishing house Heise is another big node in the European ICT discourse. They have influential magazines, including *c't* and *iX*, and active online communities on their website, www.heise.de.

A special case on the Internet is Slashdot, one of the largest and most famous independent platforms on ICT matters. Slashdot combines the idea of open source on three levels: code, content and community.[10] The open-source software that runs the weblog ('slash code') provides a user-based publishing and editorial system ('open publishing'), thus creating a critical and loyal community around 'news for nerds, stuff that matters'. Slashdot is responsible for what has been dubbed 'the Slashdot effect': the sudden increase in the number of visits to a mainstream media website when the Slashdot community debates the site in question.

But the discourse on open source is not only proliferating in media circles. During the last five years the academic sphere, with its own magazines, publications and conferences, has discovered open source as an emerging cultural practice to be explored and explained. Scholars in the fields of media studies and cultural studies increasingly conduct research on open-source issues, focusing on questions such as the motivation for developing open-source software, evaluations of innovations by communities and democratic access to technology. In addition, academics recognise several parallels between the principles of generating knowledge in the domain of open-source software and their own domain: the 'gift economy', the free sharing of knowledge, transparency and availability as preconditions for improvements, the importance of co-operation and community-building. The growing resistance to monopolist and expensive scientific journals can be seen in the same terms as the open-source battle. For instance, the Massachusetts Institute of Technology (MIT) has decided to make its educational material and academic papers freely available online on a site dubbed 'Free/Open-Source Research Community'.[11]

On the boundaries between the media and academic spheres, moreover, interesting cross-over initiatives emerge around open-source issues. These cross-overs can take the form of publications (e.g. Volker Grassmuck's *Freie Software*, 2002, Steven Weber's *The Success of Open Source*, 2004), conferences and projects. Since the 1990s, several regular meetings on open source have been held in Europe: the Wizard of OS Conferences, the

Linux Kongress in Germany and the Linuxwochen in Austria, all discussing the legal status and potential of open-source software. Organisations in the field of net culture and art are also participating in this cross-over open-source discourse. In the Netherlands, organisations such as *V2*, the Institute for Unstable Media, and the De Waag Society for Old and New Media quite often present open-source issues and initiatives at their events and festivals. The Dutch Electronic Art Festival has chosen 'Open Systems' as the main theme for its 2004 festival. These occasions provide exchange platforms for open-source spokespeople, software developers, artists, journalists, academics and even businesspeople.

It is important to note that Linux, as the alternative operating system to Microsoft's Windows, continues to be the main focus of open-source discourse in all of these domains. The representation of a kind of David-and-Goliath battle between small Linux and giant Microsoft of course appeals strongly to the imagination of subversive hackers and the general public. But we have also seen how the open-source debate has extended far beyond just Linux versus Windows, encompassing even the matter of software. Open source is increasingly becoming a public and a political issue.

How open source became a political issue

The politicisation of open-source issues cannot be seen as a kind of slogan hijacking, using the principles inappropriately for political goals. In fact, open source has had politics built into it right from the start. While open source originally just meant that executable software was delivered together with its source code, because of its far-reaching implications it came to mean much more. Providing the source code meant that other people could now look at how things worked. They could report or repair bugs, change the code to suit their own needs, create new modules, and then redistribute any changes or improvements they made. So, distributing source code implied an inherent openness to modification and redistribution. Openness is a key factor here, because it brings several other implications along with it, especially in a situation of growth and scaling-up. It implies other distribution and production models. It implies other business models for those who want to make money with open-source products.

It implies connections with user communities, and the building of such communities. It implies other concepts of copyright and ownership, along with protecting and licensing models to sustain these ideas. These implications connect the concept of open source to several domains outside the domain of plain software development, such as law, insurance, labour organisation, public relations and organisational strategies.

These domains are in a way the next-door neighbours of software production, but the open-source concept is able to move farther afield than that. We can see it travelling into public administration, politics – Howard Dean's presidential campaign of 2003 was dubbed an 'open-source campaign', as it organised fund-raising by using weblogs[12] – and even nation-state-building and geo-politics at the level of vast entities such as China and Asia.

In European discourse, the decision in June 2004 by the Munich administration to switch to Linux was a crucial moment. It apparently took a big city to gain widespread attention. The small German town of Schwäbisch Hall stepped over to Linux in 2003, but this news did not attract media attention or European-wide headlines. Now, in 2004, the battle on public administration desktops is raging: Paris and Vienna are also planning to switch to open-source systems. While these issues may be considered relatively local, the debate on the European Commission directive on software patents, including the lobbying and protests against it, is pushing the open-source discourse into the heart of European politics. At stake here is the question: will the possibility of patenting trivial software 'inventions' obstruct open-source development and implementation? Munich hesitated for a while in August 2004, wondering whether the forthcoming EU software patent directive could endanger their open-source project, but they decided to pursue it all the same.

Meanwhile, open source is being politicised not only at the level of established political institutions – there is also a grass-roots connection, inspiring a bottom-up, activist politics and more general ideas about structural social change. These connections do not come out of the blue; the concept of open source can easily travel from community-building to democracy improvement in general. It can also travel from concrete licensing formulations to abstract models of property, by claiming that open source may provide a third mode of property and production that is neither capitalist nor communist.[13]

From there it is a small step to thinking about social change in general. For example, the German Oekonux project is dedicated to debating the idea of a 'GPL society', in which the general mode of production and property would be based on the General Public License (GPL, see Annex 1).[14] The GPL is the main licence form for free software and, unlike other open-source licences, this one actively builds a commons. Oekonux (the name a blending of 'economy' and 'Linux') consists of a mailing list and regular conferences where participants theorise about how the notion of free software can 'germinate' in a socio-economic metamorphosis while migrating to other parts of society. The Oekonux project is inspired by a kind of utopian Marxism, as can be seen in the wording of the ideal of the GPL Society: 'self-unfolding as the main motivation for production; irrelevance of exchange value, so the focus is on the use value; free co-operation between people; and international teams'.[15]

While the Oekonux project operates mainly at a discursive and theoretical level, the example of Indymedia shows how open source can, both in principle and in practice, be embedded in socio-political activism. The Indymedia initiative consists of a loose collection of hundreds of locally organised, independent platforms providing online news and debates on (anti)globalisation issues, thus presenting an alternative to mainstream media. Most Indymedia Centres not only use open-source software on their computer systems and websites, they also try to implement the open-source principles of collectivism, participation and consensus decision-making at the organisational level in general.

These examples of jumps from open-source software to open-source society, social reform and revolution should not be too quickly dismissed as 'merely metaphorical'. There seems to be more at stake than just a vague metaphor for a transparent, democratic and non-private constitution. Of course, notions of 'freedom' and 'openness' appeal strongly to the social imagination, and this can easily result in utopian day-dreaming. But imagination is a necessary part of any innovation, and metaphorical associations can certainly be productive. This can be illustrated by the wild proliferation of practical initiatives with labels such as Open Hardware, Open Culture, Open Publishing, Open Access, Open Archives, and Open Theory. There is even an initiative for Open Cola.[16]

Whether these initiatives are indeed indications of a revolutionary social transformation remains to be seen. However, new social and cultural practices are emerging.

The idea of open source is spreading into society, at several levels and in several domains. It is certainly too early yet to call it mainstream; the default mode for companies, institutions and the general public is still to use proprietary software. But open source is clearly no longer a marginal idea: it appears to be heading for normalisation and mainstreaming.

Translations in the open-source network

This notion leads us to a general question: how do new things or ideas become mainstream and generally adopted anyway? The adoption process is usually analysed in terms of a 'gradual diffusion into society'. This view of diffusion assumes that a new invention or idea will find its way into society when it becomes accepted as good or true by more and more people, until it finally reaches the general public. Seen in this way, the general acceptance of a techno-scientific invention depends on the inherent, objective characteristics of the invention itself: it will become mainstream because it is technologically good or scientifically true. This can be called a techno-scientifically deterministic view of the diffusion of new inventions. A more social and historical view of diffusion foregrounds power relations in society and the subsequent acts of resistance, acceptance or ignorance by different interest-groups during the diffusion process. Nevertheless, the basic assumptions of the diffusion model are the same for both the techno-scientifically deterministic and the socially deterministic variants: on the one hand you have the new invention, and on the other groups of people who may or may not accept it.

Bruno Latour (1987) has criticised this 'diffusion model' as being too static.[17] In his view, the diffusion model wrongly assumes that a successful invention remains the same all the time, and that the social interests and powers it encounters are already pre-existing. The model cannot really explain how general acceptance can be achieved, because it cannot give an account of how both the invention itself and the social groups involved are transformed and constructed as 'diffusion' proceeds.

Latour proposes an alternative model for tracing what happens during this process; he calls this a 'model of translation', situated in an 'actor network'. Translation here means both discursive and non-discursive transformations of the invention: it concerns modifications to definitions and to rhetoric, in order to convince people, and modifications to the technical design and physical construction of the object. The invention in question is thus analysed as something 'that simultaneously changes what it is made of and whom it is convincing'.[18] If we want to trace historically how an invention became generally accepted, we have to follow the different translations it went through along its route in time and space. On this route to 'becoming true' the invention circulates between different actors, and this process transforms/translates both the invention itself and the alliances and associations between the actors. This network of translations and associations is called an actor network. In this network all kinds of heterogeneous players – people, things, concepts, inscription devices, texts, money – are at work, creating mutual alliances and associations in which the invention can become stable and indispensable. Finally, the invention may become mainstream and accepted as a 'black box', i.e., a phenomenon or thing taken for granted, a closed device with no calls for it to be opened or contested.

This model of translation is suitable not only for an anthropological history of established and taken-for-granted science and technology: it is also a strong analytical method for mapping the routings of other kinds of emerging discourse, knowledge and belief.[19] The travels of the open-source concept into different discursive and non-discursive domains appear to be particularly suited to being analysed this way, as the open-source concept mobilises so many different actors and alliances.[20]

In the next section we will sketch the actor network of the open-source discourse, first in terms of the main human actors (a 'sociogram') who are advocating, defining and representing the open-source concept, and then in terms of the discursive strategies of the actors, 'counter-actors' and intermediaries.

Who are the main human actors involved in the expanding open-source actor network, and how are they represented in the different media spheres? What do they do, what do they claim, how do they perform their persuading labour, and whom do they persuade to join in? The open-source movement has several spokesmen (yes, indeed, only men). Three of them are key figures, and we have already seen their names popping up in the samples of ICT headlines: Richard Stallman, Eric Raymond and, of course, Linus

Torvalds. All three come from the hacker culture, all have hands-on experience of developing IT applications and technologies, and they all have street credibility. As we will see, however, they use different discursive and mobilising strategies to connect the street level to other social groups and domains.

Richard Stallman, a hacker with an ethical mission

Richard Stallman can be seen as the first 'voice from the open-source revolution'.[21] His story begins in the early 1980s, when his employer, the MIT lab, decided to move over to a new mainframe computer with a proprietary operating system instead of the non-proprietary system it had been using before. Around the old, free system a hacker community had been evolving, developing and exchanging code and applications for fifteen years, but this move signalled the end of the 'free' era. Suddenly it became impossible to exchange or co-create working software, since every user had to sign a non-disclosure agreement. As Stallman (2002) writes, 'This meant that the first step in using a computer was to promise not to help your neighbour. A co-operating community was forbidden. The rule made by the owners of proprietary software was, "If you share with your neighbour, you are a pirate. If you want any changes, beg us to make them"'.[22]

Not being able to modify or share programs is fundamentally unethical, in Stallman's view, and he faced a 'stark moral choice'. He quit his job and decided to develop a free operating system, 'to make a community possible again'. This system had to be free from having to ask permission to make changes, and it had to be compatible with Unix, the dominant operating system of the embryonic Internet of that time. In 1984 he began to work on this free operating system, dubbing it GNU, a recursive acronym meaning 'GNU is not Unix'.

Of crucial importance in Stallman's project is the notion of freedom. Stallman never tires of stressing that this means 'free as in free speech, not free beer'. Free software is not about money, but about principles. The four principles of freedom include: the freedom to use, the freedom to redistribute copies (either gratis or for a fee), the freedom to modify, and the freedom to distribute modified versions without needing to ask for anyone's permission.

In order to retain this freedom, it was necessary to prevent the software from being turned into proprietary software. This was made possible by a method called 'copyleft', a kind of reverse engineering of existing copyright law: 'copyleft – all rights reversed'. Free software is licensed with the GNU General Public License (GPL), which basically states that anything added to or combined with a copyleft program is also free and copyleft.[23]

Stallman founded the Free Software Foundation in 1985 as a tax-exempt charity for free software development.[24] During the 1980s he managed to recruit a good many voluntary programmers to work part-time and to contribute machines, money and programs. Gradually, several components of GNU were developed in this way, although in the early 1990s there was still no working kernel to make it a complete operating system. Fortunately, around that time Linus Torvalds had started working on the Unix-compatible Linux project. In 1992, combining the Linux kernel with the not-quite-complete GNU system resulted in a relatively stable, free operating system. Stallman is always very keen to keep this history of GNU/Linux alive, and never tires of interrupting anyone who talks about 'Linux' with 'you mean, GNU/Linux'.

Since the 1990s, Stallman has been evangelising to spread his message, by speaking at international conferences, engaging in online discussions and reworking his manifestos. The goal is to mobilise people to use free software and to refrain totally from using non-free software. Stallman's advocacy work is based on a strong moral appeal. Free

Figure 1: Richard Stallman playing flute for a butterfly.

software is grounded in ethical principles: founding communities, helping your neighbours and friends. It is no coincidence that his book is called *Free Software, Free Society* – he believes free software will bring salvation: 'In the long run, making programs free is a step toward the post-scarcity world, where nobody will have to work very hard just to make a living. People will be free to devote themselves to activities that are fun, such as programming, after spending the necessary ten hours a week on required tasks such as legislation, family counselling, robot repair, and asteroid prospecting'.[25]

Stallman's tone is not only moral but also harsh: 'If programmers deserve to be rewarded for creating innovative programs, by the same token they should be punished if they restrict the use of these programs'.[26] Anyone who deviates from the straight and narrow path of the FSF is at least morally condemned, and we are warned against these heretics: 'Watch out though – a number of companies that associate themselves with the term "open source" actually base their business on non-free software that works with free software'.[27] Anyone who uses the term 'open source' instead of 'free software' is suspect in Stallman's eyes. The term should be avoided, as it obscures the principles of freedom and appeals primarily to 'executives and business users, many of whom hold an ideology that places profit above freedom, above community, above principle'.

Stallman's strategy can be seen as one of purification, qualifying which software and people follow the right principles and which do not. When he mentions 'Linux users', between quotation marks, he is referring to the non-pure users – magazines, advertisements and spokesmen who put convenience or business models before principle. One of these non-pure heretics is his former fellow hacker Eric Raymond, the next key figure in the open-source sociogram.

Eric Raymond, a hacker with a business model

Eric Raymond can be seen as Stallman's opponent in the open-source paradigm battle. His focus on open source is not ethical but financial. In his view, open source is basically a new mode of software production. The benefits are not only the non-alienated and efficient organisation of labour, but also technically superior products. Raymond has dubbed this new mode of production the 'bazaar mode', as opposed to the 'cathedral mode'.[28]

The cathedral mode – used by proprietary-system development companies as well as Unix developers and Stallman's Free Software Foundation (!) – is based on tight coordination, systematic planning and goal-setting. Conversely, the bazaar mode, as invented or re-invented by Linus Torvalds, emerged from 'casual hacking' and 'constructive laziness' in the context of a decentralised, collaborative, Internet community: 'quality was maintained, not by standards or autocracy, but by the naively simple strategy of releasing every week and getting feedback from hundreds of users within days'.[29] This peer-reviewed direct feedback model is an effective alternative solution to the main problem of the large, cathedral-mode systems: the exponential upsurge of complexity, bugs and communication costs. The basic idea of the bazaar is: 'Release early and often, delegate everything you can, be open to the point of promiscuity'.[30]

Figure 2: Eric Raymond at the O'Reilly Open-Source Convention.

This notion of 'promiscuity' can be seen as a key metaphor in Raymond's open-source discourse, and it should be clear that this is diametrically opposed to Stallman's purity. In Raymond's book *The Cathedral and the Bazaar* (1999), we can see how this promiscuity transforms, *en route*, a production model (aimed at products) into a business model (aimed at profits).[31] While a phrase such as 'treating your users as co-developers' may still imply a dual perspective – that of a community and a software company – the translation of the credo into 'release early, release often and listen to your customers' wholly represents the perspective of a company.[32] 'Users' have become 'customers'.

Raymond, being a hacker/programmer himself and with street credibility to boot, writes with a kind of amateur anthropological flavour, always as a participating observer. He provides detailed descriptions of the internal dynamics of the small bazaar groups centred around core developers with different leadership styles, deconstructing the 'automagic' myth of anarchic decentralised developing. Raymond shows that this is not magic; it is organised labour, in a framework of interconnecting personal itches, ego satisfaction, reputation politics, implied ownership customs, and plain hackers' enjoyment.

Raymond clearly exposes the processes of mobilising actors into the open-source actor network, describing his own strategies in detail.[33] He reveals his personal strategy of 'memetic engineering': deliberately framing the memes and myths of hacker culture in metaphors and narratives (i.e. cathedral, bazaar, inverse commons, etc.). He describes the general mobilising strategies of collecting an informal network of allies over the Internet, creating formal organisations (such as the Open-Source Initiative), attending meetings and demonstrations, giving talks, and so on. Raymond makes no secret of his main goal: this is a marketing campaign of 'spin, image-building and rebranding', aimed at big business and the general public. So it is necessary to get rid of the notion of 'free software', as this is too ideological and anti-business. Mobilising the market basically means: forget bottom-up, work on top-down, with Linux as the best demonstration case for capturing the Fortune 500.[34] In 1998 Raymond decided to become the open-source ambassador, playing with his public image as an all-American guy with a love of guns, programming and libertarianism. He grew accustomed to flying first class and riding limousines, and is now a millionaire with shares in several Linux distribution companies.

This millionaire-with-a-mission calls himself an 'accidental revolutionary'. Notice that, for Raymond, the revolution is already here. In his view, it began in January 1998 with 'a shot heard around the world', when Netscape announced it would open up the source code of its browser.[35] Raymond immediately offered Netscape his consultancy services. The second shot was fired in November 1998 when an anonymous insider from Microsoft sent him the infamous Halloween Documents, which he immediately distributed on the Internet. It is indicative that Raymond sees Netscape's announcement as a revolution. In his opinion, revolution is defined by the decisions of Fortune 500 companies. But by then Netscape was no longer a big company – it was a former big company, in big trouble because it had lost its dominance and superiority on the web browser market. Besides, until recently the open-source Netscape Navigator/Mozilla browser was too weak a product to compete with Microsoft's Internet Explorer. If we can speak of a revolution at all, it started much earlier than 1998. It started with faith, hope, and a lot of organising work to make it come true. It was Linus Torvalds, the next key figure of the open source movement, who provided the missing link between faith and practice.

Linus Torvalds, a hacker with a family

It is no coincidence that Stallman and Raymond, despite being so different in their approaches and in their interpretation of the history of hacking, both point to Linus Torvalds and Linux as the breakthrough in open-source history. Starting with a modest proposal in a Usenet posting in 1991, Linus/Linux attracted thousands of co-developers and millions of users during the 1990s. We write 'Linus/Linux' deliberately, because it is difficult to separate person from product by determining their respective roles. Was it the person Linus or the product Linux that did it? It was probably the synergy. Both Stallman and Raymond admit that Linus Torvalds is a nice guy, with a responsive and open character, so other people really want to help him. And the more people contributed their code, the better Linux became.

Figure 3: Linus Torvalds with his family.

Torvalds also published his hacker autobiography, under the significant title *Just for Fun* (2001).[36] No mention of principles or business models or metaphors: 'just for fun'. The first sentence of the book sets the tone: 'I was an ugly child'. In the first pages Torvalds talks about his nice family, and modestly about himself as having no charming personality – he was a geek, a nerd, with the wrong looks and clothes, and all he wanted to do was to play with his grandfather's calculator and computer. At the end of the chapter he mentions that nowadays his wife advises on his wardrobe.

This picture is illustrative: Torvalds represents himself as a hacker with a family. And this can be seen as a generative metaphor. His family consists not only of his intimate loved ones: it is an extended family – the open-source community. And while there are several kinds of quarrels in this family, with some of its members unable even to be in the same room with one another (Stallman and Raymond), Torvalds can get along with all of them. He can talk with the Free Software Foundation and with open-source business model developers; he can travel between the divided domains.

How does he do it? Torvalds told the magazine *Wired* how he avoids confrontation: 'Just walking away. That also allows me to concentrate on the things I do enjoy, namely the technical discussions. I can't totally avoid all political issues, but I try my best to minimise them. When I do make a statement, I try to be fairly neutral. I like being on friendly terms with most people. By staying neutral, I end up being somebody that everybody can trust. And I'm fairly comfortable with the notion of saying "Sorry, I was wrong," even in public. If I'm right, I'm right, and if I'm wrong we can go back and fix it. I think of myself as an engineer, not as a visionary or "big thinker". I don't have any lofty goals. I just want to have fun making the best damn operating system I can'.[37]

But let's be clear about it: Torvalds runs the show at the Linux project, at least as far as the core development of Linux is concerned. Though he works together with other so-called maintainers, it is he and no one else who decides which features are to be included in the next release of the kernel.[38] It is he and no one else who announces that from now on the names and e-mail addresses of individual contributors will be included in the Linux source code. Torvalds has often been called a 'benevolent dictator', and while this probably is a fitting description of his personal leadership style, it is much more than just a personal thing. What it indicates most of all is that open-source developing, notwithstanding the clichéd ideological connotations of anarchism and decentralisation, is basically a matter of organising people, artefacts, labour and decisions.

Now we have a basic sociogram of three key figures, all of them hackers with hands-on experience but with different discursive positions. Stallman, the ethical purist; Raymond, the libertarian business-model organiser, and Torvalds, the pragmatic hacker and benevolent leader. All three are necessary to keep the open-source actor network alive and kicking, each enlisting his own allies (sometimes overlapping with the others), and each transforming and speaking for different flavours of open-source products, whether they be pure or hybrids of 'free' and 'non-free' software.

But the sociogram is not yet complete. With the extension of open source from code delivery to production, and from production to licensing and copyleft/copyright matters, we enter the domain of the law and lawyers. While there are many lawyers involved, two stand out as open-source spokesmen with their own street credibility.

Lawrence Lessig and Eben Moglen: lawyers of the commons

Two lawyers who quite often feature in open-source headlines and news reports are Lawrence Lessig and Eben Moglen. Both are on the side of hacker culture and deeply involved in the legal and ideological fight to protect public cultural resources from take-overs by companies claiming copyrights and patents. Both are American professors of law (at Stanford and Columbia, respectively), and as such are important players who bring the concepts of open source and digital commons into the realm of academic discourse. This discourse does not confine itself to strictly legal issues, but explicitly connects itself to social and political matters, as can be seen from the titles of their publications. Lessig has written books such as *Code and Other Laws of Cyberspace* (1999) and *Free Culture: How big media uses technology and the law to lock down culture and control creativity* (2004). Moglen wrote *Anarchism Triumphant: Free software and the death of copyright* (1999) and *The dotCommunist Manifesto* (2003).

But they do more than just academic and discursive work. They have earned their own street credibility: Moglen works as a lawyer for the Free Software Foundation, which administers the GPL, while Lessig founded the Creative Commons Licence, an equivalent of the GPL for creative works such as texts, music, photography, weblogs and digital content in general. This licence, recently also launched in European countries such as Germany and the Netherlands, offers several variants of copyright/copyleft, allowing third parties to use, distribute and – under certain conditions – modify the creative product in question. This is another example of how the idea of open source is travelling and being extended to all kinds of digital products, not just programs.

Moglen and Lessig are frequently called communists. Indeed, it is easy to link the notion of 'advocate of commons' with this political ideology, mostly with a pejorative connotation in mind, especially in the United States. While Lessig publicly states that he is definitely not a communist, Moglen at least plays with the symbolic capital of communism. In *The dotCommunist Manifesto* he echoes the famous first lines of Marx's *Communist Manifesto*: 'A spectre is haunting multinational capitalism – the spectre of free information'.[39] This is in fact a rewriting of the *Communist Manifesto*, from the perspective of an information society trying to overcome 'information feudalism'.

Moglen clearly represents the more optimistic view. He celebrates the anarchist benefits of the copy-and-paste culture and seems convinced that the open-source revolution is already here. His views, however, do not go unchallenged. For instance *Telepolis*, the German electronic magazine for net culture, has heavily criticised his belief that a free society can be achieved through free software.[40] Lessig's view on the development of culture is more pessimistic. The threat of information feudalism, especially in the form of built-in code to control data traffic and human behaviour, is ubiquitous in his work. But both the optimistic lawyer and the more pessimistic one are important actors in the open-source network. They are necessary intermediaries between street fights and the court-room, between hacker culture and academic culture, between ethical principles and licence formulations.

Strategies of discourse

When we analyse the discourse on open-source software we notice that several discursive strategies are used by the participants to promote their message and to argue against their antagonists. In all the spheres mentioned above we can recognise strategies based on the classic Foucaultian principles of controlling a discourse:
a) prohibition, which regulates what can be spoken of, where and how one may speak, and who has a privileged or exclusive right to speak on a particular subject;
b) the opposition between reason and madness, which creates a division between irrational and reliable speakers;
c) the opposition between true and false, the Foucaultian 'will to truth', mostly represented by science and research institutes.[41]
In the open-source discourse, this comes down to three patterns of exclusion:

a) criminalising the opponent, spreading doubt about intentions or reliability, constituting and maintaining taboos;
b) proving that the antagonist's claims are wrong and irrational, constructing the truth by new evidence and facts;
c) the use of rituals, metaphors and symbols to reframe the discourse.

Fear, uncertainty and doubt

Microsoft's strategy for responding to the open-source challenge has often been described as a 'Fear, Uncertainty and Doubt' (FUD) strategy.[42] When the SCO Group claimed copyrights on parts of Linux and began to sue companies for using it, Microsoft was immediately suspected of being the secret force behind it. And indeed, the Microsoft/SCO connection became public in March 2003 when the venture-capital investor BayStar admitted that Microsoft had funded their investment in SCO and urged them to make a point of the copyright issue. Threatening any commercial usage of Linux with a potential lawsuit, SCO spread uncertainty and doubt among companies who are considering whether to use Linux or stick to proprietary software.

This is indeed an effective strategy for excluding Linux from the market and the discourse. However, it will be difficult if not impossible for the strategy to work in every domain. For a long time, open-source server software has been widely regarded as superior to Microsoft server products. Companies use open-source mostly on their network servers, and the most frequently used web server on the Internet is the open-source server Apache. The situation is different with Linux on desktops, which has been taboo for quite some time. As Michael Tiemann, Open-Source Affairs Manager at Red Hat, puts it, 'suggesting using Linux on a desktop to a customer was impossible, even if the customer had already had good experiences using Linux on a server'.[43] This was why Red Hat initially provided no desktop application products. According to Tiemann, during this period companies would exclude themselves from the market by offering Linux desktop solutions. This taboo existed for years, and pushed open-source products towards servers, away from the desktop. Most open-source software was – and still is – invisible to ordinary users, as it runs mostly on servers and modems. The taboo in fact

Figure 4 – Microsoft advertising 'An open operating system does not only have benefits'.

shaped both the market and technological products.

Microsoft's marketing focus on Linux's liabilities, bugs and 'unpleasant mutations' was made explicit in an advertisement in Germany's most prestigious tech magazine, c't, in October 2000. The two-page ad shows penguins with an elephant's nose, a frog's head and rabbit ears, with the caption: 'An open operating system does not only have benefits'. ('Ein offenes Betriebssystem hat nicht nur Vorteile.') The text continues: 'An open operating system sometimes just mutates. Conversely, Windows 2000 offers all services from a single source'.

Online Linux communities responded as expected: 'We won: MS targets Linux in German advertising'.[44] The style of the advertising seems to allude to the do-it-yourself artwork and culture-jamming that became famous through activist groups like Adbusters.[45] It is frequently used by Microsoft critics on the Internet. But for a big company like Microsoft, it is rather tricky to criticise mutations in the name of a 'pure race' in the context of German history. Besides, this strategy ignores insights from media and science studies on the productivity of modifications and mixes. Marshall McLuhan stated decades ago that hybrids produce energy and push development ahead.[46] Bruno Latour showed how, despite their obsession with purification, modern science and technology have produced a proliferation of hybrid forms that remain unrecognised.[47]

However, the culture-jamming style, which has all kinds of associations with purification and fascist ideology, is also a discursive strategy of the anti-Microsoft warriors. Their virally distributed anti-advertisements represent Microsoft – or preferably Bill Gates – as an intolerant dictator, complete with Nazi uniform and swastikas.

Considering this kind of artwork, Microsoft's anti-Linux advertisement makes some sense. But the do-it-yourself artwork of the heterogeneous multitude of open-source communities is quite different from the deliberate marketing strategy of an established multinational such as Microsoft. People who feel connected to these communities contribute not only with code jobs, but also by producing artworks, posting comments about articles on various websites or simply forwarding pictures like the ones shown beside. The interesting aspect of these demonising strategies is how technology is able to arouse people's emotions, and how this can be transformed into creative output, not only as artwork, but also at the level of discourse and symbols. The symbolic capital of Enlightenment – literacy, freedom of speech, free flow of information, liberation and democracy – provides an arsenal of discursive weapons to be used against Microsoft's monopoly-constructing market strategies. For example, the *Software Wars Map* published by Li-Cheng Tai depicts the open-source battle in terms of liberation frontiers and the Microsoft empire.

Figure 5.

Figure 6.

Marianne van den Boomen & Mirko Tobias Schäfer

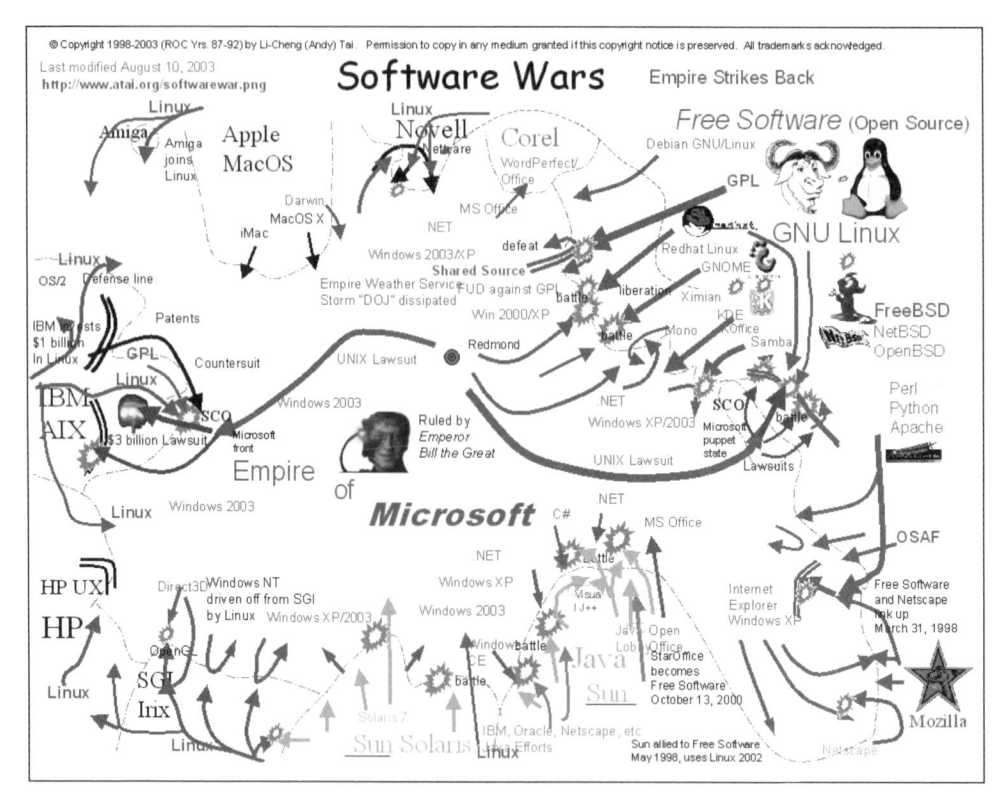

Figure 7.

Cultural practices such as do-it-yourself artwork and mapping the battlefield are not just discourse strategies, they also serve the purpose of positioning the open-source enthusiasts. As the 'most evil' antagonist in the open-source battle, Microsoft plays an important role in this process. In fact, the hegemonic company makes the cultural activity and identity of Linux protagonists possible by its mere existence, its business models and its discursive strategies. The harder Microsoft pushes its influence on parliaments, public administrations, companies, and the public sphere, the more it contributes to the identity and community-building of the open-source movement.

The 'will to truth': proof and counter-proof

In the late 1990s, one of the main reasons for companies and institutions to use open source was its price: it was practically free. Microsoft responded promptly with detailed accounts of the 'total costs of ownership' of desktop computers, which included the cost of service, maintenance and system management, claiming that their seemingly expensive products might in the end be cheaper than using Linux. In 2004 Microsoft launched a special website dedicated to the open-source debate, calling it *Get the facts*. On this website we find many links to research claiming the superiority of Microsoft products and the unreliability, or even dangers, of open source[48] – for example, a survey by the Alexis de Tocqueville Institution stating that open-source software facilitates terrorist attacks.[49] Another survey by this institution claims that Linux was not even invented by Linus Torvalds.[50] A survey published by the Forrester Research/Giga Information Group shows how companies could save up to 28% of their costs using Microsoft products instead of Linux.[51] An International Data Corporation (IDC) survey claimed that companies had higher expenses because they used Linux.[52]

This 'scientific' attack on Linux can be described as an attempt to exclude speakers from the discourse by the Foucaultian 'will to truth'. But we also learned from Foucault that truth never comes without power and organisation: several independent sources have claimed that Microsoft financially supported the Alexis de Tocqueville Institution, Forrester Research and IDC.[53]

The strategy of the 'will to truth' is not, of course, the exclusive preserve of the closed-source party in the discourse. Pro-open-source websites also provide surveys to prove the compatibility, usability and benefits of Linux.[54] Publishing success stories or case-studies on migration to open source is in fact the equivalent of Microsoft's publishing *Get the Facts*. Moreover, the Foucaultian 'will to truth' is also at work in the growing interest in open-source issues being shown by scholars from a range of different disciplines.

If you can't beat 'em, join 'em

Besides excluding Linux from the discourse by pushing its subject to the fringes of legality and reliability, Microsoft enters the discourse by pretending being open itself.

With its *Shared Source Initiative* the software company alludes to the concepts of the open-source movement, allowing licensed parties limited access to their proprietary source code. A Gartner Group survey concludes that although the software giant stresses the importance of openness it is not actually implementing these principles itself.[55] For example, the Internet Explorer review process revealed many serious security problems but did not lead to implementing any effective solutions. Microsoft's Shared Source Initiative uses the terminology of open-source principles, but it comes nowhere near to the peer-review model and collaborative production process of open-source development. It lacks practically all the freedoms Richard Stallman talks about: no public availability, no right to modify, no right to distribute.

Microsoft has taken more steps to 'join the enemy'. In June 2004 for the first time the company attended the German business fair, Linuxtag. In several statements, leading managers welcomed the competition of open source: it would lead to better products, and in the end the market would decide which was the best.[56] This is the well-known capitalist discourse of the free market allowing 'democratic elections' of the best products. But behind the scenes, and in public, Microsoft is working hard to 'enable the market to decide' in the right direction, that is: closed software as a protected business model.[57]

This strategy of 'joining the enemy' can be found in open-source circles as well. For example, Wine/Lindows is open-source software that makes it possible to run Microsoft applications on Linux systems. And approximately 25% of the open-source projects hosted on SourceForge are related to Microsoft software. In April 2004 Microsoft itself offered two projects on SourceForge for the first time ever. Surprisingly, in June 2004 these were among the most active five per cent of the more than 80,000 projects at SourceForge.

Political agenda-setting

Though we can perceive patterns like the ones above in the discursive strategies of the open-source movement, these are by no means centrally organised communication strategies. While the public discourse on open source can be shaped by the accidental or self-assigned representatives of the open-source multitudes, setting political goals and agendas is quite another thing. This is done by other players from other domains. In particular, unions, left-wing political parties and non-governmental organisations recognise in the open-source concept their traditional values of democracy, public responsibility and collectivity, and connect these values to several campaigns.

In the late 1990s the open-source discourse was framed mainly as a financial and technological issue. Open-source entrepreneurs stressed the assets of cheapness, reliability and safety. From 2001 we notice a shift in the argumentation, from costs to independence, freedom and democracy. During a year-long discussion in the German parliament about which software to use on its servers and desktops, the importance of being independent of the software supplier was a recurring argument. The German Bundestag finally compromised: it would use Linux on its 150 servers but stick to Windows on its 5,000 desktops. Nevertheless, this showed that open source was definitely on the political agenda. Now German politicians of all parties are actively promoting Linux on the platform www.bundestux.de.

In communicating their interest, politicians are extending the field of discourse to a wider public. For example, the Bavarian politician and former programmer Monica Lochner-Fischer (Social Democratic Party) launched the campaign 'More Linux, More Freedom'. Microsoft was not amused, and tried in vain to get the posters removed. In interviews, Lochner-Fischer encouraged concerned citizens and open-source activists to shift the debate from online platforms and user groups into the political sphere, by attending political meetings or writing letters to members of parliament.[58]

The Austrian Green Party launched a *'Linux for everyone'* (Linux für Alle) campaign, and distributed 5,000 copies of a bootable Linux CD.[59] The website gives arguments for using open-source software, offers a free download of Volker Grassmuck's book *Freie Software*, and the content of the Linux CD to burn at home. To encourage and support people interested in running Linux on their desktops, the Viennese department of the Green Party adopted the Linux User Groups' practice of organising Linux installation parties.[60]

The Dutch party GroenLinks (Green Left) is also actively propagating open source.[61] The party wants to stimulate the use of open source in public administrations, and is urging active support for the development of open-source solutions in the public sector. Again, the main argument here is independence from suppliers: the public administration should be in control of its own software.

Business fairs such as the Linuxtag, the Linux Worldexpo in Frankfurt, the Linuxwochen in Austria or the Wizard of OS Conference in Berlin provide platforms for discussion between politicians and open-source activists. The 2004 Wizard of OS conference released the so-called 'Berlin Declaration on Collectively Managed Online Rights' and sent it to the European Commission. In this statement copyright scholars, civil society activists and programmers urged the European Commission to revise their approach to software patents and intellectual property.[62] The Berlin Declaration is a landmark in the politicisation of the open-source discourse: it shows that the open-source multitude can become organised and is capable of formulating political goals. And this is needed badly, as the open-source discourse is being increasingly marked by battles on intellectual property, copyrights and patents. Legislation and political decision-making processes in this domain are emerging as a new open-source battlefield.

The proposed EU regulation of software patents is widely regarded as a major threat to open-source development. While copyright closure could be successfully countered with copyleft licences, this cannot be done with patents. The legislation on copyright (or copyleft) protects a specific work; the legislation on patents protects general technological inventions. Software can indeed be considered to be in between a written work and a technological invention – this is the essence of software: it is written code that does something technical. But the shift from copyright to patents implies the possibility of so-called trivial patents – patents on commonly-used building blocks or ideas. Compare this with the situation of an author writing a novel when someone has patents registered on 'the happy ending', or 'the relative clause', or the letter 'm': writing a novel would become practically impossible. In the same way, open-source development will become very difficult, as no amateur programmer would be able to go through the thousands of software patents to check whether his or her work contains possible patent infringements. It will be obvious that patenting software limits our cultural resources and slows down the innovation process in ICT.[63]

Moreover, if almost any software idea can be patented, even such common things as a toolbar, a spell checker or a double-click (all three patented by Microsoft), it will become very easy to attack any open-source program with claims of patent infringements. A recently published Hewlett-Packard memo from 2001 addresses this possibility. The memo warns: 'Microsoft could attack open-source software for patent infringements against OEMs, Linux distributors, and least likely open-source developers. (...) Basically Microsoft is going to use the legal system to shut down open-source software'.[64] On Slashdot, the memo raised a discussion with more than 350 postings. But not only open-source communities and Linux distributors are worried – European small and medium-sized businesses see these patents as a threat too.[65] And even Deutsche Bank research recently stated that 'patents on software, common practice in the US and on the brink of being legalised in Europe, in fact stifle innovation'.[66]

Increasingly diverse players representing various domains are arguing against software patents. For example, when the German chancellor Gerhard Schröder recently opened a symposium on innovation and intellectual property, a demonstration was organised by Linux groups, the Free Software Foundation Europe and non-software organisations, such as Greenpeace and Attac. Demonstrations set up to fight for open source are of course possible because the issue reflects traditional democratic values, while demonstrations for Microsoft products would seem ridiculous. In any case, this shows the public's growing interest in software patents and open source, and the political relevance of the issue. The time seems to be ripe for encouraging a public debate on open source, and drawing in those who still consider it a nerd's hobby. Open-source communities, spokesmen and other actors have demonstrated that open source matters, and that it affects much more than just the life and work of programmers. The discourse can now enter a second stage and become a major issue on the political agenda.

Conclusion: will the revolution be open-sourced?

Our explorative mapping of the open-source discourse has shown how the concept travelled from computer subcultures into various domains – economic, cultural, social, legal, academic and, especially, political. Using a actor-network approach made it possible to identify the various players, spokesmen, companies, and institutions which are busy mobilising their allies and associations, using several discursive and non-discursive strategies to transform and extend the concept of open source. It became clear that the discourse directly affects the development of technological products, and that technology, in turn, shapes the discourse.

The spokesmen of the open-source movement in fact shaped a public sphere, by representing the multitude of users and promoting agenda-setting by other players. Meanwhile, open-source developers continued to offer compatible programs, suggestions for independent technology use, open standards and free access to technology.

In the extending actor network the term 'open source' became firmly associated with democratic values, collaborative production processes, freely accessible resources and community-building.

Several actors alluded or explicitly referred to the term 'revolution'. Spokesmen such as Raymond and Torvalds call themselves 'accidental revolutionaries', and Moglen hit the spot when he translated open-source principles in terms of revolutionary communism. But revolutions can only be recognised and evaluated with hindsight, from a future in which the winners have been definitively declared. It is just too early to answer the question 'will the revolution be open-sourced?' The battle is still going on, and seems to be entering a second stage, in the domain of political agenda-setting and legal regulation.

Nevertheless, the rapid and widespread diffusion of the term 'open source' is remarkable. Starting as a practical concept from the computer subculture, the concept mobilised a huge and ever-widening discourse and technological development. It has become the major metaphor in the battle between the monopolistic establishment and distributed cultural practices, which are strongly connected with the collaborative labour dynamics of the Internet generation (Castells, 2001). While monopolistic companies and their allies try to sustain the industrial-age concepts of property, patents and copyrights, the metaphor of open source describes and mobilises the cultural practice of the digital age. Perhaps we can even describe the multitude of programmers, users, spokesmen and activists as the avant-garde developing the cultural practice of the 21st century. But what is clearly needed is a political avant-garde, or rather a broad movement, to root this in political practice. The fate of the open-source paradigm is closely connected to a public sphere which provides a legal and social framework for the ongoing circulation and modification of technologies and ideas. That is where our cultural resources reside. And it is worth the battle.

Notes

1. See for instance Raymond (1999), Stallman (2002) and Weber (2004). Following these authors, we define 'hacker culture' as the culture of passionate programmers who create their own tools. This should not be confused with 'cracker culture', i.e. vandals who destroy the tools of others.
2. See www.automatiseringgids.nl for the web archive of the weekly *Automatisering Gids* since 1997.
3. See www.opensource.org/halloween
4. These are taken from the Dutch *Automatisering Gids*, but any other European professional ICT magazine will undoubtedly reveal the same pattern.
5. The SCO Group, inheritor of the intellectual property of the Unix operating system, started its copyright claims on parts of the Linux operating system by suing IBM for more than $ 1 billion in March 2003, alleging that IBM had misappropriated SCO's Unix technology and built it into Linux.
6. Figures vary widely between research institutes. Gartner (2004) counts a 2-5% market share for Linux on PCs, Tim O'Reilly 18%. IDC (2004) estimates the server market share for Unix at 36%, Windows 35% and Linux 15%.
7. Or 'Free/Libre/Open Source' (FLOSS), with the term 'libre' to counter the ambiguity of the word 'free', which is here not intended to mean 'gratis'.
8. Gary Rivlin, 'Leader of the free world: How Linus Torvalds became benevolent dictator of Planet Linux, the biggest collaborative project in history', in *Wired* 11, 2003. See also Thomas Goetz, 'Open source everywhere: Software is just the beginning', in *Wired* 11, 2003.
9. Examples of open-source software projects organised on the Internet: Sourceforge.net (www.sourceforge.net), the Open Source Initiative (www.opensource.org), Open Office (www.openoffice.org), Mozilla (www.mozilla.org), MySQL (www.mysql.com). A long list of available open-source software is provided by Wikipedia at http://en.wikipedia.org/wiki/List_of_open-source_software_packages
10. As analysed by Berit Jimmink in her thesis *Interactiviteit bij Slashdot: Code, content en community* (Utrecht University, november 2004).
11. http://opensource.mit.edu/
12. See the book written by Dean's campaign manager, Joe Trippi: *The revolution will not be televised: Democracy, the Internet, and the overthrow of everything*. New York, HarperCollins: 2004.
13. See for instance Martin Pedersen, *Lessons from cyberspace: The Free Software movement and the configuration of ownership*. Paper presented at the conference entitled 'Imaging Social Movements', July 3, 2004, Edge Hill College, UK. Online: http://www.edgehill.ac.uk/Research/smg/Conferences2004/info/papers/pedersen.pdf
14. www.oekonux.de. See also Geert Lovink, 'Oekonux and the Free-Software Model: From Linux to the GPL Society', in *My first recession,* 2003.
15. *Free Software & GPL Society,* Stefan Merten interviewed by Joanne Richardson, online: http://subsol.c3.hu/subsol_2/contributors0/mertentext.html
16. See www.newscientist.com/hottopics/copyleft/copyleftart.jsp and www.opencola.com
17. Bruno Latour, *Science in Action: How to Follow Scientists and Engineers through Society*. Cambridge, Mass: Harvard University Press, 1987.

18 *Ibid.*, p. 139.
19 Especially since Latour's method insists on taking a *symmetrical* look at 'science in action'. Symmetrical here means: no bias, no *a priori* assumptions about social, technical, natural or scientific 'truth'. The divisions between different kinds of 'truth', and a general division between 'truth' and 'mere beliefs or common-sense' have to be analysed as the *effects* of the player-network dynamics, not the *cause*.
20 Though it remains to be seen if in this case there will ever be an accepted 'black box' in the Latourian sense, since the concept of open source itself implies an inherent resistance to such closure. Indeed, the very principle of open source is against any black-boxing.
21 Chris DiBona, Sam Ockman & Mark Stone (eds), *Open Sources: Voices from the open source revolution*. Sebastopol, O'Reilly: 1999.
22 Richard M. Stallman, *Free Software, Free Society*. Boston: GNU Press, 2002, p. 16.
23 Note that this does not forbid all 'commercial use', as suggested by Microsoft's Bradford Lee, elsewhere in this book. The GPL just forbids turning free copyleft material into proprietary material.
24 Free Software Foundation Homepage: www.gnu.org/fsf. The FSF is an actor in the network too, by providing lawyers for programmers sued because of copyright infringement, discussing recent law directives, setting the agenda for a revision of the Digital Millennium Copyright Act, etc.
25 Stallman, 2002, p. 39.
26 *Ibid.*, p. 36.
27 *Ibid.*, p. 22.
28 In 1997 Raymond presented his ideas on the bazaar model at the Linux Kongress in Germany, and published the essay online, where it immediately raised a debate. In 1999 Raymond published the essay together with other essays in *The cathedral and the bazaar: Musings on Linux and open source by an accidental revolutionary*. O'Reilly: Sebastopol, 1999.
29 *Ibid.*, p. 13.
30 *Ibid.*, p. 21.
31 In the chapter 'The magic cauldron' Raymond (1999) describes nine business models for sustainable open-source funding – two non-profit, seven for-profit.
32 *Ibid.*, p. 29.
33 Particularly in the chapter 'Revenge of the hackers' in Raymond (1999).
34 *Ibid.*, p. 177.
35 *Ibid.*, p. 196.
36 Linus Torvalds and David Diamond. *Just for Fun: The Story of an Accidental Revolutionary*. Harper Business, 2001.
37 David Diamond (2003), 'The Peacemaker: How Linus Torvalds, the man behind Linux, keeps the revolution from becoming a jihad', in *Wired* 11.07.
38 On the Linux labour organisation with several maintainers, see Paul Venezia, IDG News Service, 11-2-2000 *How the Linux kernel gets built*,
    http://www.arnnet.com.au/index.php/id;1843600829;fp;4;fpid;1854890668
39 Eben Moglen, *The dotComunist Manifesto*, 2003, online: http://emoglen.law.columbia.edu/.
40 Marcus Hammerschmitt, 'Luftbuchungen freier Software', in *Telepolis*, 21-6-2004, online:

www.heise.de/bin/tp/issue/dl-artikel.cgi?artikelnr=17676&rub_ordner=inhalt&mode=html and Stefan Krempl, 'Free Society, Von der Utopie zum Alltag', in *Telepolis*, 12-6-2004, online: www.heise.de/tp/deutsch/html/result.xhtml?url=/tp/deutsch/special/wos/17636/1.html&twords=Moglen

41 Michel Foucault, 'The discourse on language', in *The Archaeology of Knowledge*. New York: Pantheon, 1982; pp. 215-238.

42 The term FUD was first coined by Gene Amdahl to describe IBM's strategy for persuading customers to buy safe IBM products instead of their competitors' 'unsafe' products. See *The Jargon File* by Eric S. Raymond, online: http://www.catb.org/~esr/jargon/html/F/FUD.html

43 *Linux auf dem Desktop ist kein Tabu mehr*, Interview with Michael Tiemann in Golem.de, 9.7.2004, online: http://www.golem.de/0407/32066.html

44 'We won: MS targets Linux in German advertising', in *Linux Today* 22 Oct. 2000. Online: http://linuxtoday.com/mailprint.php3?action=pv&ltsn=2000-10-22-016-04-NW-CY-MS

45 See adbusters.com

46 In the chapter 'Energy from hybrids' in his book *Understanding Media* (1968, p. 95), McLuhan wrote that the hybrid, the connection of two media, is a moment of truth which produces a new kind of medium.

47 Bruno Latour, 1991.

48 *Get the Facts*: http://www.microsoft.com/mscorp/facts/default.asp

49 Kenneth Brown, *Opening the Open Source Debate*. http://www.adti.net/opensource.pdf

50 Kenneth Brown, *Samizidat*. Alexis de Tocquville Institution, 2004, http://www.adti.net/kenarbeit/samiz.release.html

51 http://download.microsoft.com/download/7/3/e/73e77129-db34-4c95-b182-ab0b9bd50081/TEICaseStudy.pdf

52 See also the Blog Deltoid: http://www.cse.unsw.edu.au/~lambert/blog/computers/tanks.html

53 For instance, Alfred Krüger, *Gesponserte Fakten*, in Telepolis, 8.1.2004; http://www.heise.de/tp/deutsch/inhalt/te/16473/1.html

54 Surveys on migration to open source: http://www.bundestux.de/themen/inlmigstud/index.html

55 John Pescatore, *Microsoft sends mixed signals about Software Security*, Gartner Group 2002, http://www3.gartner.com/resources/106700/106790/106790.pdf

56 'Microsoft Österreich-Chef im Gespräch: Heil froh' über Open Source', in *Der Standard*, 28.6.2004; online: http://derstandard.at/?id=1568721

57 See also Bradford L. Smith, *The Future of Software: Enabling the Marketplace to Decide*, March 2003; online: http://www.microsoft.com/resources/sharedsource/Articles/Future.mspx (also in this book). For a profound analysis of Microsoft's strategies see Alexander Roesler and Bernd Stiegler, *Microsoft, Medien, Macht, Monopol*. Frankfurt a.M., Suhrkamp: 2002.

58 'Mehr Linux, Mehr Freiheit', Monica Lochner-Fischer interviewed by Peter Riedlberger and Peter Mühlbauer, in *Telepolis*, 17.7.2003: http://www.heise.de/tp/deutsch/inhalt/te/15239/1.html

59 *Linux für Alle*, http://www.wien.gruene.at/linux/

60 One reason for this engagement might also be the personal background of Marie Ringler, who is responsible for technology issues in the Viennese Green Party. Ringler served for years as managing director of Public Netbase, Institute of New Culture Technologies. See www.marieringler.at

61 'Groenlinks presenteert plan Open source', 19.11.2002; online: http://www.groenlinks.nl/partij/landelijk/nieuwsarchief/dbimport/id-gldb-4001428/view
62 The Berlin Declaration, http://www.wizards-of-os.org/index.php?id=1699&L=3
63 This is also the conclusion of a US survey: Paul Horn, Eliot Maxwell, and Susan Crawford, *Promoting innovation in the on-line world: the problem of digital intellectual property. A report by the Digital Connections Council of the Committee for Economic Development*, 2004.
64 Joe Barr, 'HP Memo forecasts MS patents attack on free software', in *Newsforge*, 19.7.2004; online: http://www.newsforge.com/article.pl?sid=04/07/19/2315200
65 See *Ein Jobkiller*, Georg Greve interviewed by Stefan Krempl, in *Die Zeit*, 8.7.2004; online: http://www.zeit.de/2004/29/Interview_Patente
66 Deutsche Bank Research: *Innovation in Germany. Windows of Opportunity*; online: http://www.dbresearch.com/PROD/DBR_INTERNET_EN-PROD/PROD0000000000175949.pdf

Bibliography

BRADLEY, Dale. 'Open source, anarchy, and the utopian impulse'. M/C: *A Journal of Media and Culture* 7 (3) 2004 (http://www.media-culture.org.au/0406/03_Bradley.html).

CASTELLS, Manuel. *The Internet Galaxy*. New York: Oxford University Press, 2001.

COLEMAN, Biela & HILL, Mako. 'How free became open and everything else under the sun'. M/C: *A Journal of Media and Culture* 7 (3) 2004 (http://www.media-culture.org.au/0406/02_Coleman-Hill.html).

DIAMOND, David. 'The peacemaker: How Linus Torvalds, the man behind Linux, keeps the revolution from becoming a Jihad'. *Wired* 2003: 7.

FOUCAULT, Michel. 'The discourse on language', in: FOUCAULT, Michel, *The Archaeology of Knowledge*. New York: Pantheon, 1982, pp. 215-238.

GOETZ, Thomas. 'Open source everywhere: Software is just the beginning'. *Wired*, 11, 2003.

GRASSMUCK, Volker. *Freie Software. Zwischen Privat- und Gemeineigentum*. Bonn: BPB, 2002.

LATOUR, Bruno. *Science in Action: How to follow scientists and engineers through society*. Cambridge, Mass: Harvard University Press, 1987.

LESSIG, Lawrence. *Code and Other Laws of Cyberspace*. New York: Basic Books/Perseus, 1999.

LESSIG, Lawrence. *Free Culture: How big media uses technology and the law to lock down culture and control creativity*. Penguin Press, 2004.

LOVINK, Geert. *My First Recession: Critical Internet culture in transmission*. Rotterdam: V2_Publising/NAi Publishers, 2003.

MCLUHAN, Marshall. *Understanding Media. The extensions of man*. Cambridge: MIT Press, 1964.

MOGLEN, Eben. 'Anarchism Triumphant: Free software and the death of copyright'. *First Monday* 1999.

RAYMOND, Eric S. *The Cathedral and the Bazaar: Musings on Linux by an accidental revolutionary*. Sebastopol: O'Reilly, 1999.

RIVLIN, Gary. 'Leader of the Free World: How Linus Torvalds became benevolent dictator of Planet Linux, the biggest collaborative project in history'. *Wired*, 11, 2003.

ROESLER, Alexander & STIEGLER, Bernd. *Microsoft; Medien, Macht, Monopol*. Frankfurt a. M.: Suhrkamp, 2002.

STALLMAN, Richard M. *Free Software, Free Society*. Boston: GNU Press, 2002.
TORVALDS, Linus, and DAVID Diamond. *Just for Fun: The story of an accidental revolutionary*. Harper Business, 2001.
TRIPPI, Joe. *The Revolution will Not be Televised*. New York: HarperCollins, 2004.
WEBER, Steven. *The Success of Open Source*. Cambridge: Harvard University Press, 2004.

Pictures

Figure 1: *Richard Stallman playing flute for a butterfly*. Richard Stallman's home page
www.stallman.org/rms.jpg
Figure 2: *Eric Raymond at the O'Reilly Open-Source Convention*. LinuxDevCenter
www.linuxdevcenter.com/pub/a/linux/2001/08/02/raymond.html
Figure 3: *Linus Torvalds with his family*. The Rampantly Unofficial Linus Torvalds FAQ,
www.catb.org/~esr/ faqs/linus/le2.jpg
Figure 4: *Microsoft advertising*. Source: c't October 2000.
Figure 5: *Anti-Microsoft Page* www.theapplecollection.com/various/anti_ms/
Figure 6: *Microsoft Art Page*. http://microsoft.com.tripod.com/art.htm
Figure 7: *Software Wars*. Li-Cheng Tai, www.atai.org

Biographies

Marianne van den Boomen studied psychology and political science and has worked as an editor for several magazines. She has published several articles and books on Internet culture. Since January 2003 she has been working as a junior lecturer/researcher at the University of Utrecht, in the Department of Media and Re/presentation. She is currently writing her dissertation on Internet metaphors.

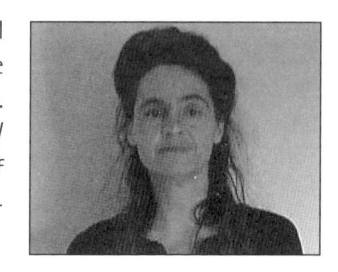

Mirko Tobias Schäfer studied theatre, film media and communication at Vienna University (A) and digital culture at Utrecht University (NL). He was organizer and co-curator of [d]vision, the Vienna Festival for Digital Culture. Since February 2003 he has been working as a junior lecturer/researcher at the University of Utrecht, in the Institute for Media and Re/presentation. He is currently writing his dissertation on "Bastard Culture! Competent Users, Networks and Cultural Industries". Mirko lives in Rotterdam (NL) and Vienna (A).

Emack & Bolio's
Cooper Square

ICE CREAM • SMOOTHIES • COFFEES

web2zone

Free as in Freedom, *not* Gratis!

An interview with Richard Stallman,
the embodiment of the dilemma of our digital commons.

Marleen Wynants

The myth and guru-esque spell of Richard Stallman originated in Marvin Minsky's AI lab at MIT at the end of the 1970s. Before the myth took off, Stallman was legendary as a software programmer. In 1984 he founded the Free Software Movement to spread the concept of freedom in programming and to develop a community of free software developers. Stallman is not merely the father of the GNU project and its associated copyleft culture, he embodies it.

Richard Matthew Stallman was born in New York City in 1953. He joined the group of hackers at the MIT Artificial Intelligence Laboratory (AI Lab) in 1971. In the 1980s, the MIT hacker community began to dissolve under the pressure of the commercialization of the software industry. A group of breakaway AI Lab hackers founded the company Symbolics. They actively attempted to recruit the rest of the AI Lab hackers in order to replace the free software in the Lab and the rest of the world with their own proprietary software. MIT made arrangements with Symbolics that declared MIT's software non-free.

For two years, Stallman duplicated the efforts of the Symbolics programmers to prevent them from gaining a monopoly on the Lab's computers. By that time, however, he was the last of his generation of hackers at the Lab. Stallman anticipated that sooner or later he would be asked to sign non-disclosure agreements and, as a precaution to prevent this from occurring, and to avoid other betrayals of his principles, he quit.

Instead he chose to share his work with others in what he regarded as a "classical spirit of scientific collaboration and openness".

So in 1984 Stallman resigned from the MIT AI Lab to work on the GNU project with the aim of developing a complete UNIX-style operating system that was free software: the GNU system. GNU is a recursive acronym for "GNU's Not UNIX". Variants of the GNU operating system, which use the kernel Linux, are now widely used; and though these systems are often referred to as "Linux" they are more accurately called GNU/Linux systems.

By officially resigning, he ensured that MIT would not be able to claim the copyright on GNU software. A year later, Stallman founded the Free Software Foundation as a tax-exempt charity for the development of free software. But Stallman was able to continue using the computers and an office at the university even though from 1984 to 1991 he no longer had any official connection with MIT.

And when, in April 2004, MIT CSAIL – the merger between the Computer Science Department and the AI Lab, under the direction of Rodney Brooks – moved into the extraordinary Ray and Maria STATA Center, designed by Frank Gehry, room 32-381 was assigned to RMS.

Saint IGNUtius

Richard Stallman did not complete a doctoral degree although throughout the years he has been awarded several honorary doctoral degrees, including the Doctor Honoris Causa award of the VUB (Vrije Universiteit Brussel). His aims are no longer academic, but purely activistic. As Stallman himself stated when walking into the First CROSSTALKS Science & Industry Dinner on 20 February 2004: "20 years and six weeks ago, I started the Free Software Movement because I was determined to live in freedom and non-free software tramples your freedom, so I was determined to escape from it...".

Stallman's philosophy is that "software users deserve to be free": if a user or fellow "hacker" can benefit from a particular piece of software it is the developer's right – and indeed duty – to allow them to use and improve it without artificial hindrance and without putting restrictions on the freedom of the person they distribute it to.

I met Richard Stallman for the first time during a weekend in February 2001 at the First FOSDEM Conference – Free and Open-Source Software Developers' Meeting – in

Europe, which took place at the ULB (Université Libre de Bruxelles) in Brussels. While the audience was awaiting the arrival of Stallman, the homepages of Slashdot.com and Mozilla.org were projected onto the wall of the auditorium. No sponsors in sight, and FOSDEM founder Raphael Bauduin promises that the Hacker Room will be functional in a couple of hours, as installation has just started.

The nervous braying in the virtually all-male auditorium (the exceptions being me and the PR women) climaxes when Stallman, the subject of the ongoing eager discussions and excitement, enters the room. RMS takes off his shoes and campus sweater, flips his long black curly hair behind his shoulders and asks with his sharp nasal voice whether he needs a microphone or not. Yes, he does. The first minutes of his talk are devoted to explaining that he is NOT affiliated with the Open-Source Movement which he thinks avoids "issues of freedom, community, principle and ethics".

His discourse then switches into a guided tour for software developers through the mazes of patents, copyrights, trademarks and trade secrecy. And all the traps associated with them.

One of the dangers looming in the near future are the negotiations between the American government and European and other international institutions on making sure that verdicts and sentences in software patents cases in American courts can be taken as examples in other courts anywhere in the world.

After more than an hour of ramifications about the differences between the proprietary open-source movement and the free software movement, about copyleft and copyright, and about GNU/Linux, the message that our creative commons are in danger has been transmitted successfully. Richard Stallman becomes Saint IGNUtius and finishes his talk with a parody on his pope-like status – he takes out his kaftan, puts a halo on his head and states: *"To be a member of the Church of Emacs, you must recite the Confession of the Faith: 'There is no system but GNU, and Linux is one of its kernels.'"*

Time to take the myth out of the man and usher him toward a quiet room for an interview. Richard Stallman first makes sure his girlfriend has found a socket to plug her laptop into, and while we head for a classroom at the ULB complex she rolls a cigarette and starts to raise some smoke in the hallway... Two years later Stallman entertains visitors to his website with a personal ad in which *the single father* appeals for a sweetheart: "... My 19-year-old child, the Free Software Movement, occupies most of my life, leaving no room for more children, but I still have room to love a sweetheart. I spend a lot of my time traveling to give speeches, often to Europe, Asia and Latin America; it would be nice if you were free to travel with me some of the time (...)".

Down through the years, Stallman has been programming on and off, depending on his availability and on physical constraints, but his main activities do indeed consist of traveling around the world advocating free software, its community and the copyleft culture. Without exception, he always gives rise to the inevitable commotion and rumors. When a panelist in De Waag in Amsterdam verbally attacked Stallman and would not let him go on with his speech, Stallman dryly said: "You can speak, I will leave." And he left.

There is also the story on his website that he got paid extra by Texas Instruments in Dallas *not* to come back and finish a series of lectures... probably because of his making nasal love to flowers on a restaurant table... Stallman continues to weave around himself mythical shockwaves of the unpredictable and vulnerable bad boy, but the only thing that really upsets him is when he feels people don't take the case of the free software movement seriously enough.

Back to the interview and to the man who made it all possible. Let's first do away with some prejudices: the Free Software Movement is concerned not only with practical benefits but with social, ethical and political issues. Free software doesn't mean you don't have to pay for it: it does not mean "free of charge" but "free" as in "freedom". Which means that with the distribution of a version of a GNU/Linux system, the source code should be distributed as well. "There are companies in China for instance that don't do that and violate the principle of free software. But since China doesn't enforce copyright laws very much, nothing can be done about it...".

What are the main challenges for the free software community during the coming years?

RMS: Our biggest challenge is not developing software, since we know we can do that. It is to prevent laws that would prohibit free software, laws such as patenting of software ideas.

How can you prevent the Free Software movement from fading away as an activist movement, or being dismissed as too radical for the real world to live with – exactly like what happened with the radical countercultural and ecological movements in the seventies and eighties?

RMS: If we are talking about rational people, people who adjust their beliefs to observed facts, there is no problem. Lots of people exclusively use free software; nowadays it isn't very hard. Twenty years ago, it was impossible to use a computer without proprietary software. Ten years ago, it was possible but difficult. Today it is pretty easy. This change is the work of the free software community. We are not just asking people to reject non-free software, we are working to help them. First we worked to make it possible, and now we are making it easier. In the future, we will make it even easier, unless governments prohibit us from doing so.

Software patents sound as if they protect the developers of software, but they don't. What is the real problem with software patents?

RMS: The main message is that software patents kill the creativity and progression in the field. Because there are so many vulnerable spots in a software program that, sooner or later, any software developer will be confronted with parts of code that are patented and that are very hard to get around or find an alternative to.

A recent study found that Linux, the kernel of the GNU/Linux system, is covered by 286 different US patents. Any other large and powerful program probably runs afoul of hundreds of patents too, but we usually don't know how many.

What can be done? Trying to avoid using algorithms that are patented, and organizing a vigorous countermovement to convince governments all over the world that the manipulation of information is not something that should be patented. And trying to convince business leaders that the patenting of software is comparable to the patenting of business methods, so that there comes a solidarity from that side too.

Software patents are a danger to all software developers except the multinational corporations, which can get many, many patents of their own and use them to counter-attack when they are threatened with patents.

Anybody else who is developing software is in danger from software patents. It's not just a free software movement issue. It is the free software community in Europe that is most aware of the danger and that is more organized to fight against it. But other software developers do have a reason, the same kind of reason, to oppose software patents, and they should read about the dangers of software patents and oppose them.

Software patents tend to be associated with copyrights or intellectual property.

RMS: Yes, people do make that association, but the point is to realize that they are different issues, different matters. To lump them together leads to unintelligent conclusions about all of them.

To have an opinion about intellectual property is foolish. I don't have an opinion about intellectual property. I have opinions about copyrights, I have opinions about patents, I have opinions about trademarks, but they are not the same opinions. These three laws do different jobs, they have different effects on society.

In the issue with software patents, the thing to realize is that a software patent restricts the development of software by others. It's a monopoly restricting what software others can develop and use.

You seem to regard software as a social product, while the rest of the world looks at it from an economic point of view. Can you elaborate on this?

RMS: I am not sure what the term "social product" would mean. Perhaps what you mean is that I think of the use of software in ethical and social terms rather than in economic terms.

People are usually taught to think of all questions in narrow economic terms, and they apply this to software. So they think the only questions are what software is available and how much it costs to use. I'm more concerned with the social conditions of using the software. In 1984, working at MIT, I could easily have used proprietary software legally without paying, without MIT's paying. (Companies like to be able to say their software is used at MIT.) Judged by most people's narrow economic terms, my situation was perfect. But I saw that computer users did not have freedom, and I wanted to change that.

Non-free software keeps users divided and helpless: divided because they have promised not to share, and helpless because none of them can tell what the program really does, let alone change it. This social system is bad for everyone. If my neighbors have promised to refuse to share with me, that hurts me – it's not just their private business. When people are part of a community and they help each other, an effort to divide them is an attack on the community.

People sometimes argue on economic grounds that a certain program won't be developed at all unless it is proprietary. I respond that we're better off without it than having it on those terms. If using a program means I'm helpless and dependent because what the program does inside is a secret, I don't want it. If using a program means I have to promise not to share it with you, I cannot ethically accept it.

So if you face the choice of developing a program as proprietary software or not at all, please don't develop it. Sooner or later someone else will be in a position to develop such a program and make it free. Freedom is worth the wait.

In your view software patents retard progress?

RMS: We see this not only from our experience. There is now economic research to back it up. There is a site called www.researchoninnovation.org where there are scientific papers backing this up. They show that in fields where innovation tends to be cumulative, patents can slow down progress. That patents are nominally intended to promote progress, but in software they don't. Some ideas still get published, but the point is that without the patent system they would be published anywhere, everywhere. Proponents of software patents like to claim that without software patents these ideas would not be published.

There is an old joke about a man walking down the street acting very strange – waving his arms in all kinds of directions, yelling and screaming at the top of his voice, clapping his hands and stamping his feet. And people were asking "Why are you doing that?" And he says "I'm keeping the elephants away!" And people say "But there are no elephants here!" Whereupon he says "You see! It works!".

The defenders of the patent system are like that. They point to the fact that there is progress and they say the progress is because of the patent system; without having an alternative universe, it is hard to prove conclusively that they are wrong, even if they are wrong.

But what we do have is the past. In the past, when there was software, there was even a software industry and it was making progress – and there were no software patents. So they will say *"That was then. Things are different today – you can't have progress without software patents."* They have no basis for this claim.

They have convinced people of a certain ideology which says that progress can never be made in a narrow area without giving somebody monopolies in this area. It's an ideology, and it's false, sometimes.

In what ways is the open-source movement a threat to the principles of free software?

RMS: People began using the term "open source" in 1998 as a way to talk about free software without mentioning the ethical and social issues that are the basis of the free software movement. They regarded this as a way to present free software to executives without making them uncomfortable. So they have adopted the narrow economic values of business. They do not talk about the issue of whether users have freedom; instead, they appeal only to short-term practical values such as how to make powerful, reliable software.

Open source ideas have persuaded programmers and companies to develop free software, and this contributes to our community. However, they fail to teach people to value freedom, and that leaves our community weak.

Their values are so different from mine that we talk completely past each other. The things that matter to me – whether you and I are free to help ourselves and help each other – they don't see them as issues.

For the breakthrough of software, do you need ideas of genius, a perfect system, or is it all about marketing?

RMS: Marketing never makes breakthroughs in anything. That's silly. Marketing just makes people use something that wasn't necessarily best for them. Marketing never has to do with progress in any sense. Progress comes from people having ideas. If there are programmers and they are engaged in programming they'll have ideas. Some of these ideas will be good, some will be bad. Where do ideas come from? They come from confronting problems. You confront a problem and it will make part of your brain think and you'll have an idea and the idea will enable you to make some part of the program better.

Writing a program is a matter of getting a lot of details correct and consistent. Getting a program to work is as much careful, rational thought as anything in the world ever is. But of course you will get ideas that will or won't work, and they come from where ideas come from for any area: you do something and you get ideas – if you've taught yourself to be open to them.

The difference between software and physical products is that physical products are rather simple, like that projector over there. Regardless of the number of people who designed that projector, how many parts are in there? Maybe a few hundred. And still it is real work to design, and to make sure that the design will really work. And that's not always so easy. So if a product is pretty simple in number of components, in terms of the size of its design, maybe there will only be one patent for that product. So it's like, one product, one patent. If it's a new product, the one who designed it will get the patent. That's how people assume it works, and in some fields it still does (more or less).

But writing a software program is different in that it is a very complicated product of which various parts or ideas already existed.

RMS: Yes, and you couldn't make it without the ideas that already existed, even if it is new.

Imagine that the German government decided in 1780: we are going to encourage the production of symphonic music and progress in symphonic music by having a patent system for musical ideas, and any composer who has a new musical idea will get a 20 year monopoly on using that idea. So they start having thousands and thousands of music patents. Then imagine that Beethoven comes along and he wants to write a symphony. He has a bunch of new ideas about things to do in symphonic music, but he is forced to use them with older ideas to write his symphony. If he had had to thread his way through this maze of patented ideas, he would have given up.

Is there a parallel between the idea of free music and free software?

RMS: Well, Napster showed that people should have the right to redistribute music non-commercially. Even to strangers. Because that is useful. And when something is useful to society, the idea of stamping it out for the sake of corporate profit is an outrage! Of course they come up with the excuse that it is for the musicians, but look at the facts and you see that the only ones making huge profits are the music factories (as I like to call them).

Since I like music and I'm a music amateur myself, the idea of a music industry simply disgusts me. Musicians making money is good, but that is not the same as having factories mass-producing hype, getting people to like crap. The music industry should get eliminated. We should look for new ways to enable musicians to make a living from playing music so that they can devote themselves to music.

Having a way to make a living is not the same as having the possibility of getting very rich. Most musicians don't even make a decent living. The current system is very bad. It gives a lot of money to a few musicians, making them rich. It enables a larger number to barely get by. And most musicians are in a horrible situation and they are getting nothing from the copyright system. Zero. Most bands that get a record contract don't get money from it. All they get is publicity. And overall, the music-industrial complex hype gives 4 % of its (total) sales to the musicians. So it is a very, very inefficient system for supporting musicians.

What's the alternative?

RMS: It's not hard to find a better system. What I propose is this: we should have a convenient cash payment system on the internet, so you could easily send somebody a few euro, and then when you play a piece of music, on the screen there will be a box and by just clicking you send the musician – let's say about 50 cent. Who is going to say "no" to such a small amount? So I think in the developed parts of the world, where people have the money to pay, they will do so. It will become a cultural thing.

Some people always donate to street musicians, others don't. The point is that they won't get more money by selling the CD. But you as music lover have to pay a lot more than that! If you do it the official way, you pay 25 times that money. So fans of musicians, who really love these musicians, will pay a small fee. And if you have twice as many people participating, you get twice as much money. I think the system will work once it is made available to enough people, once you have attained the critical mass.

For the system to be successful, it depends on how many people can easily participate. At the moment the systems for people to pay through the internet are not convenient. You have to sign up, you have to have a credit card, give the number – these inconvenience barriers make them much less desirable. But if all you have to do is click here and some money will go directly to the musicians, it would work. It will work for novels as well, and for stories, for various kinds of arts.

The send-the-money scheme wouldn't work for software, though.

RMS: Software is different. Software is functional, not artistic primarily. In that it resembles other things, like recipes, dictionaries and textbooks. They are all functional. The main purpose or reason why people want them is to get something done. For functional works it is vital for people to have the freedom to have modified versions, even commercially. The result is that you look at a typical free software package, you see that many different people have contributed to it, so if you want to send money, whom do you send it to? That becomes difficult, you see.

But with a piece of recorded music there is not much you can usefully do to modify it. Yes, people will find some things, they are going to do sampling, and I think we can handle those kinds of things. But modifying it the way we modify programs doesn't happen and isn't feasible.

So it will be enough to give the public in general the permission only for verbatim copying, in which case it is obvious who to send the money to. The send-the-money scheme works in that case. It wouldn't work as well for software. Fortunately, in the case of free software we have a vibrant free software community already developing lots of software. So we don't have a problem, or you could say we are solving the problem in various different ways already, with different solutions all together.

Not everybody needs to get money. We have lots of people developing free software which they are not getting paid for. And the point is, why are you concerned with having a way for people to get paid for doing the activity? The reason is that otherwise you may think that there is a danger that the activity won't get done. But if you look around, you see that the activity is getting done – by people who are not getting paid and who are doing it voluntarily, and they are not complaining. Then where is the problem? There is no problem. So for software, we can assume there is no problem.

For music, it is not clear because we don't (yet) have a big free music community movement developing or making lots of free music that people are listening to. We don't know if that is possible. So it is useful to look for a way that musicians could get paid – and if it doesn't work for software, that's okay as long as it works for music.

At this moment there are more than 100,000 free software developers. These people are not dying, so they are making their lives one way or another. Maybe some of them are on the dole, what's wrong with that?

It would be nice if they could earn their living by developing software, wouldn't it?

RMS: There are different solutions to this problem. Some software developers are working for companies and get their money through developing free software. At least a hundred programmers are getting paid that way. And we can expect that as the acceptance of free software goes up, it will be easier to do and more people will do it.

Another legitimate way is to get commissions to develop custom software which is not meant for publication at all in any form. Since there the ethical issues of free or not free software do not arise. So if someone says "*Write this program for me and give me all the rights and I'll pay you*", there is nothing wrong with that if he is going to use that for himself or if he is going to put it in the microwave oven. It is not really an issue.

How come so few software developers are known?

RMS: The general public doesn't make celebrities out of software developers because they are not that much interested in software. And also because we don't have a kind of hype factory. You've got to realize that musicians are made into stars as part of a marketing activity which is basically a social problem. We need to reduce the extent to which musicians, sports figures and so on get made into celebrities, because this is a marketing phenomenon which is detrimental to society. I do my bit by basically paying very little attention to any of them.

What's your view of initiatives like Creative Commons or Wikipedia?

RMS: Wikipedia is a great thing – this free encyclopedia has extended the spirit of free software into another important area. It is now the largest encyclopedia ever made.

Creative Commons is a series of licenses, ranging from free to rather restrictive, intended primarily for artistic works. For those works, these licenses are a good idea. All of them permit at least non-commercial verbatim copying, which is the minimum freedom that people should have for artistic works. However, people tend to use these licenses also for educational material, and that leads to making educational material non-free.

Let's end with two questions that came up during the CROSSTALKS public event at VUB on December 11th: does the price the end-users pay for the use of Free & Open-Source software not just shift to the services and support they need, instead of paying for the software itself, as with proprietary software?

RMS: In regard to the narrow question of who pays how much, it may be true that free software only shifts the price in this way. If so, that's great, because it means that we can live in freedom – which is the purpose of free software – without any material sacrifices.

In general, you can't expect freedom to maintain itself. People have generally had to sacrifice pleasures for it, work for it, sometimes even fight for it. That's normal – freedom is worth the price.

Can free software create new jobs and work? Or is that not an issue within the Free Software Movement?

RMS: This is not the primary issue, but it is an issue. Free software can reduce jobs in one small sector of the IT field and create new jobs in a new sector.

The sector where jobs may be lost is that of the development of software for release to users on proprietary terms. This is a small fraction of programming, which is itself a small fraction of employment in the IT field. So at worst the loss in employment will be small.

Free software also creates a new kind of job: adapting software to the wishes of clients. Free software means you're free to study and change the source code. You're also free to pay someone to do this for you. The people who you pay to do this will be programmers. There are already at least hundreds of people providing this kind of service. I do not know how many people could find such employment in a world that had switched entirely to free software.

So free software could result in a small loss of jobs, on the scale of society as a whole, or no change, or an increase in jobs. Whichever outcome occurs could depend on many specific policies.

Unemployment – or more precisely, the problems that happen in our society to the unemployed – is a serious social problem, more important "overall" than any issue concerning software. To solve the problem of unemployment entirely would be a great step forward, far more important than free software. However, maintaining jobs for 10% of the world's programmers is hardly solving the problem of unemployment. It makes no sense to subjugate computer users just to keep this minute part of society employed. There are many ways, less harmful than this, to artificially maintain such a small number of jobs.

Biography

Richard Stallman graduated from Harvard in 1974 with a BA in physics. During his college years, he also worked as a staff hacker at the MIT Artificial Intelligence Lab, learning operating-system development by doing it. He wrote the first extensible Emacs text editor there in 1975. He also developed the AI technique of dependency-directed backtracking, also known as truth maintenance. In January 1984 he resigned from MIT to start the GNU project.

Stallman received the 1991 Grace Hopper Award from the Association for Computing Machinery, for his development of the first Emacs editor. In 1990 he was awarded a MacArthur Foundation fellowship, and in 1996 an honorary doctorate from the Royal Institute of Technology in Sweden. In 1998 he received the Electronic Frontier Foundation's pioneer award along with Linus Torvalds. In 1999 he received the Yuri Rubinski award. In 2001 he received a second honorary doctorate, from the University of Glasgow, and shared the Takeda award for social/economic betterment with Torvalds and Ken Sakamura. In 2002 he was elected to the US National Academy of Engineering, and in 2003 to the American Academy of Arts and Sciences. In 2003 he was named an honorary professor of the Universidad Nacional de Ingenieria in Peru, and received an honorary doctorate from the Vrije Universiteit Brussel.

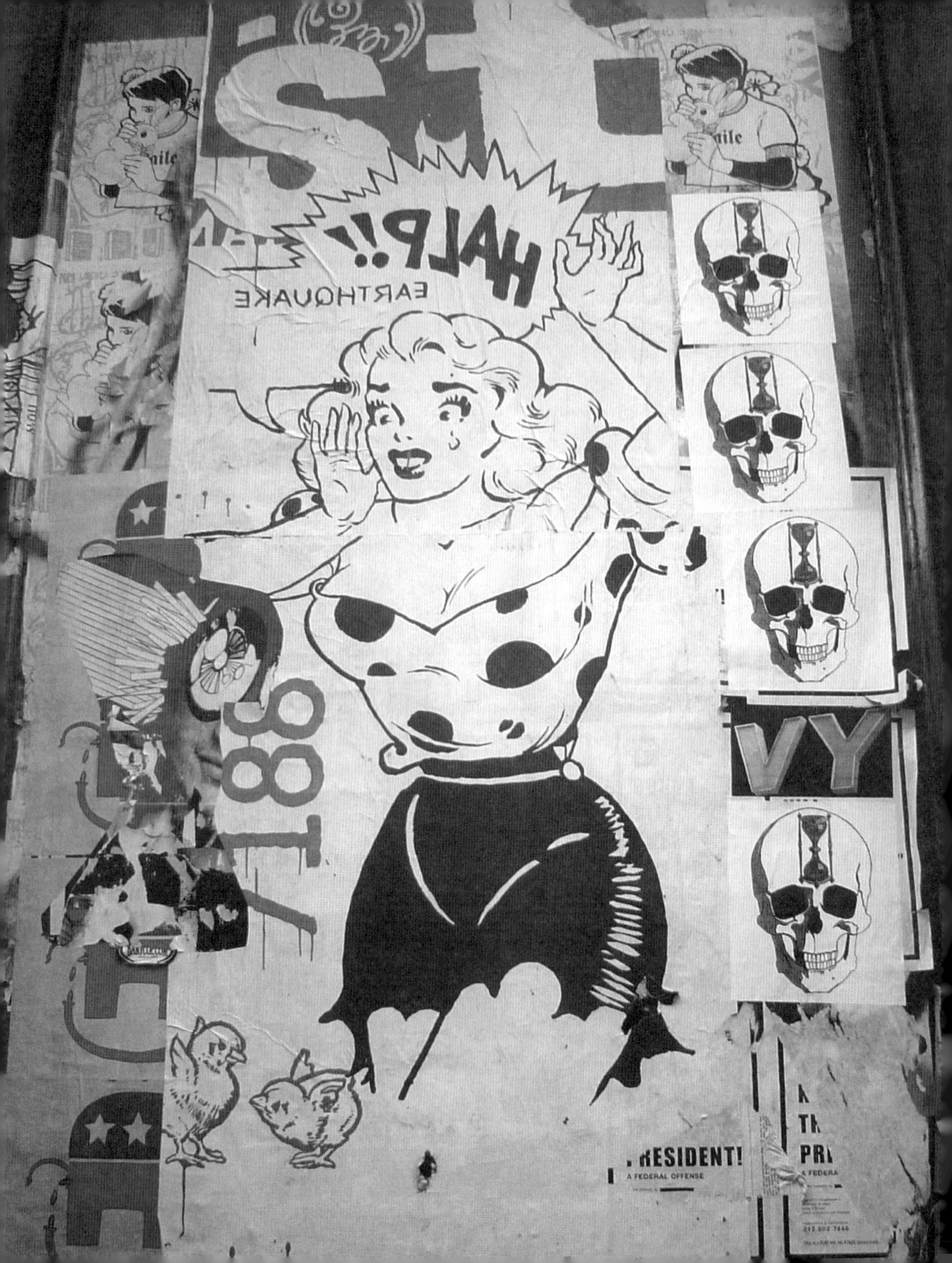
HALP!!
EARTHQUAKE
VY
RESIDENT!
A FEDERAL OFFENSE

The Open Source Paradigm Shift

by Tim O'Reilly

Paradigm shifts occur from time to time in business as well as in science. And as with scientific revolutions, they are often hard fought, and the ideas underlying them not widely accepted until long after they were first introduced. What's more, they often have implications that go far beyond the insights of their creators.

On Friday February the 20th, 2004, the first CROSSTALKS Science and Industry Dinner took place at the University Foundation in Brussels. About 20 invitees, amongst whom IT-industrials, representatives of the Belgian government and some VUB professors in computer sciences sounded out the future of computing and Free and Open Source Software. The following text is distilled out of the talk that I first gave at Warburg-Pincus' annual technology conference in May of 2003. Since then, I have delivered versions of the talk more than twenty times, at locations ranging from the O'Reilly Open Source Convention, the UK Unix User's Group, Microsoft Research in the UK, IBM Hursley, British Telecom, Red Hat's internal "all-hands" meeting, BEA's eWorld conference and at the first VUB CROSSTALKS Science & Industry Dinner in Brussels.

In 1962, Thomas Kuhn published a groundbreaking book entitled "The Structure of Scientific Revolutions". In it, he argued that the progress of science is not gradual but (much as we now think of biological evolution), a kind of punctuated equilibrium, with moments of epochal change. When Copernicus explained the movements of the planets by postulating that they moved around the sun rather than the earth, or when Darwin introduced his ideas about the origin of species, they were doing more than just building on past discoveries, or explaining new experimental data. A truly profound scientific breakthrough, Kuhn notes, "is seldom or never just an increment to what is already known. Its assimilation requires the reconstruction of prior theory and the re-evaluation of prior fact, an intrinsically revolutionary process that is seldom completed by a single man and never overnight."[1]

Kuhn referred to these revolutionary processes in science as "paradigm shifts", a term that has now entered the language to describe any profound change in our frame of reference.

The cloning of personal computers

One such paradigm shift occurred with the introduction of the standardized architecture of the IBM personal computer in 1981. In a huge departure from previous industry practice, IBM chose to build its computer from off the shelf components, and to open up its design for cloning by other manufacturers. As a result, the IBM personal computer architecture became the standard, over time displacing not only other personal computer designs, but over the next two decades, minicomputers and mainframes.

However, the executives at IBM failed to understand the full consequences of their decision. At the time, IBM's market share in computers far exceeded Microsoft's dominance of the desktop operating system market today. Software was a small part of the computer industry, a necessary part of an integrated computer, often bundled rather than sold separately. What independent software companies did exist were clearly satellite to their chosen hardware platform. So when it came time to provide an operating system for the new machine, IBM decided to license it from a small company called Microsoft, giving away the right to resell the software to the small part of the market that IBM did not control. As cloned personal computers were built by thousands of manufacturers large and small, IBM lost its leadership in the new market. Software became the new sun that the industry revolved around; Microsoft, not IBM, became the most important company in the computer industry.

But that's not the only lesson from this story. In the initial competition for leadership of the personal computer market, companies vied to "enhance" the personal computer standard, adding support for new peripherals, faster buses, and other proprietary technical innovations. Their executives, trained in the previous, hardware-dominated computer industry, acted on the lessons of the old paradigm.

The most intransigent, such as Digital's Ken Olson, derided the PC as a toy, and refused to enter the market until too late. But even pioneers like Compaq, whose initial success was driven by the introduction of "luggable" computers, the ancestor of today's laptop, were ultimately misled by old lessons that no longer applied in the new paradigm. It took an outsider, Michael Dell, who began his company selling mail order PCs from a college dorm room, to realize that a standardized PC was a commodity, and that marketplace advantage came not from building a better PC, but from building one that was good enough, lowering the cost of production by embracing standards, and seeking advantage in areas such as marketing, distribution, and logistics. In the end, it was Dell, not IBM or Compaq, who became the largest PC hardware vendor.

Meanwhile, Intel, another company that made a bold bet on the new commodity platform, abandoned its memory chip business as indefensible and made a commitment to be the more complex brains of the new design. The fact that most of the PCs built today bear an "Intel Inside" logo reminds us of the fact that even within a commodity architecture, there are opportunities for proprietary advantage.

What does all this have to do with open-source software, you might ask?

My premise is that free and open-source developers are in much the same position today that IBM was in 1981 when it changed the rules of the computer industry, but failed to understand the consequences of the change, allowing others to reap the benefits. Most existing proprietary software vendors are no better off, playing by the old rules while the new rules are reshaping the industry around them.

I have a simple test that I use in my talks to see if my audience of computer industry professionals is thinking with the old paradigm or the new. "How many of you use Linux?" I ask. Depending on the venue, 20-80% of the audience might raise its hands. "How many of you use Google?" Every hand in the room goes up. And the light begins to dawn. Every one of them uses Google's massive complex of 100,000 Linux servers, but they were blinded to the answer by a mindset in which "the software you use" is defined as the software running on the computer in front of you. Most of the "killer apps" of the Internet, applications used by hundreds of millions of people, run on Linux or FreeBSD. But the operating system, as formerly defined, is to these applications only a component of a larger system. Their true platform is the Internet.

It is in studying these next-generation applications that we can begin to understand the true long-term significance of the open source paradigm shift.

If open-source pioneers are to benefit from the revolution we've unleashed, we must look *through* the foreground elements of the free and open-source movements, and understand more deeply both the causes and consequences of the revolution.

Artificial intelligence pioneer Ray Kurzweil once said, "I'm an inventor. I became interested in long-term trends because an invention has to make sense in the world in which it is finished, not the world in which it is started."[2]

Three long-term trends

I find it useful to see open source as an expression of three deep, long-term trends:
- The commoditization of software
- Network-enabled collaboration
- Software customizability (software as a service)

Long term trends like these "three Cs", rather than "The Free Software Manifesto" or "The Open Source Definition", should be the lens through which we understand the changes that are being unleashed.

1. Software as Commodity

In his essay, "Some Implications of Software Commodification", Dave Stutz writes:

> The word commodity is used today to represent fodder for industrial processes: things or substances that are found to be valuable as basic building blocks for many different purposes. Because of their very general value, they are typically used in large quantities and in many different ways. Commodities are always sourced by more than one producer, and consumers may substitute one producer's product for another's with impunity. Because commodities are fungible in this way, they are defined by uniform quality standards to which they must conform. These quality standards help to avoid adulteration, and also facilitate quick and easy valuation, which in turn fosters productivity gains.

Software commoditization has been driven by standards, in particular by the rise of communications-oriented systems such as the Internet, which depend on shared protocols, and define the interfaces and datatypes shared between cooperating components rather than the internals of those components. Such systems necessarily consist of replaceable parts. A web server such as Apache or Microsoft's IIS, or browsers such as Internet Explorer, Netscape Navigator, or Mozilla, are all easily swappable, because in order to function, they must implement the HTTP protocol and the HTML data format. Sendmail can be replaced by Exim or Postfix or Microsoft Exchange because all must support email exchange protocols such as SMTP, POP and IMAP. Microsoft Outlook can easily be replaced by Eudora, or Pine, or Mozilla mail, or a web mail client such as Yahoo! Mail for the same reason.

In this regard, it's worth noting that Unix, the system on which Linux is based, also has a communications-centric architecture. In The Unix Programming Environment, Kernighan and Pike eloquently describe how Unix programs should be written as small pieces designed to cooperate in "pipelines", reading and writing ASCII files rather than proprietary data formats. Eric Raymond gives a contemporary expression of this theme in his book, "The Art of Unix Programming".

Note that in a communications-centric environment with standard protocols, both proprietary and open-source software become commodities. Microsoft's Internet Explorer web browser is just as much a commodity as the open-source Apache web server, because both are constrained by the open standards of the web. (If Microsoft had managed to gain dominant market share at both ends of the protocol pipeline between web browser and server, it would be another matter! See "How the Web was almost won" – http://www.salon.com/tech/feature/1999/11/16/microsoft_servers/ – for my discussion of that subject. This example makes clear one of the important roles that open source does play in "keeping standards honest". This role is being recognized by organizations like the W3C, which are increasingly reluctant to endorse standards that have only proprietary or patent-encumbered implementations.

What's more, even software that starts out proprietary eventually becomes standardized and ultimately commodified. Dave Stutz eloquently describes this process in an essay entitled "The Natural History of Software Platforms".

It occurs through a hardening of the external shell presented by the platform over time. As a platform succeeds in the marketplace, its APIs, UI, feature-set, file formats, and customization interfaces ossify and become more and more difficult to change. (They may, in fact, ossify so far as to literally harden into hardware appliances!) The process of ossification makes successful platforms easy targets for cloners, and cloning is what spells the beginning of the end for platform profit margins.

Consistent with this view, the cloning of Microsoft's Windows and Office franchises has been a major objective of the Free and Open-Source communities. In the past, Microsoft has been successful at rebuffing cloning attempts by continually revising APIs and file formats, but the writing is on the wall. Ubiquity drives standardization, and gratuitous innovation in defense of monopoly is rejected by users.

Implications of software commoditization

One might be tempted to see only the devaluation of something that was once a locus of enormous value. Thus, Red Hat founder Bob Young once remarked, *"My goal is to shrink the size of the operating system market".* (Red Hat however aimed to own a large part of that smaller market!) Defenders of the status quo, such as Microsoft VP Jim Allchin, have made statements such as *"open source is an intellectual property destroyer"*, and paint a bleak picture in which a great industry is destroyed, with nothing to take its place.

On the surface, Allchin appears to be right. Linux now generates tens of billions of dollars in server hardware related revenue, with the software revenues merely a rounding error. Despite Linux's emerging dominance in the server market, Red Hat, the largest Linux distribution company, has annual revenues of only $126 million, versus Microsoft's $32 billion. A huge amount of software value appears to have vaporized.

But is it value or overhead? Open-source advocates like to say they're not destroying actual value, but rather squeezing inefficiencies out of the system. When competition drives down prices, efficiency and average wealth levels go up. Firms unable to adapt to the new price levels undergo what the economist E.F. Schumpeter called "creative destruction", but what was "lost" returns manyfold as higher productivity and new opportunities.

The innovator's dilemma

Microsoft benefited, along with consumers, from the last round of "creative destruction" as PC hardware was commoditized. This time around, Microsoft sees the commoditization of operating systems, databases, web servers and browsers, and related software as destructive to its core business. But that destruction has created the opportunity for the killer applications of the Internet era. Yahoo!, Google, Amazon, eBay — to mention only a few — are the beneficiaries.

And so I prefer to take the view of Clayton Christensen, the author of "The Innovator's Dilemma" and "The Innovator's Solution". In a former article in *Harvard Business Review*, he articulates "the law of conservation of attractive profits" as follows:

> *When attractive profits disappear at one stage in the value chain because a product becomes modular and commoditized, the opportunity to earn attractive profits with proprietary products will usually emerge at an adjacent stage.*[3]

We see Christensen's thesis clearly at work in the paradigm shifts I'm discussing here.[4] Just as IBM's commoditization of the basic design of the personal computer led to opportunities for attractive profits "up the stack" in software, new fortunes are being made up the stack from the commodity open-source software that underlies the Internet, in a new class of proprietary applications that I have elsewhere referred to as "infoware".

Sites such as Google, Amazon, and salesforce.com provide the most serious challenge to the traditional understanding of free and open-source software. Here are applications built on top of Linux, but they are fiercely proprietary. What's more, even when using and modifying software distributed under the most restrictive of free software licenses, the GPL (see Annex I, eds), these sites are not constrained by any of its provisions, all of which are conditioned on the old paradigm. The GPL's protections are triggered by the act of software distribution, yet web-based application vendors never distribute any software: it is simply performed on the Internet's global stage, delivered as a service rather than as a packaged software application.

But even more importantly, even if these sites gave out their source code, users would not easily be able to create a full copy of the running application! The application is a dynamically updated database whose utility comes from its completeness and concurrency, and in many cases, from the network effect of its participating users.

To be sure, there would be many benefits to users were some of Google's algorithms public rather than secret, or Amazon's One-Click available to all, but the point remains: an instance of all of Google's source code would not give you Google, unless you were also able to build the capability to crawl and mirror the entire web in the same way that Google does.

And the opportunities are not merely up the stack. There are huge proprietary opportunities hidden inside the system. Christensen notes:

> *Attractive profits... move elsewhere in the value chain, often to subsystems from which the modular product is assembled. This is because it is improvements in the subsystems, rather than the modular product's architecture, that drives the assembler's ability to move upmarket towards more attractive profit margins. Hence, the subsystems become decommoditized and attractively profitable.*

We saw this pattern in the PC market with most PCs now bearing the brand "Intel Inside"; the Internet could just as easily be branded "Cisco Inside".

Back to BIND

But these "Intel Inside" business opportunities are not always obvious, nor are they necessarily in proprietary hardware or software. The open source BIND (Berkeley Internet Name Daemon) package used to run the Domain Name System (DNS) provides an important demonstration.

The business model for most of the Internet's commodity software turned out not to be selling that software (despite shrinkwrapped offerings from vendors such as NetManage and Spry, now long gone), but in services based on that software. Most of those businesses — the Internet Service Providers (ISPs), who essentially resell access to the TCP/IP protocol suite and to email and web servers — turned out to be low margin businesses. There was one notable exception.

BIND is probably the single most mission-critical program on the Internet, yet its maintainer has scraped by for the past two decades on donations and consulting fees. Meanwhile, domain name registration — an information service based on the software — became a business generating hundreds of millions of dollars a year, a virtual monopoly for Network Solutions, which was handed the business on government contract before anyone realized just how valuable it would be. The Intel Inside opportunity of the DNS was not a software opportunity at all, but the service of managing the namespace used by the software. By a historical accident, the business model became separated from the software.

That services based on software would be a dominant business model for open-source software was recognized in "The Cathedral & the Bazaar", Eric Raymond's seminal work on the movement. But in practice, most early open-source entrepreneurs focused on services associated with the maintenance and support of the software, rather than true software as a service. (That is to say, software as a service is not service in support of software, but software in support of user-facing services!)

A final lesson?

Dell gives us a final lesson for today's software industry. Much as the commoditization of PC hardware drove down IBM's outsize margins but vastly increased the size of the market, creating enormous value for users, and vast opportunities for a new ecosystem of computer manufacturers for whom the lower margins of the PC still made business sense, the commoditization of software will actually expand the software market. And as Christensen notes, in this type of market, the drivers of success "become speed to market and the ability responsively and conveniently to give customers exactly what they need, when they need it."[5]

Following this logic, I believe that the process of building custom distributions will emerge as one of the key competitive differentiators among Linux vendors. Much as a Dell vendor must be an arbitrageur of the various contract manufacturers vying to produce fungible components at the lowest price, a Linux vendor will need to manage the ever changing constellation of software suppliers whose asynchronous product releases provide the raw materials for Linux distributions. Companies like Debian founder Ian Murdock's "Progeny Systems" already see this as the heart of their business, but even old-line Linux vendors like SuSe and new entrants like Sun tout their release engineering expertise as a competitive advantage.[6]

But even the most successful of these Linux distribution vendors will never achieve the revenues or profitability of today's software giants like Microsoft or Oracle, unless they leverage some of the other lessons of history. As demonstrated by both the PC hardware market and the ISP industry (which as noted above is a service business built on the commodity protocols and applications of the Internet), commodity businesses are low margin for most of the players. Unless companies find value up the stack or through an "Intel Inside" opportunity, they must compete only through speed and responsiveness, and that's a challenging way to maintain a pricing advantage in a commodity market.

Early observers of the commodity nature of Linux, such as Red Hat's founder Bob Young, believed that advantage was to be found in "building a strong brand". That's certainly necessary, but it's not sufficient. It's even possible that contract manufacturers such as Flextronix, which work behind the scenes as industry suppliers rather than branded customer-facing entities, may provide a better analogy than Dell for some Linux vendors.

In conclusion, software itself is no longer the primary locus of value in the computer industry. The commoditization of software drives value to services enabled by that software. New business models are required.

2. Network-Enabled Collaboration

The second long-term trend I would like to elaborate on, is the network-enabled collaboration. To understand the nature of competitive advantage in the new paradigm, we should look not to Linux, but to the Internet, which has already shown signs of how the open-source story will play out.

The most common version of the history of free software begins with Richard Stallman's ethically-motivated 1984 revolt against proprietary software. It is an appealing story centered on a charismatic figure, and leads straight into a narrative in which the license he wrote — the GPL — is the centerpiece. But like most open-source advocates, who tell a broader story about building better software through transparency and code sharing, I prefer to start the history with the style of software development that was normal in the early computer industry and academia. Because software was not seen as the primary source of value, source code was freely shared throughout the early computer industry.

The Unix software tradition provides a good example. Unix was developed at Bell Labs, and was shared freely with university software researchers, who contributed many of the utilities and features we take for granted today. The fact that Unix was provided under a license that later allowed ATT to shut down the party when it decided it wanted to commercialize Unix, leading ultimately to the rise of BSD Unix and Linux as free alternatives, should not blind us to the fact that the early, collaborative development *preceded* the adoption of an open-source licensing model. Open-source licensing began as an attempt to preserve a culture of sharing, and only later led to an expanded awareness of the value of that sharing.

For the roots of open source in the Unix community, you can look to the research orientation of many of the original participants. As Bill Joy noted in his keynote at the "O'Reilly Open Source Convention" in 1999, in science, you share your data so other people can reproduce your results. And at Berkeley, he said, we thought of ourselves as computer scientists.[7]

But perhaps even more important was the fragmented nature of the early Unix hardware market. With hundreds of competing computer architectures, the only way to distribute software was as source! No one had access to all the machines to produce the necessary binaries. (This demonstrates the aptness of another of Christensen's "laws", the law of conservation of modularity. Because PC hardware was standardized and modular, it was possible to concentrate value and uniqueness in software. But because Unix hardware was unique and proprietary, software had to be made more open and modular.)

This software source code exchange culture grew from its research beginnings, but it became the hallmark of a large segment of the software industry because of the rise of computer networking.

Much of the role of open source in the development of the Internet is well known: The most widely used TCP/IP protocol implementation was developed as part of Berkeley networking; Bind runs the DNS, without which none of the web sites we depend on would be reachable; sendmail is the heart of the Internet email backbone; Apache is the dominant web server; Perl the dominant language for creating dynamic sites; etc.

Less often considered is the role of Usenet in mothering the Net we now know. Much of what drove public adoption of the Internet was in fact Usenet, that vast distributed bulletin board. You "signed up" for Usenet by finding a neighbor willing to give you a newsfeed. This was a true collaborative network, where mail and news were relayed from one cooperating site to another, often taking days to travel from one end of the Net to another. Hub sites formed an ad-hoc backbone, but everything was voluntary.

Connecting People

Rick Adams, who created UUnet, which was the first major commercial ISP, was a free software author (though he never subscribed to any of the free software ideals — it was simply an expedient way to distribute software he wanted to use). He was the author of B News (at the time the dominant Usenet news server) as well as SLIP (Serial Line IP), the first implementation of TCP/IP for dialup lines. But more importantly for the history of the Net, Rick was also the hostmaster of the world's largest Usenet hub. He realized that the voluntary Usenet was becoming unworkable, and that people would pay for reliable, well-connected access. UUnet started out as a nonprofit, and for several years, much more of its business was based on the earlier UUCP (Unix-Unix Copy Protocol) dialup network than on TCP/IP. As the Internet caught on, UUNet and others like it helped bring the Internet to the masses. But at the end of the day, the commercial Internet industry started out of a need to provide infrastructure for the completely collaborative UUCPnet and Usenet.

The UUCPnet and Usenet were used for email (the first killer app of the Internet), but also for software distribution and collaborative tech support. When Larry Wall (later famous as the author of Perl) introduced the patch program in 1984, the ponderous process of sending around 9-track tapes of source code was replaced by the transmission of "patches" — editing scripts that update existing source files. Add in Richard Stallman's Gnu C compiler (gcc), and early source code control systems like RCS (eventually replaced by CVS and now Subversion), and you had a situation where anyone could share and update free software. The early Usenet was as much a "Napster" for shared software as it was a place for conversation.

The mechanisms that the early developers used to spread and support their work became the basis for a cultural phenomenon that reached far beyond the tech sector. The heart of that phenomenon was the use of wide-area networking technology to connect people around interests, rather than through geographical location or company affiliation. This was the beginning of a massive cultural shift that we're still seeing today.

This cultural shift may have had its first flowering with open-source software, but it is not intrinsically tied to the use of free and open-source licenses and philosophies.

In 1999, together with Brian Behlendorf of the Apache project, O'Reilly founded a company called CollabNet to commercialize not the Apache product but the Apache *process*. Unlike many other OSS projects, Apache wasn't founded by a single visionary developer but by a group of users who'd been abandoned by their original "vendor" (NCSA) and who agreed to work together to maintain a tool they depended on. Apache gives us lessons about intentional wide-area collaborative software development that can be applied even by companies that haven't fully embraced open source licensing practices. For example, it is possible to apply open source collaborative principles inside a large company, even without the intention to release the resulting software to the outside world.

While CollabNet is best known for hosting high profile corporate-sponsored open source projects like OpenOffice.org, its largest customer is actually HP's printer division, where CollabNet's SourceCast platform is used to help more than 3000 internal developers share their code within the corporate firewall. Other customers use open-source-inspired development practices to share code with their customers or business partners, or to manage distributed worldwide development teams.

Open source as a natural language

But an even more compelling story comes from that archetype of proprietary software, Microsoft. Far too few people know the story of the origin of ASP.NET. As told to me by its creators, Mark Anders and Scott Guthrie, the two of them wanted to re-engineer Microsoft's ASP product to make it XML-aware. They were told that doing so would break backwards compatibility, and the decision was made to stick with the old architecture. But when Anders and Guthrie had a month between projects, they hacked up their vision anyway, just to see where it would go. Others within Microsoft heard about their work, found it useful, and adopted pieces of it. Some six or nine months later, they had a call from Bill Gates: "I'd like to see your project."

In short, one of Microsoft's flagship products was born as an internal "code fork", the result of two developers "scratching their own itch", and spread within Microsoft in much the same way as open-source projects spread on the open Internet. It appears that open source is the "natural language" of a networked community. Given enough developers and a network to connect them, open-source-style development behavior emerges.

If you take the position that open-source licensing is a means of encouraging Internet-enabled collaboration, and focus on the end rather than the means, you'll open a much larger tent. You'll see the threads that tie together not just traditional open source projects, but also collaborative "computing grid" projects like SETI@home, user reviews on *amazon.com*, technologies like collaborative filtering, new ideas about marketing such as those expressed in "The Cluetrain Manifesto", weblogs, and the way that Internet message boards can now move the stock market. What started out as a software development methodology is increasingly becoming a facet of every field, as network-enabled conversations become a principal carrier of new ideas.

Leveraging the user community

I'm particularly struck by how collaboration is central to the success and differentiation of the leading Internet applications.

EBay is an obvious example, almost the definition of a "network effects" business, in which competitive advantage is gained from the critical mass of buyers and sellers. New entrants into the auction business have a hard time competing, because there is no reason for either buyers or sellers to go to a second-tier player.

Amazon is perhaps even more interesting. Unlike eBay, whose constellation of products is provided by its users, and changes dynamically day to day, products identical to those Amazon sells are available from other vendors. Yet Amazon seems to enjoy an order-of-magnitude advantage over those other vendors. Why? Perhaps it is merely better execution, better pricing, better service, better branding. But one clear differentiator is the superior way that Amazon has leveraged its user community.

In my talks, I give a simple demonstration. I do a search for products in one of my publishing areas, JavaScript. On *amazon.com*, the search produces a complex page with four main areas. On the top is a block showing the three "most popular" products. Down below is a longer search listing that allows the customer to list products by criteria such as best-selling, highest-rated, by price, or simply alphabetically. On the right and the left are user-generated "ListMania" lists. These lists allow customers to share their own recommendations for other titles related to the given subject.

The section labeled "most popular" might not jump out at first. But as a vendor who sells to *amazon.com*, I know that it is the result of a complex, proprietary algorithm that combines not just sales but also the number and quality of user reviews, user recommendations for alternative products, links from ListMania lists, "also bought" associations, and all the other things that Amazon refers to as the "flow" around products.

The particular search that I like to demonstrate is usually topped by my own "JavaScript: The Definitive Guide." The book has 192 reviews, averaging 4 1/2 stars. Those reviews are among the *more than ten million* user reviews contributed by *amazon.com* customers.

Now contrast the #2 player in online books, *barnesandnoble.com*. The top result is a book published by Barnes & Noble itself, and there is no evidence of user-supplied content. *JavaScript: The Definitive Guide* has only 18 comments, the order-of-magnitude difference in user participation closely mirroring the order-of-magnitude difference in sales.

Treating your users as co-developers

Amazon doesn't have a natural network-effect advantage like eBay, but they've built one by architecting their site for user participation. Everything from user reviews, alternative product recommendations, ListMania, and the Associates program, which allows users to earn commissions for recommending books, encourages users to collaborate in enhancing the site. Amazon Web Services, introduced in 2001, take the story even further, allowing users to build alternate interfaces and specialized shopping experiences (as well as other unexpected applications) using Amazon's data and commerce engine as a back end.

Amazon's distance from competitors, and the security it enjoys as a market leader, is driven by the value added by its users. If, as Eric Raymond said in *The Cathedral & the Bazaar*, one of the secrets of open source is "treating your users as co-developers", Amazon has learned this secret. But note that it's completely independent of open-source licensing practices! We start to see that what has been presented as a rigidly constrained model for open source may consist of a bundle of competencies, not all of which will always be found together.

Google makes a more subtle case for the network-effect story. Google's initial innovation was the PageRank algorithm, which leverages the collective preferences of web users, expressed by their hyperlinks to sites, to produce better search results. In Google's case, the user participation is extrinsic to the company and its product, and so can be copied by competitors. If this analysis is correct, Google's long-term success will depend on finding additional ways to leverage user-created value as a key part of their offering. Services such as "orkut" and "Gmail" suggest that this lesson is not lost on them.

Now consider a counter-example. MapQuest is another pioneer that created an innovative type of web application that almost every Internet user relies on. Yet the market is shared fairly evenly between MapQuest (now owned by AOL), *maps.yahoo.com*, and *maps.msn.com* (powered by MapPoint). All three provide a commodity-business powered by standardized software and databases. None of them have made a concerted effort to leverage user-supplied content, or engage their users in building out the application. (Note also that all three are enabling an Intel-Inside style opportunity for data suppliers such as NAVTEQ, now planning a multi-billion dollar IPO!)

The Architecture of Participation

I've come to use the term "the architecture of participation" to describe the nature of systems that are designed for user contribution. Larry Lessig's book, *"Code and Other Laws of Cyberspace"*, which he characterizes as an extended meditation on Mitch Kapor's maxim, "architecture is politics", made the case that we need to pay attention to the architecture of systems if we want to understand their effects.

I immediately thought of Kernighan and Pike's description of the Unix software tools philosophy referred to above. I also recalled an unpublished portion of the interview we did with Linus Torvalds to create his essay for the 1998 book, *"Open Sources"*. Linus too expressed a sense that architecture may be more important than source code. *"I couldn't do what I did with Linux for Windows, even if I had the source code. The architecture just wouldn't support it."* Too much of the windows source code consists of interdependent, tightly coupled layers for a single developer to drop in a replacement module.

And of course, the Internet and the World Wide Web have this participatory architecture in spades. As outlined above in the section on software commoditization, any system designed around communications protocols is intrinsically designed for participation. Anyone can create a participating, first-class component.

In addition, the IETF, the Internet standards process, has a great many similarities with an open source software project. The only substantial difference is that the IETF's output is a standards document rather than a code module. Especially in the early years, anyone could participate, simply by joining a mailing list and having something to say, or by showing up to one of the three annual face-to-face meetings. Standards were decided by participating individuals, irrespective of their company affiliations. The very name for proposed Internet standards, RFCs (Request for Comments), reflects the participatory design of the Net. Though commercial participation was welcomed and encouraged, companies, like individuals, were expected to compete on the basis of their ideas and implementations, not their money or disproportional representation. The IETF approach is where open source and open standards meet.

And while there are successful open-source projects like Sendmail, which are largely the creation of a single individual, and have a monolithic architecture, those that have built large development communities have done so because they have a modular architecture that allows easy participation by independent or loosely coordinated developers. The use of Perl, for example, exploded along with CPAN, the Comprehensive Perl Archive Network, and Perl's module system, which allowed anyone to enhance the language with specialized functions, and make them available to other users.

The web, however, took the idea of participation to a new level, because it opened that participation not just to software developers but to all users of the system.

It has always baffled and disappointed me that the open-source community has not claimed the web as one of its greatest success stories. If you asked most end users, they are most likely to associate the web with proprietary clients such as Microsoft's Internet Explorer than with the revolutionary open-source architecture that made the web possible. That's a PR failure! Tim Berners-Lee's original web implementation was not just open source, it was public domain. NCSA's web server and Mosaic browser were not technically open source, but source was freely available. While the move of the NCSA team to Netscape sought to take key parts of the web infrastructure to the proprietary side, and the Microsoft-Netscape battles made it appear that the web was primarily a proprietary software battleground, we should know better. Apache, the phoenix that grew from the NCSA server, kept the open vision alive, keeping the standards honest, and not succumbing to proprietary embrace-and-extend strategies.

But even more significantly, HTML, the language of web pages, opened participation to ordinary users, not just software developers. The "View Source" menu item migrated from Tim Berners-Lee's original browser, to Mosaic, and then on to Netscape Navigator and even Microsoft's Internet Explorer. Though no one thinks of HTML as an open-source technology, its openness was absolutely key to the explosive spread of the web. Barriers to entry for "amateurs" were low, because anyone could look "over the shoulder" of anyone else producing a web page. Dynamic content created with interpreted languages continued the trend toward transparency.

And more germane to my argument here, the fundamental architecture of hyperlinking ensures that the value of the web is created by its users.

The story of Napster

In this context, it's worth noting an observation originally made by Clay Shirky in a talk at O'Reilly's 2001 "P2P and Web Services Conference" (now renamed the "Emerging Technology Conference"), entitled "Listening to Napster." There are three ways to build a large database, said Clay. The first, demonstrated by Yahoo!, is to pay people to do it. The second, inspired by lessons from the open source community, is to get volunteers to perform the same task. "The Open Directory Project", an open-source Yahoo! competitor, is the result, Wikipedia provides another example. But Napster demonstrates a third way. Because Napster set its defaults to automatically share any music that was downloaded, every user automatically helped to build the value of the shared database.

This architectural insight may actually be more central to the success of open source than the more frequently cited appeal to volunteerism. The architecture of Linux, the Internet, and the World Wide Web are such that users pursuing their own "selfish" interests build collective value as an automatic byproduct. In other words, these technologies demonstrate some of the same network effect as eBay and Napster, simply through the way that they have been designed.

These projects can be seen to have a natural architecture of participation. But as Amazon demonstrates, by consistent effort (as well as economic incentives such as the Associates program), it is possible to overlay such an architecture on a system that would not normally seem to possess it.

3. Customizability and Software-as-Service

The last of my three Cs, customizability, is an essential concomitant of software as a service. It's especially important to highlight this aspect because it illustrates just why dynamically typed languages like Perl, Python, and PHP, so-often denigrated by old-paradigm software developers as mere "scripting languages", are so important on today's software scene.

As I wrote in my 1997 essay, "Hardware, Software and Infoware":

> *If you look at a large web site like Yahoo!, you'll see that behind the scenes, an army of administrators and programmers are continually rebuilding the product. Dynamic content isn't just automatically generated, it is also often hand-tailored, typically using an array of quick and dirty scripting tools.*

"We don't create content at Yahoo! We aggregate it," says Jeffrey Friedl, author of the book "Mastering Regular Expressions" and a full-time Perl programmer at Yahoo! *"We have feeds from thousands of sources, each with its own format. We do massive amounts of 'feed processing' to clean this stuff up or to find out where to put it on Yahoo!"* For example, to link appropriate news stories to tickers at *finance.yahoo.com*, Friedl needed to write a "name recognition" program able to search for more than 15,000 company names. Perl's ability to analyze free-form text with powerful regular expressions was what made that possible.

Perl has been referred to as "the duct tape of the Internet", and like duct tape, dynamic languages like Perl are important to web sites like Yahoo! and Amazon for the same reason that duct tape is important not just to heating system repairmen but to anyone who wants to hold together a rapidly changing installation. Go to any lecture or stage play, and you'll see microphone cords and other wiring held down by duct tape.

We're used to thinking of software as an artifact rather than a process. And to be sure, even in the new paradigm, there are software artifacts, programs and commodity components that must be engineered to exacting specifications because they will be used again and again. But it is in the area of software that is *not* commoditized, the "glue" that ties together components, the scripts for managing data and machines, and all the areas that need frequent change or rapid prototyping, that dynamic languages shine.

Sites like Google, Amazon, or eBay — especially those reflecting the dynamic of user participation — are not just products, they are *processes*.

The Mechanical Turk

I like to tell people the story of the Mechanical Turk, a 1770 hoax that pretended to be a mechanical chess playing machine. The secret, of course, was that a man was hidden inside. The Turk actually played a small role in the history of computing. When Charles Babbage played against the Turk in 1820 (and lost), he saw through the hoax, but was moved to wonder whether a true computing machine would be possible.

Now, in an ironic circle, applications once more have people hidden inside them. Take a copy of Microsoft Word and a compatible computer, and it will still run ten years from now. But without the constant crawls to keep the search engine fresh, the constant product updates at an Amazon or eBay, the administrators who keep it all running, the editors and designers who integrate vendor- and user-supplied content into the interface, and in the case of some sites, even the warehouse staff who deliver the products, the Internet-era application no longer performs its function.

This is truly not the software business as it was even a decade ago. Of course, there have always been enterprise software businesses with this characteristic. (American Airlines' Sabre reservations system is an obvious example.) But only now have they become the dominant paradigm for new computer-related businesses.

The first generation of any new technology is typically seen as an extension to the previous generations. And so, through the 1990s, most people experienced the Internet as an extension or add-on to the personal computer. Email and web browsing were powerful add-ons, to be sure, and they gave added impetus to a personal computer industry that was running out of steam.

(Open source advocates can take ironic note of the fact that many of the most important features of Microsoft's new operating system releases since Windows 95 have been designed to emulate Internet functionality originally created by open-source developers.)

But now, we're starting to see the shape of a very different future. Napster brought us peer-to-peer file sharing, Seti@home introduced millions of people to the idea of distributed computation, and now web services are starting to make even huge database-backed sites like Amazon or Google appear to act like components of an even larger system. Vendors such as IBM and HP bandy about terms like "computing on demand" and "pervasive computing".

The boundaries between cell phones, wirelessly connected laptops, and even consumer devices like the iPod or TiVO, are all blurring. Each now gets a large part of its value from software that resides elsewhere. Dave Stutz characterizes this as *"software above the level of a single device"*.[8]

Building the Internet Operating System

I like to say that we're entering the stage where we are going to treat the Internet as if it were a single virtual computer. To do that, we'll need to create an Internet operating system.

The large question before us is this: What kind of operating system is it going to be? The lesson of Microsoft is that if you leverage insight into a new paradigm, you will find the secret that will give you control over the industry, the "one ring to rule them all", so to speak. Contender after contender has set out to dethrone Microsoft and take that ring from them, only to fail. But the lesson of open source and the Internet is that we can build an operating system that is designed from the ground up as "small pieces loosely joined", with an architecture that makes it easy for anyone to participate in building the value of the system.

The values of the free and open-source community are an important part of its paradigm. Just as the Copernican revolution was part of a broader social revolution that turned society away from hierarchy and received knowledge, and instead sparked a spirit of inquiry and knowledge sharing, open source is part of a communications revolution designed to maximize the free sharing of ideas expressed in code.

But free software advocates go too far when they eschew any limits on sharing, and define the movement by adherence to a restrictive set of software licensing practices. The open-source movement has made a concerted effort to be more inclusive. Eric Raymond describes "The Open Source Definition" as a "provocation to thought", a "social contract ... and an invitation to join the network of those who adhere to it."[9] But even though the open-source movement is much more business friendly and supports the right of developers to choose non-free licenses, it still uses the presence of software licenses that enforce sharing as its litmus test.

The lessons of previous paradigm shifts show us a more subtle and powerful story than one that merely pits a gift culture against a monetary culture, and a community of sharers versus those who choose not to participate. Instead, we see a dynamic migration of value, in which things that were once kept for private advantage are now shared freely, and things that were once thought incidental become the locus of enormous value. It's easy for free and open-source advocates to see this dynamic as a fall from grace, a hoarding of value that should be shared with all. But a historical view tells us that the commoditization of older technologies and the crystallization of value in new technologies is part of a process that advances the industry and creates more value for all. What is essential is to find a balance, in which we as an industry create more value than we capture as individual participants, enriching the commons that allows for further development by others.

I cannot say where things are going to end. But as Alan Kay once said, "*The best way to predict the future is to invent it.*"[10] Where we go next is up to all of us.

Conclusion

The Open Source Definition and works such as *The Cathedral & the Bazaar* tried to codify the fundamental principles of open source.

But as Kuhn notes, speaking of scientific pioneers who opened new fields of study:

> *Their achievement was sufficiently unprecedented to attract an enduring group of adherents away from competing modes of scientific activity. Simultaneously, it was sufficiently open ended to leave all sorts of problems for the redefined group of practitioners to resolve. Achievements that share these two characteristics, I shall refer to as "paradigms".*[11]

In short, if it is sufficiently robust an innovation to qualify as a new paradigm, the open-source story is far from over, and its lessons far from completely understood. Rather than thinking of open source only as a set of software licenses and associated software development practices, we do better to think of it as a field of scientific and economic inquiry, one with many historical precedents, and part of a broader social and economic story. We must understand the impact of such factors as standards and their effect on commoditization, system architecture and network effects, and the development practices associated with software as a service. We must study these factors when they appear in proprietary software as well as when they appear in traditional open-source projects. We must understand the ways in which the means by which software is deployed changes the way in which it is created and used. We must also see how the same principles that led to early source code sharing may impact other fields of collaborative activity. Only when we stop measuring open source by what activities are excluded from the definition, and begin to study its fellow travelers on the road to the future, will we understand its true impact and be fully prepared to embrace the new paradigm.

References

[1] Thomas Kuhn (1962), The Structure of Scientific Revolutions, University of Chicago Press, p. 7.
[2] Ray Kurzweil, Speech at the Foresight Senior Associates Gathering, April 2002 http://www.foresight.org/SrAssoc/spring2002/.
[3] Clayton Christensen, Harvard Business Review, Feb 2004 – http://www.tensilica.com/HBR_feb_04.pdf.
[4] I have been talking and writing about the paradigm shift for years, but until I heard Christensen speak at the Open Source Business Conference in March 2004, I hadn't heard his eloquent generalization of the economic principles at work in what I'd been calling business paradigm shifts. I am indebted to Christensen and to Dave Stutz, whose recent writings on software commoditization have enriched my own views on the subject.
[5] Clayton Christensen, Harvard Business Review, Feb 2004 – http://www.tensilica.com/HBR_feb_04.pdf.
[6] From private communications with SuSe CTO Juergen Geck and Sun CTO Greg Papadopoulos.
[7] I like to say that software enables speech between humans and computers. It is also the best way to talk about certain aspects of computer science, just as equations are the best ways to talk about problems in physics. If you follow this line of reasoning, you realize that many of the arguments for free speech apply to open source as well. How else do you tell someone how to talk with their computer other than by sharing the code you used to do so? The benefits of open source are analogous to the benefits brought by the free flow of ideas through other forms of information dissemination.
[8] Dave Stutz notes (in a private email response to an early draft of this piece), this software "includes not only what I call "collective software" that is aware of groups and individuals, but also software that is customized to its location on the network, and also software that is customized to a device or a

virtualized hosting environment. These additional types of customization lead away from shrinkwrap software that runs on a single PC or PDA/smartphone and towards personalized software that runs "on the network" and is delivered via many devices simultaneously."

9 From a private email response from Eric Raymond to an earlier draft of this paper.
10 Alan Kay, spoken at a 1971 internal Xerox planning meeting, as quoted at www.lisarein.com/alankay/tour.html.
11 Thomas Kuhn (1962), The Structure of Scientific Revolutions, University of Chicago Press, p. 10.

Biography

Tim O'Reilly (1954°) is the Irish-born CEO of O'Reilly & Associates, for many people the publishers of the best computer books in the world. Tim O'Reilly was instrumental in the early adoption of the World Wide Web; its Global Network Navigator (GNN), created in 1993 – and later sold to AOL – was the first true commercial website, the first web portal, and the first site to carry Internet advertising. In early 1997, Tim hosted the first "Free Software Summit", the meeting of free software developers that led to the wide adoption of the term "Open-Source Software" and sparked mainstream interest in projects such as Linux, Perl, Sendmail and Apache. His company's Open-Source Software Convention (http://conferences.oreilly.com/oscon) is the premier gathering for the technical élite behind all of the leading open-source projects. "Alpha geeks and early adopters show us the technologies that hold the potential for widespread adoption" says O'Reilly on his website, introducing the third annual O'Reilly Emerging Technology Conference of 2005. "In fact, people you've never heard of are changing the world."

art for teens

Develop art skills with a professional artist. Work in many media. Materials provided. Free!

MONDAYS & TUESDAYS
July through October
3:30 - 5 pm
NEW LOCATION: West Thames Park

Teen Drumming

Presented by Battery Park City Parks Conservancy

Join a drumming circle led by a master drummer. Improvise on African rhythms. Drums provided.

Tuesdays 4 - 5:30pm
Nelson A. Rockefeller Park

garden TOURS

Escape the bustle of the city by touring Battery Park City's beautiful gardens with a noted botanist. Please call 212-267-9700 to schedule a guided tour. Thursdays, 12:30 pm

Public Art TOURS

Join a contemporary art historian for an eye-opening tour of Battery Park City's 20th century public art collection.
Robert F. Wagner, Jr. Park

SATURDAYS 2 PM
MAY 22
JUNE 26
JULY 10
SEPT 18

PRESENTED BY BATTERY PARK CITY PARKS CONSERVANCY

FIX YOUR OWN BIKE

Consult an expert and learn to make simple repairs. Tools and supplies provided. Register your bike with NYPD's Bicycle Registration Program.

Saturdays, May 22 and September 18,
10 am - Noon.
Robert F. Wagner, Jr. Park

PRESENTED BY BATTERY PARK CITY PARKS CONSERVANCY

SOCCER

shoot, and dribble

Tuesdays
Nelson A. Rockefeller Park

Open Courseware and Open Scientific Publications

Frederik Questier and Wim Schreurs

Copyright law was originally designed "for the encouragement of learning" and "to promote the progress of science and useful arts". Authors received a protection against unauthorised copying and plagiarism for a limited period, before their works were passed into the public domain.

In recent decades there has been a shift from the right to protect a work against unauthorised "use" towards a right to prevent others from unauthorised access to it. This shift is, among other things, supported by a copyright protection against the circumvention of technological measures intended to protect the works, and by the 'legal support' afforded by other intellectual property rights such as sui generis database protection law.

As a result, the 'fair use' exception, and the exceptions for educational and scientific purposes, which used to be accepted in almost all countries, are endangered in today's information society. Moreover, the technological move to e-books and digital rights management systems contributes to this endangerment of the fair use and educational exceptions.

It is often hard to find good and freely reusable educational material, but as teachers and scientists are themselves the most important authors of the works they and their students need, the solution is in their own hands. Thanks to new copyright licence models – such as the Creative Commons licence – inspired by free software licences, authors themselves can define access and distribution rules which are more suitable for promoting the progress of science and art than the default copyright laws. Promoting wide redistribution helps authors to spread their knowledge and to gain recognition, which is what most educational and scientific authors want. Authors who do not want others to walk away with commercial profits from their works can still forbid any non-agreed commercial redistribution.

The Massachusetts Institute of Technology started a new trend by publishing their course material as Open Courseware under the Creative Commons licence. Projects such as the open and community-driven online encyclopedia Wikipedia (larger than any commercial encyclopedia) prove that free licences work where copyrights fail.

Some history of copyright

The large-scale reproduction of texts and books did not begin until the late 15th century, after the invention of printing technology. When book-publishing became profitable, publishers sought ways to protect their business. Often they could establish monopolies, such as the English publishing guild (the Company of Stationers). Disputes about publishing rights were enforced by common law until the birth of the first Copyright Act, the Statute of Anne (1710),[1] which attempted to break the monopoly of the English publishing guild.

As the main aim of this act was "the encouragement of learning", it tried to stimulate the creativity of authors by granting them protection in the form of copyrights. These rights were limited to 14 years plus another 14 years after an optional renewal if the author was still alive. In order to get this protection, authors had to donate nine copies of their work, one for each royal and academic library. After the period of protection had expired, the work would pass into the public domain, which meant that everybody had the right to use and build upon these works without any restriction.

In the United States of America, the first nationwide copyright law (the Copyright Act of 1790) was closely modelled on the English act, with the same opening words in the title – "An Act for the encouragement of learning" – and the same limited protection periods of 14 plus 14 years. The authority for this law was given by Article 1 of the United States Constitution: "Congress shall have power (...) to promote the progress of science and useful arts, by securing for limited times to authors and inventors the exclusive right to their respective writings and discoveries".

During that period, intellectuals argued that the Enlightenment was based on the free exchange of ideas. These ideas belong to the world and not to the individual who *discovered* them.

The French Marquis de Condorcet, for example, argued in the 18th century that copyright is not a true right, but a privilege. Copyright is a necessary evil to protect the free exchange of ideas, and must be regarded as a balance between the rights of the authors and the rights of the public. Without copyright, authors might lose their motivation to write. But with a perpetual copyright, authors could never build upon or improve other works.[2]

Over time, copyright protection periods were extended enormously. Today, copyright is considered to be an exclusive author's right without any formal condition (like a copyright notice, registration or payment), limited in time (70 years after the author's death) and subject to exceptions and restrictions. These rights and restrictions – restrictions being described as 'fair use' exceptions in common law (open system) and listed restrictedly in most European continental copyright laws (closed system) – can be found in the first copyright treaty to be adopted almost worldwide, the Berne Convention of 1886.

In particular, the Berne Convention established a general three-step test for copyright exceptions.[3] This three-step test was subsequently implemented in other international treaties such as the TRIPs Agreement (1994), WIPO Copyright Treaty (1996), WIPO Performances and Phonograms Treaty (1996) and the EU Copyright Directive (2001). On the other hand, the Berne Convention refers explicitly to exceptions for *teaching purposes*.

General problems with intellectual property rights

Despite the existence of international treaties on copyright and related rights, granting exclusive rights to authors and rights owners on the one hand and guaranteeing exceptions on the other, we can hardly deny that there exist many problems for the use of works for teaching and scientific research purposes today, especially in digital environments.

In fact, these problems reflect a general trend that is calling intellectual rights as such into question. Before going into more detail on the use of a work for teaching and research purposes, we would first like to draw your attention to what is going on with our immaterial human productions today. As we will see, it is not only copyright law that poses problems as regards the use of works for teaching and scientific purposes.

To use a metaphor, all intellectual property rights were normally supposed to be "small islands of private property" in a large ocean of free use, free flow and free exchange of information. It was considered that these 'small islands' would exist for only a limited period, and would sink after a while into the free ocean (described as the '*public* domain') and become part of it. But now, these small and temporary islands change into extensive and sometimes eternally protected landscapes of *private* property. It is quite impossible to wander in areas of research, medicines, software or other important creations without being stopped by a (digitally programmed) guard who forbids you even to *go further* without *paying* some kind of remuneration (while the immaterial act of reading, using, consuming... does not prevent others from reading, using and consuming the same information at any place and at any – even the same – time!).

However, this problem of "access to information" is *not only* a matter of intellectual property law: it is a consequence of the fact that information has become a major financial asset, produced on a large scale throughout the world and gathered in the new Fort Knox of the digital area, the Internet. And (and this is important), it is also *a matter of choice*: in the end, it is and will remain the authors (and their publishers) who decide what people can or can't do with the fruits of their creativity.

Specific problems of copyright and new technology

Together with the evolution in intellectual property, the large-scale production of immaterial goods and the protectionist attitude of the owners of works, there has also been an important evolution in the nature of copyright itself.

In theory, copyright was based on a system according to which the author or the rights holder to a work enjoyed a temporary privilege which existed only as an exclusive right for *commercial* reproduction and communication to the public. These rights were granted only *in exchange* for people having access to the works – in other words: only *if* and *after* an author gave everybody access to the work did he or she acquire an exclusive right over its *commercial* exploitation.

As a result, people could use the works for free, without consent, as long as there was no commercial use: we could share our copy with friends, destroy it, read it or listen to it as much as we wanted to, and even use it in the classroom. This was so because the work itself was incorporated in a physical device of which the owner or possessor had the material property or possession. Copyright existed only *on the information* itself, not on the physical device that contained it (book, CD, video, painting). By having control over a physical device, the users had a kind of control over the use of the work.

Now, however, these physical devices are disappearing and being replaced by hard disks and later on, by remote hard disks (accessible through internet-like communications networks). Works of science, art and literature become *pure* information *without* the existence of a device. Every use of a work becomes permanently controlled by rights owners, even if that use is exempt from copyright protection (the work has fallen into the public domain or may be regarded as a legal exception). This technological evolution poses major problems for our common access rights to information.

The introduction of technological protection measures and digital rights management systems (access control, watermarking, …) supported by copyright[4] and other laws[5] which prohibit the circumvention of it, puts rights holders in a position where they have a *de facto access right* which goes far beyond the original copyright on commercial reproduction and communication to the public.

Indeed: digital rights management systems and technological measures are generally not very fond of exceptions....

The music industry incorporates anti-copy technology in CDs to prevent private copies and, in the interest of artists and producers, sues people – young people – for *illegal one-to-one file sharing* of music files. Internet providers invade the privacy of their customers by handing over their names and addresses to organizations, such as the Recording Industry Association of America (RIAA), who search your personal computer – placed in your living room at your home – for illegal content. The movie industry uses region codes for DVDs to make them unreadable in other continents. At the moment, rights holders prepare possible claims against Google™ who uses their trademarks and copyrighted materials in a search engine. Google™ and Microsoft™ have already sued people who use similar domain names, such as Googel.nl or Lindows.com: is it even forbidden to be smart?

Besides all this, it should also be mentioned that works of art and literature are not protected by copyright *alone*. Other – new – intellectual property rights support this, like *the protection of databases* (protecting collections of information) and *trademarks* (protecting forms, signs and other expressions even if these forms and expressions are not copyrightable or have fallen into the public domain like 'Laurel & Hardy'[6] or the first 9 notes of Beethoven's *Für Elise*).[7]

Copyright exceptions

It could be said that copyright laws are not in fact the "real enemy" for students, teachers and scientific researchers. Rather, it is the introduction of new technology, and the way it is used by publishers, that is jeopardising the teaching exemptions.

The Berne Convention, almost worldwide adopted, is very clear and expressly includes a teaching exception, in Article 10(2) and (3): *It shall be a matter for legislation in the countries (...) to permit the utilization, to the extent justified by the purpose, of literary or artistic works by way of illustration in publications, broadcasts or sound or visual recordings for teaching, provided such utilization is compatible with fair practice. Where use is made of works in accordance with the preceding paragraphs of this Article, mention shall be made of the source, and of the name of the author if it appears thereon.*

The main problems with copyright issues, which are discussed today on a worldwide scale, such as the long period of protection, the prohibition of *any* reproduction or communication and the practical difficulties for copyright negotiations and contracts, are not completely relevant for teaching purposes. Even if copyright exists on a work for a thousand years, the exception for teaching purposes will still remain.

In the old, analogue system, the copyright exemptions were used by the *users* as a defence mechanism in litigation concerning copyright infringements. The user could in fact only be stopped *after* infringement. In our digital world of tomorrow, the user even *can't* infringe any more... As a consequence, users will only have a choice between either suing rights holders in order to get access to the work according to the legally binding exceptions, ... or circumventing the technological measures (which is forbidden by the E.U. Copyright Directive, see above). This puts the rights holder in a powerful position – thereby jeopardising the chances of striking a proper balance between copyright and exceptions for teaching and scientific research.[8]

When we look at the copyright and scientific research exemptions in different sets of legislation[9] – more in particular, the EU Copyright Directive of 2001 – we can see that several provisions do not fit well with the balance. First, the teaching and scientific research exceptions in the E.U. Copyright Directive are not mandatory: " Member States *may provide* for exceptions or limitations to the rights [...] in the following cases: use for the sole purpose of illustration for teaching or scientific research, as long as the source, including the author's name, is indicated, unless this turns out to be impossible, and to the extent justified by the non-commercial purpose to be achieved (article 5.3.)". This means that the Member States themselves decide whether or not to provide for the exceptions. This means that an exception in one Member State may not be provided in another.

The subsidiary principle and the autonomy of E.U. Member States to implement exceptions in national legislation, creates problems both for rights owners and consumers of information. Rights owners have to take into account the different national legislations – read: exceptions – while programming their DRM system. They will also be confronted with several problems of enforcement and international private law. Where is the infringement taking place? Which law is applicable when the work is created in France, when the rights holder is located in Sweden, when the work is accessible through the internet, when a German consumer uses his mobile phone to download while travelling through Europe?

Autonomy of the Member States in a borderless digital environment is neither advantageous for the consumer. On the contrary and more in particular: The rights owner can store the data on the server of a Member State with few exceptions in her copyright legislation, or impose to the consumer in a click-through contract the law of the Member State which has the – for the producer – most advantageous legislation...

Secondly, as mentioned above, contract law can supersede legal exceptions. This discussion about the mandatory status of exceptions has become a major issue.[10] It is possible today, because of the unavoidable access control (through technological measures), for authors and rights holders to impose contracts on users in which these rights holders alone, unilaterally, define the rights and obligations of the users, even for uses that are supposed to be exempt from copyright. The Directive devoted a separate paragraph to safeguarding the exceptions in technologically protected environments and states in Article 6.4.: *"In the absence of voluntary measures taken by rightholders, including agreements between rightholders and other parties concerned, Member States shall take appropriate measures to ensure that rightholders make available to the beneficiary of an exception or limitation (...) the means of benefiting from that exception or limitation, to the extent necessary to benefit from that exception or limitation and where that beneficiary has legal access to the protected work or subject-matter concerned"* and *"the exemptions do not apply in respect of works or other subject-matter made available to the public on agreed contractual terms in such a way that members of the public may access them from a place and at a time individually chosen by them"*. The law's attempt to preserve the exceptions for teaching and scientific purposes is subsidiary to the contractual terms and conditions of authors and rights owners!

Thirdly, we notice that not every country adopts teaching and scientific research exceptions *correctly* in their legislation. For example, Belgian copyright legislation provides no teaching exception for *communication to the public*. At present, only a *reproduction* is exempt from copyright (although new copyright legislation, to implemented the E.U. Copyright directive, is currently in preparation). This creates a problem for online learning platforms, since online reproductions of works, or parts of works, on such platforms are also regarded as communications to the public, even if only a limited number of students have access to the content.

It should also be mentioned that the default copyright protection is always a complete and comprehensive protection, whereas a limited copyright, such as the right to free use for non-commercial purposes, must be expressly mentioned by the author or the rights holder (on the document): this also makes it more difficult to organise the balance between copyrights and 'fair' use.

Intermediate conclusion

Clearly, it is the sweat of the brow of the investor, rather than the work of the author, that is increasingly protected by intellectual property rights. It is also clear that the law as such is not "that bad" as regards the use of copyrighted works for teaching and scientific purposes.

Indeed: use should be in line with fair practice, which is economically relevant, and the sources should be mentioned. On the other hand, however, the law should be improved by making most of the exceptions mandatory. The teaching and scientific research exception seems to us to be the most important one – even more important than the private reproduction and communication exception (which is economically more).

We think that the main problem, in fact, lies not in the law, but in the attitude of the rights holders themselves and the technology that they use.

In the end, the rights holders themselves decide how and when their works can be used, who should pay and who not... And they are not alone: the public, the consumers, also decide what they will read, use or listen to. The open-source software movement provides a very good illustration of the growing importance of works with limited protection. A copyleft movement is emerging.

Free licences as alternatives to copyright

The legal default protection for texts and other works has become "locked up", in defiance of the tradition in education and science. The main aim of education and science is to build upon knowledge, improve it and then share the new knowledge. Because there are now more legal and technological restrictions, educators and scientists are having increasing problems in accessing information or finding good, freely reusable educational material.

Because educators and scientists are not only consumers of these works, but also their main authors, the solution is in their own hands.

Most of the time, the main personal interest of these authors is not commercial (as they already have a job as an educator or scientist), but rather recognition. Scientists count how often their works are cited. It has been shown that works that are freely available online are cited more often.[11] We see that the first reflex of teachers is often to consider their course material as targeted only at their own students, and they do not want colleagues to copy it. That first idea often changes when they are confronted with the questions: "Would you want to share your course if all your colleagues shared their courses?" and "Would you prefer somebody else's course to be copied and become the most popular one, or yours?"

A first obvious alternative to copyright is to put one's own works immediately into the **public domain**, uncopyrighted, by adding a notice to them. This might be good for the public, but it is not satisfactory for most authors, as then anybody can modify and redistribute or sell these works without even giving credit to the original author.

Other solutions are based on free licences. Works distributed with a free licence are still copyrighted. Free distribution terms are added on top of the copyright. Legally granted user rights, such as fair use and citation rights, are in no way restricted by these free licences.

The first free licences originated in the software world. When, in the 1980s, software programmer Richard Stallman got frustrated about the growing trend of proprietary software to take away the rights of users, he founded the Free Software Foundation and the GNU project. The goal of the GNU project was to create a complete, free operating system. As this needed a free licence, in 1988 they devised the **GNU General Public License (GPL)**. The GPL grants users the right to copy, modify and redistribute the programs covered while giving credit to the original authors. The preservation of these rights in derivative works is ensured through a copyleft mechanism. This means that any modified version of the program, if redistributed, must carry the same free licence terms. Otherwise, companies could modify free software and lock it up in proprietary products (by distributing binaries without source code), effectively stripping away the freedom and rights that the original author gave to users. Many other free software licences, such as the BSD licence (Berkeley Software Distribution), do not have this copyleft mechanism. This copyleft mechanism is probably one of the main reasons why the GPL is the most popular free licence for software. The GPL is used for most of the tools of the GNU/Linux distributions, and, as of July 2004, more than 24,000 and 36,000 projects respectively on the Freshmeat.net and Sourceforge.net software repositories. The GPL not only enables individual programmers or small teams to build complex tools quickly by reusing other GPL code or tools, but it also enables programmers to work efficiently together in very large communities. The OpenOffice developing team, for example, has 12,500 contributors. Free software licences also offer users guarantees that proprietary software cannot offer: if necessary, users can themselves fix or adapt the free software; the software can be further used and developed if its company or development team ceases to exist; projects that have been abandoned for years can be taken up again; projects that were previously written for archaic computer architectures can be ported to modern systems.

Free software needs free documentation. But when free software became popular, publishers contacted the best documentation authors in order to publish their books. In return, the authors had to hand over their copyright to the publisher. Not only was this bad for the rights of the user, but it also made it difficult to adapt the documentation constantly to the evolving software, or to allow translations. In order to protect the rights of the authors and users, while still making it worthwhile for commercial publishers to invest in free documentation books, the GNU project created the **GNU Free Documentation License (GNU FDL)**. Everyone is free to copy and redistribute the GNU FDL licensed works, with or without modification, either commercially or non-commercially. On the other hand, for authors and publishers the licence preserves a way of getting credit for their work without being considered responsible for modifications made by others. Secondary sections of a work (which deal more with the authors or publishers than with the real content of the work) can be designated as invariant sections, which may not be modified. The GNU FDL is a copyleft licence, which means that derivative works must be free in the same sense as the original work. Publishers are not allowed to use technical measures to obstruct or control reading or further copying. The licence is designed mainly for manuals and instructional books, but it can be used for any textual work.

In 2002, the Creative Commons group, housed at the Stanford Law School, released an interesting set of free licences "to promote an ethos of sharing, public education and creative interactivity". The **Creative Commons licences** are inspired by the GNU GPL, but designed for a variety of non-software creative works: texts, courseware, websites, music, movies, photos, etc. Creative Commons proposes the 'some rights reserved' concept as a compromise between the extremes of 'all rights reserved' (current copyright) and 'no rights reserved' (public domain). The biggest advantage of the Creative Commons licences is their flexibility. Authors can choose between eleven licences, based on four options:

- Attribution? Should credit be given to the original author?
- Commercial? Can others use the work for commercial purposes?
- Derivative works? Can others modify the work, or is only verbatim copying allowed?
- Share alike? Must derivative works be distributed under the same licence?

Since Version 2 of the Creative Common License, the attribution option has been removed as it seemed that people always wanted attribution.

The non-commercial licence enables authors to negotiate individual commercial deals outside the licence.

Authors can choose and apply a Creative Commons licence by following four easy online steps at http://creativecommons.org/license/.

Choose License

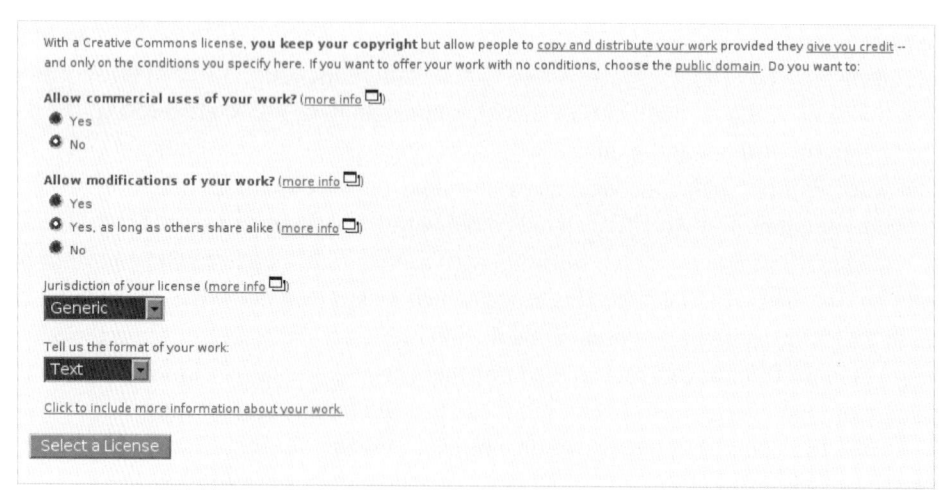

With a Creative Commons license, **you keep your copyright** but allow people to copy and distribute your work provided they give you credit -- and only on the conditions you specify here. If you want to offer your work with no conditions, choose the public domain. Do you want to:

Allow commercial uses of your work? (more info)
- Yes
- No

Allow modifications of your work? (more info)
- Yes
- Yes, as long as others share alike (more info)
- No

Jurisdiction of your license (more info)
[Generic]

Tell us the format of your work:
[Text]

Click to include more information about your work.

[Select a License]

In the first step, authors can select the Commercial, Derivative or Share Alike options; a licence specific to the copyright laws of a certain country; and the format of the work (audio, video, image, text, interactive).

In the second step, authors are presented with the resulting licence in three formats: the common deeds (human-readable), legal code (lawyer-readable) and digital code (machine-readable).

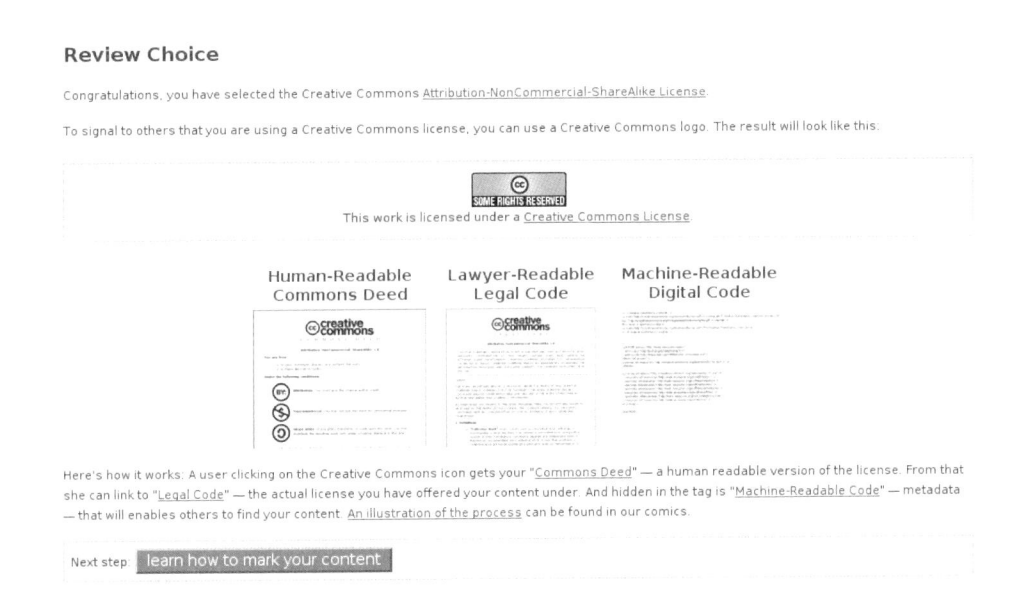

Review Choice

Congratulations, you have selected the Creative Commons Attribution-NonCommercial-ShareAlike License.

To signal to others that you are using a Creative Commons license, you can use a Creative Commons logo. The result will look like this:

SOME RIGHTS RESERVED
This work is licensed under a Creative Commons License.

| Human-Readable Commons Deed | Lawyer-Readable Legal Code | Machine-Readable Digital Code |

Here's how it works: A user clicking on the Creative Commons icon gets your "Commons Deed" — a human readable version of the license. From that she can link to "Legal Code" — the actual license you have offered your content under. And hidden in the tag is "Machine-Readable Code" — metadata — that will enables others to find your content. An illustration of the process can be found in our comics.

Next step: learn how to mark your content

In the third step, authors receive instructions on how to mark their work in the appropriate way, depending on what medium it uses (website, text not on website, mp3, PDF, etc.).

Mark Content

Now that you've chosen a Creative Commons license, you must mark your work in the appropriate way.

In order to:

- Mark your content on a web page, the HTML to display your button is as follows and be sure to follow the guidelines here:

```
<!-- Creative Commons License -->
<a rel="license" href="http://creativecommons.org/licenses/by-nc-sa/2.0/"><img alt="Creative Commons
License" border="0" src="http://creativecommons.org/images/public/somerights20.gif" /></a><br />
This work is licensed under a <a rel="license"
href="http://creativecommons.org/licenses/by-nc-sa/2.0/">Creative Commons License</a>.
<!-- /Creative Commons License -->

<!--
```

[Highlight Text to Copy] [Get HTML and email it to yourself]

- Mark an mp3, follow these guidelines.
- Mark a document not on the web, add this text to your work.
- Add your license information to a RSS feed, use the RSS 1.0 module, or the RSS 2.0 module.
- To mark a PDF or other XMP-supported file, save this template following these instructions.

Final step: [Learn how to publicize and share your work]

In the fourth step, authors learn how to publish and share their works in Open-Content archives and registers.

Publicizing and sharing your work

If you have marked your content properly, then search engines will help others find it. In addition, a number of great archives have developed which specifically identify Creative Commons content. These include:

Registries and Hosting

Common Content is a registry and directory of Creative Commons licensed works.

Archive.org's Open Source Audio and Open Source Movies offer a registry and free hosting for Creative Commons licensed audio and moving images.

Payment and Donation Systems

BitPass offers a micro-payment system that allows you to accept donations or payments for your work.

Freely licensed educational and scientific publications

The first well-known, large-scale example of Open Content in education came from the Massachusetts Institute of Technology (MIT). In 1999, they decided to provide free, searchable access to their courses for educators, students, and self-learners around the world "based on the conviction that the open dissemination of knowledge and information can open new doors to the powerful benefits of education for humanity around the world". By May 2004 they had published 701 courses under the Creative Commons Attribution – Noncommercial – Share Alike licence. Their aim is to have all their 2,000 courses published as **MIT OpenCourseWare** [http://ocw.mit.edu/] by 2008. They publish not only syllabi but also lecture notes, course calendars, problems and solutions, exams, reading lists, and even a selection of video lectures. The MIT seems happy with the impact of this openness: more than half of the site visitors come from outside North America. Educators, students and self-learners all use the content to increase their personal knowledge, but educators use the site mainly for planning, developing or improving courses or classes, while students use it mainly to find materials for the courses they are taking. Almost half of the visiting educators interviewed said they had reused, or were planning to reuse, MIT OpenCourseWare. Several universities have begun to translate MIT courses (at least into Spanish and Chinese versions, as of May 2004).

The MIT hopes that this openness "will inspire other institutions to openly share their course materials, creating a worldwide web of knowledge that will benefit humanity". And indeed others are starting to follow, the first being the Fulbright Economics School of Vietnam.

We at our university (Vrije Universiteit Brussel) are just moving to an open-source e-learning platform (Dokeos). As this enables us to adapt the platform to our wishes, we are implementing a system that allows teachers to select the access permissions for each of their documents (only for their own students, own university, or worldwide access) and the licence (plain copyright, Creative Commons License, Free Documentation License, etc.) As default access permission we would like to propose worldwide access, and as licence, the Creative Commons Attribution – Noncommercial – Share Alike licence. With our previous (proprietary) e-learning platform, teachers had no licence choices, and only class- or university-wide access options, the class-wide access option being the default. That students could only consult the courses for which they were enrolled proved to a great hindrance to integrated learning, one of our university's current focus points.

The **Connexions project** [http://cnx.rice.edu/] is a web-based environment designed to allow the collaborative development and free availability of educational and research materials. The material is organised in small modules that can easily be fitted into larger courses. The project started at Rice University in Houston in 2000, and was officially launched as an international project in February 2004. In July 2004 they had 1,800 modules online. All content is free to be used and reused under the Creative Commons Attribution Licence. In contrast to other projects such as the MIT OpenCourseWare, Connexions is open to contributions from everyone. Connexions promotes communication and collaboration between content creators, as they believe that "collaboration helps knowledge grow more quickly, advancing the possibilities for new ideas from which we all benefit". Their platform is based on the open-source content-management system Plone, and the new tools they develop are available as free software.

Merlot (Multimedia Educational Resource for Learning and Online Teaching) [http://www.merlot.org] is an online catalogue of online learning materials. Merlot is an international project, sponsored mainly by the California State University. By July 2004, it contained links to more than 11,000 learning objects along with annotations such as peer reviews and assignments. Teachers can not only contribute links to their material, they can also create a page with their collection of Merlot links. The number of times a learning object is mentioned in such collections is used as a rating measure. It is a pity that, in addition to having these interesting features, they are not promoting open content (freely licensed), but only open access. Every learning object has a meta-field "Copyright and/or Other Restrictions?" But the only possible answers are yes and no. As all free licences (except public domain) are based on copyright, this is pretty useless. Fewer than 10% of the learning objects are described as not having any copyright restrictions, and most of them simply appear to have been wrongly classified.

Wikipedia [http://www.wikipedia.org] is an online encyclopedia being written collaboratively by contributors from around the world. The site is a wiki, which means that anyone can easily edit articles, by following the 'edit this page' link that appears at the top of each page. Wikipedia began on 15 January 2001 and currently contains over 310,000 articles in English and over 530,000 in more than 100 other languages (as of July 2004), easily surpassing any commercial encyclopedia.

All text in Wikipedia, and most images and other content, are covered by the GNU Free Documentation License. Contributions remain the property of their creators, while the FDL ensures the content is freely editable, and remains freely reproducible and redistributable.

Wikipedia began as a spin-off of its more academic sister-project, Nupedia. The Nupedia software and content were covered by a free licence, but its content was written by experts and peer-reviewed. The Nupedia project was stopped in 2003, three years after its conception, with only 23 'complete' articles and 68 more in progress. The difference in success between Nupedia and Wikipedia clearly demonstrates the power of an open, collaborative community.

Wikipedia has a growing number of sister projects, grouped under the parent foundation **Wikimedia**, such as Wiktionary, Wikiquote, Wikisource and Wikibooks.

Wikibooks is a collaboratively written, multilingual collection of free and open-content textbooks, manuals, and other texts, mainly targeting education. Currently they have over 120 textbooks in various stages of development.

A new project, still under discussion for inclusion in Wikimedia, is Wikiversity. **Wikiversity** aims to create a wiki-based, free, open learning environment and community, where anyone can participate in online courses or create courses.

The Wikimedia projects in general open up perspectives for education, not only as resource, but also for assignments. Teachers can ask students to add, expand or translate articles. As every contribution is logged, this can even be used for the evaluation of students.

Another future Wikimedia project is **Wikiresearch**. Wikipedia is an interesting platform for knowledge collection, analysis and interpretation, but not for new research reports. Wikiresearch hopes to allow collaborative research with a system similar to the traditional peer review.

Open online publishing could be very promising for science: cost-saving, better access, better searching possibilities, better backup possibilities, more direct access to scientific information for public and media, etc. But publishers are standing in the way of that. While science is often government funded, scientific literature very often ends up privately owned, as authors have to hand over their author's rights to the publishers.

Michael Eisen and Pat Brown, from the Public Library of Science, wrote in *Nature* [http://www.nature.com/nature/debates/e-access/Articles/Eisen.htm, Should scientific literature be privately owned and controlled?]:

> "By any objective standard it seems absurd that publishers should 'own' the scientific literature as their private property. Journals play an important role in producing finished scientific manuscripts – they manage peer review and the editorial process. But the creativity, intellectual content and labour contributed by the publishers is minuscule in comparison to the contributions of the scientists who provide the original ideas, conduct the work, write the papers and actually carry out the peer review by serving as reviewers. And the financial investment that the publishers contribute is tiny compared to that of the institutions that fund the research itself. Should the reward for the publishers' small contribution be permanent, private ownership of the published record of scientific research, and monopoly control over how, when and by whom a paper can be read or used and how much this access will cost? No!"

Maybe scientists themselves could organise the publication process better (e.g. through a non-profit organisation). The costs would then be lower than the amounts that can be saved by their institutional libraries for journal subscriptions, and individuals, institutions or countries with limited funds would no longer have their access restricted. In any event, the average royalty for the contracting author, if any, hardly ever exceeds even 10% of the consumer price...

One of the oldest open-access projects is **arXiv.org** [e-print archive http://arxiv.org], which started in 1991 as the LANL preprint archive. It currently covers the fields of physics, mathematics, non-linear science, computer science, and quantitative biology.

In 1998 the NEC Research Institute started **CiteSeer**, also known as ResearchIndex [http://citeseer.ist.psu.edu]. Citeseer is a search engine which carries out autonomous citation indexation and caching of preprint and scientific papers about computer and information science available on the World Wide Web, usually on the personal web pages of the authors.

In 2000, the **Public Library of Science (PLoS)** [http://www.plos.org/] was founded as a coalition of scientists and physicians dedicated to making the world's scientific and medical literature a public resource. Their first act was to write an open letter calling on scientific publishers to make the archive of their research articles available through online public libraries. The open letter was signed by nearly 34,000 scientists from 180 countries. As most of the publishers did not respond positively, PLoS concluded that the only way forward was to launch their own online journals, "as a model for open-access publication and a catalyst for change in the publication industry".

By July 2004 PLoS had two journals: PLoS Biology and PLoS Medicine, both online and in print, peer-reviewed and run by professional editors and editorial boards. All PLoS articles are published under the (least restrictive) Creative Commons Attribution License. PloS not only provides Open Access, but also Open Content (giving rights to reproduce, modify and distribute the content).

The **Directory of Open Access Journals** [http://www.doaj.org/] lists more than 1,200 open scientific and scholarly journals of which more than 300 are searchable at article level.

Conclusion

Copyright laws, originally designed "for the encouragement of learning" and "to promote the progress of science and useful arts", are today having quite the opposite effect. They are no longer suited to the goals of either consumers or authors.

Legal policymakers should guarantee the mandatory character of exceptions to copyright for the use for teaching and scientific purposes. They should ensure that these exceptions are implemented at the same level in all states bound by the international copyright treaties. These mandatory exceptions should be implemented in technology and digital-rights management systems on a compulsory basis, rather than being the subject of contractual terms and conditions between the author, the publisher and the consumer. Appropriate methods of enforcing this mandatory character should be organised and applied.

Authors too must be very well aware of today's problems concerning the free exchange of information and the progress of science. They have the possibility of negotiating contracts with publishers in which both consumers' rights and their own are safeguarded to benefit of everybody. They can do as more and more authors are doing, and publish directly without the intervention of a commercial publisher, thereby making use of one of the widespread free licences. With free licences, such as the Creative Commons licence, inspired by free-software licences, authors can themselves decide on access and distribution rules that are more appropriate for promoting the progress of science and art than default copyright laws. Promoting wide redistribution helps authors to spread their knowledge and gain recognition, which is what most educational and scientific authors want. Authors who do not want others to walk away with any commercial profit from their works can still forbid any non-agreed commercial redistribution. Academic institutions should promote – and provide students, staff and public with – tools and (e-learning) platforms for the free exchange of educational and scientific knowledge. The results of government-funded research should be published as freely accessible open content.

Recent projects such as the online, community-driven encyclopedia Wikipedia show that open access and open content create new ways of collaborative knowledge-gathering and research.

Notes

[1] Statute of Anne: "An Act for the Encouragement of Learning, by Vesting the Copies of Printed Books in the Authors or Purchasers of Such Copies, during the Times therein mentioned", see *inter alia* http://www.copyrighthistory.com/anne.html

[2] On the history of copyright and status of authorship, see the interesting book by B. Sherman and A. Strowel (eds), *Of Authors and Origins. Essays on Copyright Law*, Oxford, Clarendon Press, 1994, 260 pp.

3   Article 9(2) Berne Convention for the Protection of Literary and Artistic Works, Paris Act of July 24, 1971, as amended on September 28, 1979: "It shall be a matter for legislation in the countries of the Union to permit the reproduction of such works [1] in certain special cases, [2] provided that such reproduction does not conflict with a normal exploitation of the work and [3] does not unreasonably prejudice the legitimate interests of the author" (numbering inserted by the authors).
4   E.U. Copyright Directive 2001/29/EC devoted a chapter to the protection of technological measures and rights management information and requires the E.U. member states to "provide adequate legal protection against the circumvention of any effective technological measures", while these technological measures are defined as follows: "any technology, device or component that, in the normal course of its operation, is designed to prevent or restrict acts, in respect of works or other subject-matter, which are not authorised by the right-holder of any copyright or any right related to copyright as provided for by law or the *sui generis* right provided for in Chapter III of Directive 96/9/EC. Technological measures shall be deemed 'effective' where the use of a protected work or other subject-matter is controlled by the right-holders through application of **an access control** or protection process, such as encryption, scrambling or other transformation of the work or other subject-matter or a copy control mechanism, which achieves the protection objective".
5   See S. Dusollier, "Anti-circumvention protection outside copyright – General Report for the ALAI Conference 2001"; K.J. Koelman & N. Helberger, "Protection of technological measures" in *Copyright and Electronic Commerce*, B. Hugenholtz (ed.), Kluwer Law International, Information Law Series 8, 2000, pp. 165-227.
6   Several U.S. trademarks for, among other things, "entertainment services in the nature of live performances by costumed characters", see United States Patent and Trademark Office, http://www.uspto.gov/, reg. no. 2553749.
7   Benelux Trademark "for commercial and business purposes", see Benelux Trademark Office, http://register.bmb-bbm.org/, reg. no. 535083.
8   S. Dusollier, "Legal and Technical Aspects of Electronic Rights Management Systems (ERMS)", http://www.droit.fundp.ac.be/Textes/Dusollier%203.pdf.
9   An overview of teaching exceptions in the copyright law of several countries: R. Xalabarder, *et al.*, "Copyright and Digital Distance Education (CDDE): The Use of Pre-Existing Works in Distance Education Through the Internet", http://www.uoc.edu/in3/dt/eng/20418/Questionnaires.pdf.
10 S. Dusollier, "Fair use by design in the European Copyright Directive of 2001: An empty promise", http://www.cfp2002.org/fairuse/dusollier.pdf.
11 Steve Lawrence, "Online or Invisible?", *Nature*, Vol. 411, No. 6837, 2001, p. 521.

Frederik Questier is a Free-Software and Open-Source advocate, much concerned with the ethical and social implications of restrictive software licences and digital rights management. He is employed as an educational technologist at the Educational Service Center of the Vrije Universiteit Brussel, where his main work is implementing and supporting electronic learning environments. Their recent move from a proprietary to an open-source e-learning system offers not only the flexibility needed in an academic environment, but also opportunities to promote open access and open content.

Wim Schreurs graduated from the Faculty of Law at the Vrije Universiteit Brussel in 1996 and obtained an LLM in Intellectual Property Rights from the Katholieke Universiteit Brussel in 1999. In 1998 he was admitted to the Bar of Brussels, where he still works as a lawyer in intellectual property rights, privacy and ICT. Since October 2001, he has been an assistant at the Faculty of Law of the Vrije Universiteit Brussel where he teaches methodology of law. As a member of the LSTS research group (Law, Science, Technology and Society) under Prof. Serge Gutwirth, he is involved in several research projects such as FIDIS (the Future of Identity in the Information Society – Network of Excellence, European Commission) and he is currently preparing a PhD on the legal aspects of privacy and data protection in relation to ambient intelligence.

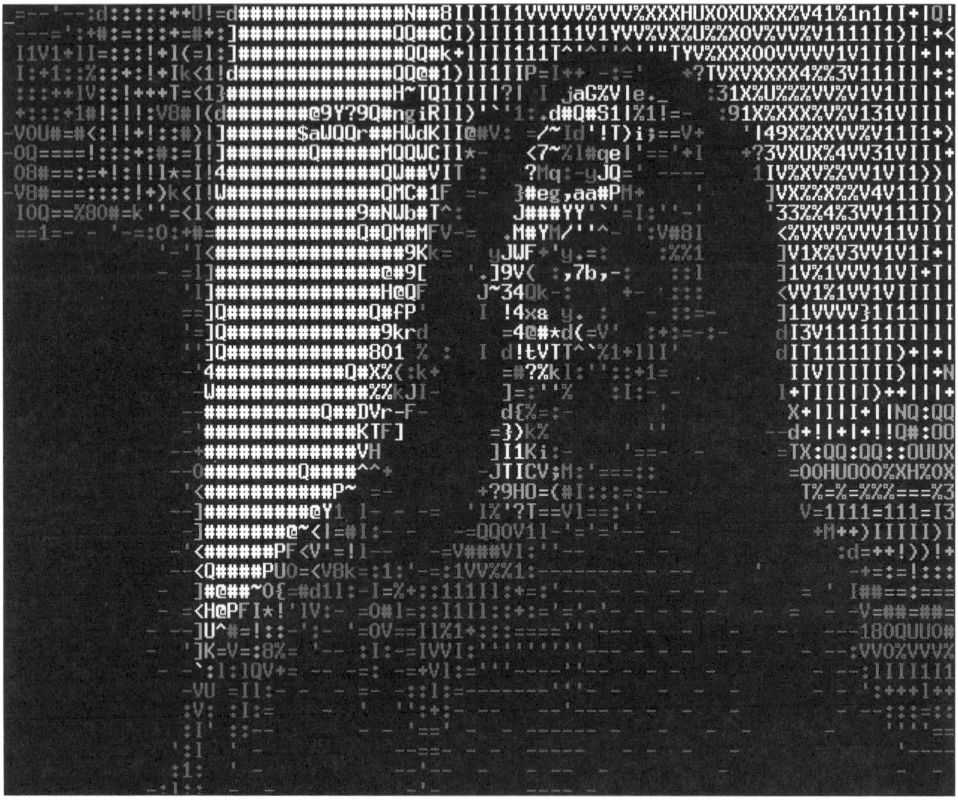

Roots Culture
Free Software Vibrations Inna Babylon

Armin Medosch

In this article I want to focus on free software as a culture. One reason for doing so is to make it very clear that there is a difference between open-source and free software, a difference that goes beyond the important distinction made by Richard Stallman. His ideas have grown legs, and now the notion of 'free-as-in-freedom' software is taken further in ways he could not possibly have imagined. Secondly, I want to show that at least one particular part of the free-software scene shows all the traits of a culture, a notion that is understood by the protagonists and is made explicit in the way they act. When it is rooted in culture, software development becomes a discipline distinct from engineering, and social and cultural values are invested in the work.

Rasta Roots and the 'Root' in Computing

The first part of the title, Roots Culture, is designed to resonate simultaneously with the hacker's pride in being the 'root' on a Unix system and with Rastafarian reggae 'roots' culture. In a file system, the root is the uppermost directory, the one from which all other sub-directories originate. In Unix-style operating systems (including GNU/Linux), 'root' is also the name of the superuser account, the user who has all rights in all modes and who can set up and administrate other accounts. Roots reggae is a particular type of reggae music with heavy basslines and African rhythmical influences. Roots reggae originated in Jamaica and is closely associated with Rastafari. Rastafari is sometimes described as either a sect/religion or a sub-culture, but neither of these definitions does justice to the diversity of the phenomenon. It is better, therefore, to follow Paul Gilroy, who suggests seeing Rastafari as a popular movement whose 'language and symbols have been put to a broad and diverse use'.[1] It originated in Jamaica in the 1930s and took some inspiration from the black nationalism, Pan-Africanism and Ethiopianism of Marcus Garvey. Through Rastafari, the African Caribbean working class found a way of fermenting resistance to the continued legacy of colonialism, racism and capitalist exploitation. It is eclectic and culturally hybrid, drawing from a range of influences, such as African drumming styles, African traditions in agriculture, food and social organisation,[2] and American Black music styles such as R&B and Soul. The central trope of the Rastafari narration is that Rastas are the twelfth tribe of Judah, living in captivity in Babylon and longing to go back to Africa, identified as a mythical Ethiopia. Making good on this promise is African Redemption.

Gilroy describes Rastas as an 'interpretive community', borrowing this phrase from Edward Said. The ideas and stories of Rastafari 'brought philosophical and historical meaning to individual and collective action'.[3] Through the enormous success of reggae, and in particular Bob Marley and the Wailers, Rastafari became popular throughout the world in the 1970s and now many non-Jamaicans sport Rasta hairstyles – dreadlocks – and dedicate themselves to the music and the activity of ganja-smoking. In the UK, versions of Rasta culture have now spread through all ages and ethnicities[4] and it is probably the most consensual popular culture in Britain today. Even though aspects of it have been heavily commercialised, and it was unfashionable for a while, roots reggae has recently made a strong comeback. The reason for this can only be that it is more than a music style or a fashion (not everybody with dreadlocks is a Rasta, and not every Rasta wears 'dreads'), and is a culture in a true and deep sense (the meaning of which I will come back to later). 'Roots' influences can now be found in Hip Hop, Jungle, Drum & Bass, 2Step and other forms of contemporary urban music.

The two notions – the 'root/s' in computing and in Rastafari – are to be understood not in any literal or narrow sense but as points of association and affinity and, therefore – tying the two narrations into a knot – as a potential point of departure for the radical imaginary. Neither Rastafari nor hacker culture is without its problems. Rastafari, for instance, is a very male culture, where homophobia is rife and women suffer a subordinated role in the midst of a supposed liberation struggle.[5] I have chosen the Rastafari theme for a number of reasons, the main one being that it has developed a language of revolution. The symbolism of this language with its focus on stories about resistance and the struggle for freedom, peace and justice has proved to be very effective, judging by the massive reception it has received. This story has resonated far beyond Jamaica and the urban African Caribbean communities in Britain and the USA. Roots Reggae, as a form of music and a liberating myth-making machine, is huge in Africa. The message from the West Indies has encouraged artists like Thomas Mapfumo, the 'Lion of Zimbabwe', to stop playing cover versions of American R&B and be true to his own African roots in his music-making, and to support the liberation struggle against the government of what was then called 'Rhodesia'. In Salvador de Bahia, the centre of Afro-Brazilian Culture, every bar is adorned with the portraits of Bob Marley and Che Guevara. Needless to add (because everybody knows), in the 1970s Salvador was the birthplace of 'Tropicalismo', a Brazilian form of 'roots' music played with drums and modern electric/electronic instruments. Thanks to its eclectic and hybrid nature, Rastafari lends itself to adoption by other communities and cultures. The experience of the diaspora, central to the Rastafari story, is shared by many people who feel displaced and uprooted, even though they may live in the land where their grandparents were born. This is well understood by some of the musical protagonists of Roots music, who encourage the 'togetherness' of all those who feel alienated in the societies they are living in. Humble Lion from the Aba Santi sound system in south London says:

> "Ultimately, people who are like us, who hold similar attitudes, will gravitate towards us, because we are aiming for the same virtues that they are, and this creates something a lot better than what society stands for. Right now, it's obvious that our societies are controlled by money, polarised, xenophobic. The major world powers back their puppet leaders and the media sanitises, separates "spectators" from reality. [...]I have to say that now it is not only the black youths who are suffering in this land, so to me, increasingly, the true inner meaning of Rasta is not concerned with colour."[6]

Hackers, young and old, have their own reasons for feeling alienated in society, one of which is the misrepresentation of their creed in the media. Originally, 'hacking' meant no more than feeling passionate about writing software and pursuing this interest sometimes outside the norms, which would not necessarily imply anything illegal. The original 'hackers', such as Richard Stallman, were in any case employees of research institutions like MIT, so they could hardly be regarded as being outside and against the 'system'. But in the 1980s, during the boom in computer-science research sponsored by the military pursuing projects such as Strategic Missile Defense and Artificial Intelligence,[7] the mood in these ivory towers of research – which had been fairly liberal in the 1970s – changed. Mavericks like Stallman left and people outside the state-sanctioned system were perceived as a potential threat to national security. In the mid 1980s, secret services and other law-enforcement agencies began their 'war against hacking', with a compliant mass media doing their best to stigmatise hackers as criminals, or even terrorists.[8] With the mass adoption of the internet in the 1990s a new type of 'hacker' emerged, the so-called script kiddies, who under the new circumstances did not have to develop a deep knowledge of computers, as cracking tools had become relatively easy to obtain. Script kiddies, who are not regarded as 'real hackers' but are called 'crackers' by others, have developed an obsession with breaking into web servers, obtaining 'root' privileges and leaving behind digital graffiti on the web server's homepage. This activity was used to legitimise an even stronger criminalisation of 'hacking', and allowed centrally owned mass media to continue to denounce computer subcultures in general with full force. Welcome to Babylon!

Hacker Ethics

The factional wars between different types of 'hackers' are bitter and full of mutual recriminations and I have no wish to put myself in the firing line, especially as the fighting sometimes rages over topics whose relevance to the bigger picture I completely fail to understand (such as which 'free' version of BSD – FreeBSD or OpenBSD or NetBSD – is the better or 'truer' one, i.e., truer to the spirit of hacking). In view of this I would warn against believing what this or that group says or what the media may choose to highlight. The denouncement of the so-called 'script kiddies' from within the hacker scene also seems to be missing the point. Certainly, older 'real' hackers are fed up because the 'kiddies' give the state a pretext for further repression of freedom on the Net. And for any system administrator, dozens of script-kiddie attacks a day are more than just a minor nuisance. Last but not least, script-kiddie vandalism can be so blind and mindless as to wipe out cultural servers like Thomas Kaulmann's Radio Orang.org, a collective resource for experimental music and radio art which was destroyed two years ago after being nursed for six years. Nevertheless, the online graffiti produced by 'kiddies' can sometimes reach the level of a native computer art that has aesthetic and political qualities of its own, and is related to other native computer arts such as the work produced by the demo scene – forms that live outside the highly rewarded and institutionalised system of computer, media and net arts. Being a script kiddie can be a step on the ladder to greater skill and social awareness.

Leaving script kiddies and crackers aside,[9] what can be identified as a common theme, transcending the internal, factional hacker wars, is the ethical code that 'real' hackers share in relation to computers and networks. Central to this ethical code is the rule that they *must not disrupt the flow of information* and *must not destroy data*. It is not my intention to idealise hackers as freedom fighters of the information age, but it must be said that their ethics stand in marked contrast to the behaviour of the state and certain industries who do their best to erect barriers, disrupt communication flows and enclose data by various means, including threats of breaking into the computers of users who participate in file-sharing networks. This hacker code of ethics has been developed as a shared commitment to a 'live-and-let-live' principle. It is an ethos that is borne out of love for the craft of hacking and the desire to let as many people as possible benefit from sources of knowledge. 'Hackers' may not represent one homogeneous group, and may be split and divided into many subgroups, but what unites them is their view that hacking is more than just writing code: it is a way of life, and it has many aspects of a culture. Hacker culture has developed its own ways of speaking, certain types of geek humour and even a kind of a dress code. Hackers regularly meet at conventions – some highly publicised, others more subterranean, with an atmosphere more closely resembling that of a large family or tribe on a picnic than any sort of formal 'meeting'.[10] From this point of view, there are similarities between hackers and Rastafari.

Armin Medosch

The Hijacking of Free Software

As Ur-Hacker Richard Stallman makes clear whenever he speaks in public, there is not much difference between open-source and free software in the way the software is developed *technically*; and most free and open-source software packages are also protected by the same licence, the General Public License (GPL) developed by Stallman with the support of New York City Columbia University law professor Eben Moglen. However, according to Stallman, there is a profound difference insofar as free software is linked with a political concept of freedom centred on freedom of speech. The term 'open source' was introduced by a group of pro-business computer libertarians in direct opposition to this political position. Eric Raymond and others proposed open source to make the idea of releasing source code and developing software collaboratively more appealing to IT investors in the USA. In that sense, this move by the proponents of open source was fantastically successful: it opened the way for IPOs by Linux companies at the height of the New Economy boom and drew the attention of companies like Sun and IBM to the existence of open source as a potential antidote to the market dominance of Microsoft. Many open-source developers make it very clear that they see themselves as engineers and engineers only, that they have no interest in politics and are glad to leave that to the politicians. It is easy to see how this more uncontroversial orientation of open source could quickly get the support of business-people and of the many software developers who mainly want to be able to make a living from their programming skills. Since the launch of the open-source bandwaggon, Richard Stallman has been on a kind of a mission to remind the world that free software is about 'free' as in 'free speech', not 'free beer'. He also keeps reminding us that the Linux kernel could not have been written without the GNU tools and libraries, and that therefore it should always be called GNU/Linux. Stallman's style of oratorical delivery does not appeal to everyone, however, and with his evangelical zeal he manages to annoy even people who like and support his concepts. The promotion of the type of freedom that is implied in free software needs support, and even his notion of freedom of speech needs some further exploration and a widening of dimensions.

The Whitewash: Hegemonic Computer and Internet Discourse and the Denial of Difference

> "Constructions of race in the form of mental images are much more than simple indexes of biological or cultural sameness. They are the constructs of the social imagination, mapped onto geographical regions and technological sites."[11]

The predominant social imagination of computer science and the internet is a whitewash. This whitewash is the product of an entanglement of historical developments, the creation of certain 'facts on the ground' and a hegemonic discourse led from the centres of Western power (which in my definition includes Japan). The starting-point here is the development of Western rationality and science, from the early Renaissance onwards, associated with heroes of the various scientific revolutions such as Descartes, Leibnitz and Newton. Cartesianism, with its positing of a space for abstract reasoning through which alone the divine rules of nature can be identified, must bear the brunt of the criticism for this botched project.[12] As Donna Harraway has pointed out, from the very beginning the rise of rationalism and the scientific worldview bore the stamp of negative dialectics:

> "..., I remember that anti-Semitism and misogyny intensified in the Renaissance and Scientific Revolution of early modern Europe, that racism and colonialism flourished in the travelling habits of the cosmopolitan Enlightenment, and that the intensified misery of billions of men and women seems organically rooted in the freedoms of transnational capitalism and technoscience." [13]

Computer science has its roots in the military-industrial complex of the Cold War era. The dominant social imagination was one of containment, of separating the world into zones of influence distributed between America and the Soviet Union, divided by electronic fences and locked into each other by the threat of mutual annihilation. Early computer projects received huge funding injections once it was recognised that computers could play an indispensable role in air defence and 'smart' guided ballistic-missile systems.[14] The cyborg discourse of Cold War think-tanks such as the Rand

Corporation and research centres like MIT generated the imaginary signification of Artificial Intelligence – a brain without a body, an intelligence that does not come from a womb but is constructed by scientists in a laboratory. It is easy to see how in this 'dream' of AI, which conducts itself so rationally, Christian ideas live on.[15] The computer brain has a god-like omni-science. With the internet, conceived in the same laboratories of the Western scientific élite, sponsored by DARPA, the AI brain was to grow nerves that would soon stretch around the globe and, via satellite, would gain a god's viewpoint in space from which the earth looks like a fragile little blue ball. Omni-science plus omni-presence equals omni-potence – but perhaps only (certainly mostly, in any case) in the imaginations of the protagonists of this 'vision'.

The internet, based on Western communication protocols, constructed by Western males, is imagined to be populated mostly by white and relatively affluent people. This may have been the case in 1995, when approximately 20 million people used it, but certainly does not match the true demography of the net in 2004, with its more than 600 million users and highest growth figures in countries such as China and India. The whitewashed mass-media discourse continues to associate the net with a Western – and in particular American – world-view and an ultra-libertarian, anti-socialist political programme. The assumption of a non-gendered, non-ethnically defined cyberspace automatically makes cyberspace 'white', a colour blindness that is inherently racist.

Academic Techno-Topia

> "Bobby Reason was born weak from typhus fever and unable to crawl away from his body of infection. He spends his time passing voltage through the pathways of least resistance to help him amplify, copy, and replay sounds. Extending his ears to where his eyes used to be, he forms lenses to put in place of his imagination. Whilst doing so he manages to split light and holds the lower end of the spectrum (radiation) with special tools he forged out of the industrial revolution to replace his hands. And after all is done, he gets out the air-freshener to replace his nose."[16]

Roots Culture - Free Software Vibrations Inna Babylon

Since the early to mid 1990s, the internet has spawned an elaborate theoretical discourse about itself in books and, mostly, on the net. The more mainstream currents of this discourse hailed the net as a force that would bring about a more democratic and egalitarian world. Unfortunately, however, the net was again imagined as a kind of homogeneous zone, free of connotations of gender, race or class division,[17] where the only distinction identified was the existence of a 'digital divide' – the realisation that the promise of the net could not be fulfilled until all people had access to it. The digital-divide discussion, well-meaning though it may have been, only proliferated another version of Western hegemonic thinking with its rhetoric of 'access': there is the net – based on open standards, egalitarian, global, democratic and hard to censor – and we have to give 'those people' down in Africa or elsewhere access to it. In this one-sided, USA/Euro-centric version of internet 'freedom', it was not imagined that the net itself could become a more diverse cultural space and that even its technical protocols might be 'mongrelised'. The narration of the internet as the success story of Western rationality and the scientific worldview did not allow for such digressions.

Theoretical internet discourse very early on embraced open standards, free software and open source. The principles embodied in TCP/IP and the GPL would guarantee freedom of expression and communication. The discourse produced by internet intellectuals tended to highlight abstract principles enshrined in code and, in so doing, by default prioritised its own values inherited from 500 years of book culture. American cyber-libertarians even went so far as to call the space of lived reality by the derogatory term 'meatspace'. The well-meaning leftist liberal discourse about the net had got caught in the classic Cartesian trap of mind/body duality.

Left-wing internet users adopted Free, Libre, Open-Source Software (FLOSS) as a potential saviour from the corporate world, yet in doing so they were following the same old patterns of thought. Too often only the abstract qualities of FLOSS are highlighted: the 'viral' character of the GPL, the net's property of being highly 'distributed', the 'meshed network topology' in wireless networking, the importance of 'copyleft principles'.[18] What receives far less consideration is the fact that these principles and abstract values in and of themselves do nothing at all without human agency, without being embedded in communities who have internalised the values contained in those acronyms. The proactive making and doing by humans – in other words, 'labour' – is once more written out of the story. The desires and passions invested in the writing of program code get little 'airtime' in FLOSS discourse. In this sense a certain type of FLOSS discourse can be seen as another prolongation of the project of Modernity with its preference for abstract reasoning and the codification of knowledge. The values and norms of society – formulated as a Bill of Rights or the Universal Declaration of Human Rights – are called inalienable and universal rights and freedoms but in fact exist mainly on paper: politicians like to quote them in Sunday speeches, but they are quickly forgotten the next morning, when business as usual kicks in.

The relationship between code as program code and as an ethical or legal code, and the importance that Western societies assign to it, is a very broad topic which I cannot explore in detail here. I would only like to say this much: generally speaking, putting one's faith in abstract truth[19] alone – truth that has cut its ties with lived reality and becomes transcendent to society – means creating a form of absolutism. The divine power of God returns, through the back door, to 'rational' discourse. Abstract, transcendent truth takes away the individual and collective freedom of people to make their own decisions, and subjects them to the rule of a truth that is already given, independent of history and the situatedness of being.[20]

If FLOSS discourse cuts itself off from the roots of culture, it empties itself of all meaning. The 'free' or 'libre' in FLOSS is not given once and for all by being laid down in the GPL – it is a freedom that needs to be constantly worked out and given new meanings by being connected to situations, to concrete social struggles. The content of this freedom cannot be understood in the abstract – it needs to be created in the actuality of sensual and bodily existence, which is, by the way, the only thing that really makes 'sense'.[21] By following the default patterns of Western rationality, academic FLOSS discourse runs the risk of generating a vacuous fiction, an idealisation that lacks body, guts, feelings, sex, pain, joy and everything else that makes life worth living.

Culture and the Social Imaginary

It is always difficult, even dangerous, to provide a definition of the term 'culture', especially in times when culture is used as a divisive issue, when a 'culture clash' is used by both sides in an armed conflict (such as the ongoing, seemingly never-ending, 'war on terror') as an ideological legitimisation for their actions. As an Austrian I am especially wary when the notions of culture and identity are tied into essentialist discourses on race or linked with hegemonic discourses on nationhood. Under the term 'culture' can be subsumed all those human activities that are not directly utilitarian, which do not serve, in a narrow way, the goal of material survival.[22] Yet at the same time culture is an indispensable component of human life without which communities or societies in the end could *not* survive. Culture provides the cohesive element for social groups, it motivates the actions of individuals and groups. Without culture, economic activity would collapse within minutes.

I do not use the term motivation here in a trivial sense, as when a sportsman or -woman is asked on television 'What motivates you?'. What I have in mind is closer to the German word 'Leitmotif', which could be roughly translated as 'guiding idea'. But it would be wrong to imagine these 'motives' as something outside culture or social reality. They are at the centre of the social life of societies, anchoring it, but also giving it direction. This concept of motives is closely related to the concept of values. It would be incorrect to say that something is 'based on' values, because values can be both implicit and explicit, internal and external. Here we cannot use architectural metaphors of foundation and superstructure. Culture is just one of the most important forces behind the creation of values and motivation, 'making sense' of and 'giving meaning' to our existence. Society, in a constant state of self-creation, develops 'social imaginary significations'[23] through cultural feedback loops. In this sense culture is not limited to cultural representations such as song, dance, poems, painting, computer games, video documentaries, etc., but is constantly reflected in the actions and inter-actions of everyday life. Culture 'finds expression' in various ways: in how people dress, what they eat and how it is prepared, in social protocols and forms of behaviour. What is expressed in those forms, in both the patterns of behaviour of everyday life and in explicit cultural representations, is the social and cultural knowledge of a society. Two things need to be said about this type of knowledge.

In Western society what has been developed, unfortunately, is a hierarchy of different forms of knowledge, with hard science at the top, the social sciences somewhere in the middle and culture *per se* at the bottom. The Positivistic Divide[24] claims that what can be described in a scientific language – logic, mathematics, theorems, etc. – is the only form of objective knowledge, whereas the rest is regarded as the soft underbelly, as a somehow lesser form of knowledge. Philosophers and historians of science have shown that it is not true that science progresses only through rational methods and in logical steps, and that in fact many other factors inform the conduct of scientific research and development: cultural and sociological factors, funding and institutional structures, belief systems and tacit knowledge. Despite the well-known masterpieces of authors such as Kuhn, Feyerabend and Harraway and an ongoing investigation into what 'informs' science from many different viewpoints (anthropology, sociology, cultural studies, etc.), the results of technoscience are presented as ideologically neutral and free of contingent forms of social knowledge. Computer science, which would conventionally be regarded as being closer to engineering than to basic research, has remodelled itself as a hard science through its close links with cognitive science, the modelling of brain functions, etc. The conventional view of software development therefore denies the link between software and culture as something that exists *before* the result. Software is seen as facilitating the production of cultural representations and influencing culture by the tools that it makes available, but it is usually not also regarded as a product of 'social imaginary significations'.

I have tried to describe the true content of culture as a form of knowledge, as 'immaterial',[25] so to speak. However, culture is quite obviously also 'material', and has various economic aspects. Cultural values define which objects are desirable, what gets produced and what not. The production of cultural representations is of course a form of human labour and therefore always includes economic transactions, whether based on money or on other forms of exchange. The commodification of the production of culture in capitalist economies was criticised by the Frankfurt School back in the early 20th century. Now, at the beginning of the 21st century, even though some of it is flawed,[26] this work is gaining in significance as the commodification of culture reaches unprecedented levels.

The culture industry has been rebranded as creative industry and is seen by many governments of overdeveloped countries, particularly in Britain, as a central plank in government strategies for economic growth and urban development (i.e., gentrification). The problems are aggravated by the aggressive conduct of the copyright industries – music, film, software, games – and the power of media conglomerates who have become highly integrated and own production companies, distribution channels and advertising agencies. Each of these industries has become highly oligopolistic or even monopolistic, and their combined influence to a large extent controls what can be seen or heard and how it is distributed. New borders have been created by various means such as copyright, patents or the gatekeeper functions of communication providers. The exchange and transmission of cultural knowledge is now in danger of being interrupted or seriously hampered by those powerful formations.[27]

In the darkness of these developments one could go even further and predict a closing-down of the cultural production of social imaginary significations. Culture is of course not the only producer of social imaginary significations and I would not even want to ascribe a special, privileged role to it in this process. But what I mean is the following. I have described two processes: one that excludes cultural knowledge from the official scientific body of knowledge, and one that encloses cultural knowledge in the products of the military-entertainment complex, a.k.a the creative industries.[28] Through both of these – exclusion and enclosure – what could happen is a lock-down on the creation of new meanings, of new powerful significations that 'rock the world'. There are already strong signs of such a lock-down in the mass conformity that is promoted by the mass media, which was only to be expected and has been going on for a long time. It was disillusioning for many to see how the internet has been tamed within a very short time-span and is running the risk of becoming just another agent of conformity. The centralisation of internet resources, whose content is created by the people, but whose surplus value is harvested with enormous financial gain by Google and others, plays into the hands of a further lock-down: websites that are not ranked highly on Google appear to be peripheral; what cannot be found easily on the symbolic battle-ground of the web appears to be marginal. However, I think that any lock-down can only be temporary and not total, that cultural production of a more radical social imaginary will not cease but has perhaps slowed down for the present. The combined totalities of government and large corporations, who both increasingly use the same forms of bureaucratic rule and are threatening to choke the life out of the cities and the countryside, are prompting powerful counter-reactions. Many people find inspiration in the language of resistance created by African Caribbeans and Americans and expressed in musical styles such as roots reggae, hip hop and underground house.

Armin Medosch

Rasta Science

Rastafari and Rasta-inspired derivatives such as Dub music have developed significations and cultural forms which either offer themselves as examples and inspiration for FLOSS discourse or show similarities in some aspects which could be explored further. These examples can be presented here only in the briefest form. They are:
- a poetically tinged criticism of Western capitalism and science based on metaphor and linguistic play
- a specific critique of the destructive power of high-tech weapons
- the development of an alternative 'dub science'
- the maintenance of an intact culture outside the commodified culture industry
- the use of the Riddim as a shared musical 'code'.

Rastas have found their own way of criticising the power structures, class and knowledge system of 'Babylon'. Rasta-inspired dub poetess Jean Breeze writes:

> *Four hundred years from the plantation whip*
> *To the IMF grip*
> *Aid travels with a bomb*
> *watch out*
> *Aid travels with a bomb*
> *They rob and exploit you of your own*
> *then send it back as a foreign loan*
> *Interest is on it, regulations too*
> *They will also*
> *decide your policy*
> *for you.*

'Aid', by Jean 'Binta' Breeze[29]

Rejecting the language of the slave-owner, and based on Jamaican Patois and Creole English, Rastas have created alternative linguistic reference systems. For instance, Rastas say 'overstanding' instead of 'understanding', because the latter would imply submission. The internet, of course, becomes the 'outernet', an interview an 'outerview'.[30]

Consistent in this critique of the West is the critique of the murderous potential of technoscience and of industrial scientific warfare in the interest of capital. Whereas fans of Bob Marley-style reggae drifted towards a hippie environmentalism and Roots Reggae lost its hegemonic grip around 1980-81,[31] the sharp edge of this critical spirit was carried on by dub poets, DJs and Toasters working with mobile sound systems and on pirate radio.

The dub style created in the early 1970s by King Tubby and Lee 'Scratch' Perry introduced a technological element into reggae music, keeping the 'roots', but working with echo, tapes, noises, reverb and other special effects. Music-making became a 'science',[32] and in the 1980s this was reflected in the names of dub artists such as Mad Professor and The Scientist. Besides the critique of Western capitalist science as producer of weapons of mass destruction – a frequent theme during the nuclear arms race in the 1980s – dub artists created their own 'science', for instance the 'African Arkology' of Lee 'Scratch' Perry:

> "I am the first scientist to mix the reggae and find out what the reggae really is. [...] The recording studio was my spaceship that was polluted by the dreadlocks in the moonlight."[33]

The culture of sound systems playing out in the open or at cultural centres (almost never in regular clubs) introduced another 'scientific' element into roots culture: the optimisation of a system of speakers, special-effect boxes and amplifiers for the specific needs of roots reggae and dub. The effect of such systems can only be translated into English by a poet. Linton Kwesi Johnson wrote:

> *Thunder from a bass drum soundin'*
> *Lightnin' from a trumpet and a organ*
> *Bass and rhythm and trumpet double up*
> *Keep up with drums for a deep pound searchin'*
> *Ridim of a tropical, electrical storm*
> *Cool doun to de base of struggle*

Armin Medosch

> *Flame ridim of historical yearnin'*
> *Flame ridim of de time of turnin'*
> *Measurin' de time for bombs and for burnin'*[34]

Sound systems have allowed roots and dub reggae styles to survive in times when they were less popular and reggae dances in the UK were stigmatised by the press as notoriously violent, with the result that Thatcher's police shut down venues or the venues cancelled raves because they were afraid of being raided by the police. Sound-system culture also highlights a number of other important aspects. Sound systems usually have a community that follows them wherever they play. The music played is often not commercially available, except on cheap cassettes or, nowadays, homeburned CDs sold at gigs. The DJs play 'dub plates', specially cut vinyls that exist only in small numbers. The music can be heard best on the sound system and is not really for home consumption. By keeping the music rare, sound-system events have aspects of cathartic rituals, an experience of love, strength and unity. Despite attempts to commercialise sound systems, this spirit is still very much alive at the annual Notting Hill Carnival in London and other carnivals around the country, the flame kept burning by sound systems such as Aba Shanti. At this year's Carnival – a carnival of anniversaries: 40 years of Notting Hill Carnival, 170 years since the abolition of slavery – Aba Shanti showed that they have lost none of their political edge, rocking a crowd of thousands with thunderous basses and lyrics about the war in Iraq.

The collective identification with roots culture leads also to another interesting phenomenon, the importance of the Riddim. The Riddim is the instrumental track of a record, stripped of the vocals. In Jamaica today it is still the norm for certain riddims to be especially popular at a certain time, so that often hundreds of artists record versions with their own lyrics on top of one of the popular riddims. This shows a direct relationship with the 'copyleft' principle in free software.

Software as Culture

> "This software is about resistance inna Babylon world which tries to control more and more the way we communicate and share information and knowledge.

This software is for all those who cannot afford to have the latest expensive hardware to speak out their words of consciousness and good will."[35]

A number of artists/engineers have started to bring software development back into the cultural realm and they are infusing culture into software. But 'they' are a very heterogeneous collection of people and it would be wrong to speak of a movement or a group. I will not try to give an overview of the entire field, but will focus instead on a few individuals and projects. Only one of the people presented here, jaromil, makes explicit references to Rastafari. This does not devalue my argument: on the contrary. Rastafari is not meant to be seen as having a monopoly on signifying otherness or cultural roots. What exists today is a range of ideas and projects with huge potential but without a single common denominator. Each of these seeds needs to be supported, disseminated, sprinkled with water, nurtured.

One of the earliest works in this area, to my knowledge, was created by a group called Mongrel which came together in London in 1996 or thereabouts. The group consists of Graham Harwood, Matsuko Yokokij, Matthew Fuller, Richard Pierre Davis and Mervin Jarmen. Coming from different ethnic and cultural backgrounds – Irish-English, Japanese and West Indian – they chose to call themselves 'mongrel', a term that is loaded with resonances of overt racism. Their inquiry began with the realisation that software tools are not neutral but charged with social significations. In their earlier work they focused on laying bare those significations. A re-engineered version of Photoshop would become a construction kit for ethnic identities;[36] a spoof of a popular search engine[37] would react very sensitively to certain search terms. If somebody was searching for 'sex', they would first get a promising list of search hits, but clicking on one of them would lead for example to a site which at first seemed like a genuine porn website but subsequently revealed itself to be a work of applied gender studies about the construction of gendered identities. Racist search terms such as 'Aryan' would lead to similar results, bringing up aggressive – but in a way also subtle – anti-racist web-pages.

Mongrel have never taken the easy route of reproducing the clichés of educated Western liberalism. Their work attacks the 'tolerance' of the middle classes as much as anything else. The name is programme. By calling themselves 'mongrels' they are stating their distance from the norms of polite society. The aggressive 'mongrelisation' of popular software programs and search engines made race an issue at a time when internet hype was getting into full swing and everybody was supposed to forget that such problems still existed, or at least to believe that the internet would somehow, magically, make them disappear. One particular work created by Mervin Jarman put the spotlight on a case of suspicious death in police custody – that of Joy Gardner, a Jamaican woman who died after having been detained at Heathrow airport.[38] The free flow of information, hailed by advocates of the 'information society', was contrasted with the practices and technologies of border control.

The Art of Listening

Mongrel later moved on from their applied critique of the social content of software to an approach that could be called more constructive – they began to write software from scratch. The social orientation of their work led them to hold many workshops during which they tried to help people from disadvantaged backgrounds to create their own digital representations. In doing this, they discovered that no existing software provided a useful platform. Either the programs were too difficult to use or they imposed a certain way of thinking on the user which alienated their clientele. So first they produced a program called 'Linker', which would enable people to bang together a website full of multimedia content without having to delve into the depths of multimedia programming or even learn HTML. But Linker, written in Macromedia Director, a proprietory software, turned out to be not the solution but only a step towards it.

Mongrel then tried a radically new approach: listening to people. They used workshops to find out what people would like to do with and expect from such a software platform: people who had previously had relatively little exposure to digital technology and who came from a variety of backgrounds and age groups. At the same time they taught themselves the skill of mastering the LAMP package – an acronym composed of the initials of the operating system Linux, the webserver Apache, the database MySQL and the scripting languages Perls, Python and PHP (which are all, needless to say, forms of free or open-source software). In a painstakingly long process they developed Nine9, an application sitting on a webserver that provides a really user-friendly interface for the creation of digital representations online.[39]

Nine9 elegantly solves one of the core problems that plague many such projects: categorisation. With any server-side web application there is always a database in the background. Computers, being completely dumb and likely to remain so for the foreseeable future, are ignorant of the type of content that is stored in them. From texts, at least keywords can be extracted by some algorithm, and used as meta tags to give some clue as to what type of text it might be. But images, audio and video do not offer this possibility. Usually the user, who uploads some 'content' to the net, is asked to categorise the content. Then it can either be left completely to the taste of the individual user to decide how to describe or categorise what, which makes it difficult later on to create a coherent, searchable database, or the categories are already predefined by the creator of the database. But Mongrel had found out that predefined categories do not usually work with their user group. Any system of categorisation, any taxonomy, contains so many cultural assumptions that people who do not share the same background find it hard to relate to it. The solution that Mongrel found was to leave the system completely open at the start, without any categorisation, but to let the relationships between the different chunks of content on the server emerge later, through usage. Graphically and conceptually, the system is an open and, potentially, an (almost) infinite plane of nine-by-nine squares, which can be squatted by individuals or groups and filled with content, linked underneath the surface by a sophisticated software that compares textual 'natural language' descriptions by users and tracks how people navigate this world.

Speculative software

> "I'm in a constant state of trying to find wings that lust after the experience of transportation while being firmly rooted to the ground. I want to see people fly from present situations to other states of pleasure and pain. Out of the gutters and into the stratosphere of the imaginary."[40]

After launching Nine9 in 2002, and using it in many workshops, Graham Harwood moved on to write what he calls 'speculative software': programs that are highly political right from the moment of conception. Each program is like a thesis, a making-visible of relations or truths that are normally hidden. One of these ideas – originally called Net Monster, now renamed GimpImage – sends out software search robots, a.k.a spiders or bots, that search the net for related combinations of two search terms (such as 'Osama Bin Laden' and 'George W. Bush'), downloads pictures and texts found in the search, and auto-assembles a picture collage out of this material using the script function of the popular OS graphical software GIMP.[41] The results are aesthetically stunning, which is probably due to the fact that Harwood has always been a very good graphic artist and has now acquired considerable programming skills.

Rastaman Programmer

The art of listening has also been cultivated by jaromil, a.k.a. Denis Rojo, a young Italian programmer with long dreadlocks and the creator of the bootable Linux distribution Dyne:bolic.[42] For a long time GNU/Linux was said to be very difficult to install, which was a deterrent to its adoption by less tech-savvy people. For quite a while now there have existed graphical user interfaces (GUIs) for GNU/Linux and other Unix-style operating systems. Once the operating system is installed on a machine, the GUI enables users who had previously worked only with Macs or Microsoft Windows systems to use a machine running GNU/Linux intuitively, without encountering many problems or having to learn how to use the command shell. The concept of the bootable Linux distribution was created to allow non-programmers to use GNU/Linux, get a taste of it and perhaps discover that it really is something for them. A boot CD is a complete operating system plus applications on a CD-ROM. If the computer is started or restarted with the CD inside, it boots into Linux, automatically detecting the hardware configuration and initialising the right drivers for sound and video card and other components. Jaromil gave the bootable Linux system a particular twist. His version, called Dyne:bolic, contains a good deal of software written by himself which allows people to publish their own content on the net. His applications – the most important of which are MuSe, FreeJ and HasciiCam – put special emphasis on live multimedia content, live mixing and the streaming of audio and video.

While the promise of the internet revolution that everybody can launch their own net radio or net tv station might in principle be true, it is seriously hampered by the fact that most programs that allow you to do so are proprietary. Here the whole litany of the perils of proprietary software could be spelled out again, but I will try to make it short. To obtain a licence to use them costs money. To use live streaming software, the source material has to be encoded in the proprietary format. The codecs are proprietary, so the dissemination of material relies on the company strategy for future developments – it is almost as if the content is 'owned' by the software company, or at least in danger of being enclosed by it. Because the source code is not released to the public it may contain backdoors and Trojan functions. In short, multiple dependencies are created. Once a self-styled net radio maker has decided on a particular software, archives will be created in the associated format, which makes it harder to switch later. And because commercial software companies usually pay little heed to the needs of financially less well-off users, they optimise their programs for high-bandwidth connections and follow the rapid update cycles of high-tech industries.

Jaromil's Dyne:bolic boot CD and the applications on it respond to these problems in various ways. Dyne:bolic is free software in the Stallman sense: everything on it is GPLed and it is designed to increase freedom. It runs on basically everything that has a CPU, doing particularly well on older computers. The source code is made available. MuSe, the main audio streaming tool, recognises the quality of a net connection and throttles the bit rate of data transmissions accordingly. Thus, on a high-bandwidth connection, it streams out top-quality audio, while on a dodgy dial-up phone line connection something, at least, is guaranteed to come out at the other end. All these decisions did not come over night and were not made automatically.

Like Mongrel, Jaromil spends a good deal of time listening to users or potential users. In 2002 he travelled to Palestine to find out what people there might need or want. One of the results of this journey was that he implemented non-Latin font sets so that Dyne:bolic can be run using Arabic, Chinese, Thai and many other character sets in the menus. His journey to Palestine was not out of character. Jaromil is almost constantly travelling. He takes his laptop with him, but he does not lead a life normally associated with software development. Sometimes he is offline for weeks, hanging out in Eastern Europe or Southern Italy, socialising with squatters or music-making gypsies, sleeping on floors or outdoors. This maybe viewed as romantic, and it probably is, but the point is that it informs his practice. Jaromil writes:

> "The roots of Rasta culture can be found in resistance to slavery. This software is not a business. This software is as free as speech and is one step in the struggle for Redemption and Freedom. This software is dedicated to the memory of Patrice Lumumba, Marcus Garvey, Martin Luther King, Walter Rodney, Malcolm X, Mumia Abu Jamal, Shaka Zulu, Steve Biko and all those who still resist slavery, racism and oppression, who still fight imperialism and seek an alternative to the hegemony of capitalism in our World."[43]

Digital Culture's Redemption

Having presented only two examples I think it is necessary to paint with a bigger brush. The vibrations of reggae music and a resistant culture are slowly beginning to infiltrate the clean white space of hegemonic computer and net discourse. Cutting the ties between culture and knowledge would mean making knowledge a monstrous thing – inhumane, value-free, above life, potentially deadly. Abstract knowledge is not a positive value in itself – only knowledge that is applied to the right cause is that. The work being done by free-software developers such as the ones I have mentioned, and by many more, is re-establishing the cultural roots of knowledge.

This work is carried forward by a rebellious spirit, but in a very kind and civic way. No grand gestures, no big words, no sensationalism, no false promises, no shouting – and therefore, by implication, no real 'career' in the usual sense and no money to spend. This softly spoken rebellion is carried by value systems that are non-traditional, not imposed from above, non-ideological. Despite everything that is going on and all the media distortion, we still 'have' values. As Raqs Media Collective quite beautifully put it, one of the major aspects of this free software culture is that people take care, they nurse code collectively, bring software development projects to fruition by tending towards shared code that is almost like a poem, an Odyssey in software.[44] People involved in large free-software projects do not share code because the GPL forces them to do so, but because they want to. This investment, however it may be motivated, mongrelises technologies and connects emotion and passion to the 'cold' logic of computers.

The developments that are emerging do not spring from some kind of mysterious, anonymous, technoscientific progress but are based on conscious choices made by people. These people develop something that they might want to use themselves, or that they see as an enriching addition to what already exists. The decision about what to do, in which area to invest, is a crucial one.

> "I'm not sure I choose a project to code/maintain – rather it chooses me – I talk to the bloke who's fixing my boiler whose life is run by computer timings or I talk to my mum who's worried by too many phone calls trying to sell her things – I see stuff – gaps in my imagination or ability to think articulately about the experience of information and guess other people feel that as well..." [45]

There are other significant projects under way in many places. One of them is the digital signal-processing platform Pure Data, a software package with a graphical programming interface used by many artists.[46] Each program can be stored as a patch and reused by others. Concrete communities of people form around such projects. Their choices are an expression of cultural values. But these values are not really abstract or immaterial: they are embedded in the lived reality of the people involved. And so is the technology that they create. The cultural vibe of the group gives the development its meaning, its significance. The 'vibe' is also important for an international group of young artists/programmers working under the name of Toplap.[47] They have started a daring experimental practice: live coding on stage. Whereas usually laptop musicians and VJs can only influence certain parameters, live coders change the control structures of algorithms themselves, on the fly, and in front of an audience, risking the almost inevitable crash of either the program or the entire system.

A new synthesis of club life, coding and collaborative geek culture is also celebrated by some elements of the international free-network communities. People worldwide have started to build wireless community networks using 802.1x technology and circumventing commercial telecommunications structures with do-it-yourself technologies. This happens for instance at a place called c-base in Berlin, where dozens of people meet every Wednesday for the 'waveloeten' meetings.[48] Besides lighter tasks, such as building antennas and discussing strategies for connecting housing blocks and city boroughs with wireless technologies, quite serious developing work in the area of dynamic, *ad hoc* routing protocols goes on. The place is buzzing because it provides a sense of belonging, of identity, of direction. Work is mixed with pleasure and fun. Nobody 'works' in the Protestant work-ethic sense. People are doing what they like to do in a social setting. Slacker hippies[49] are following their intuition and, despite all their slackness and disorganisation, as a side-effect (well, almost) the world gets the beautiful new products of a menacing software culture.

Digital culture is full of promises of revolutions, but usually the content of these revolutions is not spelled out. Discovering the roots of their cultures should help free-software developers to discover new meanings in the 'free' of 'free software' and to engage with society through their work, not just with the abstract reality of code. The language of revolution of roots reggae and dub science is surely not the only possible inspiration, but it is one pointer indicating a possibility that digital culture can make good on its promises only by leaving the mainstream and following the many currents and small rivers that connect them with the origin of their creativity.

Notes

[1] Paul Gilroy, *There Ain't No Black in the Union Jack*, Routledge, London, 1997, p. 251.
[2] African ways of living were kept alive in Jamaica by the Maroons, people who escaped from the slave plantations and survived under harsh conditions in the hills in an agricultural subsistence economy based on collective land ownership. Like the Maroons, religious Rastas are vegetarians and cultivate the smoking of Ganja – the 'herb of God' – as a religious practice.
[3] Gilroy, continuation of above quote, p. 251.
[4] For instance, a few years ago a Raggastani movement emerged: young Asians identifying themselves as Rastas
[5] See, for instance, Rastafarl Women: *Subordination in the Midst of Liberation Theology* by Obiagele Lake. Durham, North Carolina, Carolina Academic Press, 1998.
[6] Humble Lion, in an interview with the *Get Underground* online magazine

http://www.getunderground.com/underground/features/article.cfm?Article_ID=785, downloaded Sep 2004

[7] I am not claiming here that all AI research in the 1980s was sponsored by the military but that AI-related research in the US was given a second boost, after its original heyday in the 1950s and 1960s, through Reagan's Star Wars programme. For more about this see *The Closed World: Computers And The Politics Of Discourse in Cold-War America*, Paul N. Edwards, MIT Press, 1996.

[8] See the book *Underground* about the 'war against hacking' in its early stages. *Underground* is published online: http://www.underground-book.com/

[9] The book *Netzpiraten, Die Kultur des elektronischen Verbrechens*, Armin Medosch and Janko Röttgers (eds): Heise, Hannover, 2001, gives a more in-depth account of the differences between 'ethical' or 'real' hackers, crackers and script kiddies.

[10] I am talking about the Hacklabs which are held every summer now in various countries. There is a marked difference between North European and American hacklabs, which are sometimes more geek summits than anything else, and Southern European and Latin American hacklabs, which tend to focus far more on the link between Free Software, Free Speech and independent media.

[11] Harwood, Ethnical Bleaching, http://www.scotoma.org/notes/index.cgi?EthnicBleaching, last accessed 24.09.2004.

[12] I would be careful not to blame Descartes for Cartesianism, just as Marx cannot be blamed for Marxism. In his writings, he comes across as far more entertaining than the school of thought his work initiated. See for instance René Descartes, *Le Monde ou Traité de la Lumière*, Akademie Verlag, Berlin, 1989.

[13] Donna Harraway, Modest_Witness@Second_Millennium.FemaleMan·_Meets_OncoMouse‰, pp. 2-3, Routledge, 1997.

[14] Paul N. Edwards, *Closed Worlds*, MIT Press, 1996.

[15] On this topic, see for instance Richard Barbrook's polemic, *The Sacred Cyborg*, Telepolis, 1996 http://www.heise.de/tp/english/special/vag/6063/1.html, downloaded 24.09.2004; for a proper critique of the claims of 'strong' AI, look no further than *The Emperor's New Mind*, Roger Penrose, Oxford University Press, 1989.

[16] Harwood, email to the author, 31.08.2004.

[17] It should be noted that there exist serious pockets of resistance to this mainstream version of internet discourse, from the Marxist discourse of Arthur and Marie-Louise Kroker in their online magazine CTheory, to the publications put out by the Sarai group from Delhi, the Sarai Redars, and some of the writings published on mailing lists like Nettime. Afro-Futurism, Cyber-Feminism and a whole school of writers inspired by Donna Harraway are creating a growing body of work that corrects the colour-blind Western-centric vision of the net.

[18] Admittedly, I have sometimes been saying things that sound pretty similar to the mainstream FLOSS discourse. See for instance the article 'Piratology' in *DIVE*, ed. by 'Kingdom of Piracy' and produced by FACT, London/Liverpool 2002, or the article 'The Construction of the Network Commons', *Ars Electronica Catalogue*, Linz 2004.

[19] I am not against abstractions *per se*; abstractions can be meaningful, useful and beautiful, like some abstract art or minimalistic electronic music; I am only speaking against an abstract absolutism.

[20] See in this regard the remarks made by Cornelius Castoriadis in 'Culture in a Democratic Society', *Castoriadis Reader*, pages 338-348.

[21] On this point see for instance *The Phenomenology of Perception*, by Maurice Merleau-Ponty. He says that perception cannot be separated into a merely mechanical receptive organ (e.g. the eye), a transmitter (nerves), and an information-processing unit (the brain). Artificial Intelligence had to learn this the hard way in fifty years of research conducted *after* the publication of Merleau-Ponty's book in 1945.

[22] This definition is loosely based on *The Schema of Mass Culture*, Theodor W. Adorno, Routledge Classics, 1991.

[23] I borrow this term 'social imaginary significations' from Cornelius Castoriadis. In his view, 'the magma of social imaginary significations [...] animates the self-institution of society'. 'The self-institution of society is the creation of a human world: of "things", "reality", language, norms, values, ways of life and death, objects for which we live and objects for which we die – and of course, first and foremost, the creation of the human individual in which the institution of society is massively embedded'. Cornelius Castoriadis, 'The Greek Polis and the Creation of Democracy', p. 269, in *Castoriadis Reader*, edited by David Ames Curtis, London, 1997.

[24] Referring here to Logical Positivism and the Vienna Circle who tried to draw a demarcation line between what can be said scientifically and what is myth, poetry. Although the basic positivist concept of 'verification' has been dismantled by Thomas Kuhn, Paul Feyerabend and others, the Positivistic Divide continues to play a major role in Analytical Philosophy and Cognitive Sciences in the very way they are structured and approach their research subjects.

[25] I always feel a slight shudder when I type the word 'immaterial'. The discourse about immateriality has been highly damaging and in a certain sense maybe nothing is really immaterial. The so-called 'information society' is an ideological construct by rightwing libertarians. On this subject, see for instance 'The Californian Ideology', Richard Barbrook and Andy Cameron, online version: http://www.hrc.wmin.ac.uk/theory-californianideology.html, downloaded 24.09.2004.

[26] I am referring in particular to Adorno's wholesale dismissal of all products of the culture industry based on his preference for bourgeois 'high culture'. The significance or quality of a cultural representation is not necessarily determined by the economic circumstances of its production. See Footnote 21.

[27] I am keeping the critique of this process short because I assume that in the year 2004 the various frontlines of this struggle – for example music industry *vs* file-sharing, proprietary *vs* Free Software and the role of patents, etc. – have been highly publicised and are now common knowledge. Another text in this volume analyses these developments in great detail.

[28] How far this attempt to enclose popular cultural knowledge goes is best illustrated by the attempt by some lawmakers to apply patent laws to fairytales, so that grandmothers could not tell them to children without first obtaining a licence from Disney. This is a law that even the US Congress will not approve, one would hope.

[29] http://www.nald.ca/fulltext/caribb/page63.htm, downloaded 28.08.2004.

[30] In cultural studies and English-literature studies, there is a growing body of work on the Rasta use of language.

[31] For a detailed study of those developments see 'Diaspora, utopia and the critique of capitalism', pp. 200-203, in *There Ain't No Black In The Union Jack*.
[32] Erik Davis compared the experience of aural 'dub space' to William Gibson's 'cyberspace', and referred to acoustical space as especially relevant for the 'organization of subjectivity and hence for the organization of collectives', in his lecture Acoustic Cyberspace, 1997, http://www.techgnosis.com/acoustic.html, downloaded 31.08.2004.
[33] Quoted by Lee 'Scratch' Perry, pulled from various 'outerviews', on http://www.upsetter.net/scratch/words/index.html, downloaded 28.08. 2004.
[34] Excerpt from 'Reggae Sound', Linton Kwesi Johnson http://hjem.get2net.dk/sbn/lkj/reggae_sound.txt, downloaded 28.08.2004.
[35] jaromil, aka Denis Rojo, Dyne:bolic software documentation http://dynebolic.org/manual, downloaded 24.09.2004.
[36] The software is called Natural Heritage Gold: http://www.mongrel.org.uk/Natural/HeritageGold/, last accessed 24.04.2004.
[37] The work referred to is called 'Natural Selection': http://www.mongrel.org.uk/, last accessed 24.09.2004.
[38] The original work could no longer be found online. The poet Benjamin Zephaniah dedicated a poem to Joy Gardner, http://www.benjaminzephaniah.com/books.html#death, last accessed 24.09.2004.
[39] Nine9 http://9.waag.org/, last accessed 24.09.2004.
[40] Harwood, email to the author, 31.08.2004.
[41] Gimp Image, http://www.scotoma.org/notes/index.cgi?GimpImage, last accessed 24.09.2004.
[42] You can find dyne:bolic and more of jaromil's work here: http://www.dyne.org/, last accessed 24.09.2004.
[43] jaromil, dyne:bolic manual, http://dynebolic.org/manual, downloaded 24.09.2004.
MORE BROADLY, a culture of resistance ...??
[44] 'Value and its other in electronic culture: slave ships and pirate galleons', Raqs Media Collective, in DIVE, a Kingdom of Piracy project, produced by FACT, Liverpool, supported by virtualmediacentre.net and Culture 2000.
[45] Harwood, email to the author, 31.08.2004.
[46] Pure Data community website, http://puredata.info, last accessed 24.09.2004.
[47] Toplap are Adrian Ward, Julian Rohrhuber, Fredrik Olofsson, Alex McLean, Dave Griffiths, Nick Collins and Amy Alexander; website http://www.toplap. org/, recent paper http://www.toplap. org/?Read_Me_Paper, websites last accessed 24.09.2004.
[48] c-base homepage, http://www.c-base.org/, waveloeten (Eng.: 'wave-soldering') http://wiki.c-base.org/coredump/WaveLoeten, websites last accessed 24.09.2004.
[49] 'Slacker hippies' are a quite legendary 'old' hacker group who refuse to have a website or to leave many traces at all.

Armin Medosch

Biography

Armin Medosch, born in Graz in 1962, is a writer, artist and curator. He was co-founder of the online magazine *Telepolis – The Magazine of Netculture*, which he co-edited from 1996 to 2002. With *Telepolis* he was awarded the European Online Journalism Award and the Grimme Online Award. Together with Janko Röttgers he edited *Netzpiraten*, a collection of essays which portray the Internet's underworld. As a co-curator of the online project "Kingdom of Piracy" (2001 – ongoing) he produced *DIVE*, a collection of essays and a CD-ROM with free software and copyleft works by digital artists (FACT, Liverpool, 2003). His latest book, *Free Networks – Freie Netze* (Heise, October 2003), tells the worldwide success story of wireless community networks. Medosch currently writes and edits a publication for the DMZ London Media Art Festival and is preparing an exhibition about games culture by artists for the Ya Buena Vista Museum, San Francisco.

PART II

Making it Happen: Case Studies from Brussels, Belgium & Beyond

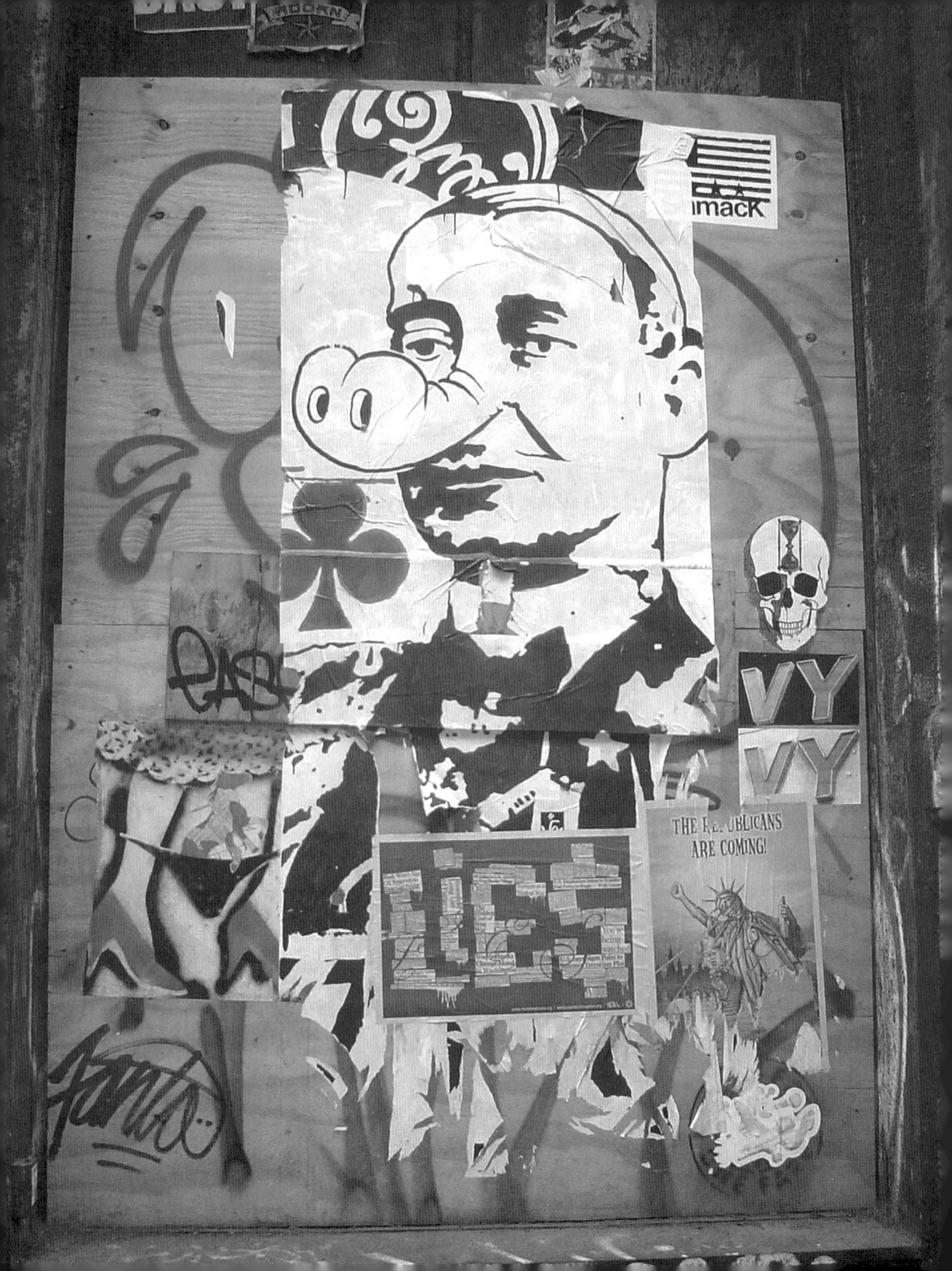

mack
VY
VY
ARE COMING!

Extremadura and the Revolution of Free Software

Achieving digital literacy and modernizing the economy of one of the European Union's poorest regions

Angel Vaca

Introduction

"Revolution". Few words are as powerful as this one. Throughout recent history, it has changed its meaning many times, inspiring awe, terror and hope.

In the present essay, however, and in order to have a reference we can hold on to, we propose a specific definition for this word: a revolution as a deep change in some area of scientific knowledge, or even in a whole society. A quick shift in the gears of Civilization's machinery, with results that help humans to improve their lives.

Please note that this definition presents quite a positive concept, departing from the more terrible meanings of the word "revolution" (i.e., destruction of what exists, violent abolition of what is established). According to our proposed definition, a revolution has a more optimistic, vital meaning, in the sense of keeping on the road, but making progress, and doing so faster.

Accepting the more constructive definition, it seems obvious that the thing to regret would be to be left out of a revolution. However, the gears of Arts, Science, Reason and human societies do not spontaneously start spinning all of a sudden. There are some conditions to be fulfilled. These conditions are necessary but, considered individually, not sufficient. All of them must be met in order for the revolution to start. They are like filters that must be perfectly aligned in order to let a powerful stream pass through them: if just one of them fails, the stream will be blocked and no power will be transmitted to the gears of revolution's machinery. Some of these filters are the socio-economic context. Others are related to local history, or to politics or even customs and traditions. In any case, there is one filter that must be present in all revolutions (as described by the proposed definition): human intelligence.

The most powerful revolutions require further conditions (i.e., more complex filters, which it is more difficult to align perfectly).

And where does free software fit into this essay? What is its role in the case of Extremadura? The key to the success of the global plan of the Government of Extremadura lies in the meaning of the terms that make up an acronym: FOSS.[1]

"F" stands for "free". Not as in "free beer", but as in "freedom of speech". Now this is one of the most important issues about the strategy of Extremadura's local administration: freedom of choice. An alternative way of doing things.

"OS" stands for "open source". The key here is "open". That "openness" strengthens the sense of "freedom" announced by the first letter in the acronym, while qualifying it: open for sharing; open for learning: in short, open knowledge for everyone to see. In the case of Extremadura, the local Administration was aware, right from the very beginning of the project, that it could not succeed if ordinary people were left out of the development of the plan. The idea was not to design a major strategy which would then be imposed on citizens in a top-down way, but to lay the foundations and then encourage ordinary people to become involved in building the edifice (but only if they wished to). And that could only be achieved if the knowledge needed for building it was open to everybody.

The last "S" stands for "software". In other words: technology, computing, digital economy, information. All the ingredients any region or country needs to join the new industrial revolution; the Revolution of our time: the digital revolution.

So, in short, in the case of Extremadura FOSS means a big saving in the public budget; an alternative that, in the opinion of the local Administration, meets the needs of the region better than previous ones; a philosophy of sharing knowledge and working together on the construction of a common building intended to benefit all citizens; and technology, information and the modernization of an obsolete, traditional, economic system.

The plan of the Government of Extremadura for bringing the Information Society to the region was born out of a need not to miss the boat, in terms of development. The plan evolved mainly thanks to the FOSS philosophy. In turn, it gave birth to several projects designed to promote the development of key sectors of Extremadura's society (focusing in particular on the educational system and the economy), bearing in mind that these would eventually become the engine that would drag Extremadura out of a situation of relative backwardness.

The plan has produced many concrete results, the most important of which is, arguably, the gnuLinEx free operating system. It embodies the spirit of the plan: it is free, it offers a powerful and interesting alternative, it encourages learning and the sharing of knowledge, and it is in many senses a tool of cutting-edge computing technology, designed not only for advanced users and programmers, but for beginners too.

It is worth mentioning that the gnuLinEx project recently won the European Award for Regional Innovation, awarded by the European Commission.

gnuLinEx is an essential part of the global plan of the Government of Extremadura to lift a poor region out of its backwardness and into the digital revolution. But it is not the only one. There is much more to it and, hopefully, there will be plenty of lessons to learn and experiences to share.

Extremadura

During General Franco's rule, the Spanish Administration suffered from a strong statism. Any decision likely to affect every part of the country was to be taken in the country's capital, Madrid.

When Spain embraced democracy and voted for a constitution, in 1978, the statist model was left behind and replaced with a new

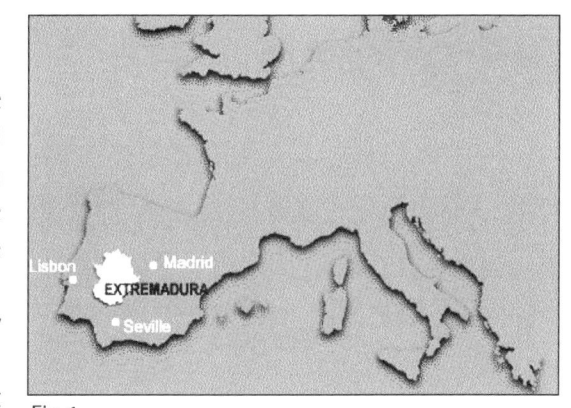

Fig 1.

one, designed to give more independence to regional Administrations. In this way, the Spanish State was politically divided into several regional Administrations known as "autonomous communities".

As time passed, local Governments even came to manage their own public education and health systems. Over the years, the "decentralized" model granted the regions so much independence from the central Administration that, nowadays, Spanish autonomous communities can be regarded, in many senses, as almost as independent and self-managed as Swiss cantons, or German Länder.

On 26 February 1983, the Status of Autonomy was proclaimed in Extremadura. The region, located in the south-west of Spain, next to the Portuguese border, then became one of Spain's independent autonomous communities. Extremadura is a vast and underpopulated region. Traditionally it has lagged behind the more developed Spanish regions in terms of economy and industrial progress. Extremadura's economy has essentially been based on an obsolete model in which farming and stock-breeding are of prime importance. It is said that the name Extremadura comes from the Latin *Extrema Dorii*, as the region is located to the south of the river Duero.

It is not hard to find places in Extremadura where no sign of civilization can be seen, from one horizon to another. Not even a single farm. In fact, Extremadura's population is roughly over 1,000,000 people (less than 2% of Spain's population), spread over an area that amounts to almost 10% of that of the country as a whole. It is thus easy to see that Extremadura's population density is far below the EU average.[2] Many urban areas in Spain (e.g., Madrid, Barcelona, Valencia, Seville, etc.) are much more densely populated than the whole of Extremadura.

There are 383 small municipalities scattered throughout the region. The three most populated towns in Extremadura are Badajoz (150,000 inhabitants), Cáceres (about 80,000) and Mérida (approximately 50,000). All three, taken together, would be less densely populated than some of the neighbourhoods in the largest European cities.

The Missed Revolution

To get back to the proposed definition for the term "revolution": it means a change, or a series of changes, that paves the way for the development of Art, Science, Knowledge or, perhaps, a whole society. The progress is always towards a situation that is better than the previous one. Changes are likely to cause a reaction and some traumatic side-effects at first, but in the long term it should be clear that the worst thing about this kind of a revolution would be to miss it.

During the 18th century, several events took place that pushed many European societies towards a new age, which some would regard as the culmination of the Modern Age. The industrial revolution, as the perfect example of the proposed definition for the term "revolution", drove entire nations towards a true metamorphosis in almost every aspect.

It would be a mistake to regard these changes as affecting only the more technical areas. A number of deep social changes were powered by the development of new tools and strategies of production within the agricultural economies and hierarchical societies of the old regimes, and they were strongly related to one another.

Throughout the whole process, several profound changes were to affect particular areas, so that new changes were sparked which, in turn, would affect more areas. It is therefore difficult to analyse each factor on its own and to distinguish clearly between them.

One of the most important effects of the industrial revolution on old societies was that it shifted the economic sectors: the primary sector (agriculture), which had until then been the dominant one, gradually lost its influence.

As the industrial revolution gained strength, the events that it sparked helped to shrink the primary sector while the secondary (industry) got bigger. Eventually, the tertiary sector (services) was to predominate over the other two. When the industrial revolution came to an end in the most developed countries, the tertiary sector, if displayed on a pie chart, would have covered an area about three times that of the other two combined.

In Spain in general, however, and in Extremadura in particular, the metamorphosis of the economic sectors happened at a much slower pace than in the countries leading the industrial revolution. The aforementioned factors needed to start off a revolution – those necessary-but-not-sufficient conditions, those complex filters that must be perfectly aligned in order to let the flow of changes pass though them – were mostly missing in Extremadura.

We will briefly point out some factors that were responsible for Extremadura's failure to join the industrial revolution.
- Low population density. Because of this, and because of Extremadura's relative isolation, during the 17th century it was particularly difficult to get to many of the towns in the region from large cities like Madrid, Lisbon or Seville. Transportation was much more inefficient and slower then than now. In addition, roads in Extremadura were sparse, narrow and in very poor condition.
- There were no big cities in the region. In the countries that led the industrial revolution, many people migrated from small towns to larger ones, making them develop into big cities that would act as a driving force, catalysing the changes.
- Large cities have traditionally failed to develop in Extremadura (as of the year 2003, more than 53% of Extremadura's citizens live in towns of less than 10,000 inhabitants[3]). In fact, migratory flows have typically been from inside the region to outside, and not just within it. Emigration was usually more intense in rural areas; nevertheless, even larger towns went through periods in which they lost a substantial part of their population because of emigration. In fact, during the 1960s, Extremadura lost up to 300,000 people who emigrated to other places, both within Spain and abroad (especially Germany).
- Lack of technical innovation. Mechanization could only arrive in Extremadura in two ways: it was either developed within the region or brought in from outside.
- The first case seemed a little improbable, considering that most of the qualified, skilled or technically trained people left the region in search of better opportunities elsewhere.
- The second did not look very promising either, because Extremadura, being an isolated and under-developed region, was not a very attractive target for these kinds of investments.
- Inefficient agricultural system. Changes in the agriculture of leading countries helped to improve crop output, thereby raising population's life expectancy. Thus their populations grew and strengthened and, as the secondary sector became more important, many people abandoned farming and left the countryside for a job in the city.
- Extremadura, however, continued to use obsolete cultivation systems which, essentialy, allowed for little more than subsistence agriculture.

- Adverse geographical factors. New industries required large amounts of raw material: coal, iron, etc. Extremadura's geographical context was no help to the development of local industry. According to the Spanish Ministry of Industry,[4] the most important mineral deposits in Extremadura consist of slate and granite, two minerals that were barely used during the industrial revolution. As opposed to this, most coal beds are located in the northern part of the Iberian Peninsula, especially in regions such as Galicia, Asturias, Aragon and Cataluña (where, not suprisingly, the industrial revolution mostly made its entrance in Spain).
- So, though some mineral beds do exist, mining has never been a relevant industry in the region. Moreover the poor quality of Extremadura's road system, already mentioned, made massive imports of coal from mines in the northern part of Spain practically impossible.
- Lack of water. Although nowadays most developed countries have the means to alleviate drought, things were very different back in the 18th century. Back then, lack of water was lethal for industry. The United Kingdom, the nation that led the industrial revolution, had a steady natural water supply. Extremadura, on the other hand, has always suffered from periodic droughts. Rain, when it came, was usually torrential, causing floods.

From missing a Train to driving the next one

So far, we have mentioned some of the factors that made Extremadura fail to take part in the industrial revolution.

Since the middle of the 20th century, Spain has played the role of latecomer country trying to catch up with the more developed nations in Europe. Extremadura thus had to overcome two hurdles: trying to catch up with Spain, while Spain, in turn, was trying to catch up with the rest of Europe.

Even when Spain managed to achieve an economic level comparable to those of the most developed European nations, Extremadura was still far from being a prosperous region. At the end of the 20th century, it was officially regarded as one of the five poorest regions in the European Union (see Table 2).

For countries like Great Britain or France, the industrial revolution meant crossing the line between the old regimes (with their obsolete economic, political and social systems) to new, modern ones.

During the last decades of the 20th century, a new technical revolution took place (again, it sparkled many deep changes in a number of areas, such as the economy, politics or even culture and philosophy). Some called it the digital revolution. It was based on new technologies (mainly telecommunications and computing), and it dramatically improved human beings' ability to keep, process and share information – that is, knowledge.

Once more, Extremadura was on the verge of missing a revolution. This time, as the region had to deal with a much more competitive context than the one that existed 200 years before, losing the chance to take part in the digital revolution would perhaps mean incalculable harm for Extremadura. And, once again, the factors needed to unleash a revolution were missing in the region. Extremadura's chances of benefiting from the new revolution, and not falling even further behind the developed areas in Europe, were very slim.

It was then that the Regional Government of Extremadura decided to look for the missing factors, to enable the region to seize what might be the last opportunity for catching up with the most developed regions in Europe. This seemed, at first, a herculean task for Extremadura's local Administration, considering the huge digital gap between the region and thriving areas such as Madrid, Valencia or Barcelona (see Table 3). A good example could be found in the zone of Las Hurdes, in the north of Extremadura. There, it is still possible to come across small villages that still keep up centuries-old traditions, which almost make them seem like relics of a pre-industrial era. In fact, as late as the 1960s many of these villages still had no electricity or phone lines.

Although it is the Internet that powers the new digital revolution, it is also a fact that, in a sense, it began when home computers became popular. When ordinary people started to see computers as more than big mainframes only large corporations could afford, a new era had begun.

Computers became popular. We could say that computing became "democratized", in the sense that the average citizen gained access to a powerful tool, designed to handle information, which until that very moment had been in the hands of the few. This is the key: as previously said, a revolution must be understood as a process that deeply changes society's very foundations; or, at least, the way of life of most citizens. If the mainspring of a society is not replaced by a better, more powerful and efficient one, or if it is not complemented by another one, the event cannot properly be called a "revolution". To quote Jack Tramiel,[5] *"computers for the masses, not for the classes"*.

Home computers were, at first, expensive items, and therefore regarded as luxuries. When their price dropped and the industry was experienced enough to manufacture better machines at a lower cost, efficiently and routinely, more average citizens (or even people with medium-to-low incomes) in developed countries could afford to buy a home computer. Computing became "democratized", as it evolved from a minor occupation for the rich to a popular commodity for average families.

Many young people immediately felt attracted to home computers. Their enthusiasm led a whole generation of future IT workers to become familiar with the tools they were to use in years to come. Tools that, soon, would become essential for modern societies. This is worth noting: when young people are impressed by some area of knowledge, it can actually end up defining their future careers.

Taking this into account, one could wonder what more is needed for the Digital Era to unfold. The answer could be: sharing information. Sharing knowledge. If the "democratization[6] of computing" had finally been achieved, then it was time to move onward: computers held information individually – now it was time to share it.

Some would say that humans are mostly gregarious and social creatures and, so, tend to share things. I for one would rather choose a different (albeit less optimistic) path, and suggest that human beings are communicative animals; not because their behaviour is best described by their tendency to share information, but because of their natural desire to gather it. All people, by their very nature, desire to know.[7] Humans feel the urge to communicate and, in essence, they want to amass data. This need is what best explains the spreading of telecommunication networks. And it is why the Internet quickly flourished.

Now it is time to get back to Extremadura, which, in the 1980s, was far from ready to take advantage of the new situation. Among the factors that caused Extremadura's relative technological backwardness, we would like to mention:

- Extremadura's mean per-capita income in the 1980s (when home computers began to become popular) was the lowest of all Spanish Autonomous Communities. Spain's own per-capita income was among the lowest in Western Europe. This was clearly not the ideal situation in which to expect most families in Extremadura to buy home computers.
- Brain drain: as the years passed, many of the young people who had managed to get a home computer in the early 1980s became highly qualified professionals and decided to leave Extremadura in search of a specialized job in the IT business.

These kinds of jobs were hard to find, and underpaid, in Extremadura. This situation posed a previously unanticipated risk: the stagnation of the region's economy, due to its loss of competitiveness as the rest of Spain was quickly turning into a modern European market, strongly based on IT. In Extremadura, the primary sector was still very important; when compared with the most prosperous regions in Spain or Europe, it appeared disproportionately large.

As the use of computers and the Internet grew more important in economies, especially in the tertiary sector, Extremadura had to face a new risk: that many of its best professionals and technicians would decide to migrate outside the region in search of jobs it could not offer them.

- The lack of the necessary infrastructure. As already stated, home computers actually became popular when sharing information was made possible, easy, fast and reasonably cheap – that is, when the Internet ceased to be a military experiment, used mainly in universities, and instead became one of the true mass media.

The more citizens and institutions gained access to the Net, the more popular it became and, thus, the more people grew familiar with computers and IT.

Telecommunications networks in Extremadura, however, were just below average, and adequate only for transmitting voice. On the other hand, only the most densely populated towns in the region had the possibility of accessing a broadband infrastructure; and, as already mentioned, most people in Extremadura lived in small towns (and still do), usually far apart one from another.

The situation was uninteresting, to say the least, for any private telecommunications company to develop an infrastructure in Extremadura.

So the situation in Extremadura looked unpromising, to say the least, to any private telecommunications company that might have been thinking of developing an infrastructure there. The technology needed was still rather expensive back then and, furthermore, the demand for the services they could provide was tiny.

A Sudden Turnabout

So far, the opening situation has been described: that was the problem. The solution would mean spreading the use of IT (especially to reach people less experienced with computers, for example elderly people, or those living in small towns). From the very beginning of the project it was clear that, in order to promote the sharing of information among the citizens of Extremadura, the local Administration had to provide an easy way for everyone to access the Internet. This, in turn, would mean training citizens unfamiliar with IT.

The plan was to leave nobody behind, but to focus on young people in order to familiarize them with computers and help them understand the role of IT in modern jobs, as a way of modernizing Extremadura's economy.

It should be noted that, from the very beginning, one of the main objectives of the global plan was to ensure that all students, regardless of their socio-economic status, could access the Net through broadband connections, from their schools. On the other hand, the objective of modernizing Extremadura's economy would not be met just by training young students in the use of IT. The Administration also had to help the IT-based private sector in Extremadura to develop and modernize.

These steps represented a global strategy consisting of simpler tactics that had to be carried out almost simultaneously. Once the foundations were laid, it was hard to decide on the best sequence of phases for the main project, as they were all so closely interlinked that it was almost impossible to analyse one of them without at the same time considering the role played by one or more of the others.

In order to implement the proposed phases of the global strategy, the Government of Extremadura decided to create several projects, built on two main pillars: the

Regional Intranet and the PAT (Plan de Alfabetización Tecnológica, or Digital Literacy Plan). These two pillars summarize the local Administration's global strategy: connectivity, sharing information and helping people get used to IT.

The Regional Intranet[8]

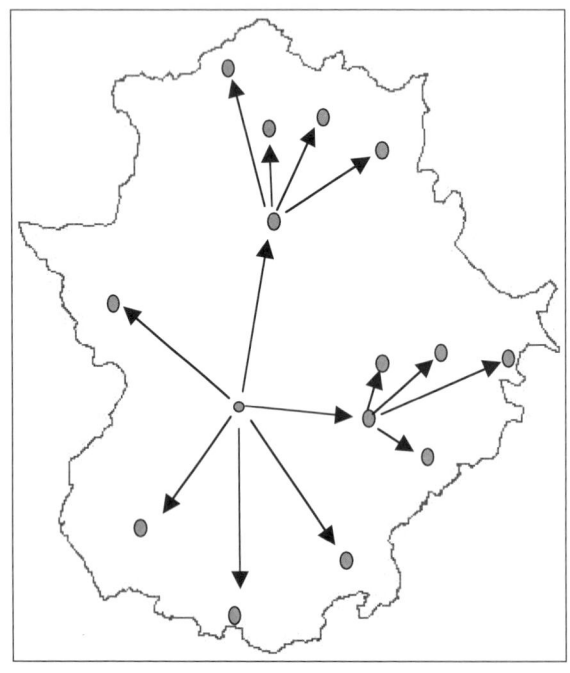

Fig 2 – diagram of main layout of Regional Intranet.

Building up a broadband network between two of the most heavily populated towns in Extremadura might, perhaps, be a reasonably easy task for private telecommunications companies with enough resources and experience. Moreover, the basic infrastructure necessary was already in place (even though it was mainly based on the old telephone lines). However, since Extremadura's population, as we have said, is scattered throughout many small towns, the effort would not be worth it.

Some would say that, without the intervention of the public authorities, many areas in Extremadura would never have been able to access the Internet. And while this assertion might be a good topic for an interesting debate, this is not the proper place to discuss it. It seems reasonable to conclude, though, that without the intervention of the local Administration the whole process of connecting Extremadura's 383 municipalities would had taken far longer than it actually did.

The main point, however, has nothing to do with the nature of the intervention by the public authorities, but with thinking about what could have happened if there had never any such intervention and the situation had just evolved freely. It seems reasonable, given the circumstances, to hypothesize that perhaps Extremadura would never have managed to be part of the digital revolution, or that, when the region was finally ready to join in, it might have been too late. From this point of view, it was not a matter of whether the whole process could have been completed thanks to the Administration, but whether it would have happened in time.

The Government had to promote the development of citizens: that is, it had to lay down the infrastructure and, from that moment on, just let citizens be free to pursue their own goals as they saw fit.

Connecting Extremadura to the Internet seemed, thus, a necessity. It was important to achieve the full connection of each and every municipality in the region, no matter what their size. The question was: where could the acccess nodes be installed? What was the most efficient solution? The answer was, obviously: take advantage of the existing roads, rather than building new ones. One should never re-invent the wheel.

Because Extremadura is such a big region, and about 70% of its population live in towns of less than 5,000 inhabitants, every single village in Extremadura has its own school.

Schools in Extremadura have the essential infrastructure (telephone lines, electricity, etc.), so they were clearly the ideal candidates for being set up as access nodes to the Regional Intranet. Moreover, we must emphasize the fact that one of the main objectives of the regional Government's plan was to familiarize students in particular, and young people in general, with computers and the Internet. Nothing was left to chance.

By installing access nodes in schools, the local Administration achieved two goals:
- Reduced costs and improved efficiency, due to the fact that all towns in Extremadura have at least one school, and every school already had the basic infrastructure needed.
- The objective of computerizing classrooms.

Alan Kay[9] has an interesting view on the role of computers in classrooms:

> "Now let me turn to the dazzling new technologies of computers and networks for a moment. Perhaps the saddest occasion for me is to be taken to a computerized classroom and be shown children joyfully using computers. They are happy, the teachers and administrators are happy, and their parents are happy. Yet, in most such classrooms, on closer examination I can see that the children are doing nothing interesting or growth inducing at all! This is technology as a kind of junk food – people love it but there is no nutrition to speak of. At its worst, it is a kind of "cargo cult" in which it is thought that the mere presence of computers will somehow bring learning back to the classroom. Here, any use of computers at all is a symbol of upward mobility in the 21st century. With this new kind of "piano", what is missing in most classrooms and homes is any real sense of whether music is happening or just 'chopsticks'."[10]

In my opinion, Dr. Kay's thoughts are very appropriate and accurate with regard to the use of computers in classrooms.

Fig 3 – An actual high school classroom in Extremadura.

His metaphor depicting the misuse of computers in school as junk food is especially enlightening. This is why we should not mistake the means for the aims. Nobody should think that the ultimate goal of the projects created by Extremadura's Administration is simply to replace old desks in every classroom with new ones specially designed to store a computer.

There is a risk of misunderstanding the digital revolution in classrooms as a mere "furniture update". The truth is that the 68,000+ computers already deployed in the schools of Extremadura are tools. Their mission is to complement, not to replace.

There is thus a risk of regarding computers in classrooms as an end in themselves. But they are only a means to achieving other aims, and to so more efficiently.

Let me focus on this concept for a moment: by definition, a tool is a medium to achieve an end. But there is something about computers that sets them apart from, say, screwdrivers or hammers. They have helped create a whole array of "sub-cultures" around them. It would be weird to think about a community of pencil-users who gather to debate on this or that topic – but this does happen when computers are involved. This is because computers are tools – but very advanced and versatile tools, designed to be used by the human intellect and human creativity. The most interesting topics of debate about computers are those related to the things that can be done with them – not their technical specifications, which are merely a secondary aspect of computers, in the same way as debating the physical characteristics of a canvas and a couple of brushes is irrelevant when compared to the things that can be done with them, and the vast array of pictorial styles seen throughout history.

In this sense, Kay's quote emphasizes our point: that computers must be regarded only as physical tools, and that we must rather focus on what can be done with them and how they can empower creativity and intelligence. In short: computers are *not* more than just tools – but nor are they just ordinary tools.

Before we go on, it might be a good idea to take a moment to think about the difference between a stand-alone computer and a computer that works as a part of a network. Without having to go into any technical aspects, the concept can be easily understood if we think of it by comparing computers to human minds.

As stated above, humans are information-loving animals. What sets them apart from other living beings is that they feel the need to gather information. There is a simple way of doing it: just by stand-alone investigation, study and analysis, individuals could learn things by themselves. But, powerful as it is, the human brain is limited by the rate at which it can absorb information, and by its actual physical capacity to retain data. In a sense, the human brain is much more powerful than the human body, so one life is too short a time in which to take full advantage of its capabilities. Or it would be, if the owner of the brain lived alone on the planet.

What boosts the learning capabilities of humans is sharing knowledge with other brain-owners, so to speak. Just as two pairs of eyes can see better than one, or two travellers can explore a wider territory than a lonely journeyman, two brains can learn much faster than one brain. Communication, the sharing of information and, in many cases, the interactive and dynamic processing of shared data (debating), dramatically improve the capabilities of the human brain. And the more people are willing to learn, to discuss and to give away knowledge, opinions and helpful hints to others, the more each individual can become a wiser person.

Now let us go back a step and recall our argument about the nature of computers: a computer is not an "intelligent machine", as some would say. As already stated, a computer is a tool. A complex, advanced and versatile tool. But just a tool, nothing more; as lifeless and inert as a microwave oven or a hairdryer. There is intelligence about computers, no question about it... but it is on the outside. So the topic of stand-alone *vs* networked computers compares perfectly with the above example, when we think that there is a human brain, an individual, ready to learn and to share knowledge, right in front of the screen.

It is up to humans to get the most out of these computer tools, to use them as a way of achieving higher goals. This is why the FOSS model was so important to us: it focuses more on what can be done with computers than on the path one must follow in order to do them. Some other models can end up regarding computers in classrooms as an end in themselves. Our idea was exactly the opposite.

Everybody knows how computers seem to captivate a teenager's imagination and creativity. The idea is to seize that enthusiasm and channel it. And this is where another of the most important parts of the global plan comes in: the deployment of computers in classrooms is a way to improve students' education, taking advantage of their fascination with computers.

In the global picture, the Regional Intranet could be regarded as the blueprint for the building Extremadura's public authorities are working hard to build, while the deployment of computers in classrooms and the possibility of connecting them to the Intranet could be regarded as the building's foundations. However, we also need the rest of the building, and that would be: making the technology helpful for students, and actually improving their education.

It should be obvious that computers are neither a panacea nor "magical machines", and nobody should think that their mere presence in schools is enough for students to feel the urge to learn. We must manage to help students awaken their thirst for knowledge. Nobody should aim for an educational system in which students only memorize data in a mindless, computer-like manner. The goal must be to help young men and women to spread their wings by themselves and then go their own way.

Let me put it this way: no one must pour a mountain of overwhelming data into the minds of young students. The objective has to be a much more ambitious one. If we think of a young person's mind as a blank book, we should steer well clear of the temptation to write our own thoughts in it, for this approach to education poses a terrible risk: if we consciously manipulate a teenager's mind, we are bound to create nothing but an unthinking robot. The point is this: do not write in a young person's blank book, but teach them how to write in it by themselves. Teach them the rules of grammar and syntax. Teach them the love of seeking knowledge, learning, understanding; the love of discovery, of improving their minds. Make them see that this is the best way for them to become free citizens, and that education, reason and developing their own personality freely (but always abiding by some minimum rules) is one of the basic foundations of freedom.

Thus is set in motion a life cycle that should describe the way of understanding civilization: individual improvement in order to achieve individual liberty (which is nothing but the freedom of thought, of reason: the freedom that allows people to distinguish facts from lies, the objective truth from subjective views); this is the only way to build free societies, made up of free citizens, none of them enslaved to the criteria some elite (of whatever kind) tries to impose on mindless, gullible people. Only free individuals can come together to make up a free society. And only in a free society can a single individual, in turn, be free.

Angel Vaca

P.A.T. – The Digital Literacy Plan

It is now time to return to the concept of "digital democratization". And we need to emphasize again the importance of not being too optimistic about the word "democratization" in this particular context. Otherwise, if we thought of "digital democratization" as just "giving away something for free to many people, regardless of their socio-economic status", we would be looking at Extremadura's classrooms and seeing only special desks with a 15" monitor on top.

We must look further. We should not think that to get our job done it is enough to distribute the tools widely. On the contrary: that is only the first step. Democracy is (or should be) much more than having the right to vote every four years. There are a number of powerful ideas (related to ethics, philosophy and politics, for example) underlying it. Thinking that deploying thousands of computers in classrooms is enough to achieve a "digital democratization" is, thus, wrong.

Computers are tools. Teaching people how to use them is the next step; but it is not the last one. There is one more step to take: participation. True participation, on the basis of an agile, transparent and efficient Administration.

Governments have always generated information. One of the most ambitious goals of a true "digital democratization" should, then, be to make it possible for any citizen to take a look at that information. Public information should be made truly public. This is not only about offering individuals the possibility of accessing certain documents, but about helping them have an overview of how the Administration manages its data. This is another of the keys for the building of a healthy democracy: transparency.

The PAT (Plan de Alfabetización Tecnológica, or Digital Literacy Plan) is aimed at people with little or no experience of computers or the Internet, and its goal is to make these people feel more comfortable with IT.

The Plan was started in 1999, when six special centres opened their doors in several towns in rural areas. These centres were supported by local town councils and certain civil-society organizations. In the second stage of the Plan, 14 new centres were inaugurated. Finally, in the latest stage so far, 12 new centres have been inaugurated, several of them in impoverished areas in towns of more than 20,000 inhabitants. This, however, is not the last stage of the Plan: the idea is that, over time, each and every

Fig 4 – The gnuLinEx 2004 desktop.

municipality in Extremadura will have at least one Nuevo Centro del Conocimiento (NCC, or New Knowledge Centre).

What is gnuLinEx?

The planning, implementation and maintenance of the Regional Intranet required a huge effort, in both human and economic terms, but once it was finished there was still a problem to face: we had to decide which software we were going to use in all the

68,000 computers deployed in all the Region's educational centres and Intranet access nodes. If we decided to install proprietary software in all those computers, the price to be paid would – because of the licence fees – skyrocket.

But that would not be the only problem – the Administration would have to rely on third parties if it needed to modify, improve or update any of the applications used in the educational centres. Moreover, it was obvious that nobody wanted to encourage people to make illegal copies of proprietary software, so we needed a solution that could provide us with an alternative kind of software. We needed a solution that mainstream standards appeared unable to provide.

Now, to get back for a moment to the introduction to this essay, let us recall the acronym FOSS and the way in which the Government of Extremadura understood it.

So, what about the "F" for Freedom? For the Administration, abiding by the most popular software licence system today would have meant relying on a third party. When you are only renting a software solution, you are bound to accept the true owner's rules. You turn yourself into a perpetual client, never actually getting to own the piece of software you have paid for. This posed a definite problem for the regional Administration: the global plan was a very ambitious one indeed, which strongly encouraged people to be creative and to learn. These seemed difficult goals to achieve when the software used was, in a sense, limiting a portion of the creative potential of the most advanced users.

If we accept that sharing information is an essential part of the human desire for knowledge, limiting it right from the start would, clearly, limit the expected outcome. If you do not wish to encourage people to make illegal copies of licensed software, it is obvious that you have only two alternatives: either you pay for the licences, or you stop using licensed software.

Please note that while the financial issue was of very great importance to the Administration when it decided to choose an alternative to proprietary software, there was an ethical and philosophical background as well, and it was this that, at the end of the day, proved decisive.

The Government of Extremadura wanted citizens in general, and students in particular, to share knowledge and information. Paying a high price for having the privilege to share information freely, without restrictions, could well have put a premature end to the project. Worse still, it would have undermined the credibility of the ethical part of the plan, in other words, the principle that knowledge is free. One can only imagine what would have happened to modern science if, for instance, Johannes Kepler's *De Revolutionibus Orbium Coelestium* or Isaac Newton's *Principia Mathematica* had been kept for the eyes of payers only, and they, in turn, had been legally bound to keep them secret.

Let us not forget that one of the main focuses of the plan was to change the way students learnt things at school. So it should be clear that it was not just a financial issue that prevented the local Administration from choosing a proprietary solution – it was that it just could not encourage students to break the law, nor was it willing to accept that some knowledge (regarding science, history, biology, philosophy, etc.) is private property.

Perhaps the standard, most widely-known proprietary solution would satisfy entry-level users. But we wanted to go further. And, to put it simply, one cannot learn how a car engine actually works if the bonnet is locked and one cannot read any books on the subject.

This is where the "OS" part of the FOSS acronym comes in: Open Source. The software the Administration wanted to use would have to allow users to understand how an operating system works – or any other piece of software, for that matter. This began as a purely technical concern, but it can be extended to a much deeper issue involving ethics and philosophy.

In the end, what summarizes everything is the word "transparency". Transparency for the software. Transparency in the way the Administration uses it. Moreover, open-source software allows users to add their own contributions to the existing pool of computer applications, thus encouraging them to learn, to investigate and to become even more expert in the use of IT, by studying the very fabric of operating systems and modern computing.

At a more practical level, the software needed had to be network-optimized, as it was to be installed in thousands of computers, and was destined to power a broadband network covering an area the size of a small country.

We decided that the only logical conclusion was to use free software. And, thus, gnuLinEx, our own version of GNU/Linux, was born. This software has all the advantages we were looking for, plus some others, such as freedom (not only in a "zero cost" sense, but also in the sense that it is software anyone can use, copy, distribute or modify, freely and at no cost) and transparency.

Being open source, gnuLinEx and all the applications it features can be studied and freely modified by anyone with enough knowledge. Thus citizens can actually see how the Administration manages its data, and even propose ways to optimize it. This would be totally impossible had we chosen a solution based on proprietary software.

Note that the we did not reject proprietary software on the grounds that it reflected a different philosophy or business model, but because it could not provide us with the solution we needed, while FOSS did.

The Projects

The global plan of the local Administration is divided into several projects which, in turn, are based upon the two pillars already mentioned: the Regional Intranet and the Digital Literacy Plan. The projects are coordinated by Fundecyt[11] and the Ministry of Education, Science and Technology of the Government of Extremadura.

N.C.C. – The New Knowledge Centres

The NCC project is mainly responsible for spreading the Digital Literacy Plan. As already mentioned, since 1999 several centres have been inaugurated from which the NCC staff carry out their activities, in areas where the presence of IT is almost nonexistent.

In these centres, NCC members have the task of popularizing the use of computers in general and the Internet in particular. They can be regarded as teachers of basic computing for beginners. Their task is essentially an informative one, and their aim is, on the one hand, to make people who have never used a computer feel comfortable using one, and on the other to act as access points to the Regional Intranet, and thus to the entire Internet.

The Internet is a window onto a huge ocean of information, which makes it a great way for improving the education of the inhabitants of remote villages or impoverished areas in larger

Fig 5 – NCC & PAT.

towns. It is worth noting that the NCC staff not only help young people interested in learning about computers, or youngsters who do not have a computer or an Internet connection at home: there are also a number of elderly people who had never used a computer before and who now go to their nearest NCC centre to discover their possibilities.

Each NCC centre is managed by two staff members. One is always a computer technician, while the other acts as an organizer of various activities that initiate people into the basics of computing.

Not all the activities organized by the NCCs are aimed at beginners, although it is obvious that the first steps must always be taken with their needs in mind. There are some elderly people in remote villages who have never handled a computer mouse or typed on a computer keyboard. When activities are organized with people like them in mind, they have to consist, literally, in a physical description of computer components: what they do and how they are used. Over time, though, the objective is to make people understand the role of computers and the Internet in modern societies and their economies.

There are already a number of activities and projects that have been developed in small villages, by people who, before there was an NCC centre in their area, had never used a computer: from websites in which people talk about the traditions of their home town or, perhaps, keep an archive of old photos, to chats with teenagers or people from Extremadura currently living in other regions or countries. The possibilities are endless.

Vivernet – The Breeding Ground for new IT-Based Companies

The Government of Extremadura understands the key role played by a modern and cometitive economy, with a thriving tertiary sector powered by the enormous possibilities IT has to offer.

The Vivernet project has a long-term goal of helping the economy of Extremadura to modernize, and improving its competitiveness and its orientation towards the Services Sector. In a shorter term, the objective is to help young businessmen and businesswoman to establish their own IT-based companies.

Fig 6 – ViverNet.

Currently, Vivernet has two offices in Extremadura's two most heavily populated towns (Badajoz and Cáceres). In order for their projects, opportunities and ideas to reach even the most remote villages easily, Vivernet also has a "roaming team" that travels all over the region. The idea is to support young people, encouraging them to create their own IT-based businesses. This is why Vivernet periodically organizes courses and meetings on topics related to the use of IT in a modern and dynamic economy. The project also offers advice and technical information to anyone who might need them.

Any young businessman or businesswoman with a good idea for starting up a new IT-based company in Extremadura can count on the staff of the Vivernet project for support and training.

Many new IT business opportunities have flourished thanks to the Vivernet project, such as Estudio3D (http://www.estudio3d.com),
Baselga & Associates (http://baselga.vivernet.net),
Bittacora (http://www.bittacora.com), Creaxia (http://www.creaxia.com),
Inmolandia (http://www.inmolandia.com),
Contenidos e Innovación (http://www.coein.net),
Deex Software (http://www.deex-software.com),
Stork Designers (http://www.gestiondeobras.com), all devoted to software development, multimedia designs, consulting, etc.

C.F.N.I. – The Regional Observatory for the Information Society

Fig 7 – CFNI.

The acronym "CFNI" stands for Centro de Fomento de Nuevas Iniciativas (Centre for the Promotion of New Initiatives).

In 1997, the Government of Extremadura launched what was then called the Infodex Plan for cooperation between regions. The project was founded by both the European Union and the local Administration, and was managed by Fundecyt.

The Infodex Plan was initially designed to operate as a Regional Observatory for the Information Society. Its mission was to monitor the spreading of IT in Extremadura, analyse citizens' needs in terms of the Information Society, detect which areas needed help in order to develop faster, and infer future tendencies.

Another of the goals of the Infodex Plan was to take advantage of the possibilities of the Regional Intranet. Just as the decision to deploy thousands of computers in Extremadura's schools was to be regarded as the first step of a more ambitious plan, the Regional Intranet is far more than just a broadband network spreading all over the region and interconnecting its municipalities: it must be guaranteed to be a way to access useful content, so that citizens can get the most out of it.

This is why digital literacy courses were organized to teach professionals from various fields (such as the health or education systems) how to access and browse the Net. Some other projects were also developed, including the preparation of a complete, interactive course on the Portuguese language. The Infodex staff was also responsible for the design, development and maintenance of the official website of the Government of Extremadura.

It was then that the Infodex Plan slowly began to take on a more technical role. The number of projects in which the Infodex staff was involved began to grow at a steady pace; at the same time, these became more important and complex. This is why, in the year 2002, the Infodex Plan became the CFNI, as it is known nowadays. Its new mission is to face the new challenges with renewed strength and more resources, while keeping the old ones.

As proof of the philosophy of keeping on the old projects in which the Infodex Plan was involved, the CFNI is still generating contents for the so-called RTE (Red Tecnológica Educativa, or Technological Educational Network), without this meaning that the old ones have been abandoned.

On the other hand, to emphasize the fact that the CFNI was created bearing in mind the idea that it should go further than the Infodex Plan had done, it is worth mentioning that several agreements have been signed with a number of institutions and regions, from both Spain and abroad. For example: the CFNI is currently cooperating with institutions in Latin American countries (Brazil, Colombia and Argentina, among others), is involved in several projects founded by the European Union and is working in the e-Extremadura project (also founded by the UE), devoted to the development of IT-based innovative actions within Extremadura.

But perhaps one of the more important milestones introduced by the CFNI is the development of the gnuLinEx custom-built operating system.

gnuLinEx is currently installed on the tens of thousands of computers deployed in the classrooms of Extremadura. Nowadays, the CFNI keeps a highly qualified international team of developers working to update and improve Extremadura's FOSS operating system.

The GNU Licence

gnuLinEx abides strictly by the GNU licence, which can be summarized in the so-called Four Freedoms of GNU:
1. You have the freedom to run the program, for any purpose.
2. You have the freedom to modify the program to suit your needs. (To make this freedom effective in practice, you must have access to the source code, as making changes in a program without having the source code is exceedingly difficult.)
3. You have the freedom to redistribute copies, either gratis or for a fee.
4. You have the freedom to distribute modified versions of the program, so that the community can benefit from your improvements.

Note that these freedoms do not mean it is impossible to earn money from your software – you can, although you need a different approach from the one most frequently used nowadays.

You can sell the services your software provides to the user, but you cannot sell the software itself. You can also sell copies of it, but you are actually charging for the physical media, manuals, etc. And you must always bear in mind that you have to give away the source code along with the software.

It is because we decided to abide by the GNU licence that we decided to modify a Debian GNU/Linux distribution in order to create our own customized distribution, gnuLinEx. But we are not stopping there: we continue to develop more programs, such as Facturlinex and Contalinex, or special tools for teachers, to make gnuLinEx more versatile. We do not have to rely on third parties to update our code. And, of course, we always give away our code, so that anyone can study and modify it. This way, tools can be adapted to users, and not the other way round.

A good example of this way of thinking is one of our newest projects which consists of promoting the use of Squeak in schools.

Squeak is an open-source media authoring tool[12] written with the SmallTalk programming language. It allows teachers to be the ones who generate their own contents in whatever way they like. Of course, there must be a common background for all students and schools: the concept of gravity, for instance, is the same everywhere, but individuals are welcome to choose the way to teach it to students. Or better still: they are welcome to encourage students to prove that they have understand the concept by making a project on the topic, using a free, open-source and fully customizable computer tool. We already have many projects by teachers and students from all over Extremadura.

Squeak provides us with this very versatile and intuitive tool we were looking for. It allows young children to learn about complex concepts. It is surprising how a piece of software can spark students' creativity and imagination, while they are learning, in a very natural way, the very essence of subjects such as maths, biology, computing, statistics, physics, and so on.

Squeak makes it possible, for instance, to build simple programs just by dragging and dropping items on-screen, helping children to grasp abstract ideas.

A popular example among Squeak developers is the "little car project", in which a student draws a small car on-screen and then associates a couple of variables to control its speed and turning rate. In a very intuitive way, young children are learning abstract concepts such as magnitude or the difference between a positive figure and a negative one. The aim is that, in the short term, students will manage to understand how mathematical formulae work and how they are used to simulate the real world.

This is quite an innovative departure from certain traditional methods of teaching, which tend to focus on specific details and encourage students to memorize data. While this is not necessarily a bad thing, we think that memory alone is not enough to make a free-thinking, rational person. Abstraction is needed too. In fact, abstraction is the very first step to be taken. This is a top-down system: concepts first, details later.

We are working to integrate Squeak into the gnuLinEx project, and we have already begun to translate all the available documentation (including on-screen text) and to train teachers and developers in the use of Squeak and SmallTalk.

gnuLinEx Technical Specifications

As a final remark, here are some of the technical specifications of the latest instalment (called gnuLinEx 2004) of our own GNU/Linux distribution:
- A modified Debian[13] GNU/Linux distribution.
- Uses the Gnome 2.6 desktop manager.[14]
- The latest kernel is version 2.6.6.
- Uses a modified Anaconda (Red Hat Linux) installer.

We are committed to developing an operating system which is user-friendly, since we are aiming at people with little experience in using computers. This is why we chose to customize the default Gnome desktop, adding icons that refer to local topics (such as famous landmarks or characters). To put it simply, it is easier for an older person living in a remote town to memorize names such as "Espronceda" (a famous 17th-century writer from Extremadura) or "Guadalupe" (a local monastery) than "Open Office" or "Ximian Evolution".

In our latest version, and as a result of the agreements with Andalusia and several regions in Latin America, we have also added icons that refer to topics widely known among people there.

In any case, we want gnuLinEx to be a powerful and versatile operating system that highly qualified professionals can also use, to the fullest extent. So, bearing in mind these advanced users who, in many cases, are already familiar with the GNU/Linux operating system, we have included an option that returns the customized icons and names to the original ones.

Further Reading

gnuLinEx official website — http://www.linex.org
SqueakLand — http://www.squeakland.org
"Powerful ideas need love too", by Dr. Alan Kay — http://minnow.cc.gatech.edu/learn/12
WikiPedia, the free online encyclopaedia — http://www.wikipedia.org
ViverNet official website — http://www.vivernet.com
NCC & PAT official website — http://www.nccintegrared.org
Fundecyt official website — http://www.fundecyt.es
Government of Extremadura official website — http://www.juntaex.es

Appendix: Tables, Facts and Data

Table 1 – Population distribution in Extremadura and Spain[15] as of 2003

Municipalities	Extremadura	Spain
< 2,001 inhabitants	20.7%	7.1%
2,001 - 10,000 inhabitants	33.9%	15.9%
10,001 - 100,000 inhabitants	32.7%	36.4%
100,001 - 500,000 inhabitants	12.8%	23.4%
> 500,000 inhabitants	0.0%	17.1%

Table 2 – Gross income (euro per capita)[16]

Year	Extremadura	Ratio (Spain = 100)	Spain
1991	5696	83.24	6843
1992	6078	83.13	7312
1993	6389	84.55	7556
1994	6713	86.22	7786
1995	7131	84.14	8475
1996	7654	86.03	8897
1997	8129	87.03	9341
1998	8693	87.03	9984

Note: As of 2003, Spain's GDP was 95% that of the European Union, Extremadura's only 62%.

Table 3 – Information technology and communications[17] as of 2003

IT and communications	Extremadura	Spain
Homes with cell phones	65.8%	73.7%
Homes with an Internet connection	14.3%	25.2%
Homes with a broadband Internet connection	14.5%	35.5%
Homes with a computer	32.1%	43.3%

Table 4 – Illiteracy rates as of 2003

Region	Illiterates	No studies	Primary school	Secondary school	University
Extremadura	6.5%	32.5%	29%	27.1%	4.9%
Spain	3.2%	21.6%	34%	34.2%	6.9%

Notes

[1] FOSS stands for "Free, Open-Source Software".
[2] In fact, the population is five times less dense.
[3] By comparison, only 23% of the Spanish population live in towns with under 10,000 inhabitants. Up to 17.1% of Spanish citizens live in cities of more than 500,000 people. Please remember that the biggest town in Extremadura has 150,000 inhabitants. Source: Spain's Ministry of Public Administrations (http://www.map.es). See Table 1.
[4] Official website at: http://www.min.es
[5] Jack Tramiel was the founder of Commodore Business Machines, a very popular company which, in the 1980s, manufactured quality home computers at a very reasonable price that many average families could afford.
[6] I repeatedly quote the term "democratization" in this particular context because, in my opinion, "democratization" means much more than a mere "popularization" of something. We must handle this idea very carefully in order to avoid confusing readers into thinking that "computer democratization" could be the equivalent of "indiscriminate distribution of computers regardless of socio-economic factors".
[7] The words with which Aristotle begins his *Metaphysics*.
[8] The Regional Intranet consists of more than 1,400 nodes, and guarantees a minimum bandwidth of 2 Mbps. It uses mainly fibre optics.
[9] Dr Alan Kay is President of the Viewpoints Research Institute, Inc., and Senior Fellow at Hewlett Packard Labs. He is best known for the ideas of personal computing, the laptop computer, and the invention of the now ubiquitous overlapping-window interface and modern object-oriented programming. His deep interest in children and education were the catalysts for these ideas, and they continue

to be a source of inspiration to him. (Excerpt from Dr Kay's biography. Full text can be found at http://www.squeakland.org/community/biography/alanbio.html).

10 Taken from an article entitled "Powerful ideas need love too!", written by Alan Kay. Source: http://minnow.cc.gatech.edu/learn/12

11 Fundecyt (Fundación para el desarrollo de la Ciencia y la Tecnología en Extremadura – or Foundation for the Development of Science and Technology in Extremadura) is a half-private, half-public foundation whose main objective is to act as a bridge between private companies, the University of Extremadura and the local Administration.

12 Or, as the Squeak official site puts it: "Squeak is [...] software that you can download to your computer and then use to create your own media or share and play with others". More information on the Squeak official website: http://www.squeakland.org

13 We decided to go for a Debian distribution mainly because it is the most independent of all GNU/Linux distributions – i.e., it is not directly supported by any company, and it is the most freely modifiable distribution available.

14 Some would prefer the KDE desktop manager but, in our experience, basic users tend to feel more comfortable with Gnome desktop managers, whose appearance and feel resemble those of the most popular graphic user interface.

15 Source: Spanish Ministry of Public Administrations (http://www.map.es)

16 Source: Regional Government of Extremadura (http://www.juntaex.es)

17 Source: Spain's Ministry of Public Administrations (http://www.map.es)

Biography

Angel Vaca Quintanilla studied computer enginegering at the University of Seville. In 2000 he worked with RedIRIS where he designed and implemented a distributed FTP protocol using only free software. This helped shape his professional career, as it was one of the main reasons for his move, in 2002, to the Centro de Fomento de Nuevas Iniciativas (CFNI) in Extremadura, where he was involved in the gnuLinEx project as a technical advisor and developer. It was during this period when he was introduced to the CROSSTALKS project. In September 2004, he left the CFNI and joined Sevilla Ingenieros, a thriving IT company located in Seville and currently working for many institutions, including the Andalusian Regional Government, which, following the example of Extremadura, decided to develop their own version of gnuLinEx, called Guadalinex. Angel Vaca is currently studying philosophy at the U.N.E.D. University in Spain and is an amateur astronomer.

1 • PUT THINGS BACK, YOU ARE NOT ALO[NE]
0

Building Open Ecosystems for Collaborative Creativity

Peter Hanappe

The fact of openly sharing creative works on the Internet may have a profound impact on the contents industry. A new ecosystem may emerge, with the potential to take over an important share of cultural production. If it is to reach its full potential, however, a better understanding is needed both of the incentives for participants and of the technical tools for supporting and stimulating this ecosystem. Social aspects and intellectual stimulation may outweigh financial rewards as the main reason why authors participate. If we succeed in accentuating these aspects, we may see the development of a collaborative creativity that is a hopeful answer to alarmist views on the commoditisation of culture.

Introduction

Recently, I have been listening a lot to *icotec*'s music. icotec is a Norwegian artist who makes Drum'n Bass music. I have about 40 songs of his on my computer, all of which I have downloaded from the Internet. I downloaded these songs legally. I did not get a "ripped" or illegal copy that someone had made available. No, icotec puts his music on the Web for free – almost four CDs' worth. Since I enjoy his music, and I assume others do too, why, then, did icotec choose to make his music available instead of signing a contract with a music label? When I asked him, he said: "... because of a very simple reason: I enjoy it greatly. I'm not so occupied with the thought of earning money from the music anymore – I guess I try to follow the flow of what entertainment on the Internet is all about, so I merely want to be a part of that".

There are many more musicians like icotec who make their music freely available. I don't have any precise figures to illustrate the size and importance of this free music phenomenon. Let me just mention two websites: ElectronicScene.com and Magnatune.org.[1] Over little more than a year, the number of MP3 files downloaded on ElectronicScene more than doubled to over 140,000 a month.[2] ElectronicScene hopes to have one million unique visitors annually by the end of the year. The site has become a victim of its own success, and access to it has currently been restricted until an improved infrastructure is in place. What is surprising is that the site is run mainly by a single person, Gideon Marken. The second website, Magnatune.org, started only in 2003, and about a year later 160 artists have made almost 4,000 songs available. Although the size of these two sites is not comparable to the size of the music industry, they are steadily growing.[3]

The Internet, as a distribution medium, challenges the established distribution channels for content. The uncontrolled sharing of content on the Internet has triggered a widespread debate on copyright. The purpose of copyright is to stimulate the broad availability of an extensive creative production.[4] It does this by giving the author of a work a monopoly. With this monopoly, the author can ensure she gets a financial return on her work. By making content freely accessible, however, an author undercuts a possible source of income. In such a situation, are there still enough incentives for authors to create works? If so, what are they?

In this article, I discuss what I call open ecosystems for creative collaboration or, in short, creative communities. I analyse the production and free dissemination of creative works in a connected society. I will try to take a broad view. There has been a lot of discussion in the press about music distribution. But distribution is just one aspect of the creative process. Instead, I think it is essential to take a step back and analyse all interactions and exchanges between participants. In particular, I will consider the incentives and rewards for authors, reviewers and the audience. Only when we have a good understanding of the whole ecosystem can we make interesting, new propositions. This text does not aim to offer conclusions or solutions. I think it is too early for that. However, where possible, I will refer to concepts found in the social and economic literature that may help in constructing a theoretical framework.

The text is organised as follows: in the next part, I discuss various issues that relate to the current discussion, including Free/Open-Source Software and the Creative Commons. I will also give a brief overview of alternative forms of *capital*, that is, alternative forms of resources that can be invested, and the returns on those investments.

The second part focuses on creative communities. First, I will analyse the incentives for authors to participate in creative communities, and secondly, I will discuss the technological aspects and see what tools may be needed to support creative communities.

In the last part, I will present experiments designed to observe some interactions. These experiments are very tentative in their approach. From them, I hope to gain a better insight into the possibilities and requirements – but also the obstacles – associated with establishing creative communities.

1. Current topics / current state

This section discusses several issues that are relevant to the present text. First, I will review various forms of capital found in the literature of economics and sociology. Then I will analyse two distinct *ecosystems*: the traditional music-business model, and the exchanges in the Free/Open-Source Software communities. I finish this part with a short presentation of the Creative Commons project.

1.1   Forms of capital

Later in this text we will discuss incentives for authors to create works. These incentives are generally understood to be financial reward. Indeed, the copyright law was introduced to ensure such a "fair return" to authors for their work. Since I will examine an alternative form of content production and distribution, it is worthwhile examining alternative forms of capital, other than financial. Capital is any form of resources that is invested and that yields a return on the investment. Capital refers to the initial resources invested, but also to the profits made. Marx's description of the production cycle led to the classical theory of capital. According to this view, the capitalist converts money into means of production and engages labour and land to produce commodities that are sold in the marketplace in order to yield a profit. Capital then refers to the physical means of production, such as the factories and the raw materials. Over time, the definition of capital has been broadened. Of interest to us are the theories on human and social capital. The following overview is largely based on Nan Lin's text [32].

Human capital arises from an investment in knowledge and skills. Through education and work experience, a person invests in human capital. The return on the investment is obtained through the labour market where job positions and salaries are negotiated. In the classical theory of capital, labourers are replaceable and are paid the minimum wage necessary for their subsistence needs. In the human capital theory, labourers acquire skills that allows them to negotiate higher incomes that more than cover their subsistence needs. Human capital is thus an investment with expected returns.

The second form of capital discussed is social capital. Social capital is an investment in social relationships. The return on the investment is the higher chance of success when a person engages in a purposeful action. An example of such an action is applying for a job. Whereas human and cultural capital are associated with the players themselves, social capital is associated with the player's social relations. Through these social relations, the player may access resources that are otherwise unattainable. I will say more about social capital in section 2.1.3, on incentives in creative communities.

These new theories regard capitalisation as a process that engages both players and hierarchical structures. They describe the choices made by those players to obtain better positions within those structures. These theories focus on processes that are associated with a person and in which individual actions play an important role, in contrast to the macro-level analysis of classical capital theory.

With a better understanding of various forms of capital, I will now analyse two distinct production models for creative works. The first analysis concerns the traditional music-business model. The second analysis discusses Free Software, or Open-Source Software.

Building Open Ecosystems for Collaborative Creativity

1.2 The traditional music-business model

Since the invention of the phonograph by Thomas Edison in 1877, it has been possible to record sound onto a physical medium. Over more than a century, many different recording technologies have been introduced, but one thing they all have in common is that the audio recording is fixed on a physical medium. The physical media – the disks and cassettes – can be distributed and sold. They have become the basis of a new industry, the recording industry: musicians make a recording, the record company copies the recording onto disks and sells the disks through music retailers.

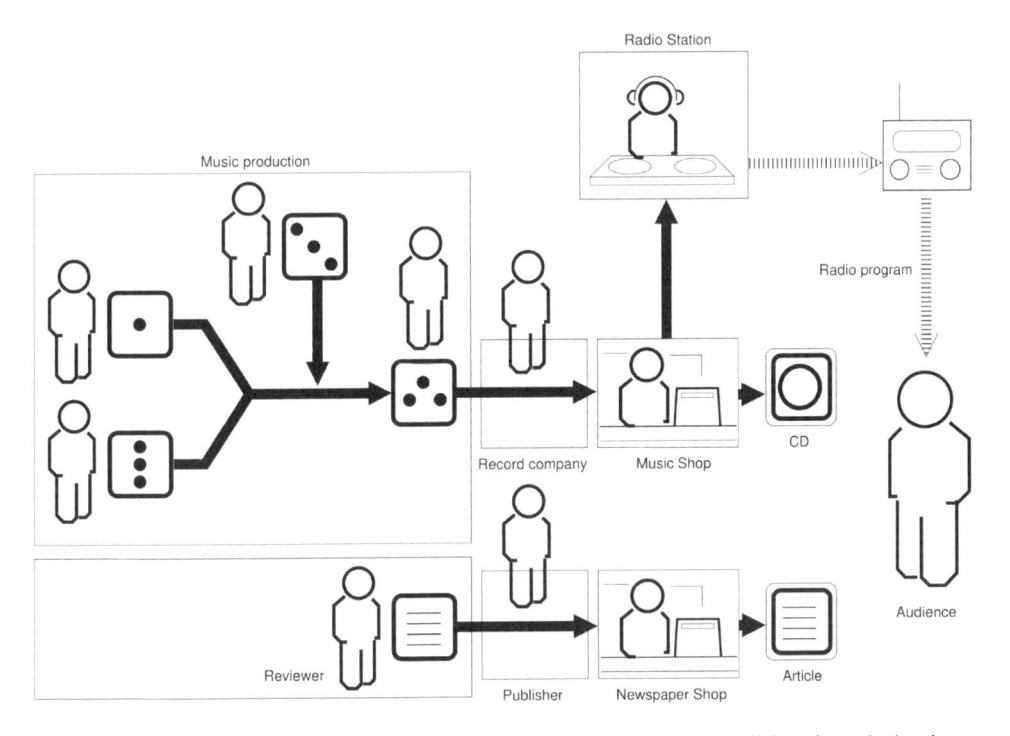

Figure 1 – A simplified view of the flow of music and reviews in the traditional music-business model.

The picture I will draw of the traditional music industry will necessarily be simplified. I am interested in tracing the flow of ideas and contents, and the types of benefit to those who participate in the system. In most cases, the recording is the work of many people: musicians, composers, arrangers, song writers, sound engineers, and many more. There are many possible types of collaboration, contracts and intermediaries between these participants, but ultimately the most important contract is the one with the record company. The record company oversees the production, distribution, sales and promotion of the recordings. In parallel, the music also reaches an audience through radio stations and TV channels. The written press, radio and TV also play an important role as reviewers, by making a selection and publicising their appreciation of available music (see Figure 1).

Concerning the benefits to participants, I will discuss mainly the financial reward. The record company hands back to the authors a percentage of its revenue from a recording, i.e., the money it has obtained by selling it. From the sale of a $14.98 CD, an artist may expect an (all-in) royalty of $0.447 [28] (see also [21]). A second stream of revenue comes from performing-rights organisations, which tax radios and TVs on their broadcasts. For many artists, income from the sale of their recordings is small and probably only a few authors can live off that alone. This means that other benefits must also play an important role. The journalist is paid by the publisher, often a fixed amount for every published article. The audience is in it for the enjoyment of the music, of course, but probably not only that. Listening to music or discussing it with others – the social aspects – may be an important factor too.

I would like to make a couple of observations. First, in this model, there is little direct feedback from the audience to the authors. The audience are very much at the receiving end of the distribution channels. Secondly, even though the organisation of the music production may be very ad hoc and may involve many people, in this model the record labels play the central role. Lastly, the audience has no simple way of seeing how the recording is structured – i.e., how it was composed and recorded – nor can it reuse any of those components. The end products – the recording, the reviews, and also the radio programmes – come in a non-editable format.

In this short overview I deliberately did not mention the concerts and other public performances by the artists. The characteristics of these public performances are sufficiently different from those of the recordings to be treated separately. Certainly, concerts are part of the ecosystem, as they strongly influence record sales, and vice versa. However, creative communities – the subject of this text – may have a bigger structural impact on the recording industry than on the concert scene. In fact, while the free music phenomenon seems to increase ticket sales for concerts, it does not significantly alter other aspects of a concert (for some accounts, see [21, 42 and 33]).

Before I continue with the next section, I would like to mention the changes currently affecting the recording industry. I will start by introducing the term *excludable*, which is used by economists to refer to goods[5] for which it is possible, or not too costly, to prevent someone from enjoying that good. For example, the good "going to a concert" is excludable because it is easy to sell tickets and have someone check the tickets at the entrance to the theatre. The classical example of a non-excludable good is a lighthouse: it is too complicated to make passing boats pay a tax to cover the cost of the lighthouse and prevent boats that do not pay from passing. Lighthouses are, however, very useful. They are therefore provided as a "public good".

A musical recording on a physical medium is excludable: it is impossible for anyone to obtain the disk without being noticed, as you have to go to a music shop to buy one.[6] This changed, however, with the advent of digital audio and the Internet. It has become common to distribute music worldwide, and it is very costly to prevent someone from doing so. Music recordings are no longer excludable, which makes the old business model harder to maintain. The solutions that have been proposed to remedy the situation all aim at reintroducing excludability. A first category of solutions seeks to ensure that only the person who bought the music, and no one else, can play her copy. These solutions are based mainly on encryption technologies and try to reduce the possibility of copying a work [50, 34, 15 and 24] (see also [3 and 38]). A second category of solutions tries to make the contents "traceable" so that when the music becomes freely available on the Internet the authorities can trace the file back to the original buyer. These solutions embed some personal information about the buyer in the music, and are often called watermarking. Both solutions are generally referred to as Digital Rights Management or DRM. The introduction of DRM may come at a high cost, but when it is successful it allows the recording industry to translate the old business model to the new medium of the Internet.

1.3 Free/Open-Source Software

This section discusses a very different "business" model, that of Free and Open-Source Software, or FOSS. Although most people may not regard software as typical "content", it is nonetheless protected by copyright law. Since the FOSS philosophy is inspiring people outside the realm of software, it is important to have a better understanding of this phenomenon.

Free/Open-Source Software is software that is protected by a specific licence, a Free Software or Open-Source licence. What these licences all have in common is that they give anyone the right to use, copy, modify and redistribute the source code of the software.[7] FOSS licences are legally rooted in copyright law. The author of the software claims the authorship of the source code, and the work is thus protected by copyright law. This gives the author a monopoly of the distribution rights to the source code. Using these rights, the author then guarantees the "freedom" of the code. The freedoms granted include the freedom for anyone to run the program, study how it works, adapt it to their own needs, redistribute copies, or improve the program and release these improvements to the public [47, 22].

The FOSS movements began with a philosophy and a licence, but over the past twenty years it has evolved into a complex ecosystem for software production and distribution. Consider, for example, SourceForge.net. This has become the biggest exchange platform for FOSS: it hosts more than 80,000 software projects and has over 800,000 registered developers. Consider also the *distributions*. Distributions compile and bundle software to form a coherent system.[8] The Debian GNU/Linux distribution, for example, is developed by 1,308 people, providing 8,710 software packages for 10 distinct hardware architectures.[9] The Debian project also has it own constitution and voting policy. This illustrates how much the ecosystem has evolved beyond the initial licensing scheme.

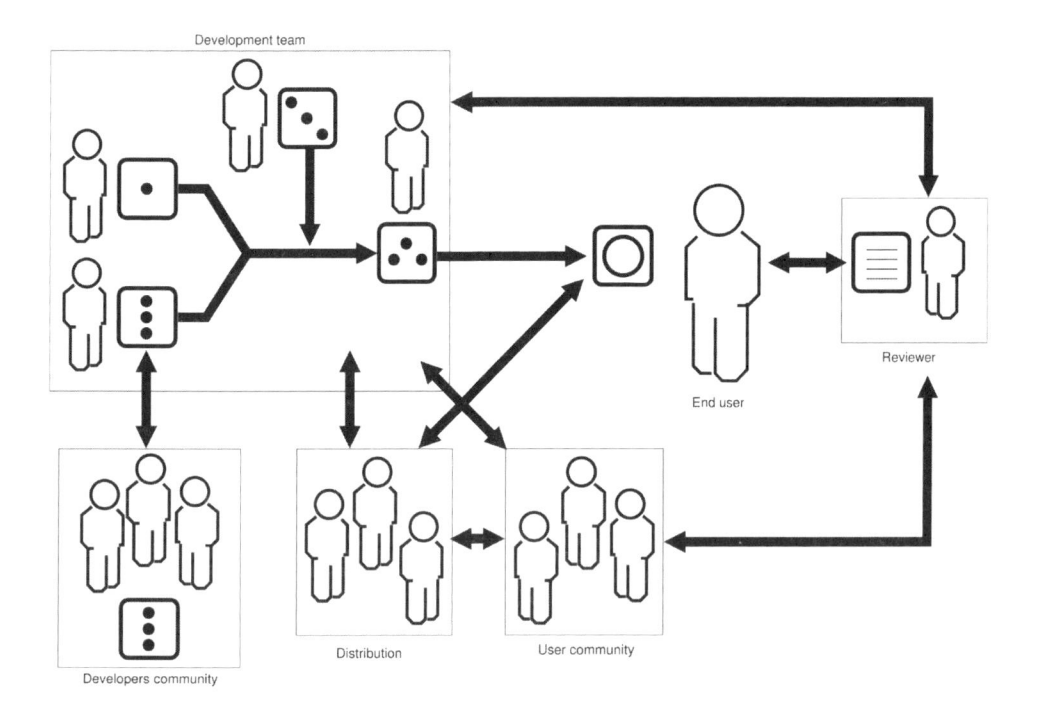

Building Open Ecosystems for Collaborative Creativity

Figure 2 – The various roles in the FOSS system and the relations between them.

The developers of FOSS software are often a "loosely-knit team of hackers across the Net".[10] The software is a collaborative effort but the participants are in general very clearly defined, and each developer often manages one particular module of the software. The core development team interacts with a larger development community. This community provides feedback and enhancements, and often modifies the software for its own purposes. It regularly happens that a developer from the community joins the core developer team. The software user may obtain the software directly from the core developers and may also interact with them directly. Most users, however, install the software provided by a distribution. The organisation that manages the distribution itself involves many people. These distributions may be commercial – selling the compiled software as a service – or they may be managed by a community, such as Debian.[11] The user community is often in close contact with the developers and the distributions. They provide feedback, enhancements and documentation and offer help to other users. Lastly, there are also people who review software, describing the merits and inconveniences of alternative software solutions, or documenting the complete software setups. Many of these reviews are published on the Web although commercial, paper editions are available. Interactions and exchanges between all these participants take place mainly on the Internet, through websites and mailing lists. When we look at the financial benefits for the participants, it is clear that they are not very substantial. Users may pay for a distribution but all distributions, even the commercial ones, can be obtained for free. The Hacker Survey indicates that 30% of developers are financially compensated for their contributions. These developers are mainly professionals who need FOSS for their work or are paid by their employer to develop FOSS [29]. That leaves 70% of developers contributing for reasons other than financial. I will talk about some of these incentives in section 2.1.

1.4 Creative Commons

Creative Commons was founded in 2001 and is "devoted to expanding the range of creative work available for others to build upon and share" [11]. Inspired by the FOSS licences, the Creative Commons project proposes a set of licences that authors can use for their work. Under all these licences, the work in question can be copied, distributed, displayed or performed in public or on the Web, or converted to another format. Certain other rights, however, can be reserved by the author. For example, an author can stipulate that their work must not be used for commercial purposes without their explicit consent (the *non-commercial* clause). This means that if, for example, a company wants to use a recording – released under the Attribution/Non-Commercial License – in an advertisement, they will have to negociate the contract and terms of use with the author.

It is difficult to evaluate how well the Creative Commons licences are currently being adopted. In many countries, they are being adjusted to national jurisdictions: they have been introduced in Brazil, Germany, Belgium and the Netherlands, and translations for many other countries are underway. As an illustration: the BBC plans to make its archive available under a Creative Commons licence [10]. And Magnatune, mentioned earlier, publishes all music under a Creative Common licence.

2. Open Ecosystems for Collaborative Creativity

What do I mean by *open ecosystems for collaborative creativity*? In this article, I focus on two issues: 1) incentives and reward in creative communities, and 2) the technologies needed to support and/or stimulate the establishment of creative communities.

Before I start, let me try to characterise open ecosystems for collaborative creativity. The main constituents of this ecosystem are the participants and the works. On a higher level, we find the organisation of participants and the process of creating the work. First, the works. In an open ecosystem, these works can be distributed, modified, enjoyed, reused freely, possibly with *some rights reserved* as discussed in the previous section. So the content is fairly "open" and resides in a shared space. The second point concerns the participants. Compared with the ecosystem of the traditional contents industry, there is probably a freer exchange, and all participants have more opportunities to add value to the creative process. Also, the various roles in the organisation are not strictly defined or distinct. As Steven Weber puts it, in relation to FOSS: "there is no consciously organized or enforced division of labor. [...] Users merge into the production process itself in profound way" [51]. The last point concerns organisation. It will probably be a distributed organisation without centralised control. Instead of a one-way channel from authors through publishers to the audience, there will be a more open exchange between all participants. Since the notion of a finalised product disappears, the creation process may generate multiple intermediate versions of an idea in a work rhythm that knows no stringent deadlines. This characteristic has produced a work methodology for software development that is quite different from the methodology that prevailed in commercial software development. Although these characteristics may seem very general, they represent a major shift from the established model.

A form of collaborative creativity can also be found in the development of the Web. Someone publishing a HTML page is and remains the sole author of the page. No one can modify it. However, the HTML code of the page is visible to anyone and can be reused to create new pages. The openness and decentralised nature of the Web stimulate exchange and creativity.

Collaborative creativity does not mean "collaborative works". Every author retains sovereignty over her own work and does not have to participate in discussions on it. A large body of literature exists on collaborative writing, for example. That is not what is meant in this text. Having several people writing a poem together is unlikely to yield a great result. However, having people give feedback to the poet or create new versions of the poem can be stimulating for all and may translate into a new and interesting work. Collaborative creativity, then, probably has more to do with the established practice of peer reviewing than with collaborative writing.

Open ecosystems for collaborative creativity is not the same as the Creative Commons. The "creative commons" refers to the shared works or the abstract space in which these works reside. However, putting a work in this space, i.e. publishing it under a Creative Commons licence, is not in itself enough to maximise the possibilities for collaborative creativity. Other aspects, both technical and social, should be taken into account. In the text below I will address some of these aspects. The point I want make is that for FOSS, a licence may have been sufficient to get the movement going. For creative works, however, we may need more than just a licence. In this text, I make a modest attempt to gain a better understanding of how creative communities may function. I will concentrate on two issues. First, I will discuss the incentives for people to participate in creative communities. Then I will focus on the technological aspects of creative communities.

2.1 Incentives in Creative Communities

When considering collaborative creativity, we need to ask what the benefits to the participants are. The following discussion in organised around the various types of capital discussed earlier.

2.1.1 Financial reward

I begin this section with two observations about FOSS. First, it seems to me that the software landscape is growing more and more polarised between commercial software and FOSS. Both commercial developers and FOSS developers defend their ground, very vocally. The result seems to be that there is almost no middle ground any more. A second observation is that FOSS did not start out with a clear business model and will probably never have one. FOSS licences do not rule out the possibility for the author of a program to sell the software and earn an income from that. But as a FOSS licence grants everyone free access to the software, income from sales only is practically impossible. If direct, financial income for FOSS writers is difficult, indirect income may be possible.[12] Even if that is the case, I think it is fairly safe to say that, although the *utility* value of FOSS is comparable to the utility value of commercial software, the revenue streams generated by FOSS are probably only a fraction of those generated by commercial software. As a result, the majority of FOSS developers never see any financial income from their work.

Does this mean that something similar may happen in the contents industry? Possibly. On the one hand, digital-rights management technologies aim at a very closed and protected delivery of content but can ensure some direct income to the artists. On the other hand, the Creative Commons provides content free of charge and, like FOSS, still has to prove that it can provide authors with a financial reward. However, it may be easier to establish a middle ground than in the case of software. First, it is important to note that it is currently not easy for musicians to earn money in the old business model either, as we have seen in section 1.2. Finding a record label to distribute the music is time-consuming, and the financial return from such a deal is often very small. Making the music available for free is not necessarily a big financial loss for many musicians. As icotec says: "Another reason [for making music available for free] is that it's simple, it doesn't require too much time for my part – I only need that time for composing new music and to upload it as MP3 files". (For a discussion on this issue see also [7 and 8].) However, if the traditional music industry can reduce the cost of transactions and contracts, they may be able to deliver the same advantages but still guarantee some income [25].

A second point, which may prove to be less important than I think it is, is that right from the beginning Magnatune.org has made it possible for the audience to buy an album even if it is freely available – they can even set their own price, between $5 and $18. However, the fact that this option has been introduced from the start, and in an organised way, may make it easier for people to adapt to this mentality. Some FOSS developers include a PayPal link on their website and ask for contributions (SourceForge now adds a "donate" link on the project pages), but for FOSS this option seems much harder to introduce so late in the day. People also feel a very different attachment to content and to software. Some people may have very strong feelings about the software they run on their computer, but for most other people software is nothing more than a utility. Creative works, however, are valued mainly for the experience they provide. Providing better-quality audio recordings, for example, may be a service for which people are willing to pay ("Water is free, but a lot of us drink bottled water because it tastes better" [20]).

Public funding schemes may also gain in importance. Although there are many political and financial hurdles blocking the transition to generalised public funding schemes, some do already exist, which should simplify future extensions [16, 14]. There are also some interesting alternative propositions, such as the Street Performer Protocol or the Potato System. These solutions are largely untested, but they do leave some terrain to be explored [26, 19].

Designers of peer-to-peer file-sharing applications are also studying how to introduce micro-payments.[13] Peer-to-peer applications struggle with "free riders", people who take advantage of the system but do not contribute to it. This work may yield new solutions for payments on the Internet [1, 37, 35].

Using the non-commercial clause in the Creative Commons licence, authors can retain the right to stipulate that a work cannot be used freely for commercial purposes. If someone wants to use it for commercial purposes, she has to negotiate a contract with the author. Commercial uses include advertisements, commercial films and commercial CDs. It may also include use on commercial TV and radio, or in bars or shops.

Although the fact that content is freely accessible seriously reduces the possibilities of making direct income, the situation may not be hopeless. There are still many possibilities to be explored.

2.1.2 Skills and human capital

The Hacker Survey by the Boston Consulting Group questioned 684 FOSS developers on their motivation for participating in software projects. The top two reasons given by the hackers were that the code they wrote for the project was intellectually stimulating, and that it improved their programming skills. Ninety-two per cent of the interviewees mentioned that the increase in their personal knowledge base was the most important benefit of participation [29]. This is an important fact. It suggests that many creative people are not "in it just for the money". Rather, it suggests that learning, skill improvements, and fun can be important stimuli to participate. Similar arguments may hold in the creative domain. icotec seems to indicate as much: "Many musicians work together as well, doing remixes and listening to each other. That, I think, is one of the best parts of the ElectronicScene community. […] I try to participate in this community as much as I can, and for some 30 % of my new music I seek feedback from other musicians using the forum. This is rewarding as I get feedback on both a technical and a musical level. I also try to listen to and actively share my opinion with other musicians on their music, as much and as often as I can".

2.1.3 Social capital

Social capital is the ability to access resources through social connections. If social capital is an important benefit of participating in creative communities, then what kind of resources does it provide access to? To give an example, Linus Torvalds, the originator and main developer of the Linux kernel, was invited to take a job at Transmeta after Peter Anvin had suggested this to the company's management [49]. Although the offer was not triggered by an explicit action by Linus Torvalds,[14] it is an indication that the social network of FOSS developers may be useful for finding jobs. This is related to, but not the same as, the human capital discussed in the previous section. Before the managers of Transmeta could assess Torvald's skills, someone had to point him out to them and say: "There's a valuable person for your organisation". This flow of information is facilitated by social networks, and is one of the reasons why social capital works.

A last issue I would like to address is the role of *gatekeepers*. Gatekeepers decide whose works are produced, promoted or performed. Gatekeepers are the producers, the radio programmers, the gallery owners, and so on. Staying on good terms with these decision-makers can be important for an artist's success. The promise of the digital networks as an open distribution medium is that anyone can now publish their work, bypassing gatekeepers and reaching the audience directly. Worldwide distribution is now within the reach of anyone, and there is a new opportunity for artists to be heard and to have their works broadcast. They can effectively build up a reputation within a social network. This reputation, and a stronger tie with the audience, may result, for example, in higher ticket sales for their concerts. This phenomenon has been given by many musicians as one of the main reasons why they are in favour of free music distribution [21, 42, 33].

2.1.4 Other observations

Although giving content away free makes it difficult to obtain any material returns, it can be an interesting investment for human or social capital. I am not saying that financial reward is impossible. However, I find it worth exploring the idea that there may be other reward systems, possibly based on social or human capital, that can provide enough incentives for authors. Such reward systems probably do exist. The question then is, is there a way to make them more tangible? Human capital – knowledge and skill – is "traded" in the labour market, and software developers can browse job offers to get an idea of the demand for certain skills. For content creators, such skills are probably harder to assess and evaluate. Social capital is even harder to measure. There are attempts to measure reputation, in particular for business transactions [31]. Technologies exist for evaluating sellers and buyers, such as on eBay. Trust, accountability and reputation are widely discussed in the literature on Internet applications [18]. However, it is still unclear how to apply these approaches to creative production. Do we actually want to make social capital explicit, and put a figure on the value of our social relationships? According to Lin, someone who is high up in the hierarchy of one type of resource has easy access to other types of resources. That means that if someone has a good deal of human or social capital, access to financial capital may be easier. If this can be confirmed, then there may be no need to measure human or social capital explicitly.

Since, in the Western world, the material needs of the majority of people are satisfied, it may seem possible for human, cultural or social capital to become more important than financial capital. Nan Lin writes: "[W]e are witnessing a new era in which social capital will soon supersede personal capital in significance and effect"

([32] p. 214). Jeremy Rifkin seems to agree: "[I]n a society that has conquered material scarcity, immaterial values take precedence and the quest for self-fulfilment and personal transformation becomes the goal. In such a society, the right not to be excluded from a 'full life' becomes the most important property value a person holds" ([45] p. 239).

2.2 Technologies to support Creative Communities

In the previous section I discussed the incentives for authors to participate in creative communities. The emergence of FOSS communities owes much to the availability of inexpensive digital communication technologies and other tools. Without a doubt, technology also plays an essential role in the ecosystem of collaborative creativity. On the one hand, there is the technology needed for the creation itself – this includes authoring tools, but also standardised formats and descriptive languages. On the other hand, there are the technologies that enable the sharing and retrieval of content. I will discuss some of the necessary and/or desirable elements of both parts in the next two sections.

2.2.1 Authoring

The availability of a common development language, such as the "C" programming language, and development tools, such as **gcc** and **make**, has certainly contributed to the establishment of the FOSS community. It makes a difference when people who are working together have access to the same tools. Lawrence Lessig stresses that by providing a "neutral platform, open source invites a different kind of innovation" [30]. A neutral platform for content creation is probably essential too.

Before discussing this issue further, I have to make a brief excursion into file formats. It is important to understand the difference between a flat, binary file format and one that retains the structure of the data. When a digital work is created, whether software or content, it is generally distributed in a binary format, such as MP3 audio files or software executables. This binary file was assembled from various elementary data sources that have been organised and combined by the author to yield the final work. For software, we call the initial description the source code, which is stored as human-readable text files written in a programming language. For content, there are a plethora of languages and formats in which to store the description of a work. Several efforts have been made to define standardised languages for describing content. The Motion Picture Experts Group (MPEG) and the Web Consortium are working on several such standards. If the works are accessible in the editable format, we begin to see the same phenomenon as what has happened with HTML and FOSS: people start building upon each other's work.

I will now list the characteristics of those descriptive languages I consider important for supporting collaborative creativity. First, the specifications of these languages have to be open and standardised. They must be unambiguous and completely specified, so that applications built to render these files all produce the same output. There should be some facility for building version control systems (see also below). For this, textual file formats are easier than binary formats. Since we want to be able to combine content from various sources, it should be possible to incorporate links to external sources.

Descriptive languages alone are not sufficient. Alan Kay said in an interview about the Web: "[T]he people who did web browsers I think were too lazy to do the authoring part" [27]. We need open, reliable authoring tools and players. These authoring tools should not be reserved solely for the authors, as it should be easy for anyone to make changes to a work.

2.2.2 Exchange platform

Uploading files to a website is the most straightforward way of making content available. For an effective, large-scale distribution, the use of a well-designed exchange platform is essential. This exchange platform also handles the communication between participants, file-sharing, reviews, user comments, authorship management, meta-data, version control, usage statistics and, possibly, the reputation system.

First, we need tools for communication. Many artists may choose not to communicate, but we should at least make sure that communication is easy when it is desired. These communication tools may be used by the audience to give feedback to the authors. For many artists feedback may be a source of inspiration in their work, but for the audience it is motivating, too. As an example, the German band Einstürzende Neubauten has put up a website where fans can follow the progress of their music creations [36].

As is common practice in software development, content creators may benefit greatly from version control. This version control is very important (imagine FOSS without version control!).[15] If reuse is to be promoted, and the primary way of reusing material is to link to it rather than to copy it, then the author has to have a guarantee that the original link will provide the same content, even if the original author continues editing it. So an author provides a link not only to some content on the web, but to a particular version of that content.[16]

Like version control, authorship management should be a fundamental feature of the exchange platform. The goal of authorship management is to ensure that a work, or a part of a work, is credited to its authors and that this link is difficult to erase. At present, in FOSS, the authors of a project ensure the correct crediting of all authors whose work or contributions they use. This is done manually. If creative communities are to flourish, this management should be done transparently by the authoring tools. In addition, it should be possible at any time to query a work and obtain a lists of all the contributors to it. Search engines and database tools can be built that trace the lineage of a work. It is important to note that, even under FOSS, authorship is well defined. Even though everyone can obtain the source code and can make changes to a private copy, or propose changes, access to the official copy of the source code is well protected and its authors are clearly defined. However, this credit information is not registered in a structured way. There is no search engine that will retrieve all the FOSS projects in which a developer has participated, and what exactly she has contributed. Most FOSS projects maintain a file, generally called AUTHORS, in which all participants in a project are mentioned. But this information is coded relatively freely, and as far as I know no attempts have been made to build a searchable database of contributors.

Authorship information is a form of meta-data. Meta-data is data about data. For example, the title, the names of the authors, the genre, and other descriptions of a work are all meta-data. It is important for meta-data to be available and easily accessible. Meta-data is necessary for searching and accessing a work in large databases, for relating one work to another, and for allowing users to create a personalised view of a contents database [40]. If a considerable number of works, or parts of works, become available, it becomes increasingly difficult to find and value a work. In that sense, the value of a work is dependent not only on its content, but also on the amount and quality of its meta-data.

Reviews and user preferences are another form of meta-data. The use of user preferences for searching content is generally called Collaborative Filtering. Another form of reviewing is peer reviewing, which is widely used in the scientific field. Peer reviewing also works for software and it is regarded as one of the main factors contributing to the quality of FOSS. Is peer reviewing possible for content? In my view, there are two sides to the answer. The first thing to note is that, in software development and science, it may not always be possible to say if one proposal is better than another, but at least it is possible to point to flawed, incomplete or unclear proposals. For software as for science, there is some notion of "better": "better functionality" for software or a "better model" for science. But for content? I do not think that there is an easy answer to that. And this makes peer reviewing more difficult. However, it is often the discussions between "experts", among other factors, that give a work a place in a culture. So some form of peer reviewing is important and should receive a central place in any exchange platform.

The distribution of the content itself may require specific technologies. Traditional client-server technologies are costly and do not scale well with increasing numbers of clients. It is desirable for a creative community to be built using peer-to-peer technology [37]. Content distribution networks, such as FreeCache, or file-sharing networks using peer-to-peer technologies, such as BitTorrent, may be appropriate solutions. Distributed file systems, such as OceanStore and PAST, also handle persistent storage and version control, which is desirable, as noted above.

Open ecosystems encourage the reuse of content, but this openness must be compensated for by better authorship management. This trade-off works as long as the authorship management is effective and/or participants play by the rules. For these reasons there have to be tools that allow participants somehow to "monitor" the exchange platform to ensure that everyone plays fairly. Clearly, the exchange platform will have to be open and will have to publish all possible information to its members.[17]

3. Projects

In this section I will present two projects. These projects have quite a small scope and are designed mainly to test some of the concepts of collaborative creativity. Through these projects, I hope to gain a better understanding of creative ecosystems. The key question is whether creative communities are possible at all. If so, we may hope to gain an insight in the social interactions that define collaborative creativity, and the technology that supports it. The first project, called Fofito, is an attempt to give visitors to an exhibition the opportunity to express their views and leave a trace of their visit. The second project, called EcoScene, which is still being developed at the time of writing, aims to create a small, contained ecosystem of music production based on the FOSS philosophy.

3.1   The Fofito project

The Fofito project is a collaboration between Luc Steels and the author. We first experimented with the project at the exhibition "Social Capital: Forms of Interaction", organised by the Whitney Independent Study Program in New York, USA. The project is an experiment in audience participation and feedback. We put ourselves at the receiving end of the traditional distribution channel and investigate possible user contributions. Using new technologies, we try to engage visitors in the loop of the creative process so that they can become an active part of it. Cécile de Varine makes the following observation about visitors talking about the works in a museum [12]:

> L'objet exposé devient le receptacle d'une multitude d'interprétations. Les formes composées des tableaux organisent à leur manière l'ordre d'un discours culturel en chantier, en cours de construction. Comme des cathédrales de mots, les regards parlés construisent du sens, interprètent, déplient les œuvres... [...] Mais que deviennent toutes ces paroles, tous ces regards qui se construisent et circulent entre oeuvres, visiteurs et médiateurs? Il n'en reste bien souvent pas trace dans la littérature des musées. [...] Comment prendre en considération et rendre compte des regards singuliers ou collectifs de ceux qui viennent au musée confronter leur expérience du monde et leur compétences aux objets exposés?

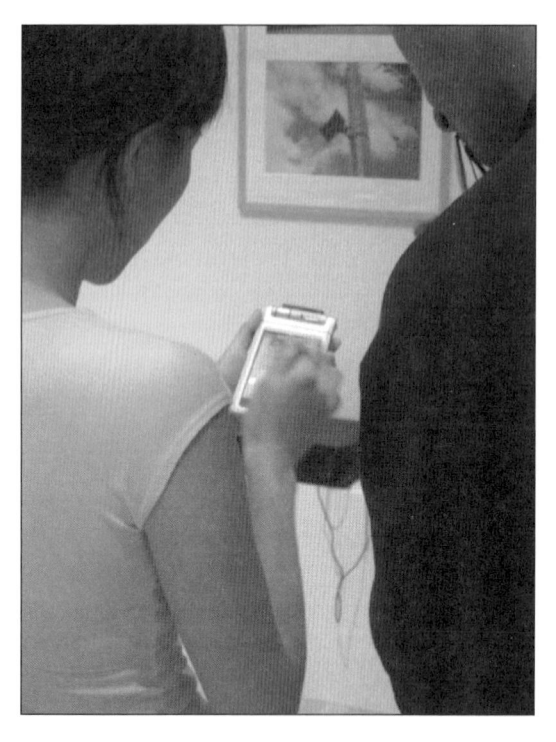

In the project we give visitors to the exhibition a chance to express their views on the works displayed and to participate in the discussion around them. The tool we developed allows the visitor to take pictures of the works and annotate them with text. It also allows them to browse the pictures and texts that have been previously entered by other visitors.

People can borrow a hand-held device or personal digital assistant (PDA) during their visit to the exhibition. In the near future, we assume that visitors will have their own electronic devices with which they can participate, probably their cell phones. The PDA is connected to a local server over a wireless network (WiFi or 802.11b). The server hosts a website with information about the exhibition. The website is organised in three sections, entitled *expo*, *catalogs*, and *you* (see Figures 3 and 4). The first section, *expo*, provides information about the works on display in the exhibition. Each one has a dedicated web page displaying a picture of the work, naming its authors and giving its title and technical information aout it. The page also provides links to the *catalogs* that discuss the work. A list of all available catalogues can be found in the second section of the website. A catalogue is a list of pages with pictures and text. A page can be related to a work, in which case it will show the title of the work and the names of the artists. Navigation through the information on the website is very straightforward and intuitive. The third section, entitled *you*, concerns the visitor's input. Every visitor has her own catalogue, which can be edited in this section. The PDAs we used have a built-in camera that the visitors can use to take photos in the gallery. These pictures can then

Building Open Ecosystems for Collaborative Creativity

Figure 3: Two screenshots of the Fofito interface. On the left, the expo section which displays the list of artists. On the right, the catalog section with the list of available catalogues. The first catalogue in the list is an electronic adaptation of the official catalogue by the curators. The other catalogues are those made by the visitors. Note that the website was developed to be viewed on PDAs, which is why the screenshots have a slim shape.

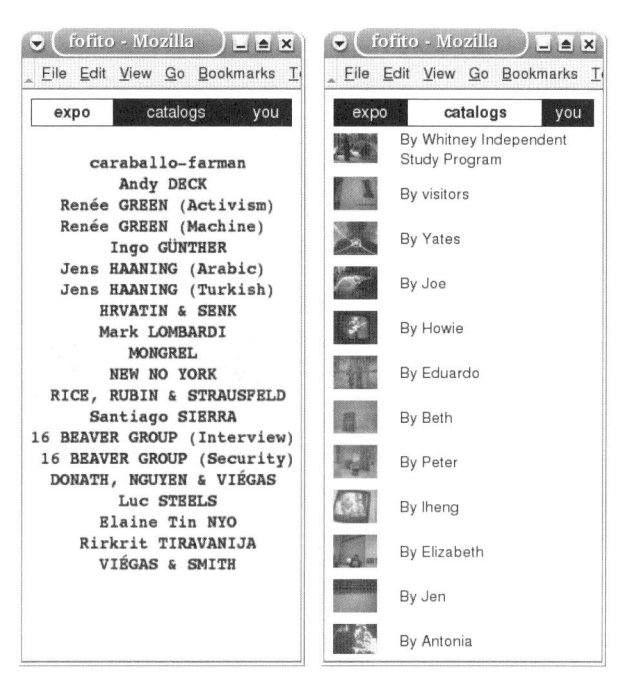

be annotated and inserted into their catalogue. The interface developed for the Fofito project can be used in several ways. It could be used to keep a personal record, a memory, of the visit to the exhibition. It could also be used to express a point of view that complements the works of the artists or the texts of the curators.

The wireless network and the web server provide a shared space, making all contributions visible to everyone. This shared space is not limited to the gallery. It is accessible from outside the exhibition space and visitors can continue their participation at home, adding more pictures or texts, or showing their input to friends and family. The website remains visible at http://fofito.csl.sony.fr.

It is still quite difficult to draw any conclusions from this experiment. Overall, reactions were positive. After overcoming an initial hesitation, most people enjoyed taking photos of the works on display. Many were intrigued by the novelty, although some preferred not to use it because they did not feel comfortable with the technology.

221

Figure 4: Two screenshots of the Fofito interface. On the left, a detail of a page in a catalogue. This page has been linked to a work and the work's artist and title are displayed. On the right, the you section, which allows a visitor to edit her catalogue.

Some people started using it creatively, but only a few people used it to write down an opinion. This may be due in large part to the fact that the textual input on a PDA is still awkward, especially when it is used for the first time. Most people contributed by taking pictures. In fact, most people took straighforward pictures, much like those you find in an official catalogue. This is perfectly acceptable. Taking the pictures – however "normal" they may be – is the first step to looking at a work from a different angle. It is a first, important step towards re-interpreting and re-appropriating the works on display. However, several people took more personal pictures.

The interface, which is developed in standard HTML, makes file-browsing to select the pictures and switching between the camera application and the Web browser less intuitive. As a result, I helped most visitors to upload the pictures and create the new pages in the catalogue. However, these problems can easily be solved by using a specifically designed interface. If the Fofito system was not readily used as a medium for expression, this was partly due to these shortcomings in the software. The feedback we received from the visitors was encouraging enough to convince us that such devices and interfaces could become a new means of interaction with museums and artists.

3.2 The EcoScene project

The EcoScene project is an attempt to create a small, contained ecosystem for music production. It focuses on the creative process and the possibility of exchanges between authors, reviewers and audience.

In this project, three composers work for two months on a music project of their choice. The only constraint is that their work, even while it is being composed, is made visible to all other participants in the project. The works are stored in their structured formats – that is, not as an audio file (an MP3 file, for example) but in an editable format. All intermediate versions of their work are kept, and remain available to anyone. During the project, an audio file is produced, however, to simplify listening to the music with simple players. The composers are free to reuse any sounds or material of another composer, but a record of what material is being reused has to be kept. The composers remain the sole authors of their work and are encouraged, but not obliged, to participate in the discussions on their work.

A music critic is invited to review the music regularly and to write down his impressions in a blog. And, of course, several people participate as an audience. There is a mailing list to which everyone is subscribed – composers, reviewer and audience. Anyone from the audience can also have a personal web page for the project, on which they can post their comments. Reuse of the musical material is not restricted to the composers: anyone from the audience can also start making modifications to their personal copy and publish it on their web page.

At the time of writing, the project is still being worked out. It is scheduled for autumn 2004, so as yet we have no conclusions to report. From the beginning, however, it was clear that to generalise such a project it would be very difficult to define a common music platform accessible to everyone. This indicates that it is far from easy – indeed, it is almost impossible – to define a common description language or authoring tool for music. Readers can follow the evolution of the experiment at http://ecoscene.csl.sony.fr.

4. Conclusion

The following are some of the points I would like to make:
- New forms of content creation and distribution are seeing the light of day, particularly in music. Inspired by FOSS, they allow free access to content. "Free" should be read not only as "gratis" but also as in "freedom".
- It is not clear how sustainable or important this phenomenon is. In the end, there will have to be enough incentives for artists to participate.
- Financial incentives may or may not be possible. This issue is currently receiving a good deal of attention in the media. Chances are that some intermediate solution will arise.
- Instead of concentrating on financial awards, I find it interesting to consider other forms of rewards, such as human capital and social capital. For many people, the social and learning aspects may be reason enough for participating. Can these forms of rewards be made more tangible? Can they become more important than financial rewards?
- To stimulate these other forms of rewards (human capital, social capital), new technologies and tools may have to be developed. I have discussed some of them.
- Judging by our experience so far, people seem excited about the idea of participating but are still uneasy about doing so. Also, technology still appears to be a barrier for the "general" audience today. Composers also seem interested, but are perhaps still a little uneasy about working in the open. They may feel uncomfortable having to discuss in public how and why they create something.

To conclude this text, I would like to comment on some of the discussions on the experience economy. Rifkin wrote an alarming book, *The Age of Access*, in which he casts doubt on the experience economy and the future of culture [45]. He quotes Herbert Schiller, professor emeritus of communications at the University of California at San Diego, as saying: "speech, dance, drama, ritual, music, and the visual and plastic arts have been vital, indeed necessary, features of human experience from earliest times. What is different is the relentless and successful effort to separate these elemental expressions of human creativity from their group and community origins for the purpose of selling them to those who can pay for them" (p. 140). Rifkin adds, "access will no longer be based on intrinsic criteria – traditions, rights of passage, family and kinship relations, ethnicity, religion, or gender – but rather on the affordability in the commercial arena. ... [C]apitalism is making its final transistions into full-blown cultural capitalism, appropriating not only the signifiers of cultural life and the artistic forms that interpret those cultural signifiers but lived experience as well" (pp. 140 and 144). And there does indeed appear to be such a tendency. Pascal Nègre, president of Universal Music France and of the Société civile des producteurs phonographiques,[18] states in an online interview: "Je revendique à 100% la marchandisation de la culture. Le seul endroit où la culture n'est pas marchandée c'est lorsqu'elle est d'Etat... Je n'ai aucune fascination pour l'art mussolinien, stalinien... L'art choisi par les princes" [13].

In my opinion, there are more options available to us than submitting culture to the control of either commercial or government institutions. A third solution lies within the realm of communities themselves. And FOSS has shown that this solution can be powerful indeed. If creative communities develop, the experience economy may take on a very different appearance from that described above. Rifkin comes to the conclusion that "the commercial sphere is offering something it cannot, in the final analysis, deliver: access to a life of deep communion and personal transformation" (p. 247). Instead of the commoditisation of culture, culture will probably stay what it was all along, a "complex web of shifting patterns that link people".[19]

5. Thanks

This work is funded by the Sony Computer Science Laboratory. I would like to thank Luc Steels, François Pachet and Atau Tanaka for the many discussions we had, which have greatly contributed to this text. Kudos goes to Marleen Wynants for her confidence and feedback on the article. Special thanks also to Howie Chen, Leta Ming, Allison Moore and Nadia Perucic of the Whitney Museum Independent Study Program for allowing me to set up camp in their exhibition space, and to icotec and Gideon Marken for taking the time to reply to my inquiries and for making the music available.

Notes

1. For an overview of other free music sites, see also reference [41], below.
2. This number does not include the files that are streamed, i.e. that are played immediately without being saved to disk. The number of files streamed per month is over 80,000.
3. In 2003 the RIAA shipped about 800 million units – CDs, cassettes, music videos, etc. – and brings out close to 30000 new albums each year [44, 52 and 5]. Compare also with Apple's iTunes Music Store, which sold 70 million songs in one year in the USA alone and offers a catalogue of 700000 songs [4].
4. This is made clear in the initial discussion of copyright and is confirmed by subsequent statements of the American Supreme Court. See also [2].
5. Goods are products in economic parlance.
6. It is possible, of course, to copy a cassette or a CD. However, this copying has always remained fairly marginal and was mainly limited to copying for friends and family. Large scale copying for retail, however, was traceable and actively pursued legally.
7. The distinction between Free Software and Open-Source Software is largely philosophical. For Free Software advocates, the freedom to access the source code is an ethical issue. For Open-Source advocates, this access is more an issue of praxis and methodology: "[The Open Source Initiative] is a pitch for 'free software' on solid pragmatic grounds rather than ideological tub-thumping" [23]. I will not go into details in this text. The interested reader can consult the following references: [48, 43 and 6].
8. Distribution offers much more than just binary versions of software. A software application often depends on other software applications or software libraries. The distribution keeps a list of all these dependencies and ensures that all the correct versions of the required software is installed. It also provides installation media – CDs, DVDs, diskettes – and installation *scripts* that help the user install and configure the software and ensures that the software integrates well with the existing setup. They also provide security updates, documentation and communication channels for support and debugging.
9. The figures are for the "stable" release. The "testing" release contains more than 15,000 packages.
10. A *hacker* is a developer. The term has been misused in the media and, as a result, has gained a negative connotation.
11. For an overview of available distributions, see http://www.distrowatch.com.
12. Some projects, like MySQL, sell support. Others make the documentation proprietary and sell it as a service. This is the case with jBoss. (However, the Free Software Foundation disapproves of making the documentation not free [17]). Even for companies selling support, since the core product – the software – comes almost at no cost, customers may be less willing to pay more for the extras [9]. Companies benefit from FOSS probably because of the reduced budgets for writing and maintaining their own software. According to Eric Raymonds, more software is written for use than for sale [43]. If this is the case, using FOSS may reduce the internal costs of software development. Also, making the software a commodity may help to increase revenue from complementary products such as hardware or support services [46]. This seems to be the strategy of both Apple and IBM.
13. Micro-payments are not necessarily financial: they can be a service – for example, providing disk space for others, or doing some computation.

14 Following Nan Lin's definition, the action of obtain the job position should have been a purposeful action initiated by Linus Torvalds in order to count the connection with Peter Anvin as part of Linus' social capital.
15 Version control for contents may be even more important than for software because software developers usually write code that uses a specific *application programming interface*, or API. It is the version of the API that is important, even if the implementation of the API changes. For contents, any modification will change the end result.
16 If some form of version control was embedded from the start in the specifications of the Web we may have had less problems with broken links.
17 For the need for monitoring, see also Elinor Ostrom's work on common-pool resources [39].
18 The recording industry association of France
19 Taken from Wikipedia, the collaboratively developed encyclopedia (http://www.wikipedia.org).

References

[1] Aytan Adar and Bernardo A. Huberman. Free riding on gnutella. *First Monday*, 5(10), 2000. http://www.firstmonday.dk/issues/issue5_10/adar/.
[2] Patrick Aichroth and Jens Hasselbach. Incentive management for virtual goods: About copyright and creative production in the digital domain. In *Virtual Goods 2003*, Ilmenau, Germany, May 2003. http://virtualgoods.tu-ilmenau.de/2003/.
[3] Ross Anderson. 'Trusted computing' frequently asked questions, 2003. http://www.cl.cam.ac.uk/ rja14/tcpa-faq.html.
[4] Apple. itunes celebrates its first anniversary; over 70 million songs purchased, April 2004. http://www.apple.com/pr/library/2004/apr/28itunes.html.
[5] Moses Avalon. Nielsen rating system at odds with riaa's claim of "lost sales". *Music Dish*, April 2004. http://www.musicdish.com/mag/index.php3? id=9452.
[6] Joe Barr. Live and let license. *ITworld.com*, 2001. http://www.itworld.com/AppDev/350/LWD010523vcontrol4/.
[7] Yochai Benkler. Coase's penguin, or Linux and the nature of the firm. *Yale Law Journal*, 112, 2002. http://www.benkler.org/CoasesPenguin.html.
[8] Yochai Benkler. "Sharing nicely": On shareable goods and the emergence of sharing as a modality of economic production. *Yale Law Journal*, 114, 2004, forthcoming. Electronic version: http://benkler.org/SharingNicely.html.
[9] John Carroll. Open source: Supply and demand. *ZDNet UK*, June 2004. http://comment.zdnet.co.uk/0,39020505,39157438,00.htm.
[10] BBC creative archive pioneers new approach to public access rights in digital age. Press Release, May 2004. http://www.bbc.co.uk/pressoffice/pressreleases/stories/2004/05_may/26/creative_archive.shtml.
[11] Creative commons. http://creativecommons.org.
[12] Cécilia de Varine. Regards parlés. In *L'Exposition, un média*, Volume 9 of *Médiamorphoses*. INA, 2003.
[13] Le Journal du Net. Pascal Nègre (universal music france): "Je ne crois pas à l'avenir à moyen terme du peer to peer", January 2003. http://www.journaldunet.com/chat/retrans/030117_negre.shtml.

[14] Peter Eckersley. The economic evaluation of alternatives to digital copyright. In SERCIAC, editor, *SERCIAC*, Northampton, Massachusetts, June 2003. Society for Economic Research on Copyright Issues.
[15] FairPlay. http://en.wikipedia.org/wiki/FairPlay.
[16] William Fisher. *Promises to Keep: Technology, Law, and the Future of Entertainment*, Chapter 6: An Alternative Compensation System. Stanford University Press, 2004. Currently in print. An electronic version of the chapter is available at http://www.tfisher.org/PTK.htm.
[17] Free Software Foundation. Free software and free manuals. http://www.gnu.org/philosophy/free-doc.html.
[18] Tyrone Grandison and Morris Sloman. A survey of trust in internet applications. *IEEE Communications Surveys*, 2000.
[19] Rüdiger Grimm and Jürgen Nützel. Security and business models for virtual goods. In *ACM Multimedia Security Workshop*, pages 75-79. ACM, 2002.
[20] Janis Ian. Fallout – a follow-up to the internet debacle, 2002. http://www.janisian.com/article-fallout.html.
[21] Janis Ian. The internet debacle: An alternative view. *Performing Songwriter Magazine*, May 2002. http://www.janisian.com/article-internet_debacle.html.
[22] Open Source Initiative. The open source definition. http://www.opensource.org/docs/definition.php.
[23] The Open Source Initiative. Frequently asked questions. http://www.opensource.org/advocacy/faq.html.
[24] Intertrust. http://www.intertrust.com.
[25] Fred Kaplan. D.i.y. meets n.r.l. (no record label). *The New York Times*, 4 July 2004.
[26] John Kelsey and Bruce Schneier. The street performer protocol and digital copyrights. *First Monday*, 4(6), 1999. http://www.firstmonday.dk/issues/issue4_6/kelsey/.
[27] David Kirkpatrick. A pc pioneer decries the state of computing. *Fortune*, Thursday, July 8, 2004. http://www.fortune.com/fortune/fastforward/0,15704,661671,00.html.
[28] M. William Krasilovsky and Sidney Shemel. *This Busines of Music: The Definite Guide to the Music Industry*. Billboard Books, 2000.
[29] Karim R. Lakhani, Bob Wolf, Jeff Bates, and Chris DeBona. The hacker survey. Technical report, Boston Consulting Group, 2002. http://www.osdn.com/bcg/.
[30] Lawrence Lessig. *The Future of Ideas: the fate of the commons in a connected world*. Vintage Books, 2002.
[31] Richard Lethin. *Peer-To-Peer: Harnessing the power of disruptive technologies*, chapter on Reputation. O'Reilly, 2001.
[32] Nan Lin. *Social Capital: a theory of social structure and action*. Cambridge University Press, 2001.
[33] Brian Mansfield. When free is profitable. *USA Today*, May 2004. http://www.usatoday.com/tech/webguide/music/2004-05-20-file-sharing-main_x.htm.
[34] Microsoft. Windows media drm. http://www.microsoft.com/windows/windowsmedia/drm/default.aspx.
[35] Dejan S. Milojicic, Vana Kalogeraki, Rajan Lukose, Kiran Nagaraja, Jim Pruyne, Bruno Richard, Sami Rollins, and Zhichen Xu. Peer-to-peer computing. Technical Report HPL-2002-57, HP Laboratories Palo Alto, March 2002.
[36] Einstürzende Neubauten. http://www.neubauten.org.

[37] Andy Oram, editor. *Peer-To-Peer: harnessing the power of disruptive technologies*. O'Reilly, 2001.
[38] Andrew Orlowski. Biometric drm is 'empowering' says ivue maker. *The Register*, June 2004. http://www.theregister.co.uk/2004/06/11/biometric_drm_interview/.
[39] Elinor Ostrom. *Governing the Commons: the evolution of institutions for collective action*. Cambridge University Press, 1990.
[40] François Pachet. Content management for electronic music distribution: The real issues. *Communications of the ACM*, April 2003. http://www.csl.sony.fr/downloads/papers/uploads/pachet-03a.pdf.
[41] Jon Pareles. No fears: Laptop d.j.s have a feast. *New York Times*, September 10, 2004. http://www.nytimes.com/2004/09/10/arts/music/10INTE.html.
[42] Andy Raskin. Giving it away (for fun and profit). *Business 2.0*, May 2004.
[43] Eric S. Raymond. The cathedral and the bazaar. http://www.catb.org/esr/writings/cathedral-bazaar/.
[44] RIAA. Year-end marketing reports on u.s. recorded shipments. http://www.riaa.com/news/marketingdata/yearend.asp.
[45] Jeremy Rifkin. *The Age of Access*. Penguin Books, 2000.
[46] Joel Spolsky. Strategy Letter V, June 2002. http://www.joelonsoftware.com/articles/StrategyLetterV.html.
[47] Richard Stallman. The free software definition. http://www.gnu.org/philosophy/free-sw.html.
[48] Richard Stallman. *Free Software, Free Society: Selected Essays of Richard M. Stallman*, chapter entitled "Why 'Free Software' is better than 'Open Source'". Free Software Foundation, 2002. Available online at http://www.gnu.org/philosophy/free-software-for-freedom.html.
[49] Linus Torvalds and David Diamond. *Just for Fun*. HarperBusiness, 2001.
[50] Trusted computing group. https://www.trustedcomputinggroup.org.
[51] Steven Weber. *The Succes of OpenSource*. Harvard University Press, 2004.
[52] George Ziemann. Riaa questions validity of own information, 2003. http://www.azoz.com/news/0023.html.

Biography

Peter Hanappe studied electronic engineering at the University of Ghent, Belgium. He began his research in computer music at the IPEM (Institute for Psychoacoustics and Electronic Music). In 1994 he moved to Paris, where he wrote his PhD thesis on music and sound environments at Ircam - Centre Georges Pompidou (Institute for Research and Coordination in Acoustics / Music). After working for three years as a freelance developer, Peter Hanappe joined the Sony Computer Science Laboratory in Paris where he continues his research on new modes of content creation and distribution.

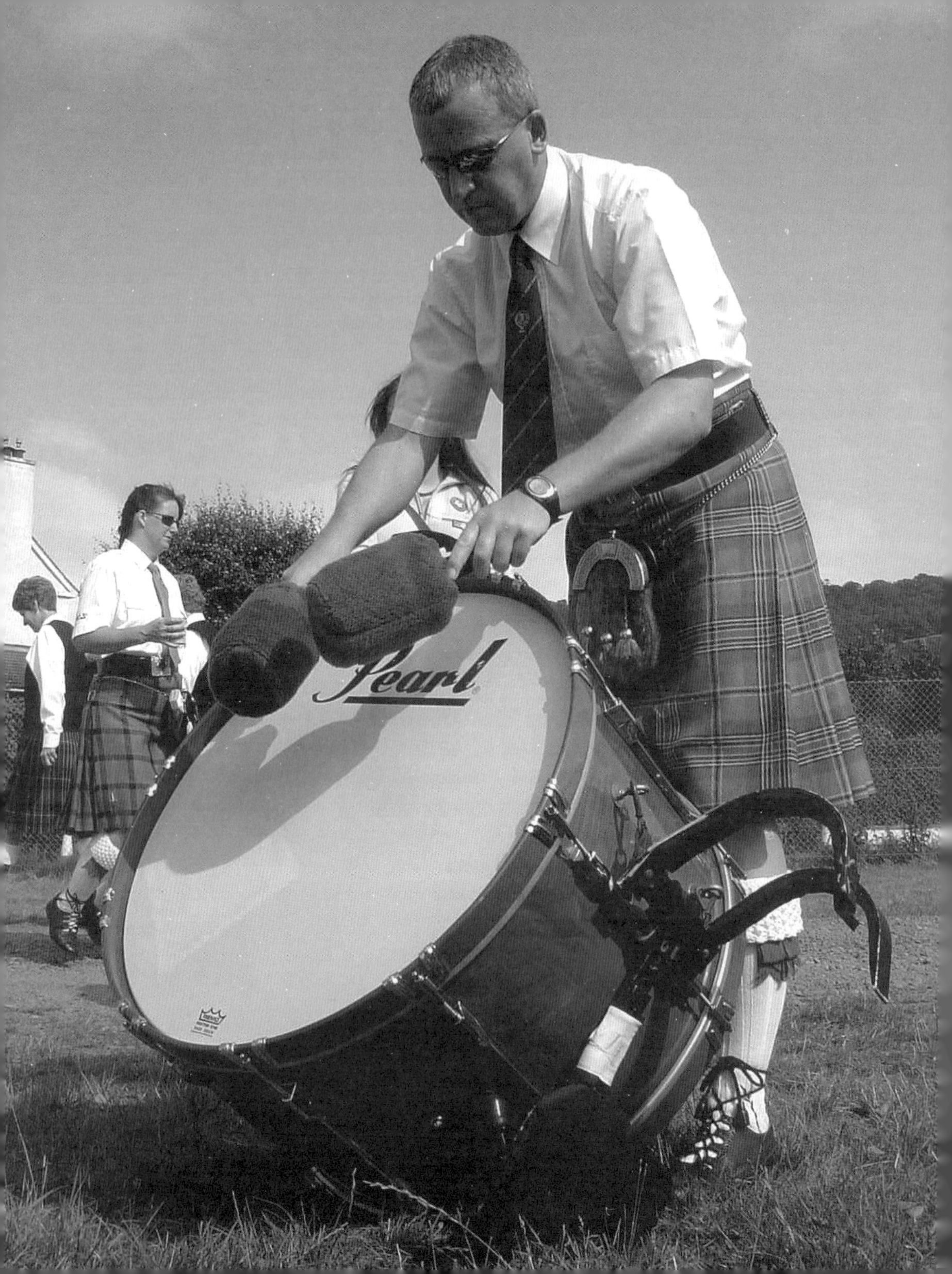
Pearl

A Walk through the Music Bazaar –
Reflections on the Future of Music

Sara Engelen

Introduction

> "We become what we behold. We shape our
> tools, and thereafter, our tools shape us."
> Marshall McLuhan

Anyone who logs on to the Internet nowadays inevitably enters a jungle of sound data, an "audio hyperspace", where music consumption, production and distribution is explored to the maximum, prospecting the mutability of digital data in the open-endedness of the World Wide Web. Today, not only sophisticated users are kicking the digital-music experience up a notch or two. The enormous possibilities of manipulating audio resulting from the playfulness of the digital medium and the synergy of peer-to-peer networking have unleashed music into a digital realm of so-called free space, thereby questioning the prevailing structures of the music business. Digital technologies with user-friendly interfaces allow solitary musicians and digital experimenters to draw on a full spectrum of sounds, tools, and programs, hence removing musical sophistication as a requirement for producing sophisticated sound. Music has become a digital fluid, an instrument of cross-fertilization between media, genres, cultures, arts and sounds, supporting the intrinsic idea that the free flow of information results in better products. The age of digital (re)production seems to embrace the idea of a free market-place, where the freedom is granted to express thoughts and ideas, to create and (ex)change content, to copy, cut and paste, and to rip, mix and burn.

Meanwhile the music industry has been ringing the alarm bell for quite some time. The other side of the "free market"-coin is regulation, and regulation is meaningless if it cannot be enforced. Digital reproduction undermines the idea of scarcity, and the immense popularity of file-sharing services such as Napster, KaZaA and Gnutella put the very essence of the ownership of music and copyright laws under review, turning it into a hot potato on many dinner tables in music-land, resulting in a massive controversy between grassroots movements, the government and the music industries.

Nevertheless, the industry's watchdogs, the Recording Industry of America Association (RIAA) and the International Federation of the Phonographic Industry (IFPI), have been carefully protecting their business since its early days. Today, RIAA members create, manufacture and distribute approximately 90 per cent of all legitimate sound recordings produced and sold in the United States.[1] During the last decade, the industry's largest companies and their subdivisions have been making a mass move by consolidating, re-organizing, downsizing and merging between themselves. Hence the architecture of the world's largest music market is easily mapped: five major conglomerates are in control of 75 per cent of business profits, with Universal Music Group in pole position, followed by EMI, Sony Entertainment Group, Warner and BMG. The rest is divided between thousands of independent labels. The international umbrella organization IFPI, which is generally regarded as the "global" counterweight of the RIAA, represents 1,500 record companies and distributors in 76 states.[2]

Worldwide, a movement of heterogeneous communities – some declaring themselves techno-libertarians – is not only taking a stand against the core of the music industry but expanding the debate to government control and media accessibility. From this perspective, the roots of free distribution go back to Richard Stallman's Free Software Movement of the eighties, which launched the concept of common, free content and collaborative creativity, from software programs to music. These movements explore the boundaries of free speech and creative expression in two realms which, although they harbour the idea of an open landscape and liberty, have become regulatory swamps for the professional, the audiophile and the occasional passenger. That is, both the internet and modes of digital (re)production make alternative gateways to the world of content possible. Music is content. From the early days of recorded music to Reboot.fm, music has come a long way.

This article sketches the ongoing controversy around the concept of "open music" as a result of the historic battle for more content, starting from the predigital era (see Part I) and continuing through the new technologies of the digital revolution. Although these new technologies inevitably embrace the idea of a free culture, this free culture is, as Lawrence Lessig states, "*like a free market, filled with property. It is filled with rules of property and contract that get enforced by the state. But just as a free market is perverted if its property becomes feudal, so too can a free culture be queered by extremism in the property rights that define it*"[3] (see Part II). That is exactly where the innovative power of digital audio meets free and open-source software as a *partner in crime*. The increasing popularity of Eric Raymond's alternative business model of the bazaar seems quite suitable for digital audio as well. Digital distribution, consumption and creation seem to combine all the conditions for creating a common space for music: tuning in for online music entertainment is tuning in to a music bazaar, a virtual dynamic market-place in which to exchange files, formats and programs, composed of worldwide file-sharing networks (see Part III). These developments are likely to transform the broadcasting spectrum into a gateway to the commons (see Part IV).

Part I - A Slice of History

> "Music is prophecy: its styles and economic organization are ahead of the rest of society because it explores, much faster than material reality can, the entire range of possibilities in a given code. It makes audible the new world that will gradually become visible..."
>
> Jacques Attali: Noise (1977)

The Early Days

Two centuries ago, nobody would have believed it was possible to record the human voice, let alone music, until Thomas Edison presented his talking machine in 1877 in the New York offices of the *Scientific American*. This cylindrical phonograph, a "marriage between the telephone and the telegraph", was to undergo many attempts at improvement, but it would have to wait almost twenty years until Berliner transformed it to the flat recording disc in 1896. More than ten years later, the US Copyright Act was amended, and Tin Pan Alley publishers established the American Society of Composers, Authors and Publishers (ASCAP) in 1914, as a basis for royalty payments for recorded music, and not just live performance.[4] Today, with over 175,000 member-owners, including the greatest and newest names in American music, ASCAP is a vital, leading-edge organization that over the last three years has distributed nearly $1.7 billion dollars in royalties.[5]

With the invention of the radio in the roaring twenties, a time of American prosperity and optimism, the second foundation was laid for a music business that has today become the bouncing heart of a million-dollar business. In October 1919 America's first radio concern was formed, the Radio Corporation of America (RCA).[6] From the twenties on, radio stations started to pop up like mushrooms, run by radio-set manufacturers, electric utilities, churches and newspapers, without any rules. It became obvious to lawmakers that some type of regulation was needed. Starting in 1926 a Federal Radio Commission, the predecessor of the FCC, was given responsibility for apportioning wavelengths. This allowed corporate broadcasting companies to gain control of the market, with financial mergers greatly accelerating the process. RCA, as both the largest manufacturer of radios and the leading broadcaster, dominated the industry. In 1934, the Federal Communications Commission was formed as the end result of the Communications Act of the same year, charged with regulating interstate and international communication by radio. Almost a century has passed and the FCC has now become one of the most influential organs in US legislation, directly responsible to Congress and responsible for regulating interstate and international communication by radio, television, wire, satellite and cable.

Radio rocks

With regard to the recording industry, it is remarkable that, at first, recording companies did not recognize the immense prospects of radio as a means of distribution, but rather perceived it as a fearsome new technology. Steadily, however, it began to dawn on people that listening to radio was a powerful instrument for increasing business sales. At this time, the "commonwealth" of music was exclusively defined by the captains of industry. Companies like RCA had grasped the market for commercial radio and defined the architecture of broadcasting, organized around demographics and advertisers' interests, and tending towards a coherent musical sound, with ASCAP pulling the strings. As proprietors of the compositions of their members, these organizations exercised considerable power in shaping public taste.[7] As the fifties approached, however, times were about to change. As a response by many broadcasters to the corporate control of the music business, Broadcast Music Incorporated (BMI) was created in 1940. Many broadcasters felt that ASCAP engaged in monopolistic practices and price-fixing, that they ignored the needs of alternative music and discriminated against genres such as country music and rhythm and blues – "hillbilly" and "race" music, as they were called then. Also, in search of cheaper forms of programming, independent radio turned more and more to recorded music. For a time, independent local radio DJs became pivotal figures in the music industry.

Alan Freed – a disc jockey and concert producer – is a personality famous in music history for having unleashed the logical successor to these mouthshut genres on the airwaves as "rock and roll". A white man, Elvis Aaron Presley, fused elements of black and white music into a style that came to be called "rockabilly", a hybrid of black rhythm and blues and white hillbilly music which was acceptable to a "whites-only" society that would not directly embrace black performers. For the first time in music history, music appeared to have an implicit capacity for social change. Moreover, although the genre was immediately rejected by the old generation and branded as "a subversive tool of communism", immoral and despicable (referring to the hidden subtextual sexual allusions), young white America was bitten by the rogue spirit of rock, and the imaginary line between white and black quickly evaporated on the dance floor.[8] The music business itself was touched to the core: *"Small independent record companies called "indies" were experiencing phenomenal growth rates by producing rock and roll records. And the well-established record companies which concentrated on the traditional music were losing a major share of the market".*[9]

Sara Engelen

The transistor radio entered the music market in 1954, and sparked the music revolution as a portable playmate during daytime on the beach and a secret soulmate under one's pillow at night-time. By the mid fifties the independent record companies, united in Broadcast Music Incorporated, had broken the majors' stranglehold on airplay, and BMI-licensed songs dominated the charts.

Cassette underground

But perhaps the most significant conflict between the record and audio industries and the public in the second half of the twentieth century can be found in the controversies surrounding popular uses of the cassette tape.[10] Whereas the sudden rise of independent labels and the exploding popularity of DJs – as mouthpieces for a broad range of "the suppressed" – considerably lowered the threshold for alternative content, the crusaders of innovation could sail with the wind astern with the emergence of the Philips compact audio cassette in 1963. In its handy format and reusability, the cassette tape concealed the power to democratize the audio market-place. Blank tapes were selling like hotcakes, as the empty cassettes enabled music fans to exchange music, copy friends' records or music from the radio, and produce bootlegs, unauthorized concert recordings.

The Grateful Dead, originally a rather obscure band, gained enormous popularity by authorizing people to tape their concerts. People could now record their own music themselves, make compilations of their favourite songs, break them up into pieces and tape everything back together again: the "do-it-yourself" (DIY) generation was born. "Garageband" musicians and artists no longer needed to bargain over their music with recording companies, or collect a small fortune in order to record their music in a professional audio studio: "*Home recording became to music what the single-lens reflex camera was to photography: a means for a mass audience to pursue mass production*".[11] The gates to musical and cultural freedom were irrevocably opened. Precisely because the cassette technology was portable and recordable, it was also used in the production, duplication and dissemination of local music and in the creation of new musical styles. New voices and new kinds of music found new avenues for expression. William

Burroughs, always avant-garde and one of the figureheads of the beatnik generation, saw the Philips cassette recorder as a way to turn words into weapons, ploughshares into swords.[12] For instance, a *World Press* review noted that the significance and extent of cassette tapes became apparent for the first time in 1979 when they were the medium by which the Iranian Revolution spread across the country.[13]

Home taping is killing music

One of the famous success stories of the cross-fertilization between genres, technology and media is hip-hop music: "*To the subculture of hip-hop and rap culture, the mix of audio tape, vinyl and radio was crucial. The radio was only important as a source of sounds to be taped... The "hip-hoppers" stole music off the air and cut it up. Then they broke it down into its component parts and remixed it on tape. By doing this they were breaking the law of copyright. But the cut 'n' mix attitude was that no one owns a rhythm or a sound. You just borrow it, use it, and give it back to the people in a slightly different form*".[14]

Already in this "premature" state of music sharing and copying, the practice of home taping was condemned by the music industry as piracy, through RIAA slogans such as "*Home taping is killing music*", and the recording industry began pursuing the US Congress to amend the copyright laws. Home taping, the industry reasoned, is copyright infringement.[15] Because of the impact of the compact cassette, and the urge to bring the US into line with international copyright law, practices and policies, the US Copyright Act was reviewed. The 1976 act superseded all previous copyright law.[16]

Nevertheless, thanks to "master hoppers" like DJ Kool Herc and Grand Master Flash, hip-hop's boundaries were redefined from a neighbourhood novelty to a worldwide phenomenon that grew into a million-dollar business. They turned the record deck and the turntable into instruments of the gods, and threw pieces of funk, soul, jazz and other music into the melting-pot. Dick Hebdige spoke of the implications of this move in his 1987 book *Cut 'n' Mix*: "*In order to e-voke you have to be able to in-voke. And every time the other voice is borrowed in this way, it is turned away slightly from what it was the original author or singer or musician thought they were saying, singing,*

Sara Engelen

playing... It's a democratic principle because it implies that no one has the final say. Everybody has a chance to make a contribution. And no one's version is treated as Holy Writ."[17]

Today, hip-hop's exuberant and boasting attitude may be disapproved of by some as megalomaniac and discriminating, while for many others the genre still voices the rebellious spirit of going from rags to riches. Moreover, according to the RIAA's 2003 Consumer Profile, rap/hip-hop music is currently the second most frequently purchased genre.

As the above anecdotes from music history illustrate, the evolution of the music industry, in sync with the development of new technologies, can be characterized as a grassroots struggle for more diversified content and greater access to the channels of artistic liberty in the commonwealth of music. The digital revolution was to struggle on: welcome to the next level.

Part II – Going Digital

> "The dark side of the digital revolution can be seen in the aggressive efforts of businesses to enclose the cyber-commons by erecting new proprietary barriers of control over infrastructure, information, and users."
>
> David Bollier

"In the future, records will be made from records" – John Cage (1956)

The spirit of experimentation and play that was once so characteristic of hip-hop music is now more recognizable than ever in digital music. Where these early experimenters were bound by the limitations of the analogue domain for music, digital production elevated the creation of music to an unprecedented artistic creativity and freedom in cyberspace. Programs like Cakewalk Homestudio, Audiotools or Apple's

Garageband considerably lower the threshold to music creation and turn a household computer into a powerful multitrack studio. The great songs of the past are now fragmented and deconstructed to create new content and reshape meanings: techno, drum 'n' base, house music – it all comes together as producers and musicians engage in a dialogue of dazzling speed.

It might be difficult to see how one could add to the genius of the original, but JXL, for example, established a monster hit in 2002 with a remixed version of Elvis's "A Little Less Conversation": by twisting it, bringing up the beats and adding a few echoes here and there he polished the gold until it shone again[18] – a brilliant move even tolerated by Elvis's heirs. DJ Shadow's "Endtroducing", an expansive, intricate and morose tapestry of samples that wove brass, pianos, filtersweeps and hip-hop beats together, became a cult record that found mainstream success, attracting serious hip-hop chinstrokers and casual music fans alike.[19] But let us not jump ahead...

Digital Home Recording

After the punches it had received from "piracy" in a period of economic recession, for the recording industry the advent of Compact Disc Digital Audio in the early 1980s meant solace. Once the market was adopted to the new conditions of the digital music experience, in quick succession a variety of digital and optical storage methods flooded the market, tempting and harassing consumers with a plethora of carrier formats and playback devices. When Sony introduced the Minidisc, it was regarded by many as primarily a recording medium, and hence as the logical successor to the cassette tape, as the CD was to the record. Philips also had a go at grasping the market with the Digital Compact Cassette (DCC) in the early 1990s. Pitched as a competitor to Minidisc, it never caught on with the general public. It shared its form factor with standard analogue cassettes, and players were designed to accept either type of tape. The idea was to provide this backward compatibility so that users could adopt digital recording without having to make their tape collections obsolete. In reality, however, it turned out that consumers are often ready to adopt new technology without such backward compatibility.[20] Cassette sales were steadily declining.

Sony attempted to replace the venerable compact cassette by the Digital Audio Tape (DAT) in 1987. Although this new consumer standard was not using data compression, the format never gained widespread popularity in its intended market, except in professional recording circles. However, the prospect of exact digital copies of copyrighted material was sufficient for the music industry in the US to force the passage of the Audio Home Recording Act (AHRA). The 1992 Act represented a compromise between those who wanted to codify a consumer's right to tape music at home and those who wanted to ensure that the advent of perfect digital copies did not bring about industry-crippling piracy. According to the AHRA, the manufacturers and importers of digital audio recording devices and media must pay a royalty tax to the copyright-holders of music that is, presumably, being copied, in order to compensate them for royalties lost when consumers copy audio recordings at home.[21] On the other hand, the Act offers consumers and digital audio equipment manufacturers immunity from suit for the non-commercial copying of music, but requires that digital audio recording devices should incorporate technical measures to permit only "first-generation" copies of digital music files.[22]

Ten years ago, however, Congress did not anticipate that these technical measures would be inadequate to contain the impending home digital recording explosion that was galvanized by the Internet.[23] Most of the computer software and hardware that pertains to digital music is not covered by the AHRA, because it is not used exclusively for copying music.[24]

Ripping & Burning

With the advent of the recordable and rewritable CD and MP3 technology, CDs could be ripped in no time to MP3 using a personal computer, sent to the other side of the globe at the speed of light, and burned five minutes later on a blank CD. In the wake of the mix, rip & burn revolution of the 21st century, the Fab Five of the music industry hence increased readiness. The recording industry was facing the challenge of the century.

Thousands of FTP sites emerged around the Internet, many maintained by high-school or college students, who used the freely available MP3 software to rip their CD collections into digital computer files, as at that time compact discs did not yet include any copy protection mechanism. The immensely hyped peer-to-peer file-sharing simplified things a little more – as it enabled masses of users to access other users' hard drives and to find and copy their music files.

In 1999, 19-year-old Shawn Fanning was sitting in his dorm room at Northeastern University, Boston, listening to his roommate complain about dead MP3 links, when he came up with the idea for Napster: a sophisticated, online, central music database, with an attractive and synoptic user-friendly interface, where swappers could easily – and free of charge – exchange and download their MP3 files: bootlegs, rare tracks and the latest new releases from major artists. Once completed, Napster was a huge success and became one of the fastest growing sites in history.[25]

The visionary site MP3.com also wrote music history at the turn of the century: a free music-sharing service, with no charge for downloading music. As artists could transfer their music to the site to promote their work, it became a renowned resource for independent musicians. The website featured charts defined by genre and geographical area, as well as statistical data for artists, telling them which of their songs were the most popular. For many artists, the MP3 site became a true vehicle of artistic expression.

As these pioneering downloading sites made the format flourish on the Internet, persistent rumours and misunderstandings about its legality flourished as well, and established its reputation on the market as both revolutionary and controversial. Revolutionary in the sense that it greatly reduced the amount of data required to reproduce audio, while still offering near-CD quality. On the other hand, the blurry guidelines concerning the legitimate use of MP3 caused confusion. Although it is generally considered completely legal to make copies for personal use or to download music when permission is granted by the copyright-holder, it is considered illegal to distribute, trade or sell copies of songs without the permission of the copyright-holder.[26] Perpetrators are accused of piracy.

However, as the guidelines for the legal application of MP3 were subject to multiple interpretations, ripping CDs and distributing songs through sites such as Napster and MP3.com became a commodity for a generation of whizz-kids, artists and, gradually, for the masses. Consequently, as "piracy" became as easy as clicking a mouse, pirates were leaving shore *en masse*.

Copyright

Despite the Internet and MP3's raging popularity, the fruit of progress tasted bitter to the data-lords of industry. As with the Philips compact cassette, the double-edged sword of technology again cut into corporate control. MP3 encouraged a business model that linked artists directly with consumers, bypassing the record companies completely.[27] The government was forced to take action.

As a result of the burst of public acceptance and usage of the Internet, Congress passed the Digital Performance Rights in Sound Recordings Act (DPRSRA) in 1995.[28] This Act gave copyright-owners exclusive rights over public performance by means of digital audio transmission and the exclusive right to receive compensation for the public performance of their music. This allowed record companies to collect a royalty on digital "performances" of sound recordings. In 1998 President Clinton signed the controversial Digital Millennium Copyright Act (DMCA), which changed copyright law in two significant ways. "*First, it provides safe harbors from liability for copyright infringement for online service providers that meet certain conditions. Second, it created two new causes of action, one for manufacturing, using, or distributing products that circumvent technological measures designed to protect copyrighted works from unauthorized copying, and one for impairing copyright management information.*"[29]

Although the DMCA was designed to protect copyright-holders confronted by a new digital world, it could not foresee the future scenarios of the industry. Many, moreover, regard the DMCA as a vague law leaving much room for abuse. Lawrence Lessig stated in *Free Culture*: "*The uncertainty of the law is one burden to innovation. [...] The internet is in transition. We should not be regulating a technology in transition. We should instead be regulating to minimize the harm to interests affected by this technological change, while enabling, and encouraging, the most efficient technology we can create*".[30] The Napster case would put the brand-new battery of laws immediately to the test.

The Napster Case

With its lawsuit against Napster in 1999, the RIAA set a historical precedent in deterring illegal file-sharing. Digital piracy and the fight against it became a hit in media headlines. On behalf of recording industry giants like AOL Time Warner Music, BMG, EMI and Sony Music, Napster was sued for breach of copyright law, as it was accused of founding an illegal business based on the use of copyrighted material that they were not entitled to distribute. The whole file-sharing movement would cost the music industry millions in falling sales and unpaid royalties, while Napster argued that it was merely providing a service – relying on the DMCA – and that it was the users who were doing the distributing.[31]

After an interpretative tournament in court on the applicability of the DMCA and Audio Home Recording Act (AHRA), Napster was found guilty. For instance, Napster believed that shutting down their company was in violation of the AHRA, which immunizes all non-commercial consumer copying of music in digital or analogue form, as the Napster service was intended for the sole purpose of "non-commercial consumer" usage.[32] Napster supporters contended that the law applies to music downloads because the music being copied is for personal use, not redistribution for profit. Many others, however, including the U.S. Justice Department, disagreed because this act was based on digital audiotapes, not Web music.[33] Eventually, the District Court of Appeals refuted all of Napster's defence tactics – also the DMCA's "*safe harbors from liability for copyright infringement*" provision was found irrelevant – and ordered the company to stop allowing its millions of users to download and share copyrighted material without properly compensating the owners of the material.

From 2000 on, legal online music services started popping up on the Internet. In 2002, Roxio acquired Napster and in May 2003 it also acquired the online music service Pressplay, a partner company of Sony and Universal Music. Now in possession of a digital music distribution infrastructure and catalogue rights with all five major music labels, Roxio relaunched a legal version of Napster on the market in 2003. Similar services, like MP3.com, were also tracked down by the RIAA, and were forced to redefine themselves in a legal framework.

Decentralize it

According to Clay Shirky, the RIAA has slowly altered the environment in such a way that relatively efficient systems like Napster were killed, thereby opening up a niche for more decentralized systems like KaZaA and Gnutella: "*Napster's problem, of course, was that although Napster nodes acted as both client and server, the central database gave the RIAA a single target. Seeing this, networks like Gnutella and KaZaA shifted to a mesh of nodes that could each act as client, server, and router. These networks are self-assembling and self-reconfiguring with a minimum of bootstrapping, and decentralize even addresses and pointers to files*".[34]

In spite of these measures, these music-sharing communities have been battling with the same copyright and legal issues as Napster. However, KaZaA is still an operational P2P file-sharing service (and still doing battle with the RIAA) where users can freely download copyrighted files. Gnutella, an open-source program, is especially worth mentioning as an example of community spirit and perseverance. It was invented at Nullsoft, a subsidiary of AOL, and released in March 2000 to the general public from the Nullsoft website. Once it was known that Gnutella was capable of doing the same as Napster, and with AOL merging with Time Warner Music at the time, AOL forced Nullsoft to remove all links to Gnutella from their website. It was too late, though, as in the few hours that the program was on the website it had been downloaded by a large number of people. Once Gnutella was out on the Internet, people who had been able to download it set about reverse-engineering the protocol. As different people had gone about doing the reverse engineering, many different programs using the Gnutella protocol became available on the Internet, e.g. Morpheus, LimeWire, GNUcleus and others.[35]

Ever since, the RIAA has been proved to be very persistent in its prosecution strategy. 2003 was a true *annus horribilis* for file-sharing communities, followed by a new wave of individually targeted lawsuits against hundreds of file sharers during the spring of 2004. Since the beginning of the anonymous lawsuits in September 2003, more than 3,200 file sharers have been charged, the aim being to *"send a message of deterrence, protect the rights of property owners, and foster an environment where the legitimate market-place, both online and at retail, can flourish,"* as Cary Sherman, President of the RIAA, stated.[36] In Europe, it took a little longer for the IFPI to undertake action, but since the spring of 2004 the IFPI has followed the RIAA's policy in filing lawsuits against individuals – aged from 12 to 88.

Piratology

As Katherine Bowrey and Matthew Rimmer (2002) put it:[37] "*One thing that the Napster phenomenon brought unambiguously to the fore was the question of the politics of copyright law*". In the controversy surrounding the digital reproduction of copyright material and its distribution through P2P-networks, much comes down to the interpretation of "fair use", an important doctrine of copyright law. It is obvious that the notion of "fair use" does not apply to large-scale "commercial piracy", defined in IFPI's Commercial Piracy Report[38] as the "*illegal pirate sales of pressed discs, manufactured on factory production lines; CD-Rs, where music albums are copied from a variety of sources onto blank discs using CD burning equipment; and pirate cassettes*". These practices focus on massive export and pursue huge profits by bypassing copyright laws, and have little to do with P2P networks.

However, according to RIAA piracy definitions, even the occasional downloader with no criminal intentions can easily be accused of piracy. Amongst many other categories of music piracy, the RIAA labels as "pirate recordings", for example, "*the unauthorized duplication of only the sound of legitimate recordings, as opposed to all the packaging, i.e. the original art, label, title, sequencing, combination of titles, etc. This includes mixed tapes and compilation CDs featuring one or more artists*". "Online piracy" is defined as "*the unauthorized uploading of a copyrighted sound recording and making it available to the public, or downloading a sound recording from an Internet site, even if the recording isn't resold. Online piracy may now also include certain uses of "streaming" technologies from the Internet*".[39] Although the swiftness of sharing, downloading and sampling music easily triggers the illusion of free distribution and space for personal creativity and experiment, the above-mentioned guidelines leave the music fan with pretty well nothing much left to do with his or her digital freedom.

Fair Users

Furthermore, there is a huge difference between people who use P2P file-sharing to get free music (as in "free beer") and people who actually do something with the music they get from the net (who reserve the right to transform the original). These consumers become 'prosumers' who download, MIX and then burn, who actually become creative. And then there is the huge world of patch programmers, of people who sample not music, but patches, who create music digitally and use each other's patches for sound effects. For this very broad and heterogeneous category of users, P2P file-sharing provides a vibrant cultural feedback loop through community networking (see below).

Piracy is a flag that covers many issues. As Armin Medosch[40] has argued: "*Piracy does not simply exist because there are bloody-minded people who don't care for the rules and laws of the civilised world. It tends to emerge whenever there is a hegemonic power that asserts itself by establishing a trade monopoly. A monopoly, by its very nature, cuts out competition by other traders and destroys existing means of trade. People deprived of their traditional way of making a living resort to criminal activity. The hegemonic power, itself not averse to using violence to force others into submission, considers itself to be the law and defines others' activity as piracy [...] Hollywood film studios, software giants and multi-national record companies have chosen to use the term 'piracy' to cover all kinds of copyright infringement. This might turn out to backfire [...]*".

And it did: the immense popularity of Napster and the perseverance of its successors have vividly shown that there is a huge demand for alternative methods of distribution, for more alternative gateways to content, and for more versatile methods of consumption in music. From a users' perspective, media coverage of the Napster case exposed a public need by publicizing the complaints of defiant Napster users, supported by prominent "alternative" musicians. For them, "*copyright law disempowered creative talent and led to the ripping-off of artists and fans alike, it was argued. The law entrenched corporate greed*".[41]

Some Facts & Figures

From the industry's perspective, in turn, many musicians, music studios and recording companies do equate Napster with piracy. For them, "*copyright is the main way of *encouraging investment in new artists, and simply allocates what is justly deserved".* From this angle, *"digital piracy sponsored by unauthorized file-sharing technologies forestalls the development of new media services, preventing consumers from getting the best possible legitimate access to digital media as well as damaging the income potential of past and future artists and the corporations that support them".*[42]

A conclusive study of the impact of peer-to-peer file-sharing and music downloads on the record industry is difficult to obtain, and each side can show figures to their own advantage. There is a swamp of inconsistent information and articles on the Internet about industry-related facts and figures. While the RIAA, for example, states that there has been a 31 per cent drop in sales of recorded music since file-sharing became popular,[43] many critics mention other factors that can be held responsible for sales drops, such as the decline in new releases, market trends, and the rise of the DVD. A recent report from the Harvard Business School and the University of Carolina kicked up more dust by pointing out that illicit file-sharing has an effect on record sales that is *"statistically indistinguishable from zero".*[44] Other sources have demonstrated that P2P actually encourages sales, by introducing listeners to new material which is then purchased in CD format.

Nevertheless, Metallica, for example, a heavy metal band, unambiguously joined the RIAA opinion and filed a suit against Napster, accusing the company of shoplifting, copyright infringement and racketeering. *Exit light*: more than 300,000 Napster users were fingered as copyright violators. In contrast, a Web-based survey by the Pew Internet Project 2004[45] pointed out that 60 per cent of the musicians and songwriters it surveyed did not believe the RIAA's efforts to halt file-sharing through lawsuits would benefit them. Additionally, 35 per cent of the survey believed free downloading had helped their careers, 37 per cent believed it had not had any effect and only 5 per cent believed it had exclusively hurt their careers. While the file-sharing battle leaves many musicians caught in the middle, artists like Chuck D and bands like Public Enemy and Ween openly promote file-sharing and the downloading of their music. The Pew Internet Project, quoted above, found that 83 per cent of those interviewed had provided free samples of their music online, of which a significant number say free downloading has helped them sell CDs and increase the crowds at their concerts.

Sara Engelen

Giving the Wookie what he Wants

Expanding the debate to the Free and Open-Source community: an article dating from 2000, entitled "Linux Leaders: Beware of Napster"[46] quotes Linus Torvalds, refining: "*Of course you should be able to sue over copyrights. The one good lawsuit in the whole Napster case is the one by Metallica: a suit by the actual authors*". The article also quotes Stallman, giving the other side of the story: "*Indeed, Richard Stallman, long known for arguing that there shouldn't be any commercial-style software at all, says Napster was a 'good idea' because it helps draw people to concerts. Though many music-industry analysts disagree, Stallman argues that musicians make their real money through concerts and other merchandising, since, he says, most of the profit from CD sales is going to the music labels*".

Tim O'Reilly in particular has added some interesting food for thought to the argument. In his article "Piracy is Progressive Taxation, and Other Thoughts on the Evolution of Online Distribution",[47] he formulates some lessons from his experience in the publishing world that also apply to the music industry. In fact, these lessons provide a glimpse into the future.

Summarizing Lesson 1: Obscurity is a far greater threat to authors and creative artists than piracy. "*Many works linger in deserved obscurity, but so many more suffer simply from the vast differential between supply and demand. Tens of thousands of musicians self-publish their own CDs; a happy few get a recording contract. Of those, fewer still have their records sell in appreciable numbers. The deep backlist of music publishers is lost to consumers because the music just isn't available in stores.*"

Lesson 2: Piracy is progressive taxation. "*For all of these creative artists, most laboring in obscurity, being well-enough known to be pirated would be a crowning achievement. Piracy is a kind of progressive taxation, which may shave a few percentage points off the sales of well-known artists (and I say "may" because even that point is not proven), in exchange for massive benefits to the far greater number for whom exposure may lead to increased revenue.*"

Lesson 3: Customers want to do the right thing, if they can. "*Online file sharing is the work of enthusiasts who are trading their music because there is no legitimate alternative. Piracy is an illegal commercial activity that is typically a substantial* problem only in countries without strong enforcement of existing copyright law. The simplest way to get customers to stop trading illicit digital copies of music and movies is to give those customers a legitimate alternative, at a fair price."

Lesson 4: Shoplifting is a bigger threat than piracy. *"Because an online copy is never out of stock, we at least have a chance at a sale, rather than being subject to the enormous inefficiencies and arbitrary choke points in the [analogue] distribution system."*

Lesson 5: File-sharing networks don't threaten book, music, or film publishing. They threaten existing publishers. *"Over time, it may be that online music publishing services will replace CDs and other physical distribution media, much as recorded music relegated sheet music publishers to a niche and, for many, made household pianos a nostalgic affectation rather than the home entertainment center. But the role of the artist and the music publisher will remain. The question, then, is not the death of book publishing, music publishing, or film production, but rather one of who will be the publishers."*

Lesson 6: "Free" is eventually replaced by a higher-quality paid service. *"Services like Kazaa flourish in the absence of competitive alternatives. I confidently predict that once the music industry provides a service that provides access to all the same songs, freedom from onerous copy-restriction, more accurate metadata and other added value, there will be hundreds of millions of paying subscribers. That is, unless they wait too long, in which case, Kazaa itself will start to offer (and charge for) these advantages."*

Lesson 7: There's more than one way to do it. *"And that's the ultimate lesson. 'Give the wookie what he wants!' as Han Solo said so memorably in the first Star Wars movie. Give it to him in as many ways as you can find, at a fair price, and let him choose which works best for him."*

Legalise it

With the introduction onto the market of online music stores and MP3 players, the industry obviously came across in *"giving the wookie what he wants".* Although Apple's iPod was not the first digital audio player on the market, it was certainly the one that grabbed worldwide media attention. With the introduction of the iPod on the music market, the best of both worlds – downloadable and legal music – was conceived as a portable digital audio player with the smooth integration of an online music service.

Showing up on the market in 2001, the iPod started out as a high-end music device for sophisticated gadgeteers, but subtle refinements, price decreases and media attention transformed it into a truly mainstream product. Offering different capacities for storage, and available also in a mini-version, this gadget – fast, easy, and flashy – is clearly riding the waves of high-speed communication.

With Apple's iPod and the recent introduction of its complementary iTunes Music Store, Apple CEO Steve Jobs marked out a clear path for the future and established a solid position for online music on the legitimate market-place. In 2003, *Time* magazine called the Music Store the coolest invention of the year. Featuring a huge music library offering songs from all major music companies and sophisticated extras, the iTunes Music Store has become a smash hit with music fans, professional musicians and the entire music industry. Nevertheless, fast technologies demand fast adaptation. In the meantime, many competing manufacturers have shipped a series of MP3 players with iPod-esque capacities and sizes but lower prices. For example, after launching its own sophisticated digital audio-player, VAIO Pocket, Sony declared outright war on Apple with the introduction of its online music store Connect and the new Network Walkman.

Part III – Open Source can be an Ally

> "... He who receives an idea from me, receives instruction himself without lessening mine; as he who lights his taper at mine, receives light without darkening me..."
>
> Thomas Jefferson

So far the babbling bazaar

Raymond describes the Linux community as "*a great babbling bazaar of differing agendas and approaches... out of which a coherent and stable system could seemingly emerge only by a succession of miracles*".[48] In the previous section, an attempt was made to situate existing agendas in the music community. Without claiming to give an exhaustive overview, in the following paragraphs we will sketch some music-industry trends and some approaches adopted to try and cope with the current transitions, ranging from the industry's adjustments to their implications for the consumers and artists. Although the latter may have defined how they want their music served, and got it – in some way, the industry is still the *chef de cuisine*. It seems that record companies can still dictate what music can be made and when and how it can be sold. By treating music as a close-content and close-source product, the industry is far from creating any stable or open environment, nor for the distribution and consumption of music, nor for its creation.

However, to return to the source – the endless process of music creation – a free and open-source spirit is unquestionably present: "*Digital technology and the Internet can empower artists to reach a worldwide audience and to build upon each other's ideas and imagination with extremely low production and distribution costs. Many software developers, through both the open-source software initiative and the free software movement, have long taken advantage of these facts to create a vibrant community of shared software that benefits creators and the public*".[49]

Planet Spreadsheet

Now that a variety of online music services have hit the market, consumers are beginning to experience some of the less obvious consequences of the online music hype. In the arena of digital technologies, the panic about piracy – "*one swapped file more is one sale less*" – has for several years prompted record companies to toy with protecting CDs against copying. Thousands of CDs incorporating anti-copying technology have already been sold to unsuspecting consumers. Furthermore, MP3 is no longer the only bar in town when it comes to compressing audio for computer storage.

New online music services include technology known as digital-rights management (DRM), which can "lock" copyright-protected songs, create artificial scarcity, and make it harder for consumers to share that music illegally. However, the lack of a "holistic" view in the music industry is forcing the music consumer to migrate to a kind of "planet spreadsheet"[50] in order to enjoy music. A wave of competing and incompatible DRM products has now hit the market from Microsoft, Apple Computers, Sony, IBM, Real-Networks and others, creating interoperability headaches for consumers.[51] Moreover, many companies with their own online music stores only support their own digital audio players with their own software and music data-compression formats. Record and distribution companies can all too easily turn DRM into a powerful tool for locking customers into proprietary technologies. The notion of secure downloading of digital files also raises another key issue: that of consumer privacy. Any secure downloading process would probably involve the collection of personal information about the user such as name, credit card number or e-mail address.[52]

The struggle for access

Another consideration regarding these new forms of digital distribution is that the historical battle for more access to content certainly does not end here. As Shirky states in his article "The Music Business and the Big Flip": *"Industry harvests the aggregate taste of music lovers and sells it back to us as popularity, without offering anyone the chance to be heard without their approval. The industry's judgment, not ours, still determines the entire domain in which any collaborative filtering will subsequently operate. A working 'publish, then filter' system that used our collective judgment to sort new music before it gets played on the radio or sold at the record store would be a revolution"*.[53]

Online music sale does not change the top-down filtering system of the industry. Instead, it changes the form of distribution. Downloading individual songs offers some flexibility, helping overcome the long-entrenched "tyranny" of the album – notice the sudden proliferation of compilation albums – but it does not expand the music menu. There is still a long way to go. For instance, the lack of songs by the Beatles – amongst many others – has been an oft-cited gap in the supply of online music stores. Some artists (or their publishers) are reluctant to support the pay-per-song-system. For example, Madonna and Radiohead simply "won't allow" single-song downloads, the latter still arguing that its songs are an integral part of a conceptual whole – the album.⁵⁴ This contrasts with P2P networks, where the variety of titles is limited only by the imaginations of each one of the tens of millions of P2P users, and where "unpublished" artists can freely provide their music, being independent of the majors for releasing material. New technologies to track down "illegal networks" are looming, however. Audible Magic, for instance – supported by a big lobby of RIAA affiliates – is a company that provides appliances (described by critics as "the silver bullet for P2P infringement") that can passively monitor a network's data traffic and provide a range of reporting and control functions specific to P2P transactions.⁵⁵ Last year a test was conducted with the technology at an American university, but it was ended after students complained about invasion of privacy.

To recall Tim O'Reilly's lessons: *File-sharing networks don't threaten publishing. They threaten publishers.* Various voices from artists' circles suggest that the tide may indeed be turning, as they are putting the "old" architecture of music publishing under reconstruction. To start with some heavyweights: two musical pioneers who have shaped, succeeded in and challenged the last three decades of popular music have joined forces under a new mandate. Early in 2004 rock veterans Peter Gabriel (also co-founder of DO2, Europe's biggest business-to-business digital music provider) and Brian Eno introduced a provocative new musicians' alliance at Midem, one of the world's largest music festivals. This alliance would go against the industry grain by letting artists sell their music online instead of only through record labels, indicating that the music industry is finally beginning to react to the challenges it faces. MUDDA, short for Magnificent Union of Digitally Downloading Artists, aspires to offer alternatives throughout the entire process of music-making, and even to change the nature of content. For example, they no longer see a song as a finished piece of content, but rather embrace the new capacities of digital reproduction and modification to sell mixes of songs, selling music as a process, not a product. Ideas include having an artist release a minute of music every day for a month, as a teaser, or posting several versions of the same song. To quoting Peter Gabriel: "*It's a critical time where the music business is being transformed – some voluntary changes and some involuntary changes, [...] unless musicians think about what's going on and how it could change their situation both creatively and commercially, [musicians] will be at the end of the food chain as usual*".⁵⁶

Sara Engelen

Nomad Netizens

Seen from a bottom-up perspective, "*Musicians are often unwilling to speak out against the tight constraints of their record labels, afraid of biting the hand that feeds. But an increasing number of artists are embracing the changes in digital technology as a potential revolution which may free them from the shackles of the commercial record industry*",[57] as the composer Miriam Rainsford put it.

After the relentless pursuit of Napster, many netizens felt oppressed by the tightening forces of industry. The constraining regulations, the lawsuits, the track-down technologies and the piecemeal supply of incompatible formats considerably restrict the *Lebensraum* of many artists and fans. For them, restricting the use of the Internet and, consequently, the possibilities of P2P-networking, is like cutting the connection to the mother ship – the source of information. As Cascone (2002) pointed out: "*Composers of glitch [electronic, postmodern] music have gained their technical knowledge through self-study, countless hours deciphering software manuals, and probing Internet newsgroups for needed information. They have used the Internet both as a tool for learning and as a method of distributing their work. Composers now need to know about file types, sample rates, and bit resolution to optimize their work for the Internet. The artist completes a cultural feedback loop in the circuit of the Internet: artists download tools and information, develop ideas based on that information, create work reflecting those ideas with the appropriate tools, and then upload that work to a World Wide Web site where other artists can explore the ideas embedded in the work*". [58]

In order to offer some resistance to the iron grip of the big players of the music industry, many alternative visions have been circulating on the net, many of them inspired by the Free and Open-Source Movement.

Given enough eyeballs, all bugs are shallow

As a response to the aggressive "crush the connector" tactics of the RIAA, darknets emerged, reminiscent of the cassette underground of the seventies. As Shirky[59] observed: "*[it's] a kind of social Visa system... instead of being able to search for* resources a certain topological distance from you, you search for resources a certain social distance from you". Freenet for example is free software that lets you publish and obtain information on the Internet without fear of censorship. To achieve this freedom, the network is entirely decentralized and publishers and consumers of information are anonymous. A short comment from the 25-year-old project founder, Ian Clarke: *"Copyright is just one way of encouraging artists to create. And, ultimately, free speech is more important than your current copyright laws"*.[60]

Similar forms of digital networking enable musicians and fellow music enthusiasts to interact on a horizontal level. Moreover, artists' feedback on songs and digital data tools can in a way be regarded as an implementation of Linus's Law – *given enough eyeballs, all bugs are shallow.* So it is for music: as a practical implementation of Linus's Law, Garage-Band.com, for example, leaves the "debugging" to the artists. In response to the growing number of musicians who view peer-to-peer as a valid and useful promotional avenue, GarageBand.com is a site that hosts independent music and uses a peer-review process to identify hot bands – instead of the "filter, then publish" system of RIAA members. The site has focused its efforts on building a community of musicians. Artists themselves must rate 30 other songs before they can upload their music, and the most popular songs land in the charts.[61] This collaboration by many small gatekeepers in the field of expertise guarantees a more democratic choice and supply of music, genres and styles.

Whoops, I Did It Again

Even fans can become part of the cultural feedback loop. Artists might disapprove of piracy on the record, but off the record they admit that so-called pirates or hackers can do them a great favour. Through file-sharing, they can contribute to an artist's commercial success. For example, it seems it has become an off-the-record commodity in artistic circles to supposedly "lose" unpublished records in cyberspace. Stars including Madonna, Eminem, Sir Elton John and Britney Spears have all condemned unauthorised downloading, with Oasis branding fans who downloaded their latest album as "thieves". But when Eminem's last album was mysteriously leaked to the public, the industry agreed that it actually helped boost sales.

Proving once again that a CD does not have to be commercially available to be pirated, in 2003 Radiohead's album *Hail to the Thief* was leaked onto the Internet some three months before its scheduled street date. *"Despite the band's seemingly blasé attitude towards the leak, it's particularly interesting to note that Greenwood (a band member) sees the Internet as a viable distribution medium for recordings that may otherwise go unreleased"*. Progressive taxation indeed. *"A seasoned, critically acclaimed band like Radiohead likely doesn't have a problem finding labels to pick up its recordings, but for smaller, less-established artists, the Internet can be an incredibly effective distribution tool"*. [62]

A growing number of artists are apparently following the trend, with rapper 50 Cent selling four million copies in two months despite being leaked onto the Internet. Rock group Linkin Park imposed strict security on their latest album, *Meteora*, avoiding Internet leaks – selling 800,000 copies, while their 2001 debut sold 4.8 million copies in the US – but was reported to have been downloaded as many as another eight million times.[63]

Copyleft

Richard Stallman's concept of copyleft licensing offers a valuable alternative to artists who feel that DRM practices and constraining copyrights go against the free spirit of music. *"By adapting this principle to suit creative works, musicians have a means to license the sharing of their works without unnecessary technical constraint. The Open Audio License and Larry Lessig's Creative Commons project are examples of the practical application of copyleft principles in the arts, which musicians may easily utilise without the need for specialist legal knowledge"*.[64]

The Open Audio License (OAL) is an attempt to give artists a chance to release songs, musical works or audio recordings that anyone may freely copy, share, perform and adapt. In exchange for receiving rights from the artist in excess of those granted by copyright itself, the user is required to give proper credit to the author for his or her creation and gift to humanity.[65] As the preamble of the OAL explains, this licence is designed to serve as a tool of freedom for artists who wish to reach one another and new fans with their original works. It allows musicians to collaborate in creating a pool of "open audio" that can be freely modified, exchanged and utilized in new ways. Artists can use this licence to promote themselves and take advantage of the new possibilities for empowerment and independence that technology provides. It also allows the public to experience new music, and connect directly with artists, as well as "super distribution" where the public is encouraged to copy and distribute a work, adding value to the artist's reputation while experiencing a world of new music never before available.[66]

Both GarageBand.com (see above)[67] and Opsound – an experimental record label – offer Creative Commons licences. Opsound is a kind of music laboratory that explores the possibilities of developing a gift economy among musicians: anyone is invited to contribute their sounds to the open pool, using a copyleft licence. Work in the open pool is available to be listened to, reconfigured, recombined and remixed, and also released by Opsound (and other) microlabels both on the Internet and in the physical world.[68]

Open music

Many free and open-source audio tools have already been developed by collaborative communities of software users and music makers, as a radical statement against the digital cage of music, created by copyright and proprietary technology. They not only adapt the open spirit that is already audible in the new digital world but have really implemented free and open-source software, providing a real alternative to expensive commercial software and professional gear. To name but a few: *Audacity* is an open-source sound-editing program that makes changing complex sounds as easy as using a word-processor. The application truly has a global audience – it has been translated into over 16 languages. SourceForge.net announced the program in July 2004 as project of the month.[69]

There are high expectations of *Ogg Vorbis,* a new professional audio file format, which is hailed by many as the logical successor to MP3. The Vorbis project was started following a September 1998 letter from Fraunhofer Gesellschaft announcing plans to charge licensing fees for the MP3 format. In contrast, Ogg Vorbis usage is completely unrestricted and licence-free, meaning that anyone can use it for any purpose they like without having to use proprietary software or pay licensing fees. Vorbis's specifications are in the public domain, its libraries are released under a BSD-style licence, and its tools are released under the GPL.[70]

Another initiative to increase awareness of the issues related to free expression and contemporary artistic tools sharing the spirit of free software is the *Agnula* project. The main purpose of the Agnula project is to develop two GNU/Linux distributions devoted to audio and multimedia that are based completely on free software. The project began in April 2002 and is a European Commission-funded accompanying measure running under Key Action IV.3.3 (Free software development: towards critical mass), one of the themes of the Fifth Framework Programme.[71]

Pd (aka Pure Data) is a real-time graphical programming environment for audio, video and graphical processing. It is the third major branch of the family of patcher programming languages known as Max. Pd was created to explore how to refine further the Max paradigm with the core ideas of allowing data to be treated in a more open-ended way and opening it up to applications outside audio and MIDI, such as graphics and video. The work of many developers is already available as part of the standard Pd package, making the whole package very much a – rapidly growing – community effort.[72]

As for the Open Audio License, such projects help foster a community of creators and performers who are free to share and build on each other's work. These "prosumers" are allowed to experiment, recycle and remix in the cultural feedback loop made possible by copyleft licensing and free and open-source software. Like the digital case that holds the music and the tools that created it, creations can be endlessly redefined. Through networked communication, the social dimension of music production, distribution and consumption is expanded, as these peer-to-peer networks create platforms to learn and become skilled in an open dialogue between masters and disciples and between artists and their fans: "*This also frees their audience to share works that they enjoy with others, all for the purpose of creating a rich and vibrant public commons*".[73]

Part IV – Broadcasting to the future

> "Freedom of speech does not exist in the abstract. On the contrary, the right to speak can flourish only if it is allowed to operate in an effective forum – whether it be a public park or a radio frequency."
> William J. Brennan Jr.

Reclaiming the Airwaves

Although public broadcasting is now almost the default model for broadcasting in the Western world, and is generally supposed to be "free from political interference and commercial pressure", radio has gone through many periods of revolt and experimentation. Back in the early 1930s Bertolt Brecht launched his historical critique, noting that radio was a one-sided medium when it should be two-sided, and advocating a system of open communication by recommending an apparatus that would allow the audience to receive as well as transmit, and to speak as well as hear.[74] Many grassroots initiatives for more access to the airwaves have characterized the history of broadcasting. Whether called pirate radio, free radio, community radio or independent radio, they all strove to gain more access to the airwaves and to minimize government control and commercial despotism.

Nevertheless, according to Bollier, "*the loss of a public commons in broadcasting must be counted as one of the twentieth century's great civic and cultural losses*".[75] For instance, the USA 1996 Telecommunications Act raised a storm of protest among media critics, academics, journalists and cybercitizens alike, as it dismantled existing laws designed to protect the public's access to diverse media content. The Telecom Act singled out radio for sweeping ownership deregulation and paved the way for Clear Channel to expand from 40 stations to 1,225, and, in the process, exert unprecedented control over the industry. Local radio stations were gobbled up by conglomerates like Clear Channel, allowing it not only to dominate the airwaves, but also to become America's predominant concert-venue owner and tour promoter. Since 1996 there have been 30 per cent fewer station owners, resulting in less local news and local programming, as formats are programmed at headquarters.[76]

From the perspective of a radio station, one would be eager to think that the digital era has provided the freedom necessary to allow the medium blossom, to let it finally become what it was originally designed to be: a public asset, not private property. Considering all the benefits of digital broadcasting – that is, more choice (more stations can be broadcast within a comparable amount of radio spectrum), simple tuning, great reception, no interference and nice extras like text and information ("metadata") on your digital radio set – it does seem as if the digitization of the medium should be able to overcome the impediments of the past. However, free-radio activists strongly condemn digital audio broadcasting (DAB) because of the high costs involved, which are prohibitive for small broadcasters. For local communities, analogue radio broadcasting still is a powerful weapon, as acting locally can produce results globally.

Free Radio Berkeley

In the United States, Free Radio Berkeley was instrumental in helping to create an ever-growing movement to promote micropower broadcasting – i.e. radio broadcasting on a very low wattage to a small local group within a limited reach – movement to liberate the airwaves and break the corporate broadcast media's stranglehold on the free flow of news, information, ideas, cultural and artistic creativity.[77] The issue of micropower broadcasting was brought to the forefront by an African-American, Kantako, who started his own 10-watt FM station – "Human Rights Radio" – in Springfield, USA, to serve his small community in 1986. Inspired by Kantako and as a direct response to the Gulf War and the media coverage of the conflict, Stephen Dunifer began Free Radio Berkeley in 1993. A social activist, he stated that control of the airwaves by those whose interests were those of the government was to say the least disturbing, and a direct threat to civil rights. The initiatives of both Kantako and Dunifer were tracked down and they were prosecuted by the FCC. Dunifer was accused of infringing broadcasting licences, harming the regulatory scheme itself, interfering with other broadcasters and causing irreparable harm to the community.

Ever since, the case of Free Radio Berkeley has walked a long trail of lawsuits and court hearings at which the FCC has kept insisting that Free Radio Berkeley was an illegal initiative. As a reaction to the corporate predators in the media, the "Reclaiming the Airwaves" project was launched, organized by affiliates of Free Radio Berkeley. Through a broad range of community networking – over the Internet and over the airwaves – it has prompted hundreds of micropower broadcast stations to take to the air across the United States, and in other countries as well. The book has meanwhile become an illustrious manifesto for popular free radio. "Reclaiming the Airwaves" eventually had the desired effect. Recently, an independent study found that low-power stations *"do not pose a significant risk of causing interference to existing full-service FM stations. In response to the finding, a senator drafted the Low Power Radio Act of 2004"*.[78] Under the proposed rules, restrictions that have made it impossible for any low-power station to be licensed in any of the top 50 radio markets would be made overdue. Community-radio activists hope the bill will eventually lead to a flowering of small broadcasters in urban areas where the radio spectrum is dominated by large commercial stations.

Casting over the Web

With respect to local broadcasting initiatives, it is assumed that online audio streaming, or webcasting, is an interesting prospect for radio. As the digital downbeat of low-power radio, webcasting stations can provide programming to meet the needs of specific and under-represented groups. They can provide a forum for cultural minorities and religious and linguistic communities, and can address issues that are too small to attract much attention from mainstream, ratings-driven media. Recording and performing artists, in particular, can benefit greatly by gaining more outlets for airplay, especially on a local or regional level, or in genres that are currently under-represented on commercial radio.

However… As a result of the Digital Millennium Copyright Act (DMCA), webcasters were required to compensate performers or record companies for the use of their recordings. Consequently, many small-scale webcasters were forced into bankruptcy by high sound-recording royalty rates. Once again the DMCA was hotly debated by the defenders of free speech and music, as this measure was not in line with previous practice: analogue broadcasts have always been exempt from the requirement for sound recording performance licence. This prompted the US non-commercial web broadcasting community to launch a successful campaign against the regulations proposed in the DMCA. In 2002, college radio stations all over the United States stopped broadcasting music over the Internet for one day, in protest against the new regulations.[79] This led to the drafting of the Small Webcaster Settlement Act, under which the royalty-collection organizations were to take a fairer, more balanced approach to small webcasters.

Opening yet another door in the free distribution of music, P2P-networking can be webcasting's sparring partner. *Last.fm* – which started out as a small-scale open-source project – appears to point in this direction. Last.fm offers a streaming radio service, where users build up their individual music profiles by listening to customized music streams. Through collaborative filtering, software users can quickly find new music by connecting up with people who have similar tastes in music.[80]

Wireless Future

As the next stage is high-speed wireless communication, Wi-Fi is likely to be facing a future of blue skies. Short for "Wireless Fidelity", Wi-Fi is wireless technology that operates under the Federal Communications Commission's rules and regulations for unlicensed radio frequency communications. The popularity of Wi-Fi comes from its low cost, flexibility and ease of use. Just like a household cordless phone, Wi-Fi relies on low-power radio signals to communicate between a computer and a base station with a broadband Internet connection. The unlicensed status of Wi-Fi means that no access charges or service fees are required for using the airwaves. The open Wi-Fi standard means that dozens of competing companies manufacture Wi-Fi equipment, leading to lower prices and higher quality. Because of the low cost and wide availability of Wi-Fi hardware, many models have emerged for deploying and sustaining community wireless networks.[81]

In this context, the concept of "open spectrum" for managing free-data networks goes one step further in offering an alternative and more open approach to the distribution of the airwaves. Open spectrum is a plea to transform the broadcasting spectrum available to all as commons, instead of treating it as a scarce resource. According to Werbach,[82] "*open spectrum would allow for more efficient and creative use of the precious resource of the airwaves. It could enable innovative services, reduce prices, foster competition, create business opportunities and bring our communications policies in line with our democratic ideals. Despite its radical implications, open spectrum can coexist with traditional exclusive licensing, through both designated unlicensed wireless "parks" and "underlay" of non-intrusive communications in licensed bands. Both approaches should be encouraged. The risks are minimal, while the potential benefits are extraordinary*".

In this data network topology, Armin Medosch sees a new premise of freedom which he describes "*not as a metaphysical concept and not even on the level of political philosophy, but on a very pragmatic level as a hacker type of freedom – the freedom to access and use communication networks under a minimum of restrictions, empowering individuals and communities to make the best use of those networks as they see fit [...] Over the last few years, loosely connected groups all over the world have started to build free networks, networks which are owned and maintained by their users and are largely free of state and corporate influence. This fledgling free-network movement is not one coherent group, campaign or strategy, but another one of those multitudes, a free association of individuals who work together for a common goal under a loose umbrella of a few principles and with a lot of enthusiasm*".[83]

Predictions for the future envision a new era in mobile computing, made possible by combining Wi-Fi with the new cellular-data networks the phone companies are rolling out. Considering the various combinations of digital music, online distributing, community networking, streaming audio and good, old-fashioned radio broadcasting, the future of music may indeed be bright.

CASE: Reboot.fm – Against corporate control of radio

At the crossroads of the diverging fields of force of technology, various online platforms for the global new media art community have emerged against the *narrow-*

casting of music industry – avoiding the mainstream. These platforms support the creation, presentation, discussion and preservation of contemporary art and music that uses new technologies in significant ways. For example, Rhizome.org,[84] the Xchange Network,[85] and Radioqualia[86] are pioneering international projects in combining digital music, free and open-source software, networking technologies and new explorations of radio over geographically dispersed communities, including artists, curators, writers, designers, programmers, students, educators and new media professionals.

In this line, Reboot.fm[87] was (and is: today Reboot.fm is still providing streaming radio and fighting for a new frequency) a temporary, Berlin-based radio project that ran from 1 February until the end of April 2004. Reboot.fm was part of the third edition of the Berlin biennial for contemporary art, housed under Bootlab, a Berlin-based media centre which hosts over 30 groups and individuals working with media-related projects including digital audio and video production and similar areas of digital production. As a local and international peer-to-peer network of groups, individuals and non-commercial radios, Reboot.fm combined the advantages of traditional radio and new open-source software, to broadcast on 104.1 and provide streaming audio for 100 days.

In a four-pronged approach to free radio, Reboot.fm combines good old "terrestrial" radio with digital media and open-source software in the larger context of streaming media. Reboot.fm engages in the battle against highly regulated media architecture, widespread commercial media concentration and industrial ownership of the production and distribution of music. As a perfect symbiosis of "old" and new technologies, this project is once again a plea for more commons in music, on the airwaves and on the net.

Open Radio

The first element in the Reboot.fm[88] project is low-power radio. Legalizing low-power FM frequencies in larger cities, like Berlin, is a precondition for allowing more variety. Those stations must be run on a non-commercial basis, reaching nothing like the large audiences targeted by commercial radios.

Secondly, Reboot.fm embraces the net as the most open and most deregulated of all the available options, in combination with free-software development. This means more than just the obligatory live stream: it means using the net as a tool for decentralized, collaborative production and exchange. Reboot.fm relies on existing local nodes, in Berlin and elsewhere, that are already producing potential radio shows in abundance, and provides both an infrastructure to make them audible and a context to give them the resonance they deserve. By including a simple but strictly open model of editorial in the software which manages the radio schedule, additional hierarchies of mediation and representation are avoided or become part of social organization. The scheduler supports a decentralized editorial model and remote access. Local editors can be far away, and far-away editors can be local, as long as there is Internet access. Different groups of editors select and organize their own programme in the form of "time slots", which are again dealt with within a general programme scheme.

Thirdly, Reboot.fm is also a software development project, and as such it wants to be to commercial radio software what Control-Alt-Delete is to the average Windows computer: a reboot from scratch. Every product is determined by the technologies that are used to create it, and so the founders of the project are convinced that talking about free radio is impossible without talking about open source: "*We think of free software as more than just a more transparent, more inclusive, more secure and cheaper alternative to closed, commercial code. Beyond these obvious advantages, free software takes into account that all software is social software: the structures it creates shape the working environment of its users. So, rather than reproduce the technological restrictions that reduce the job of most radio editors to the administration of an autopilot, the aim is to make available a system that allows both individual and collective decisions at any stage of the process*". Reboot.fm for example provides streaming audio using the open-format Ogg Vorbis, described above.

Last but not least, Reboot.fm is part of the struggle for the free exchange of cultural data – be it the development of technologies to distribute digital music in decentralized networks, or practical resistance to restrictive copyright legislation. The organizers are convinced that neither radio producers nor radio listeners need so-called Rights Management Systems imposed on them, to decide what they are allowed to copy, download, play or listen to – they should be perfectly capable of managing all that on their own. A syndication network must allow radio editors to browse, preview, download and rebroadcast any radio program whose original creator has agreed to make it distributable. "*In the end, radios produce not only live broadcasts, but also great archives – and we don't see how these can be legally bound to just gather dust.*"

With a tactical combination of campaigning, research, open-source programming, editorial process, media politics, open licensing and open archives, and endless debates, Reboot.fm takes a holistic and incremental approach to software development and the largely commercially defined area of software culture. However, Reboot.fm is aware of the contradictions that surround it: how can you keep a radio free without relying on endless hours of unpaid work? How can you keep a radio open without just broadcasting any random piece of nonsense? And how can you deny the professionalism of commercial radio without sounding amateurish? Their answer is simple: "*When it comes down to these questions, we know that we are working on problems, not on solutions. The best result that we can imagine is a radio that makes audible the very conditions under which it is produced. The selection of news and music will differ from other stations, they will not be separated from each other according to a strict set of rules, but mixed just as people think it is appropriate. Some moderators will talk too fast, some records will have scratches, and a lot of things will happen that normally never happen on the radio. As a whole, Reboot.fm will be a radio that has edges, and that's not really something we intend to fix*".

Discussion: From hot potato to food for thought

This article's chronological overview of technological (r)evolutions in the music business, and the controversies that go with them, shows a constant field of tension between consumer culture on the one hand and the corporate music industry on the other. The digital revolution has changed the form rather than the content of the debate. The potato has become digital, but it is hotter than ever.

A quote from Lawrence Lessig's article "Protectionism will kill recovery!" captures the debate in a nutshell: "*Intellectual property is vital to growth. [...] [Copyright and patent laws] should be to encourage competition and innovation. It should never be to *protect the old against the new*".[89] File swapping and new forms of broadcasting – over the net and over the airwaves – open up a wide horizon of possibilities for production, distribution and consumption in the music industry. As these technologies are still in transition, the legal framework they operate in needs to be balanced fairly, to serve the interests of both the givers and the receivers of the goods this industry produces, in a flexible interpretation of the notion of "fair use".

The grassroots battle for more accessibility to the tools of communication is a swelling cry for attention in the face of concentration and globalization trends in the music industry, and their regrettable consequences. This social dynamism, made possible by peer-to-peer networking and the open spirit of the free and open-source movement, is tangible in every corner of the industry. Following the conclusions of Axel Bruns's study on cultural communities and networking,[90] "*culture has emerged from a tactical underground or consumer subculture to now establish institutions of its own; [...] this was also aided by the vacuum of strategic control over emerging computer-based consumer and communication technologies, which allowed users to form structures of use and communication of their own*", as was the case with Napster.

Throughout the history of music, the communities that emerged from this vacuum of control (cassette underground, P2P networks, pirate radio) have always functioned as platforms for alternative visions and controversy. These communities are therefore indispensable for progress and innovation, whether or not they eventually go on to be licensed. Hence, considering the trend to segmentation at the grassroots levels of the music industry, in contrast to the homogenizing principles of corporate control, it is particularly interesting to note Bruns's conclusions. To McLuhan's much-quoted concept of a homogenized global *village*, Bruns preferred the image of a global *metropolis* that is shaped by the communication pandemonium of the Internet. "*Instead of the overarching structure of the 'global civil society', various different 'suburban' communities [...] can live in this metropolis [...] with its own individual neighbourhoods, consisting of suburban main squares that are surrounded and serviced by electronically interconnected specialist stores and offices [...], suburban newspapers and their offices [...], libraries [...], and information boards [...]*". The music bazaar is inevitably part of this image. Both the free and open-source movement and an expanding network of artists, producers and amateurs find themselves, in a colourful market-place, shouting on the same side, negotiating the best deal.

Sara Engelen

Almost a century ago, the industrial revolution inspired the cold, mechanical, industrial *Metropolis* of Fritz Lang's expressionistic movie where machines controlled the repressed, impoverished masses. The digital revolution has enabled the mass to become the wired (soon wireless) multitude. Community-based initiatives like Garage-Band, Creative Commons, Pure Data and Reboot.fm are all striving to tear down parts of the big Music Machine, reverse-engineering it towards an open and self-fertilizing common space for music. As Tim O'Reilly put it: *"There's more than one way to do it"*.

Notes

[1] Recording Association of America. Retrieved from http://www.riaa.com/about/default.asp.
[2] International Federation of the Phonographic Industry. Retrieved from http://www.ifpi.org/site-content/about/mission.html).
[3] Lawrence Lessig (2004). *Free Culture*. New York: The Penguin Press.
[4] Paragraph based on R. Garofalo (1999). From Music Publishing to MP3: Music and Industry in the Twentieth Century. [Electronic Version] *American Music* (Fall 1999). University of Illinois Press. Retrieved from http://www.findarticles.com/p/articles/mi_m2298/is_3_17/ai_62052928/pg_2.
[5] American Society of Composers, Authors and Publishers. Retrieved from http://www.ascap.com.
[6] F. Sicart (2000, Feb). AOL, RCA, and The Shape of History. Retrieved from http://www.goldeagle.com/bears_lair/sicart020200.html.
[7] R. Garofalo, *op. cit.*
[8] T. Shacklett (?). African Influence on Early American "White" Music. Retrieved from http://home.earthlink.net/~tshack2/termproject/shacklett/preface.htm.
[9] J.G. Hornberger (1990). Racism, Control, and Rock and Roll. Freedom Daily. *The Future of Freedom Foundation*. Retrieved from http://www.fff.org/freedom/1090a.asp.
[10] R. Garofalo, *op. cit.*
[11] S. Jones, (1990). The Cassette Underground. The Cassette Mythos. *Autonomedia*. Retrieved from http://www.halcyon.com/robinja/mythos/SteveJones.html.
[12] W. Levy (1990). The New Orality. The Cassette Mythos. *Autonomedia*. Retrieved from http://www.halcyon.com/robinja/mythos/WilliamLevy.html#LEVBBC.
[13] S. Jones, *op. cit.*
[14] S. Jones, *op. cit.*
[15] S. Jones, *op. cit.*
[16] Association of Research Libraries (ARL) Staff. TIMELINE: A History of Copyright in the United States. *Association of Research Libraries*, Washington, DC. Retrieved from http://www.arl.org/info/frn/copy/timeline.html.
[17] Dick Hebdige. *Jahsonic.com*. Retrieved from http://www.jahsonic.com/DickHebdige.html.

[18] C. Long (?). Elvis vs. JXL – A Little Less Conversation. *BBC*. Retrieved from http://www.bbc.co.uk/manchester/music/reviews/singles/2002/06/10/a_little_less_conversation.shtml.

[19] N. Southall (2003). DJ Shadow – The Private Press. *Stylusmagazine.com*. Retrieved from http://stylusmagazine.com/review.php?ID=301.

[20] DAT. *The Free Dictionary*. Retrieved from http://encyclopedia.thefreedictionary.com/DAT.

[21] AHRA. *Drmwatch.webopedia.com*. Retrieved from http://drmwatch.webopedia.com/TERM/A/AHRA.html.

[22] J. Laferrera (2004). Limits to the Copying of Digital Content: Where We've Been and Where We're Going. *Tech Law Bulletin*. Retrieved from http://www.gesmer.com/publications/new/14.php.

[23] T. Hall (2002). Music Piracy and the Audio Home Recording Act. *Duke Law & Technology Review*. Retrieved from http://www.law.duke.edu/journals/dltr/articles/2002dltr0023.html.

[24] C. Jones (2000). Metallica rips Napster. *Wired News*. Retrieved from http://www.wired.com/news/politics/0,1283,35670-2,00.html?tw=wn_story_page_next1.

[25] S. Crosse, E. Wilson, A.M. Walsch, D. Coen, C. Smith.Napster. *P2P Networks*. Retrieved from http://ntrg.cs.tcd.ie/undergrad/4ba2.02-03/p4.html.

[26] T. Costanzo (1999). MP3: overview and issues. *Library and Archives Canada*. Retrieved from http://www.collectionscanada.ca/9/1/p1-261-e.html.

[27] R. Garofalo, *op. cit*.

[28] Seongkun Oh (1996). Legal Update – The Digital Performance Rights in Sound Recordings Act of 1995: Exclusive Performance Rights for Digital Transmission of Copyrighted Works. *Boston University Journal of Science & Technology Law*. Retrieved from http://www.bu.edu/law/scitech/volume2/2JSTL17.pdf.

[29] B.R. Socolow (2000). Recent Decisions Shed Light on Digital Millennium Copyright Act. *Loeb&Loeb*. Retrieved from http://www.loeb.com/CM/Articles/articles25.asp.

[30] Lawrence Lessig, *op. cit*.

[31] S. Crosse, E. Wilson, *et al., op. cit*.

[32] Napster: First Amendment Right? *Freeessays.cc*. Retrieved from http://www.freeessays.cc/db/14/cia63.shtml.

[33] Napster Case. Retrieved from http://www.e-businessethics.com/napster.htm.

[34] C. Shirky (2003). File-sharing Goes Social. Clay Shirky's Writings About the Internet. *Economics & Culture, Media & Community, Open Source*. Retrieved from http://www.shirky.com/writings/file-sharing_social.html.

[35] E. Creedon, D. Humphreys, B. Kelly, S. Kinane, K. Elstner. *P2P Network*. Retrieved from http://ntrg.cs.tcd.ie/undergrad/4ba2.02-03/p5.html.

[36] A. Jordan (2004). RIAA Intensifies Fight Against Music Piracy. *TechNewsWorld.com*. Retrieved from http://www.technewsworld.com/story/34021.html.

[37] K. Bowrey & M. Rimmer (2002). Rip, Mix, Burn. *First Monday*. Retrieved from http://www.firstmonday.dk/issues/issue7_8/bowrey/.

[38] The Recording Industry Commercial Piracy Report. *IFPI*. Retrieved from http://www.ifpi.org/site-content/library/piracy2004.pdf.

[39] Anti-piracy. *RIAA*. Retrieved from http://www.riaa.com/issues/piracy/default.asp.

40 A. Medosch. Piratology. *Dive/Kingdom of Piracy*. Retrieved from http://kop.fact.co.uk/DIVE/cd/text/index.html.
41 K. Bowrey & M. Rimmer, *op. cit.*
42 K. Bowrey & M. Rimmer, *op. cit.*
43 N. Strauss (2003). NYT Musicians Speak Out Re: File-Sharing Music and RIAA. *Free-Music-Now*. Retrieved from http://www.free-music-now.com/music_sharing/file_sharing_music/file_sharing_music_msg31527/file_sharing_music_msg31527.shtml.
44 Profs debunk myth of file-sharing Armageddon. *Dmeurope.com*. Retrieved at http://www.dmeurope.com/default.asp?from=f&ArticleID=1380&cachecommand=bypass&Print=true.
45 L. Rainie & M. Madden (2004). Pew Internet & American Life Project. *www.pewinternet.org*. Retrieved from http://www.pewinternet.org/pdfs/PIP_Musicians_Prelim_Findings.pdf.
46 L. Gomes (2000). Linux leaders: Beware of Napster. *The Wall Street Journal Online*. Retrieved from http://zdnet.com.com/2100-11-520941.html?legacy=zdnn.
47 P. O'Reilly (2002). Piracy is Progressive Taxation, and Other Thoughts on the Evolution of Online Distribution. *OpenP2P.com*. Retrieved from http://www.openp2P.com/lpt/a/3015.
48 M. Truscello (2003). The Architecture of Information: Open-source software and Tactical Poststructuralist Anarchism. Retrieved from http://www.postanarki.net/truscello.htm.
49 EFF Open Audio Licence. *Radio Parallax*. Retrieved from http://www.theparallax.com/radio/stuff/oal.html.
50 M. Grebb (2004). Record Industry Wants Still More. *Wired News*. Retrieved from http://www.wired.com/news/digiwood/0,1412,63332,00.html.
51 Recording industry and online music services battle over copyright laws. *CNN.com*. Retrieved from http://www.cnn.com/2000/LAW/05/16/mp3.napster.suit/.
52 T. Costanzo, *op. cit.*
53 C. Shirky (2003). The Music Business and the Big Flip. Clay Shirky's Writings About the Internet. *Economics & Culture, Media & Community, Open Source*. Retrieved from http://www.shirky.com/writings/music_flip.html.
54 Glimmer of hope for music industry? *The Staronline*. Retrieved from http://star-techcentral.com/tech/story.asp?file=/2004/2/10/itfeature/7246609&sec=itfeature.
55 http://www.audiblemagic.com/.
56 E. Mitkos (2004). MUDDA: Musicians' Alliance Cuts Against Industry Grain. *DigitalJournal.com*. Retrieved from http://www.digitaljournal.com/news/?articleID=4052.
57 M. Rainsford (2003). A Musician's Take on File Sharing, DRM, and Copyleft Licensing. *Open P2P.com*. Retrieved at http://www.openp2p.com/pub/a/p2p/2003/06/10/musician_pov.html.
58 K. Cascone (2002). The Aesthetics of Failure. *Mediamatic.net*. Retrieved from http://www.mediamatic.net/cwolk/view/8470.
59 C. Shirky, File-sharing Goes Social, *op. cit.*
60 X. Jardin (2002). P2P App's Aim: Defend Free Speech. *Wired News*. Retrieved from http://www.wired.com/news/technology/0,1282,56063,00.html.

61 http://www.garageband.com.
62 S. Gassior (2003). New Radiohead CD leaks onto Internet early. *The Tech Report*. Retrieved from http://tech-report.com/onearticle.x/4939.
63 Gloom settles on global CD sales. *BBC News*. Retrieved from http://news.bbc.co.uk/2/hi/entertainment/2931589.stm.
64 M. Rainsford, *op. cit.*
65 EFF Open Audio Licence. Retrieved from http://www.eff.org/IP/Open_licenses/20010421_eff_oal_faq.html.
66 EFF Open Audio Licence, *op. cit.*
67 K. Dean (2004). GarageBand.com Leaves Door Open. *Wired.com*. Retrieved from http://www.wired.com/news/digiwood/0,1412,63720,00.html.
68 http://www.opsound.org/opsound/about.html.
69 http://sourceforge.net/potm/potm-2004-07.php.
70 Ogg Vorbis. Retrieved from http://en.wikipedia.org/wiki/Ogg_Vorbis.
71 AGNULA – GNU/Linux Audio package. *Electronic Music*. Retrieved from http://www.em411.com/show/alert/372/1/agnula_gnu_linux_audio_package.html.
72 About Pure Data. Retrieved from http://puredata.info.
73 EFF Open Audio Licence, *op. cit.*
74 Bertolt Brecht on Radio and Interactivity. *City of Sound*. Retrieved from http://www.cityofsound.com/blog/2004/02/bertolt_brecht_.html.
75 D. Bollier (2002). "Reclaiming the Commons." *FreeRepublic*. Retrieved from http://www.freerepublic.com/focus/news/727212/posts.
76 M. Ivins (2003). Media Concentration is a Totalitarian Tool. *Boulder Daily Media* on Common Dreams Newscenter. Retrieved from http://www.commondreams.org/views03/0131-09.htm.
77 Free Radio Berkeley. *Freeradio.org*. Retrieved from http://www.freeradio.org/.
78 R. Singel (2004, June 5). Senators Back Low Power Radio. *Wired News*. Retrieved at http://www.wired.com/news/digiwood/0,1412,63731,00.html.
79 Webcasting. Retrieved from http://www.slais.ubc.ca/courses/libr500/02-03-wt1/www/S_Goard/webcasters.htm.
80 http://www.last.fm.
81 A. Townsend (2004). Neighborhood Wireless Networks: Best Practices. *Wireless Commons*. Retrieved from http://www.wirelesscommons.org/.
82 K. Werbach (2002). Open Spectrum: The New Wireless Paradigm. *New America Foundation Spectrum Policy Program*. Retrieved at http://werbach.com/docs/new_wireless_paradigm.htm.
83 A. Medosch (2004). Not Just Another Wireless Utopia: Developing the Social Protocols of Free Networking. *[RAM]5 Open-Source Media Architecture*. Retrieved at http://rixc.lv/ram/en/public07.html.
84 http://rhizome.org/info/.
85 http://xchange.x-i.net/.
86 http://www.radioqualia.net/.
87 http://www.reboot.fm/.

[88] Paragraph based entirely on information on the Reboot.fm site and the press release on *Openserver*, retrieved from http://openserver.cccb.org/modules.php?name=News&file=article&sid=72.
[89] L. Lessig (2004). Protectionism will kill recovery! *Wired.com*. Retrieved from http://www.wired.com/wired/archive/12.05/view.html?pg=5.
[90] A. Bruns (1998). 'Every Home Is Wired': The Use of Internet Discussion Fora by a Subcultural Community. Retrieved from http://www.nicoladoering.net/Hogrefe/bruns/www.uq.net.au/~zzabruns/uni/honours/thesis.html.

Acknowledgements

Many thanks to Armin Medosch, Tadek Krzywania, Marleen Wynants and Hugo Bulteel for their valuable comments and inspiring suggestions.

Biography

Sara Engelen (born 1978) graduated in Communication Science at K.U.Leuven and obtained a Masters in Applied Audio-Visual Communication Sciences. The European Erasmus exchange project enabled her to live in Barcelona and complete her studies at the Universitat Autònoma de Barcelona (UAB) – Facultat de Ciències de la Comunicació. Her thesis was entitled "Future Females: The image of women in science-fiction movies of the 80s and 90s". She has worked on the editorial staff of regional television stations and as production assistant at various international cultural events, amongst other odds and ends. Since 2004 she has been part of the VUB R&D Interface Cell team and co-developer of the VUB CROSSTALKS network.

CYCLING	WALKING
SKATING	RUNNING
←	→
BIKEWAY	WALKWAY

Open Source, Science and Education

Marc Nyssen & Frederik Cheeseman

Starting from our personal experience and taking an historical perspective, we analyze the impact of "Open Source" on ICT, mainly in scientific and educational applications. Illustrated with our own observations and anecdotes from the past 30 years in the field of scientific and educational computation and networking.

Personal experience

When Bell Labs started sending versions of the UNIX system to academic institutions, including ours, we got tapes containing the source code of the full system. For quite some time, the only advantage of this was the mere fact (often overlooked in the open-source discussion) that this allowed us to upgrade the software to make use of improved versions of the compiler and improved versions of the libraries. But then our research in biomedical image processing suddenly required additional functionality, quite specific to us and of little or no commercial utility at the time. Thanks to our access to the system's source code, and with the help of several correspondents of Usenet newsgroups otherwise unknown to us, we were able to develop the necessary drivers, incorporate them into the system and perform our experiments successfully.

The "production line" of researchers and educators requires computer support at all stages: from simulation through data acquisition, processing and the extraction of relevant conclusions, right down to archiving. There is no such thing as a single, "vertical" software package that includes support for all these needs.

Researchers and educators are typically, computer users who have to put together their own computer tools, tailored to their own particular needs, from the building blocks of "horizontal packages" – each of which meets a specific need, but none of which is able to cater for their full range of needs.

This "building blocks" concept – resulting in small, specialized programs – was the concept behind the traditional UNIX applications: the operating system reinforces it by providing straightforward inter-process communication channels.

Talented (and some less talented) programmers have built components to fulfill their own needs and put their achievements in the public domain for others to share: if any technology lends itself to sharing, software does!

In this context, the GNU C compiler, a portable compiler for the C programming language, has been a major enabling tool. The GNU C compiler can quite easily be adapted to new computer architectures, and will then compile itself on the new machine, after which any system or application can be installed on it.[1-2]

Over the past 25 years, this has been a major tool in support of porting operating systems and applications to new hardware platforms. The GNU C compiler, on which many programmers collaborated, is reason enough in itself to advocate open-source technology.

The advent of networking, and the very positive collaborative spirit that characterized the early networking days (in the 1970s, 1980s and early 1990s), increased researchers' potential to design their own software working environment (on a UNIX/Linux platform) "with a little help from their friends". The real people behind the birth of the Internet (and their attitudes) are well described by Salus[3] and Naughton.[4]

Personal experience 2

The maintenance of a classroom full of personal computers, to be used by students on a day-to-day basis for their practice sessions, is a system administrator's worst nightmare. The instability of the Windows environment and its security shortcomings are well known to all of us. Viral infections, user-installed programs (it's rumored that students at some universities like to play games), system crashes that destroy the system's integrity, stealthily installed spy-ware that interferes with the normal functioning of the machine are just some examples of the many things that can go wrong, and that are bound to go wrong.

Faced with this ongoing, time-consuming chore, we decided to use the open-source GNU-Linux, (currently Fedora Core 1) to streamline the daily maintenance of Windows machines, which are needed by several colleagues. The main idea behind this set-up for our infrastructure was to make use of network file systems for users' files: all user data would reside on a network file server, so that data would become independent of the workstation, but accessible from anywhere on the university.

No matter where you log in, you will find the directories with your data to work on. Data residing on the hard disk of the workstations (client machines) would be considered completely unprotected and would be liable to be lost at any time.

Data on the server, however, would be protected and backed up regularly.

So, how did we do this?

We configured the machines as multi-booting systems that can start up in Windows or in GNU-Linux (currently Fedora Core 1), enabling those who wish to do so to use the Windows environment but also enabling users and system administrators to work in the Linux environment.

Installing

The machines came with a pre-installed version of Windows which took up the whole hard disk. There was only one partition: the Windows partition. So we had to create free space for the new GNU-Linux partitions. After shrinking the Windows partition which used to occupy the whole hard disk, we used the newly freed disk space to create the new GNU-Linux disk partitions we needed. Here we installed the GNU-LINUX system within its own partitions – "swap" and "root" – where system files and user directories reside.

Once the installation of GNU-Linux was complete, it "saw" the Windows 98 partition and integrated it into the GNU-Linux boot process – and it also ensured that the

Windows partition could be accessed by the (running) GNU-Linux system through the use of the well-known *mount* command, i.e.:

```
mount -t vfat /dev/hda1 /w
```

will mount the Windows 98 partition /dev/hda1 on the directory /w, created by us. The *-t* option of the mount command has *vfat* as an argument (parameter in the command line) because Windows uses long filenames on the FAT filesystem, e.g.:

```
[root@minf13 /]$ mount -t vfat /dev/hda1 /w
[root@minf13 /]$ ls -l /w
total 1504
drwxr-xr-x   4 root    root    8192 Oct 23 2001 My Documents
```

and

```
[root@minf13 /]$ mount -t msdos /dev/hda1 /w
[root@minf13 /]$ ls -l /w
total 1512
drwxr-xr-x   4 root    root    8192 Oct 23 2001 mydocu~1
```

The last mount command has -msdos as an argument instead of vfat and so we only get part of the long filename. On the GNU-Linux partition we installed a complete bit-to-bit – local to the machine – backup of the Windows 98 partition with the the well-known UNIX *tar* archiver program, i.e.:

```
[root@xxxxxx]$ mount
/dev/hda1 on /w type vfat (rw)
tar czvf windows.tgz /w
```

In this example the compressed (-z option of the tar command) tar file *windows.tgz* file is created (-c option of the tar command) using verbose output (-v option of the tar command) on the screen, with the tar-archive windows.tgz as output file.

Access to the server file system, on which the users' files reside, is accomplished by "nfs mounts" under Linux and via the Windows Explorer application in Windows, fed by the "SAMBA" open-source file server on the main campus server machine. In both cases, one "sees" the same files becoming accessible.

Maintenance

A small shell script named *cl* (clear) living on the GNU-Linux partition allows us to reset Windows completely in its pristine form.

The content of this *cl* script is:

```
mount -t vfat /dev/hda1 /w
rm -rf ./w
tar xzvf windows.tgz
```

Resetting a whole classroom (20 systems) using this *cl* script takes only about 30 minutes.

An extra backup of the Windows 98 installation in its tar archiver form (windows.tgz) is also stored on one of our central GNU-Linux servers. These central servers are accessed with the open-source secure file transfer program, or sftp.

This method also allows us to make the maintenance of two laptop classes (one for each VUB campus) manageable.

Based on our own experience over some thirty years, we can conclude that the only applications surviving over the long term are those that were available in open source. Indeed, most commercial vendors have disappeared, gone bankrupt or been gobbled up by other companies, and support for their applications has evaporated with them into the mists of time. Moreover, application platforms are constantly changing – resulting in "improved" (but different) runtime libraries and graphical interfaces.

Source-code availability has proven to be the only guarantee of the long-term survival of an application.

Peer review

From a completely different viewpoint comes the question of a "peer reviewable" code. Source code can be peer-reviewed, whereas binary code cannot. Although this argument may be considered somewhat academic, from time to time a really nicely written program can achieve the quality of techno-poetry. Another aspect is quality control.

The peer review concept, the repeatability/control of the experiments and permanent questioning are deeply rooted in our scientific tradition, making us suspicious of "black box" software packages.

Although software researchers have spent huge amounts of energy "proving" software correctness and generating automatically "correct" programs, they have not yet come up with the magic formula, and a mere visual inspection of the code or computer-assisted tracking, using an on-line debugger, is the best we can achieve right now.

For this we need the source of the program in question ("May the source be with you!"). The well-known "annotated code of the UNIX operating system" by John Lions,[5] the development of the MINIX system by Andrew Tanenbaum,[6] and Linux source code, are all irreplaceable educational and learning tools for software engineers.

File formats

A subtle and dangerous way in which companies and other entities try to gain a hold over users is by imposing proprietary file formats. Recent history has shown that changes in management, or a company take-over, can lead to legal harassment concerning the use of file formats that have been tolerated for a long time but then suddenly, without warning, are no longer – as illustrated by the Unisys company's threat to charge for the use of the "gif" image format.[7] Naive users will not even be aware of exactly what file formats they use every day; scientific users should be aware of this, as should official bodies (see "institutional concerns", below).

Economic aspects

This means that we have to organize! Networking and computational logistics for research and education are far below industry standards.

Three tools can enable us to continue working:
- open-source and free software
- improved efficiency, making investments last longer

- flexibility, allowing users to play an active part in meeting their own infrastructural needs.

In the majority world, open-source and free software often represent the only economically viable possibility, as financial resources are lacking. To put it another way: free software is a real blessing for these countries, as it potentially enables them to work in complete legality without a software budget.

Institutional concerns

The Open Source concept appears to have been discovered only recently by the institutional, legal and political worlds. In our view, the matter of software patents – protecting the meritorious inventor – is completely overshadowed by the potential for legal actions initiated by financially strong companies purely in order to kill competition, either by paying better lawyers or by prolonging a case beyond the financial reserves of the weaker party. The absence of patentability is the only guarantee that such legal actions will have no grounds. In a recent (January 2004) opinion to Minister Van Mechelen, a committee set up by the Flemish Scientific Council made following recommendations:[8]

1. There is a need for a better understanding of the meaning of "open-source software", "proprietary standards or data formats", "open specifications", "free specifications" and "open standards"
2. The authorities should not regulate "open-source software"
3. "Open standards" should be encouraged
4. Specific action in research, awareness-raising and ICT normalization can encourage the use of "open standards".

This wise series of recommendations first defines clearly what we are talking about and then states that there should be no *a priori* rules for or against any software technology: it says that the most appropriate should be used, but comes out clearly in favor of open formats.

Reading between the lines, however, we may conclude that the public authorities cannot force citizens to buy proprietary software to enable them to exchange information with the administration – otherwise they would be going against recommendations 2 and 3.

So far, we have seen little evidence of this in everyday practice. Indeed, official electronic documents and forms – for submitting project proposals, tenders, etc. – are often distributed in proprietary formats, forcing citizens to buy proprietary software.

Let's hope that the change in awareness that is developing, will change this in the near future.

Conclusions

Thanks to the concept and existence of open-source software, scientific and educational users can build and take part in building the support for their own production lines, in accordance with their needs and within the scope of their limited resources. In doing so, they can collaborate with and contribute to the work of their colleagues who are facing the same problems. The integration of commercial, non-open-source software is possible, but in our experience these commercial solutions usually work for only a very limited time-span.

Notes

[1] The GCC homepage: http://gcc.gnu.org/.
[2] Richard M. Stallman and the GCC Developer Community, *Using GCC: The GNU Compiler Collection Reference Manual*, October 2003, ISBN: 1-882114-39-6.
[3] Peter H. Salus, *Casting the Net*, Addison-Wesley Publ. Co.; 1st edition, 21 April 1995, ISBN: 0201876744.
[4] John Naughton, *A Brief History of the Future: the origins of the Internet*, Weidenfeld and Nicolson, September 1999, ISBN: 1585671843.
[5] John Lions, *Lions' Commentary on UNIX 6th Edition with Source Code*,??ASIN: 1573980137.
[6] Andrew S. Tanenbaum, Albert S. Woodhull, *Operating Systems Design and Implementation*, Prentice-Hall Inc., ISBN 0-13-630195-9.
[7] Michael C. Battilana, "The GIF Controversy: A Software Developer's Perspective", http://cloanto.com/users/mcb/19950127giflzw.html.
[8] Werkgroep Open-Source Software, Vlaamse Raad voor Wetenschapsbeleid, Rapport "Advies 86 – Open-Source Software", 22 januari 2004.

Biographies

Marc Nyssen is Professor of Medical Informatics at the Faculty of Medicine, Vrije Universiteit Brussel, in Jette.

After graduating in electrical engineering (electronics and computer engineering) and obtaining a PhD, he was one of the architects of the VUB's early Internet, in the early 80s. As an eager and grateful user, he is in daily contact with open-source developments, their creators and their teachers.

Frederik Cheeseman is a commercial engineer who has a good deal of experience in telecommunications thanks to the time he has spent in the Belgian Army (Signal Corps) and the Belgian State Railroad Company. Added to that professional experience are the years working as a systems and network administrator at the Vrije Universiteit Brussel. Frederik has a strong preference for open-source projects.

**Les Bruxellois paient 15% des impôts du pays.
6% seulement sont attribués à Bruxelles.**

Open Standards Policy in Belgium

Peter Strickx & Jean Jochmans

Introduction

The basis of this text was created in December 2003 after nightly discussions with some colleagues on standards and interfaces. Despite the fact that the existing e-gov building blocks from FEDICT were all built with open standards – the Federal Network (FedMAN – TCP/IP), Middleware (Universal Messaging Engine – XML/HTTP(s)), the Federal Portal (www.belgium.be – HTML and support for Internet Explorer, Mozilla, Opera) – there was a need for a more formal agreement between the different Federal Administrations.

Our goal is to create a framework to enhance the flexibility and interoperability of the various back-office systems. In order to benefit from new technologies like PDAs, digitaal thuisplatform, etc., in bringing government information and applications to citizens, enterprises and civil servants, we wanted an information model that was not tied to any platform or product but based on open specifications/open standards.

The members of the PICTS (Permanent ICT Steering Committee) provided invaluable feedback to help keep this text above all pragmatic. Key contributions came from Jorg Leenaards (IT director Foreign Affairs) and Frank De Saer (IT Director Economic Affairs).

These directives and recommendation are but a first step in improving the information flow between the federal administrations, their customers (citizens, enterprises, employees) and partners (other governments and public services).

The next paragraphs state the objective, define the key terms and present the directives and recommendation.

1 Objective

In compliance with the State Secretary for e-government's strategic memorandum, government services can only be improved via rapid, transparent, user-friendly, efficient and effective communication with their customers (citizens, enterprises and civil servants). The basic principles are:
- transparency: hide the complexity of the internal organization;
- unique data collection: "authoritative sources" will collect and update information, and other public services will have to consult these "authoritative sources" first;
- simplification of administrative formalities;
- customer focus: ultimately, certain rights will need to be granted automatically;
- intention-based services and information: government services and information will be communicated according to customers' interest rather than the different internal roles and responsibilities;
- protection of privacy;
- avoiding the digital divide: the integration of new technologies must increase the efficiency of public services, irrespective of the channel (people/computers) used to deliver these services;
- no additional costs for the user, and reduction of costs in the long term;

In order to create a truly "connected" government, the seamless integration of the various back-office systems and interoperability between different levels of government is essential. The communication protocols and data formats therefore need to be standardized.

Owing to the ever-increasing pressure on government budgets in general, and more specifically on the ICT budget, an efficient use of government's financial resources is mandatory. In order to re-use (totally or partially) "custom-built" software, limit dependence on service providers and at the same time guarantee long-term support for these applications, the federal administrations need the unrestricted availability of and access to the source code.

Depending on the actual problem, the use of open-source software, commercial software or a combination of both will represent the best value for money. The federal administrations are best placed to decide what is most appropriate.

The next paragraph defines the key terms used in the directives and recommendation.

2 Definitions

2.1 Open specification

An "open specification" must be free of charge, available on-line and detailed enough to develop an implementation (a reference implementation).

2.2 Free specification

A "free specification" must be open (ref. 2.1) and must not involve legal restrictions (other than "open-source licences") that complicate implementation, distribution and/or use.

2.3 Open standard

An "open standard" is a "free specification" (ref. 2.2) and must be approved by an independent standards organization.

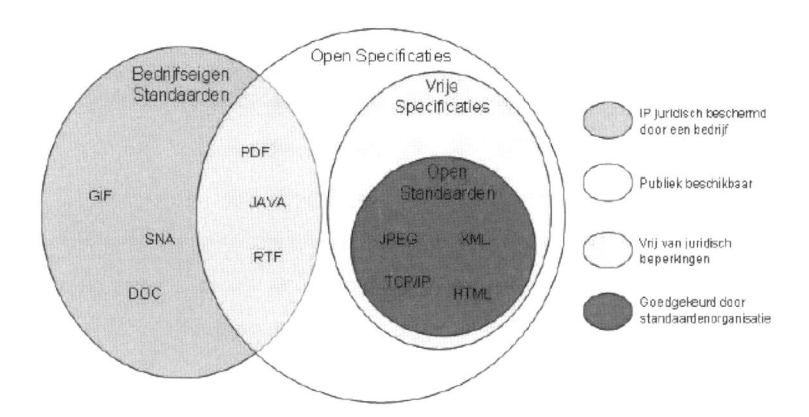

Current examples of open specifications, free specifications and open standards.

2.4 Proprietary platform

A proprietary platform is defined as a computing system (hardware, software or a combination of both) where the applications depend on elements for which there are no open specifications and/or open standards.

2.5 Federal administrations

The federal administrations are defined in this document as: the federal public services, the public planning services, the public social-security institutions, the federal semi-public services, the State Council and the Audit Office.

3. Directives[1]

3.1 The federal administrations agree to use exclusively open standards/open specifications for data archiving and data exchange/communication. These will be defined by consensus by the PICTS (Permanent ICT Steering Committee) and will begin to be used after a formal agreement by the federal administrations.

3.2 The federal administrations will develop and implement migration plans for "legacy" applications to comply with directive 3.1 The migration period will be part of the formal acceptance of an open specification/open standard by the federal administrations.

3.3 The federal administrations will have "ownership rights" to all "custom-built software". A formula of "co-ownership" with the software developer is a possible alternative allowing for re-use and distribution within federal administrations without the formal consent of the software developer. The custom-built software will always be supplied in source code and without any licensing rights. The federal administrations will be able to make this software available to other federal administrations as "open-source software".

3.4 When purchasing software, the federal administrations will preferably have recourse to public procurement, whose allocation criteria are based on criteria such as TCO (Total Cost of Ownership) (such as the costs related to *business continuity*, compatibility with existing equipment, etc.) and value for money, while complying with directives (3.1), (3.2) and (3.3).

4. Recommendation

When purchasing ICT products and services, the federal administrations will seek to avoid lock-in to proprietary platforms.

Note

[1] This directive and recommendation do not apply to the defence computer systems which are used to support operations.

Bibliography

Open-source software use within the UK Government
    http://www.ogc.gov.uk/index.asp?id=2190&
Guide to the choice and use of open-source software licences for administrations (France – ATICA)
    http://www.adae.pm.gouv.fr/article.php3?id_article=172
Open Source for the Federal Administration (DE)
    http://www.kbst.bund.de/Themen-und-Projekte/Software-,74/Open-Source.htm
QinetiQ Report "Analysis of the Impact of Open-Source Software" is available at:
    http://www.govtalk.gov.uk/interoperability/egif_document.asp?docnum=430
IDA OSS Migration Guidelines (November 2003)
    http://europa.eu.int/ISPO/ida/export/files/en/1618.pdf
Further information on OSS is available at: http://www.demo-transit.douane.gouv.fr
Open-Source Software (Vlaamse Raad voor Wetenschapsbeleid - Flemish Science Policy Council)
    http://www.vrwb.vlaanderen.be/pdf/advies86.pdf

Biographies

Peter Strickx holds an MSc in Computer Science with a specialization in Artificial Intelligence from the Vrije Universiteit Brussel where he graduated in 1987. From 1987 to 1989 he worked as a research assistant with Prof. Luc Steels (VUB). During his decade at Sun Microsystems Belgium he held various management positions in Sales & Marketing as well as in more technical areas such as sales support.

Jean Jochmans has been involved in Belgian social security IT matters for more than 20 years.

After having been responsible for the implementation of the electronic employer's quarterly declaration to the social security in the late eighties, he took over the management of the IT department of the Crossroads Bank for Social Security in 1995.

As such he also takes part in federal and European IT committees where he represents the Belgian social security institutions.

Part III

Ethics
&
Bottlenecks

NO STANDING ANYTIME

←→

DEPT OF TRANSPORTATION

The Patenting of Life

An interview with VUB scientist Lode Wyns about the dangers of patents in biotechnology and the pressing need for ethics in law

When Jonas Salk developed the polio vaccine in 1955, and was questioned about patenting it, he replied, "A patent? Could you patent the sun?" Salk regarded his invention as something for the people, he was doing something in the public interest and patents were out of the question. But attitudes changed, and from the 1980s on patents could be issued on living things *sui generis*. Which meant that you could get a patent if you discovered a virus or altered a plant or found a gene and isolated it. A new gold rush had begun.

Only a few decades ago, it was quite unthinkable that universities could be stimulated, let alone pushed, to produce patents. Nowadays, the production of patents is often an element in the evaluation of university staff. "This is not necessarily bad, and certainly not in a number of particular cases, as long as it is not compulsory", says Lode Wyns. "What is more of a problem, however, is that universities are led to believe that patents will provide them with a huge and decisive extra income, even though their income from patents adds up to no more than 10% of a university's funding, even in the best cases".[1] Nevertheless, the temptation to put far too much energy into the patenting effort and to focus aberrantly on the applied sciences is very real. In 1965, universities were awarded 95 patents, in comparison to 3,200 in 2000 and more than 3,600 in 2002.

Lode Wyns experienced the evolution and change in attitude in his field concomitant with the shift from molecular biology and biochemistry to biotechnology. Wyns has known a time in which nobody even mentioned patents – people in biology were all enjoying the constant astonishment about DNA, proteins... The foundations for biotechnology were laid about 30 years ago with money from society. Then, with the advent of genetic "engineering", the story changed: "(...) until the fruit is on the tree and ready to be picked, everything gets paid by society – but from the moment you can go to the market or have to start production, then society does not have the equipment or the money to start doing production, since it's a completely different job". So says Lode Wyns. In fact, this should not present a major problem. The truly creative challenge with most developments is often limited but you need an immense and specific organization, and that organization is called industry. "The frustration, however, starts as soon as some people in industry – and the authorities even more so – express an almost one-sided interest in short-term results and applications and forget about the origins and the long-term potential of the initial fundamental research. And then there is the obligation in some 'academic' funding contexts – but alas, they are the most important ones – to produce patents. Luckily I have some people who are very good at that, who notice the potential in the research, are enthusiastic about it. I can appreciate that, but the emphasis that is put on it nowadays is aberrant and endangers the basic function of universities in research and education. What I observe is that truly fundamental research gets oppressed. Moreover it is very clear that upstream research should never get patented. However, there is a definite tendency to patent more and more technologies and fundamental methods. Today, if people were allowed to patent Newton's law, they would do so – and today rather than tomorrow."

And that's exactly where one goes beyond the basic principle of a patent.

Lode Wyns: Right. The basic principle is that knowledge gets freed, distributed, whereas what we are seeing more and more are exercises in blocking that knowledge. Including with regard to software. I think that the patent laws state that there are two things you cannot patent: mathematical formulae and scientific concepts. Computer science, with its algorithms, is typically situated between formulas and concepts. In our field, we see that the large companies, meaning the large chemical concerns, have sold part of their chemistry and are launching themselves solely in the field of biotechnology. At the same time, bio-informatics institutes are set up to "data-mine" and patent genes, if possible many series of genes. So here again we're dealing with aspects related to computer sciences, with algorithms, and you end up in a fundamental conflict with the fact that you can't patent concepts. The risky biomedical research is still largely done in the public sector but the translation of this knowledge is left entirely up to the industry, which is slapping a 20-year monopoly on everything it develops. So once you start to translate the major breakthroughs of molecular biology into drugs, and develop pharmacy, you enter a different world.

One of the crucial questions remains: up to what level is something still merely an idea, and at what point does it become a concept, or develop the potential for a commercial or industrial application?

Wyns: You can't draw a line here but in the field of biotechnology, of medicine and food, as these two are drawing closer and closer together, of pharmaceuticals, nutraceuticals, smartfood, whatever, it's more about the ethics of law than anything else. So on the one hand you have an industry that by its nature depends on patents, while on the other hand there are the conflicts about health, about the position of the third world, the position of Fortress Europe and Fortress USA. Typically you can't avoid coming back to the case of Myriad Genetics and patents on BReast CAncer or BRCA-linked genes. Myriad had taken out a patent on these genes, and a few years ago the company decided that the genetic tests for breast cancer would only be available in the USA. At the same time, the price for these tests was increased exorbitantly: in practice, this would result in the end of their application. Years before that, in a commission I chaired, I had used this case as an example that would have negative consequences for both the research and public health. But some of the highest-ranking university and governmental policymakers were very critical of that and the example got minimized as a footnote, since it was not relevant or opportune to talk about it. Still, for me the BRCA case is an extreme but now real example of one out of many dangers associated with patenting: you have genes that are related to breast cancer, a company that owns the patents and a health insurance that can't pay for it. What's even worse is if the company does only diagnostics and only limited therapy research, or none, so that if you want to continue to do research on the issue you're forced to obtain the licenses from the company.

What happened next?

Wyns: From what I understand of recent developments, at the European Patent Court the whole issue came to a halt, and not even on the basis of content but mainly for purely technical legal reasons. It's understandable that a legally-minded person should work that way, but I'm not a legally-minded person and part of me can't accept that.

Patenting medical data was absolutely unthinkable a few years ago, so how did this develop?

Wyns: Pharmaceutical companies have always run on patents. It's a pretty crucial element in their business. If they lose a patent, or if one of their patents expires, it can lead to an immediate dip in their income. I remember that when the Valium patent expired, its developer Roche was in real trouble. It's amazing to see how a pharmaceutical company can often depend on just one or a few crucial products for its profits. So their concern about patents is understandable, as it's an industry sector where patents are fundamental to the process. But there are other areas where patents are being introduced and where they turn against us.

When I'm confronted with the text of a law on patents that states: "*(...) genes and series of genes can be the object of an invention if there has been a technical operation applied in order to isolate them and if afterwards there has been an industrial application (...)*", I ask myself, what are we talking about here? When it says "genes and series of genes", that immediately suggests that the people drafting this law aren't aware of the full meaning of "genes and series of genes...". You have to realize that sometimes you have a gene with a particular function but there is a certain redundancy in our genome in the sense that nature invents something, a gene or a function, and, just like with human beings, you get variations on a certain theme and start to use it in many contexts. So you get genes with related but not identical functions. That means that one gene can be a representative of a complete series of genes, but that also means that by indicating one gene you can establish a monopoly on a whole series of functions. Secondly, we know that a gene in a fruit-fly, in yeast or in a human being – or even in a bacterium – can be identical, or at least very similar. So when you patent one gene, you can start patenting transversally through any kind of organism. The major problem is that these patents are drafted in the broadest possible terms. So we are not talking about genes, but about series of genes through all kinds of organisms... And there is an even deeper concept, which at first sight is seemingly innocent, and that is the concept of master and slave genes: a master gene can be a master control gene for lots of circuits and regulatory networks that play a fundamental role in the development of an organism. So in a biological development this gene can play a specific function in a specific type of tissue or cell that you are developing but that you also develop in a liver, a lung, a stomach or an intestine.

It's upsetting, though, that a lot of people concerned with the issue don't seem to be aware of what's written in that legal text. What does it mean, (...)"*if there has been a technical operation applied in order to isolate them*"? Isolating a gene today, or isolating DNA, has in a number of cases become a kindergarten activity. This is how I describe the situation to my students: DNA? It's wonderful. We isolate it, we put it in isolamyl alcohol, in phenol, we put it at minus 80 degrees Celsius, you can sit on it if you like, you can do whatever you like with it. Isolating a gene is often a very simple thing to do, and you can call it a technical operation but that doesn't mean a thing. It's not about technical virtuosity or sophistication. The whole thing would be rather like taking out a patent on a wheel from a wheelbarrow. If I draw up the patent as broadly as I can, the result is that, at a stroke, I also have a patent on the wheels of cars, trucks, trains, airplanes, and so on.

On the other hand, the world of patents is a very specialized world of experts and legal technology.

Wyns: Yes, a recent report from the French Parliament stated that the people who concern themselves with patents form a very closed world of technological and legal experts whose representatives think that what they have been applying for years in certain domains can be extended or applied universally. At least that's what they do: the rules and the conditions attached to a patent for plastic, or a patent for steel, are suddenly mapped onto the pharmaceutical industry. Even human health and food get patented in the same way. But you can't simply map the context and conditions for one patent automatically onto anything else. You can't just extend that in a linear way.

There is an enormous contradiction emerging between the lawyers and their tremendous legal knowledge on the one hand, and their absolute ignorance about science and biology on the other.

How do you deal with the patenting issue within your own research group?

Wyns: It's a major problem. The most important work – often the most fundamental and difficult – is rarely patentable. It's often easier with the more obvious work, so people working on downstream materials or processes get more chances to produce patents than the others. This patenting issue is a very asocial thing within a research group, especially when a lot of money may be linked to a fortunate researcher with a fortunate topic. As such it is very difficult to deal with since there is an obvious unfairness inherent in the system.

But I think patents are not only the problem of university research groups, I think they can be even more of a problem for the industry. I've talked a lot with people from large companies who have had major conflicts with truly large companies, with multinationals, and at a certain point even the fairly large companies have to give in because the patent business is a prohibitively expensive business, in some cases even a scandalously expensive business. When you think that with the development of the most high-performance type of corn, no less than about 36 patents were taken out by about 14 different patent holders... It's not hard to imagine the patent aerobics involved in these kinds of products. But the high invoices that are presented in such cases, by the best and most specialized patent offices, are out of reach even for fairly large companies. So the smaller ones can certainly forget about it. And the main consequence is that in certain fields you get a constipation of patents.

Daniel De Beer mentions this in his paper, when he talks about the tragedy of the anti-commons. And he points out its worst consequence: the under-exploitation of certain disciplines and subjects.

Wyns: Right. As an academic group you can't afford to pay for specific licenses as they're too expensive. And the industry doesn't invest in these subjects or in research in general unless they already have a very solid patent portfolio themselves. So in terms of expertise and competition, these patents become the central players.

It sounds like property speculation and the empty houses that are wasting away just because somebody is out for future profit. Of course it doesn't mean that private property should be abolished, but excesses like that can ruin neighborhoods and are not exactly constructive initiatives.

Wyns: It's exactly the same! Excesses like that, or extreme examples like the BRCA case, can block research of supreme human and social importance. But other companies or researchers don't intervene and everybody waits for the patent's expiry date. Another direct and obvious consequence of that accumulation of patents is, of course, the creation of monopoly positions.

But then how can a small country like Belgium or a small university like the VUB still aim at breakthrough or top research?

Wyns: We can't. It's as simple as that. When talking about Fortress Europe, we can already state that even though Flanders invests quite a bit, we have to stand on the tips of our toes to be of any scientific relevance to the outside world. We can't reach the level of some of the British – and in particular, American – universities. People don't look enough at the budgets of American universities when talking about their impact and quality. Look at the endowment of Harvard! For years I've been drawing people's attention to it, and I thought it must now be about 18 billion dollars. But I was wrong: very recently I learned it's 22.5 billion dollars! These universities have access to amounts of money that we find it hard even to imagine. So in any kind of competition, we'll lose. But okay, we're still able to participate at a certain scientific level. But the third- and fourth- and fifth-world countries can forget about any level – and, under today's rules of the game, irreversibly. But if then, on top of this strictly scientific threshold, you put a second obstacle, consisting of superior expertise in patent laws, it will make the existing disadvantageous position even worse. Is that the intention? Maybe, but once more it is the expression of a very specific form of globalism: a selfish and asocial one.

In a discussion with Jean-Claude Burgelman and Jan Cornelis on this issue, it seemed that the only possible major breakthrough for free and open-source software would come from the East... That if a country like China, which actually could afford transgressing international rules, the WTO or agreements on industrial competition, if they suddenly decide to go for open source, they can create the volume, they can push the development along and can redress the big imbalance that exists now.

Wyns: It's a very anarchistic answer and the only possible one. At one point I remember that, during a meeting, I asked Marc van Montagu[2] about the patents on genetic engineering and the risk of monopolization and he replied: "Well, but China doesn't bother at all!" The sad thing is indeed that the only argument is an anarchistic one because many countries will never be able to compete. If one threshold after the other is imposed, not only scientifically, but technically, structurally, and then the experts ensure that every step is blocked by a legal hurdle, they will never be able to get on an equal footing.

The Human Genome Project is often cited as a wonderful example of an open and collaborative project. So why does this patenting of genes suddenly becomes a rat-race?

Wyns: The problem with the Human Genome Project is that you have to subscribe to some commercial databases and this means that all the data becomes less accessible... But the main rule of the game at the moment is that you can patent a gene provided you can associate the gene with a function. The result is, you get a race – a race to grab as many genes as you can, attach a function to them as fast as possible and without any specification about how broad or how narrow that function may be. So it's a very simple cycle: pick a gene, add a function and patent it, and write the patent as broadly as you can. And this last aspect, especially, is maybe the most dangerous one. When I take a look at what I do in my lab, I would never have been able to imagine the kinds of fields we protein chemists, we crystallographers, have ended up in – you work with proteins that bind sugars and I enter the world of bacterial infections that can be uropathogenic or central in a veterinary context. I work with proteins that behaved funny in bacteria associated with the binding of metals and I enter the world of environmental remediation. You work on proteins that break down sugar polymers and you enter the world of paper-recycling. The technologies that you need are always the same: take a gene, put it in a context, bring it to expression, clear the proteins – there is a complete world of basic technologies that bring you into widely differing fields. But then you notice that Bayer or DuPont have suddenly started to sell chemical parts and start buying biotechnological parts. You notice mergers between the food sector and the pharmaceutical sector. The whole pharmaceutical sector is about mergers and the chemical sector is becoming biochemical, and agricultural – it's turning into a sector that has implications for just about everything. And the corporate systems are getting bigger and bigger. That's where the real danger lies, as eventually there will be only a few players in the market and – thanks to the very general nature of the technologies – they will be playing on every possible field – and this will have an impact on health, vaccines, food, the environment, medicine, and so on.

What will be the short-term consequences of patenting in biotech research?

Wyns: With regard to our field, and in a university lab environment, I think we'll feel it most quickly, and most acutely, in the cost of research. In lots of the products you buy, the patenting is included, so we pay more for the same. PCR technology – the polymer chain reaction – was the latest marvel years ago and was a patent that Roche bought for – I was told – two billion euro. So it has to be paid for. But an even bigger danger nowadays is that exchange between universities is being blocked – more information and research is being protected instead of distributed. Your own university will declare you a fool if you give away research results in which they saw potentially patentable things. It's an illusion that spin-offs and patents will bring in money for universities – in *Science* there was a list of top universities and if these got ten per cent of their income from spin-off activities and patents, it was an absolute record. Most of them only get five per cent, and in my view universities would be better off sticking to their core business. But the effect is that whereas before you used to exchange results and research more quickly, and unconditionally, nowadays lots of universities go through agreements and regulations before exchanging research. In industry the danger is even bigger, in that if you're not a patent holder or you're not in a position to achieve a solid patent position in a particular sector, then you don't even think about starting with the research. If the BRCA for example were to say, "OK, let's start therapy research on breast cancer", but another company has the patent, then the second company, even if it has the better tools, will never start the research since they would only be working for the first one. Things like that do block a lot of research, as I said before.

What quarter will the solutions to the "protecting versus sharing" problem come from?

Wyns: There are only two ways to tackle this: one is not to give up the struggle. The BRCA case with its ongoing legal struggles is one among many. The universities should also become aware that they must not expect any miracles from these kinds of activities. A few years ago there was a statement by the European Federation of Chemical Industry and it said, about applied sciences at the universities: *"they should be given the opportunity but there is no need..."*. Major industries sometimes realize that the university has one function and they have a different one. In a small, middle-market landscape, like in Flanders, it's not so clear. The matter gets complicated, as you have politicians who want to support local industry, and engaging university labs in direct results and short-term thinking is one way of doing so.

In some Scandinavian companies I've seen a new business model emerging because people have started to realize that they will no longer be drug producers but drug providers. If they do business with a continent like Africa, it won't any longer be a matter of delivering containers with pills, but the challenge will be to develop a broader technical, medical and social structure to cover such a country. You'll say, OK, a new kind of business model, a new kind of R&D... but who is going to produce it? The major companies of course.

The only thing we, scientific researchers, can do is to continue sparking and facilitating the discussion. But even within universities this is sometimes difficult, given the absurd idea that some universities have, that they should score like a company! One way of doing this is by showing a portfolio of patents. Or by showing a growing number of spin-offs. But I think that the true function of a university lies elsewhere. If you have good science teachers and researchers, it allows people and students to look at the world from a distance, to put things in perspective, to reflect on things, to instruct some people about what the scientific method is and to act according to it.

And, last but not least, there is also this thing called history, and we should not forget that. When you asked me about solutions a while ago, I wanted to be nice and tried to enumerate some of them, to come up with an answer. If we look back at history, we have to admit that there is an elasticity in continuing to live in terrible situations and that true change only occurs when there is a catastrophe. How will the confrontation with the third and fourth worlds and the rest develop? Except for the Velvet Revolution in Prague, where luckily there had already been a prelude, all the other revolutions have turned out to be catastrophes. In the nice constitutional solution versus the anarchist one... so far the anarchistic one is winning... What is going to happen in China? In Africa? My colleague Dr Els Torreele is working there and she is worried particularly about research on diseases that we are not concerned with. What is happening at that level? Next to nothing! We're seeing a decrease in the kind of pharmacy that is being done. The gamma of research is getting leaner, you get a few big players in the top ten of illnesses of the western world who want to keep their stakeholders happy. Products for the control of cholesterol for an over-obese society are one major target, Viagra is another. But the general supply and range of medication has decreased. They perform market studies and all arrive at the same few target objectives and public and that's where they compete. And at some point the cost becomes so enormous that only the big concerns can actually pay it: the research, the administrative part, the legal part... the profits are high, but we should not forget that the investment is enormous too.

What strikes me is that the debate on this whole issue is at its height. Every week there are solid discussions on these kinds of matters from every possible angle. Even in the USA, in *Science*, in *Nature*, whatever. This is all good for discussion, but it looks as if the main forces are still heading the other way: against the current form of globalization, against free-market rules. Some sectors stick to the old rules and the open-source spirit doesn't have the means to enable them to achieve what they want. Our innovative potential is slipping towards third-world situations and we don't know where it's all going to end. Nobody seems able to formulate a perspective or a credible solution for that. The best comparison is US military research – the military budget is immense, which isn't surprising when you consider that close to 90 per cent of the military research that happens in the world happens over there. Alas, it is also very strong research, since you go according to the scenario of the survival of the fittest.

But if I look at the exponential growth of working costs in my lab, it's devastating. In genetic engineering, costs are rising, since at every level at which I want to perform an action there is a brand-new gadget, and if I don't buy that one it'll slow down the research and I'll end up behind all the others. In chemistry you have two worlds: thermodynamics, working on balance and kinetics, working on speed, on fastness. If people think in terms of equilibrium, they feel good. And everybody pretends and keeps acting as if everything is in balance, but in actual fact the whole economy is a rat-race and you're no longer out for equilibrium but for kinetics: the fastest wins. In my research field, the same thing happens. Not having the budgets we need for doing competitive research is one of the main reasons why our European universities are in such terrible shape. And we don't have that American culture, we don't want to depend on charity and endowments, but at the end of the day, we'll lose... It's really a terrible dilemma.

Notes

[1] *Science*, August 2004: "Patent royalty and licensing revenue provides an insignificant portion of the total university revenues in Commons-based strategies and the problems of patents".

[2] Marc van Montagu is professor emeritus and an internationally acclaimed scientist who in 2000 founded the Institute for Plant Biotechnology in Developing Countries at the Ghent University in Belgium. Already in the 1970s, the Ghent Unversity harbored scientists as Walter Fiers, Jef Schell, Joël Vandekerckhove and Van Montagu who developed a strong reputation for high-quality fundamental molecular biology with an emphasis on biomedical and plant genetic research.

Biography

Lode Wyns has a PhD in chemistry and is a professor at VUB. His research field is biochemistry and biophysics. Wyns is the director of the Department of Molecular & Cellular Interactions at the Flemish Interuniversity Institute for Biotechnology (Vlaams Instituut voor Biotechnologie, or VIB). This department resides within the Institute for Molecular Biology and Biotechnology at VUB and represents a multidisciplinary collaboration between the research groups on cellular and molecular immunology, microbial interactions and ultrastructure research. His major line of research concerns the fundamental theme of protein structure-function correlation.

From 1994 to 2000 Lode Wyns was president of the Flemish Science Policy Commission and from 2001 to 2004 he was Dean of the Science Faculty of Vrije Universiteit Brussel. Wyns is vice-president of the Flemish Institute for Science and Technology Assessment, associated with the Flemish Parliament, and he is the Belgian representative in the European Synchrotron Radiation Facility.

← 13-26
RECTOR ST

ONE WAY

DEPT OF TRA SPORTAT

Fostering Research, Innovation and Networking

Jan Cornelis

Introduction

Our knowledge society is governed by fast evolution. Little time is left for the development of long-term visions and ideas. Nevertheless, long-term thinking is the basic tool that research people at universities and in companies need to make progress in their own field and to develop intellectual and technical resources for the future. Preserving these long-term thinking processes is one of the key objectives of each university in its mission to foster the discovery of new knowledge, to capture this knowledge, to disseminate it and to exploit it in innovative inventions.

For research management in a medium-sized university in a European context, the main challenges are on the one hand to maintain the quest for excellence and creativity through fundamental research, and on the other to meet the increasing short-term requirements that society imposes on a university. The paper describes a long-matured policy and underlying management model for R&D and the sustainable valorization of scientific research, aimed at achieving both.

Jan Cornelis

Why a paper like this, in the context of the debate on proprietary, free and open-source software?

Personally, I knew of the existence of the free and open-source movement, but did not feel very concerned about its underlying principles, evolution or societal impact. I think I am not far off the mark in saying that the whole open-source movement, interesting as it may be, attracts limited active interest in our university. When one looks at the engineering faculty, for example, only a few people seem really concerned about it, while in the faculty of science two groups exist: those who view it pragmatically, and a small group of hard-core activists. I acquired a deeper understanding of the issue during the CROSSTALKS discussions and the editing of this book, and so became aware of its implicit impact on societal processes. Nevertheless, although I only recently began to understand the true nature of the open and free-source movement, I was able to assimilate many of my earlier proposals for the strategy and implementation of the university's R&D management to what happens in this movement. That is the main reason why I took the initiative to write this paper in the context of the CROSSTALKS debate on free, open and proprietary software. That is also one of the reasons why I would not go as far as some people in this book, who claim that the open-source movement has *steered* social, economic and organizational processes in society. I think the open-source spirit is in *one of the mainstream spirits* of this era, and that society is a good deal more subtle and complex than the open-source issue. To see it as the driving force behind a variety of different (r)evolutionary processes is to overrate it. It is part of these processes, yes, but no more than that.

The university's R&D management model

Since the management model described in the paper is based on the context in which the university operates, a brief overview of the R&D scene in Brussels, Flanders, Belgium and Europe will be sketched.

In the context of the typical requirements for the university support of the knowledge society, particular emphasis is put on a specific type of large-scale projects/programs that encompass generic research with the clear goal of achieving benefits for society and/or industry, with a typical time-scale of between three and ten years, i.e., *strategic research*. In the context of a knowledge society, a different kind of research management is needed than the kind people were able to rely on years ago. Our society's development and future call for a kind of research that focuses on interdisciplinarity, complex systems, organization and planning – research that is usually supported by large-scale initiatives, teamwork and networking. This, in a nutshell, is what I mean by *strategic research*. To be successful in a university context, it requires input from fundamental research, triggered by the curiosity of the *individual researcher*, and ways to support *excelling research groups*, which both continue to be the main resources for innovation breakthroughs and progress in science and technology. Moving into the domain of strategic research only makes sense if the *development* aspect of R&D is also considered as a focus of attention, implying knowledge and technology transfer: the ability to translate fundamental research into feasible applications. In order to avoid clashes or abrupt transitions between the fundamental research and the development phases, we have to build program-oriented ways of thinking, which bridge the gap between the two. This program-oriented approach to strategic research is quite different from and complementary to classic research-project planning processes. The organization of what I have called strategic research requires a global, dynamic approach that is different from the traditional academic one. The model that has evolved at VUB is one in which different research types can interact and are supported and evaluated on their own particular merits. Internally, it has to keep abreast of the needs of researchers while at the same time, externally, it has to accommodate the expectations of the university as an educational and knowledge institute with an important societal task. One thing is obvious: the one-fits-all model does not apply to successful R&D. So at the VUB, the research management policy has set out one series of interacting models that support the university research culture, complementing another series that fulfils the requirements imposed by society. Keeping a balance between them, in a fast-changing society, continuously raises new policy questions. In the recent past, a series of initiatives were taken to support both – some examples are described below. The structure of the university's Interface Cell is an example of a strategic set-up offering the most efficient and variable support to researchers on issues of technology/knowledge exploitation and transfer, whenever they ask for it. Internal quality assessment, the setting-up and organization of a university research council and the bottom-up development of both a profile for PhD students & promotors and a structured PhD process, are all initiatives that should primarily respond to the researcher's needs. All these were initiatives pioneered by the VUB, showing our research management's interest first of all in the quality of the scientific research carried out and collaborative efforts to stimulate the research community, and secondly in the excellence of the education taking place.

The relation between university R&D management and a brain-storming initiative around free and open software

As Richard Stallman puts it himself, "the free software movement is not only concerned with practical benefits but implies social, ethical and political issues". It is undeniable that the open attitude of the free software movement is not isolated from the general societal forces that tend to increase transparency, a property that we also try to display in the attitude of research management towards researchers, research groups and society. Although the free software movement has probably never really functioned as a driving force for a larger societal movement, except in limited circles of initiates, it is undoubtedly an expression of a larger socio-cultural trend within society which is primarily cultivated in universities and centers of independent thinking. The profile of the VUB is based on free inquiry – 'free as in freedom, not gratis' – which manifested itself in an open attitude towards research, one that is unlimited (except financially), as opposed to what is observed in more traditional universities. Today this is still reflected in the research themes of some of our leading research groups (e.g. the medical social sciences with their end-of-life studies; the life sciences with forefront fertility and genetic studies) and in our capacity to push research to the point where it has a real impact on society and industry. The second characteristic of the VUB is its diversified composition in terms of social classes, nationalities and ideas, while the fact that it is situated in Brussels fosters this variety which makes the VUB unlike any other university.

This positive attitude towards "free inquiry" gives us no excuse for escaping from organizational efficiency. VUB is intent on quality research and fosters the cohabitation of individuals and large, dynamic groups who are seeking excellence. With regard to *strategic research* it means that we deliberately have to define strategic areas and themes for development, as in the case-study discussed in Section 3.3. As explained below, the need for these thematic choices must never come into conflict with the basic concepts underlying our research management strategy: flexibility in the support offered to the researchers, the freedom to decide whether to participate in all or a subset of research types, and encouragement of the true spirit of collaboration in the sense of the *universitas* idea.

Open, free and proprietary software: reflections on the university's attitude

With regard to the free and open-source issue, as a university, VUB supports open standards at all levels, but it is not up to the university to impose a particular system. VUB prefers to adopt a pragmatic attitude, in the following sense:

- We indicate the risks involved with proprietary software and those accompanying the use of free and open-source software, we prefer to concentrate on the workability and efficiency of a tool used in research (and software for many researchers is only a tool, a means to pursuing other goals without caring or deciphering how it is made), but we insist on saving the results in an open (documented) format to ensure sustainable access and interchange. In this context we are aware that changes in management, or a company take-over, can lead to legal harassment concerning the use of file formats that have been tolerated for a long time but then suddenly, without warning, are no longer.
- We use open standards and open-source software as the basis for the educational platform, but provide user access through the most widespread proprietary and open-source software applications.
- The university is by nature an excellent breeding-ground for defenders of the open/free software movement in all its gradations; institutionally we will continue to provide an open forum for discussions, where all major points of view have to be confronted.

The university as an institution does not share the extreme view of some of its computer scientists who would like to *enforce* the generalized use of open-source software. Whenever users have good reasons for using proprietary software that suits their needs, their choice is accepted provided no excessive recurring costs are anticipated. In this respect, the main recommendations made to the government by the expert group of the *Vlaamse Raad voor Wetenschapsbeleid* (the Flemish research council) are followed: (i) there is no need – nor is it advisable – for the government to issue regulations on open-source software, mainly because it could create a precedent in favoring one kind of technology; (ii) open standards should be promoted to increase interconnectivity, transparency and readability; (iii) as far as possible, the government should communicate using open standards and formats in order to observe strict neutrality when disseminating information through electronic channels and to ensure it reaches the largest possible audience; (iv) action in research, awareness-raising and ICT normalization will promote the use of open standards.

The evolution of the knowledge society and the ways of contributing to its construction undoubtedly outweigh the issues involved in open/free and proprietary software, but they will rely, in their processes and communication, on the tools and engineering concepts underlying the building of our digital commons.

Identity card – the VUB in a nutshell

VUB is a 9,218-student, full-service university serving Flanders and the Brussels Region. While it is a small to medium-sized institution within the Flemish academic landscape, in numbers it is the biggest Flemish employer in the Brussels region, with 2,511 employed at the university itself and an additional 2,500 at the university hospital. Of its staff, 38% are administrative/technical personnel, 62% are academic staff, and 34% are female. VUB has retained an emphasis on free and unfettered, progressive, scientific research and teaching, and includes an English-language liberal arts college, Vesalius College. The multicultural student body and faculty enhance the academic and social environment of the university. Turning this *diversity* into an asset for high-quality research and education is one of the major components of our mission statement and constitutes a continuous challenge. The university also belongs to a university association (UAB) which includes one high school (Erasmus) with 4,302 students and 505 employees [Annual Report VUB – 2003].

Research budget 2003
Government funding: 126.627.333 kEuro
External bunding: 36.880.310 kEuro
Research budet: > 50.000 kEuro

- 27%
- 19%
- 33%
- 21%

■ VUB research funding (1)
■ Government funding 'fundamental research' (2)
■ Government project funding 'strategic & applied research' (3)
■ Private sector (4)

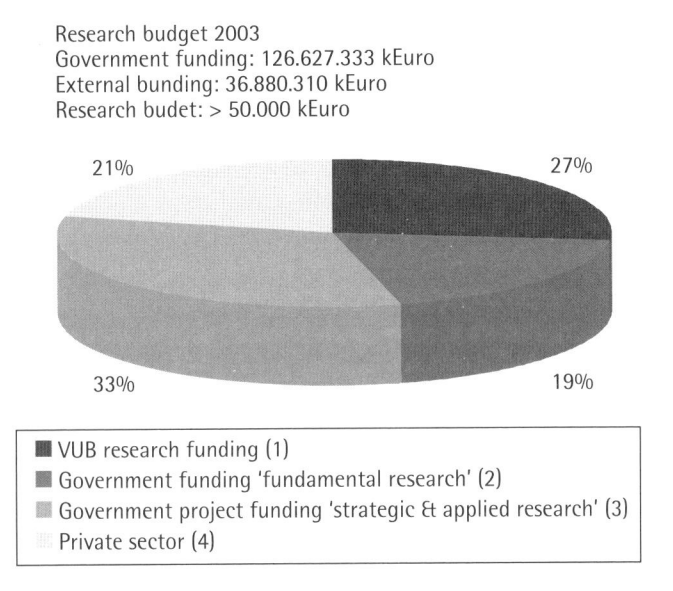

Figure 1 – Origin and size of the research budget of the Vrije Universiteit Brussel in 2003: (1) governmental funds, allocated internally by the Research Council for fundamental research; (2) regional and national government funding for fundamental research obtained in competition with other universities, high schools and industry; (3) regional, national and international funding for strategic and applied research; (4) contract research with industry.

1. Commitments to the VUB research community

Although there are no strict boundaries between the research types, modularization is useful in order to reduce the complexity of research management. *It is my conviction that a university should support all research types, including trajectories leading from scientific discovery all the way to development and implementation. Each of the three main stages along this trajectory requires appropriate management attitudes.*

Types of research

Research Types	Funding channels in interuniversity competition	Intra-university funding channels	Steering	Normalized budget per project or program/ amount of projects or programs	Type of players/ results
Fundamental research	FWO (grants & projects)	BOF (grants and projects)	No thematic steering; only quality control	1 euro / 100	Explorers/ Discoveries & Knowledge expansion
Strategic research	SBO (society and industrial impact)	IOF (economic impact)	Thematic steering based on university policy	10 euro / 5	Inventors/ Innovation & Knowledge structuring
Industrial research	IWT and contract research	--	Economic and society steering	100 Euro / 1	Developers/ Products, Services & Knowledge consolidation

Figure 2 – Research categorization in 3 types: fundamental research, strategic research, industrial/societal research.
Column 1: research types;
Column 2: channels where funding can be obtained in competition with other universities and research institutes (FWO), industry and high schools (SBO, IWT); FWO = Science Foundation; SBO = Strategic Research; IWT= Institute for Science and Technology;
Column 3: intra-university funding channels, based on government funding divided among universities with criteria derived from global performances and needs; BOF = University Research Council; IOF = University Fund for Industrial Research;
Column 4: level and type of steering;
In the next columns, the numbers should be interpreted as very rough estimates of orders of magnitude: they serve to clarify the main differentiations between research types. Exceptions exist, certainly in "Big Science" requiring exceptional infrastructures (e.g. CERN).
Column 5 (a): Normalized budget per project or program: for each euro spent on fundamental research, typically 10 euro is needed to carry the results up to the level of inventions with a potential impact on economy and society, and a extra 100 euro is needed at the development and business level;
Column 5 (b): the amount of projects needed to come to one successful, marketable end result is 5 to 10 at the level of strategic research and 100 at the level of fundamental research;
Column 6: typical players in the research process, and type of results that can be expected.

Research Trajectories

Support for creativity is essential. The typical players in the area of fundamental research initiated on the personal initiative of researchers and research groups can be qualified as *explorers*. The main management tasks for this type of research are to monitor quality and implement internal remediation of organizational flaws in order to improve support. The main challenge for research management is to avoid steering the content.

An investment in fundamental research (i.e. investigator-initiated research which above all has the goal of advancing knowledge and understanding) is crucial in the process leading from *discovery* to *invention* and *development*. Figure 3 shows the typical evolutionary phases of this process for a given technology or knowledge domain. The vertical axis has no units but carries the meaning of *direct impact, visibility, involvement of financial resources* and *scale*. The horizontal axis stands for *time*, but should not be interpreted as a purely causal, unidirectional dimension: many feedback and cross-fertilization loops exist between the evolutionary phases. The *discovery stage* characterizing fundamental research is hardly visible on the far left of the graph. The *invention* phase usually takes place in a program-driven mode, where R&D partners are collaborating under consortium agreements. This is the stage when larger groups of people are becoming aware of the societal, market and economic potential. Finally, at the stage of *product development and design of services*, project-driven approaches usually become dominant, because of the competition between different players on similar markets.

A major handicap in attracting government attention to fundamental research is the latter's limited direct visibility for policy-makers, politicians and captains of industry, combined with its long-term nature. We should not forget, however, that under-investment in fundamental research leads to a reduction in the number of sources of S-curves (like the one in Figure 3), and certainly prevents S-curves from reaching high plateaus in the project-driven stadium.

Fundamental research is crucial
Technology Lifecycle

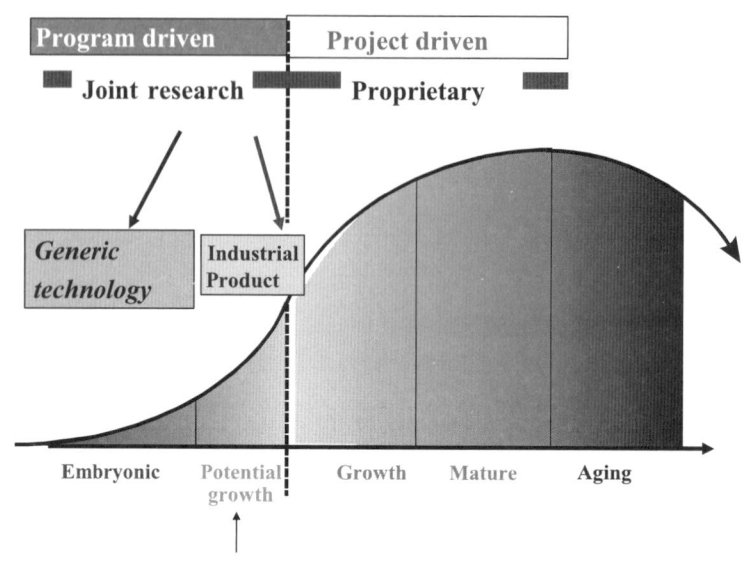

Figure 3 – Evolutionary stages from discovery to invention up to development of products, services and transferable knowledge

Commitments

External recognition results in reputation; internal recognition builds a sense of community within the university that is essential for a flourishing research culture. The support structure and its flexible dynamics are there (i) to support on the one hand the local and interdisciplinary research culture, on the other hand the international relevance of VUB research, (ii) to protect the multi-level valorization of the research results (industrial contract research, patent policy, spin-off creation, incubators, science communication) and (iii) to guide and support the research and its financing at every possible level, primarily at the request of the researchers. The primary commitments of research management to the VUB research community can be summarized as follows:

- For *fundamental research* no thematic steering will hamper the initiatives of individual researchers or research groups. Support for bottom-up initiatives and quality assessment are the main keywords for R&D management; motivation, curiosity, patience, striving for quality and perseverance are the keywords for the researchers. Regardless of temporarily dominant trends and political imperatives, fundamental research has to be supported by the university as a unique source of discovery and knowledge creation. After all, Wilhelm Conrad Roentgen was not looking for a method to look into the inside of the human body when he discovered X-rays, he was merely experimenting (playing) with cathode-ray tubes. If we follow the drift towards goal-oriented (strategic) research too much, we will end up doing nothing more than confirming what we already know or expect, without creating opportunities for fortuitous hits and the discovery of new insights and knowledge. The application of these discoveries is of secondary importance at this stage. Finally, research management in a university should guarantee that the evaluation of the main research processes and results occurs through the consultation of *scientific peers*.
- Besides the strong commitment to fundamental research, *strategic research* in support of innovation, requiring sustainable program-oriented rather than project-oriented funding, is also part of the universities' mission. Bottom-up initiatives, *emanating from excellent groups*, are supported, provided they are built upon the results of the fundamental research or specialized expertise. The typically high cost of this level of research necessitates thematic top-down selection and comparison with societal and economic perspectives. An efficient, dynamic system for identifying *excellence*, which also allows for renewal by emerging new *excellence pools*, is under construction. It should replace the implicit and not very well-defined trajectory that groups now follow to acquire the label of excellence. Limitation of access to the funds for strategic research should be supported by a regulation that is perceived by the research community as being equitable and just.
- For those who wish to push through to the level of commercial or societal valorization, the university has made a commitment to offer a full support structure, covering legal advice, contract negotiation, patent filing, venture capital

for spin-off creation, incubation environments and science parks. A pro-active approach to creating awareness of this type of valorization has been introduced through technology scouting and entrepreneurial initiation and training sessions.

2. Main funding sources for the different types of research

The Belgian context for research funding is a very particular one, in the sense that there are two main levels of research policy and associated funding sources: the *regional/community level* – i.e., for VUB, the Brussels-Capital Region as well as the Flemish region/community – and the *federal level*. It is worth mentioning that at all levels the policy-makers for research have loosely committed themselves to reaching the Barcelona norm by 2010, namely, spending 3% of their gross domestic product on R&D (1% government – currently in Flanders we have reached approximately 0.75%; 2% industry). For the Flemish Government, this implies a cumulative effort of – at a minimum – 60-100 million euro/year. In the 1990s the Belgian budget for R&D was amongst the lowest in Europe. In ten years, a great deal has changed, and Belgium is now catching up with its neighbors, although this is almost entirely thanks to Flanders.

The Flemish level – yearly budget of approximately 1,400 million euro (850 million euro going directly to R&D; 400 million euro to fundamental research)

Since 1993, primary responsibility for research policy has been transferred from the Federal level to the Communities and Regions. This includes education and training for researchers; the stimulation of fundamental research for the enrichment of our knowledge base; industrial and societal application-oriented research and the valorization of the results of scientific research; the creation of opportunities for international and industrial collaboration in matters of R&D. The whole range of scientific research types is covered: (i) fundamental research going beyond the boundaries of current state-of-the-art knowledge, (ii) strategic research with an industrial, economic or societal purpose, (iii) applied research and finally (iv) the industrial and societal valorization of research results. The largest funding stream for the Flemish universities, including VUB, originates from this Flemish level.

The Federal level – yearly budget of approximately 650 million euro

Federal science policy manages research in certain specified areas, e.g. *space research* (Belgium's budget for ESA is about twice that of the Netherlands or Sweden), and certain explicitly formulated actions (e.g. *sustainable development*, earth observation, science and society, social sciences and governance, telematics and federal governance, Antarctica research, citizens and legal protection, sustainable mobility, normalization, peace and security, marine sciences, etc.), in the context of the federal government's areas of competence. Important actions for the Belgian universities are: (i) long-term science networking among Belgian research groups and international partners (e.g. IUAP – interuniversity attraction poles), (ii) the bilateral agreements with other countries, and (iii) technological networking (e.g. TAP – technological attraction poles). Moreover, the mission statement of the federal science policy includes support for the federal scientific institutes and the Belgian communication network for research (BELNET).

The European level

The European Commission supports research, development and demonstration activities through its multi-annual (five-year) framework programs (FPs) for research. Each FP stipulates the priority research fields and the funding conditions. The current FP6 aims to create a European Research Area (ERA), a kind of internal market for science, technology and research. Better coordination and cooperation between all the relevant players should boost scientific excellence, competitiveness and innovation, through consistency in the approach to research.
- The largest portion of the FP6 budget goes to research that enhances networking and collaboration between researchers in a selected number of fields that are relevant to Europe. Seven priority research fields have been identified, with an extra one for policy on supporting research. The traditional research projects with scales

used in previous FPs still exist, but have to a large extent been replaced by *Integrated Projects* (IPs) and *Networks of Excellence* (NoEs), which are characterized by greater autonomy in project management to go with their increased scale.
- Secondly, the European Commission wants to reinforce research capacity by providing *resources for researcher mobility* (Marie Curie actions) and for research infrastructure.
- To stimulate the coordination of research activities with the national and regional programs, the Commission provides support for the so-called *ERA networks*. Its goal is to ensure that program managers – i.e., national and regional "funding agencies" or ministries that manage a national/regional program – gradually increase the coordination of their activities.
- *Technology Platforms* bring together companies, research institutions, the financial world and regulatory authorities to draw up a common research agenda which should mobilize a critical mass of (national and European) public and private resources. This approach has been, or will be, adopted in areas such as energy (hydrogen technology, photovoltaic solar energy), transport (aeronautics), mobile communications, embedded systems and nano-electronics. This entails in particular identifying the legal and regulatory conditions needed in order to implement the common research agenda.
- The creation of the *European Research Council (ERC)*, which will operate as an agency and will be controlled by the scientific world, like the National Science Foundation in the USA, is imminent. Research financing will follow sound, transparent principles, in a competition between individual research groups and researchers whereby scientific excellence will be the single evaluation criterion.

Generally speaking, it is my opinion that besides mobility, EU funding mainly *supports strategic research and industrial R&D*.

The Brussels level

The Brussels-Capital Region primarily supports R&D with an economic goal (e.g. industrial research and pre-competitive research – collective and international research, innovation in areas compatible with an urban society such as Brussels, initiatives to encourage participation in EU programs). Research with non-economic objectives is also supported (e.g. "Research in Brussels" – a system of grants for foreign researchers coming to the Brussels region, and "Prospective Research in Brussels" – project funding in areas of direct importance to the region). More than its R&D funding capabilities, the image of Brussels as the only real international city in Belgium constitutes a powerful asset in the debate on *brain drain* and *brain gain*.

Structuring the information on R&D funding opportunities is a major challenge in the Belgian microcosm of scientific research

Although there is definitely a will to distribute responsibility for R&D in a rational way among the different layers of government within Belgium, failure to reach sensible agreements leads in reality to an even more complex situation than the one described in the summary of funding sources given above. The major tasks of university R&D management (VUB is dependent on the Flemish community for research matters directly related to education, on the Flemish and Brussels regions for its R&D and research valorization, and on the federal science policy department for specific domains and actions) include structuring the relevant information, timely dissemination of funding opportunities, organizing selected mailing groups within the university, and maintaining a well-informed help desk. The complexity of the R&D funding landscape is a feature of many federal states, but it has reached a record level in Brussels and the VUB, because of the latter's exceptional situation within the Flemish community *and* the Brussels Region.

3. The R&D support structure

For a better orientation of the reader within the university's R&D landscape, Figure 4 sketches the main areas of responsibility of the R&D department, organized in three layers (R&D structure, Tools and Networks). Within the R&D structure, two well-established activities may be observed (Fundamental Research and Interface), as well as an emerging third one on Strategic Research. As an extra beacon for the reader, the educational sector is shown on the right-hand side of Figure 4.

R&D						Education					
Interface cell (commission industrial relations)			Research department (research council)			Lifelong learning			Department of education (council for education)		
Industr. Contract research	Patent policy & Management	Spin-off creation	Industrial Research Fund (IOF)	Bureau Research Council (BOZ)	Science Communication (WEC)	IPAVUB	Seminars & courses	...	New ways of education	International Relations	Curriculum ...

'TOOLS'					
BI³ Incubation Fund	IICB ICAB Incubators	Science Parks		Legacy & special donations (in	Chairs preparation)

NETWORKS							
CROSS-TALKS	...	Research Communities & IUAP	EU NOE	...	Alumni	Institutional Relations	...

Figure 4 – Organizational structure of the R&D sector. Two main interacting administrative sections may be seen: the research department and the interface cell. The context of the educational sector is sketched on the right of the table.
IPAVUB: continuing education,
WEC: science communication,
CROSSTALKS: the university's business network,
NoE: Network of Excellence (EU, Framework Programme 6),
IUAP: Inter-University Attraction Pole.

3.1. Fundamental Research

The research cell acts under the academic responsibility of the *Research Council* (OZR – Onderzoeksraad), assisted by the *Executive Bureau* (BOZ – Bureau van de Onderzoeksraad) and the *Science Communication Working Group* (WEC – Werkgroep Wetenschapscommunicatie). The main responsibilities of the Research Council/Research Department are: research policy, project evaluation, allocation of funding and human resources, science communication, internal quality assurance, preparatory studies for policy-makers, monitoring of research performance, structuring of the information on VUB research, delivery of VUB research parameters to the government, awards to encourage researchers, structuring of the PhD process and accompanying measures, contribution to the debate and design of science policy at the regional, national and European levels, advice to funding and science-management agencies, administrative support for projects and grant-holders, legal advice, and internal dissemination of information about research programs and funding opportunities.

Quality assessment and levels of project evaluation in accordance with the amount of funding

Generally speaking, three levels of project funding are considered:
- the *seed level*, offering project opportunities for (i) developing bright, explorative, new, sometimes even isolated ideas, (ii) giving new postdoctoral researchers the opportunity to gain some independence in implementing their first projects, (iii) the early exploration of new research lines, (iv) supporting projects that are set up around the work of PhD students;
- the *incubation level*, typically for research groups in the phase of growing towards excellence, whereby the funding is attributed based primarily on the soundness of the project and the principle of matching funds (a research project that has been financed, albeit partially, by an external funding organization is assumed to have obtained a positive peer review by that external funding agency, and can therefore obtain extra university funding);

- the *excellence level,* reserved for research consortia that have already acquired internationally acknowledged excellence, for which we have a system of concerted actions (GOA – Geconcerteerde OnderzoeksActie), evaluated by external peer review only.

This three-level approach allows for a good trade-off between a reasonable evaluation workload and high evaluation quality, going from lightweight internal towards more external evaluation and leading, finally, to full external peer review for the large projects receiving the highest amounts of funding. Grants for individual researchers are also provided, on the basis of the evaluation of the accompanying project proposals.

Decentralization of R&D responsibilities

The research council supervises three domain-specific advisory boards (*Human Sciences, Natural and Applied Sciences, Biomedical Sciences*). Each of these three advisory *sub-committees* has proprietary project-screening and fund-allocation procedures, adapted to the particular needs and characteristics of the research domain it covers, and each conforms to the general rules and quality control procedures of the Research Council.

Thematic partitioning of the available research budget

The yearly distribution of the research budget among the *sub-committees* is calculated using a well-documented mathematical model taking into account research needs and performance parameters. The rationale behind this approach is (i) the acknowledgement that different cultures exist in different research domains and (ii) the impossibility of comparing the quality of projects that differ greatly in scientific discipline. Shared evaluation and funding by different advisory sub-committees is provided for multidisciplinary projects, and a *central funding line exists for transdisciplinary projects (the so-called horizontal research actions, or HOAs).*

Departments and research groups

The research itself is carried out in the context of *departments* (within a faculty) that have a permanent nature. Since they also have an educational task and administrative identity (accounts, etc.), each member of staff is allocated to one or more of these departments. Optionally, *research groups* can be created on demand, after their proposals have been screened by the Research Council, either (i) to give an identity to a group of people dealing with a highly specialized subject within a department, or (ii) to allow for cross-faculty and departmental research. They should fulfill criteria of critical mass, and are evaluated every three years. Some research groups are temporary, and act as vehicles assisting a group of researchers to work towards a common (temporary) goal, while others provide a structure for ongoing collaboration and inter-university framework agreements.

What is the role of the faculties in R&D organization?

Currently, faculties play an important role in those research matters that come partly under the educational sector, such as PhD accompanying programs and the yearly follow-up of the progress made by each PhD student. These roles are justified by their proximity to the work floor.

Notice, however, that *faculties do not formally appear in the research hierarchy* from Research Council and Sub-Committee up to Department/Research Group. At present, the primary task of faculties is concerned with education (educational programs, student supervision, schedules for courses, etc.), but they also manage logistics (personnel, room allocation to departments, etc.).

Working with three advisory *sub-committees*, rather than with eight faculties, greatly facilitates trans-faculty R&D. The supervision of the *Executive Bureau* of the *Research Council* ensures that multidisciplinary and transdisciplinary research gets a fair chance, even when it crosses the borders of the thematic areas for which the sub-committees are responsible. Day-to-day experience shows that this thematic modularization provides a good trade-off between research management complexity on one hand and, on the other, an (excessive) partitioning of the research budget, resulting in bias and lack of robustness in the mathematical fund-allocation model, when applied to small research communities.

However, in my opinion, the main drawback of the system is the mismatch between the areas of competence of faculties and advisory sub-committees. Most importantly, this creates inconsistencies in the management of personnel, nowadays a typical responsibility of the faculty. For understandable but not justified reasons, meeting the educational need to ensure a full educational program is given priority over research imperatives. Sometimes, research performance is insufficiently taken into account in new appointments and promotions. These two facts restrict successful research groups in their growth: once the academic staff covering the educational program in their domain of expertise is at hand, no further expansion is possible since there is no long-term university career as a researcher without a professorship.

As faculties primarily have an educational responsibility, there is a tendency to let the size and diversity of education supply grow beyond reasonable limits. The current European-wide Bachelor/Master reform will hopefully limit this tendency through the supra-university accreditation procedure for Master programs, which have to be based on a meaningful research capacity. Faculties also show insufficient comprehension of the space needed for R&D and of the flexibility requirements for logistical support. Moreover, faculties are implicitly hampering cross-disciplinary research, a major issue for example in *strategic research*, which has to respond to the increasing complexity of the problems posed by the knowledge society.

To solve these problems, a university-wide restructuring is needed: merging of departments, relieving the eight faculties of their duties as regards personnel and logistics management, definition of three middle-management structures whose spheres of competence coincide with those of the advisory sub-committees, so that the "*coherent management of research* and *education* and *logistics*" can be achieved.

The proposed structure has several advantages: (i) conformity with the growing trend towards tightly coupled research and education in Master's programs, (ii) adaptation to the increasing scale of research projects and networks (see for example the EU's FP6 and FP7 initiatives, described in Section 2), (iii) increased flexibility of resource management, (iv) increased capability for multidisciplinary research, (v) greater flexibility in the organization of administrative support and (vi) critical mass needed for strategic research in support of the government's and industry's demands for innovation. In the new organizational model, faculties would become lightweight entities, administratively speaking, but they would retain important powers when it came to establishing educational programs, local quality control of education, educational trajectories, and matters related to student affairs.

Virtual institutes, cherishing the best talent without fragmenting or duplicating effort or investment

Going beyond university R&D policy matters, in general I believe that carrying out research in institutes that also have an educational vocation creates maximal opportunities for the emergence of new talent. In this context I strongly support the Flemish government's policy of creating so-called *virtual institutes*. Basically, such a virtual institute has a lightweight central management structure dealing with administration, quality control, legal assistance, networking, IPR management and domain-specific valorization of results, while the research is done by the university partners, based in their local labs. The model behind these virtual centers is interesting and deserves a more detailed analysis:
- Contact with training and education, and hence with students, is maintained – the investment is not solely in technology and gaining knowledge, but also in the creation of new talent.
- Thematically oriented initiatives based on the background of the various partners will, in the long run, create a Flanders Research Area, in which the best from each research domain will be involved, irrespective of their university roots. This seems to me preferable to selecting one "top research" university, surrounded by a number of other "less prestigious" universities which would primarily have teaching obligations.
- The virtual centers make it possible to bridge the gap between the different monodisciplinary research domains and to cross over the borders of faculty areas of competence (at university level, the notion of a *research group* was also created for that purpose – see above, Section 3.1). This is extremely important for exploring innovation at the boundaries of research domains and application fields.

- Coherence of action within the virtual institute can be ensured by global, dedicated performance criteria defined at the outset, the establishment of a road map, research programs and a long-term vision. Funding is made dependent on the degree to which the performance criteria are met.
- Virtual centers also allow for balanced, mixed leadership and policy-making between industry, university and other socio-economic partners.
- The virtual-institute model inherently provides more flexibility than a centralized facility, mainly in terms of the down- and up-scaling of certain themes on the basis of the evolution and importance of the research domain. Owing to the flexibility with which universities shift research domains and employment, within the framework of their multiple missions, social dramas can be reduced or avoided.

Examples of these virtual excellence centers and/or networks in which VUB participates are: Flanders Drive, Flanders Mechatronics, VIB – Flemish Institute for Biotechnology, IBBT – the Institute for Broad-Band Technology, DISC – Decision, Information, Science and Communication (the ICT knowledge centre of the Brussels Capital Region). Each has its own different operating mode and mission statement.

3.2. The bridging mission of the Interface Cell

The Interface Cell bridges the gap between industry and the university's research and expertise. An important deal flow is achieved mainly by research projects with economic potential, but also through assistance in the creation and follow-up of spin-off projects, services offered for patenting and a wide range of support, advice and mentoring.

The mission of the Interface Cell is to make the results of innovative research available to society in close collaboration with the researchers who are the basis for these newly developed technologies or concepts. To this end, it plays what is for a university a fundamental role: that of mediator in the gathering and dissemination of knowledge. It is imperative that this mission be organized in an efficient way: the cost of the "valorization process" is high, risks are everywhere and a university plays a different game from industry. More specifically, it is important for the Interface Cell to concentrate on supporting those projects that are *based on the university's research results, areas of special competence or unique skills* – conform to the university's mission – so that we are not merely providing a cheap substitute for what external organizations could do better themselves.

The Interface cell aims at creating awareness among young researchers about the ownership and protection of intellectual property, about "patent and publish" strategies and about the possible exploitation of their applied research. Through seminars and on-site visits, these aspects – which are fairly new to most researchers – are presented and individual guidance is offered. The university pre-finances all the costs involved in patenting, and the Interface Cell draws up contracts and negotiates commercial opportunities, in consultation with the researchers by means of technology transfer to existing companies or, if opportune, by patent licensing or establishing a spin-off. Appropriate regulation protects the rights of the inventors and provides for a return for the research groups, the inventors and the university that has borne the cost of setting up this valorization procedure. This ensures that the greatest proportion of the income is re-invested in further research.

Why does a university have to make this shift to the commercialization of knowledge, and why is it no longer sufficient to bring the results of research into the public forum by means of peer-review publications? Many researchers struggle with the notion of accepting money for delivering knowledge to a few market players who might try to steer their further choice of research plans. They do not wish to accept that a whole new and parallel research "literature" has developed in the form of patent data, and in some (rare) cases they even try to deny this completely. Hence the deeper, underlying mission of the Interface cell: to find out, with the researcher, what is the most appropriate way to make results available to society without neglecting our researchers' concerns or objections and without jeopardizing the possibility of creating an added value that can generate new income for further research.

What about academic freedom? It is a highly valued principle at the VUB, and this is reflected in all regulations, including those on structured valorization. Researchers may consider the public dissemination of results more appropriate than protection. The VUB accepts this right and provides for a procedure whereby, after notification of the patentable material to the Interface Cell, there is a round of consultations to discuss the desirability of patenting or not. The aim is to come to a collectively taken decision – the researchers, however, have the last word.

This can lead to situations were within one research group the decision is taken to patent a valuable new discovery with many applications in the health sector and to exploit it in a VUB spin-off company, whereas another invention is deliberately brought into the public domain at once, in order to prevent any commercial exploitation or monopolization that could harm developing countries.

As international patents (EPO and USPTO) are becoming more important as an output parameter for the researcher as well as for the university – comparable to publications and citations – the Interface Cell tries to stimulate a debate on patenting issues. It does not steer, but informs, in order to make well-considered decisions possible.

In this way the VUB keeps open the possibility of playing an active role in an environment were protection of IP is an absolute prerequisite, without, however, losing touch with academically, ethically and socially inspired considerations.

The challenges of valorizing research results through licensing and spin-off creation – a closer look at the process

Until the early 1990s, no formal financial or managerial support was given to the valorization of scientific research. The valorization of the VUB's intellectual capital, as in many other European universities, was left to individual effort on the part of the researchers. Licensing and spin-offs happened, independently from and often even unnoticed by the university. In 1997, the VUB adopted a university policy and regulation on valorization, and created a Technology Transfer Cell within the industrial liaison office (known as the Interface Cell) which is an integral part of the Research and Development Department.

The record of spin-offs until that time (i.e., until 1996) had, indeed, proved that such valorization was valuable and worthwhile. Nonetheless, it escaped the university without benefiting it either financially or organizationally. For all spin-offs created since 1996 – and certainly since the VUB regulation on valorization became effective in 1997 – the relationship between the mother university and its spin-offs has been formalized in a contractual arrangement between the two parties. In some cases, the VUB is a shareholder in its spin-offs; in most cases the university also benefits financially from its spin-offs' business success through contract research fees, license fees, royalties or other types of payments. All spin-off companies created up to now have originated in one of the following faculties: science, applied science, medicine and pharmacy, or physical education and physiotherapy. Recently, ideas with valorization potential through spin-off creation have also been put forward by researchers from the human sciences.

Critical to the launching of the valorization process is an early assessment of the scientific as well as the business and financial value of the research in progress. When the Interface Cell deems that support needs to be given to allow scientific work to be taken to a level where it may be financially valorized, as well as protected by intellectual property rights, a specific plan of action is drawn up in collaboration with the researchers, with financial support from the university's budgetary resources.

Within the framework of its contract research with industry, the VUB aims to increase its financial returns by negotiating contract terms stipulating that a fair share of the income earned by the company is transferred to the university, certainly if the research results are successfully exploited by the industrial partner. In that sense, licensing is a valuable tool for the valorization of university research, and in some scientific areas, such as medicine or pharmacology, it is often the most appropriate one.

To generate a commercially viable spin-off, however, one needs to proceed from a patent or pre-patent research to a commercial application thereof that proves viable. This means that more financial and managerial resources are needed to fund "translational" research and the development of a sound business plan and business model. To this end, and at the critical stage between pre-seed and seed capital, it was found that another financial and managerial tool was needed.

All Flemish universities have established incubation or investment funds for their spin-offs. The VUB was the last one to act and create its own fund: the BI^3-fund (BI^3-fund: http://www.vub.ac.be/infovoor/bedrijven/startkapitaalfonds.html). But as a result it was able to learn from the management problems that had beset some of these funds' activities and resulted in a slender output of spin-offs. The BI^3 Fund's main objective is to provide capital – in the form of seed capital and financial and business-related know-how – to VUB spin-off companies, both within Belgium and abroad. Ventures that are focused on scientific research, technological development and the commercialization of their research results are, typically, companies of interest to BI[3], on condition that the transfer of the university's academic knowledge and technological developments between the VUB and these companies is guaranteed. The BI[3] Fund not only provides capital to VUB spin-off companies during their start-up phase: in addition, as a closed fund it is financially capable of providing initial follow-up financing as well.

The financial and managerial challenges facing a fund are twofold. First, there is the challenge of an adequate "pipeline". This requires an investment by the institution in the origination and preparation of dossiers and the maintenance thereof. The second challenge concerns the winnowing-down of this prospect list to a few viable spin-off projects. Pre-seed funding and institutional support play a role in getting these ventures off the ground. Of equal importance to finding financial partners for the fund is the establishment of a network of external experts who can add value to the dossiers submitted to the fund and to the VUB's valorization effort as a whole: what is sought is not only financing but also a network, and the capacity to invest time and energy, through advice and support, in project preparation and appraisal.

In its establishment documentation, the fund stresses its acceptance criteria. Here, a seamless interplay with the Interface Cell is mandatory. It is this Cell that provides the "pipeline" of projects to the fund. It regularly alerts the fund as to the overall valorization "pipeline", allowing for a dialogue between fund and Cell so they can coordinate action in the preparation of ventures. No project will come forward to the fund until and unless it has been scientifically validated through the Interface Cell and its underlying scientific idea has undergone an initial test of marketability.

VUB's intellectual property and/or know-how is transferred to the spin-off company in consideration of license fees and royalties based on the company's turnover or, in most cases, in consideration of equity. Where an incubation project is accepted by the fund, an a priori valuation of the university's contribution of intellectual property and/or know-how is made by the definition of a bracket, i.e. the university's minimum and maximum shares in the future company's capital. This means that expectations of future shareholdership on the part of the researchers/founders and the financial investors do not compromise the subsequent incorporation of what could be a successful spin-off company. The individual researchers receive some of the university's shares, in accordance with the *University Regulation on Valorization*, and, where this has been agreed between all future shareholders, additional founder's shares. The researchers/founders are also expected to participate financially in the company capital. It is the policy of the university not to invest financially in the company itself. This is the role (or one of the roles) of the university fund.

Research Parks

Companies focused on research and seeking collaboration with the VUB can find suitable accommodation and infrastructure in one of the university's two *research parks* (Zellik in the Flemish Region and Neder-over-Heembeek in the Brussels Region).

Incubation facilities

An important support option for spin-off initiatives and small and medium-sized high-technology enterprises wishing to establish or maintain an R&D relationship with the university is the *incubation facility*, located at the Zellik research park, close to the VUB's Academic Hospital (Centre for Innovation and Incubation – IICB). In addition, the green light was recently received for the construction of an incubator facility at the "Arsenaal" site, close to VUB's main campus at Oefenplein. The "Arsenaal" Incubation Centre (ICAB) can rely on a renovation budget of more than 5.3 million euro, and is designed to house and support VUB spin-off initiatives and other technological companies involved in research collaboration with the university. The ICAB is expected to become operational in the spring of 2007. We are counting on the proximity (walking distance) of the university's Oefenplein Campus, which hosts excellent groups in engineering, the basic sciences and information technology, to facilitate the creation of new synergistic collaborations in R&D and technology transfer.

The VUB business network: CROSSTALKS

"Today we no longer have the right to pretend that we command a unique position from which we can view the truth about the world. We must learn not to judge different areas of knowledge, culture, or art, but to combine them and to establish new ways of coexistence with those who enable us to meet the unique demands of our time" – Ilya Prigogine & Isabelle Stengers, *Man's New Dialogue with Nature*, 1979.

Our goal, with the CROSSTALKS initiative, is to develop a new exchange dynamic, a model based on interdisciplinary, multi-level and confrontational interfaces between science, industry and society. Through a series of workshops and meetings, and transparent communication about the insights and knowledge generated, CROSSTALKS aims to promote interdisciplinary and long-term thinking as the crucial path towards innovation. The network should be the support structure through which we valorize that particular kind of university knowledge that cannot directly be transferred in a classic technology/knowledge transfer process (i.e., initiated by direct contact between researchers and (specialized) R&D divisions in industry), but which is valuable for enterprises as a whole. Indeed, several types of research, particularly in the human sciences, could be valuable for industry but fall outside the direct interest focus of its R&D divisions.

The objectives of CROSSTALKS

The goal of CROSSTALKS is three-fold: (i) to build a networking framework for out-of-the-box thinking, (ii) to challenge existing and visualize future prospects and (iii) to contribute to a competitive knowledge-based society.

The *networking* aspect aims to produce win-win situations for the university and its business partners by means of the following:
- establishing a new platform and new visibility for academic researchers and industrial decision-makers: networking disseminates VUB research, stimulates its key players and encourages social responsibility and innovation on the part of the business partners;
- bridging the gap between academic research, industry and society while respecting the particular characteristics of each yet stimulating confrontational but constructive exchanges;
- generating the necessary and critical pre-trajectory path for innovation in a fast-evolving, knowledge- and economically oriented society;
- anchoring knowledge at different levels within society, within the industry and within the academic world;

- translating the emerging viewpoints, contrasting perspectives and future economic or social models into a readable, non-academic book;
- offering interdisciplinary coverage and new insights – out-of-the-box thinking – to everybody involved;
- identifying role models – still a major stimulus for young people – to encourage engagement in scientific studies and careers.

In these respects the CROSSTALKS network goes far beyond the spontaneously emerging R&D networks, and also the institutional ones, which are primarily educationally oriented. It also complements the normal *interface* activities described in Section 3.2 above.

The themes and activities of CROSSTALKS

- Future economic and social scenarios based on free and open-source software, including a public debate (Windows by Day, Linux by Night), a science and industry dinner (Open Source: the Paradigm Shift), and a book (*How Open is our Future?*).
- Keeping up with the changing population profile, a theme that emerged as a highly topical issue in a series of prospective conversations and interviews with CEOs from Belgian industry, regional and federal policy-makers and researchers from the VUB (coming soon: The Limits of Medicine, Privatization and Solidarity in a Risk Society, New Interfaces for Older People, Ageing in Brussels).

The anticipated impact of CROSSTALKS

CROSSTALKS aims at valorizing multidisciplinary knowledge in workshops, leading to a series of white papers and reports. A network such as this currently falls outside the strict mission statement of the university and is hence not funded by the government. The main challenge at present is to attract private (industry) partners to fund an initiative that is crucial for the consolidation of knowledge in a complex knowledge-based society, but that does not produce direct, tangible results, and thus has no impact on the next quarterly financial report of the companies involved.

Solid business networks from respected American research institutes such as the Santa Fe Institute, with 50 business partners each contributing 30,000 dollars a year, have become major platforms for exchange both for the academic researchers and for the affiliated business members. There is no reason why this type of networking concept should not succeed with European-based companies – although its scale might be more modest during the initial phase. A major success factor is the excellence and interdisciplinary approach of the scientists involved and the unconditional financial support from the industrial members. A second condition is the establishment of a structural framework and *follow-up* on the events and on the relationships, various forms of collaboration and content emerging from them – through summer courses, educational programs, books and working papers.

3.3. Strategic Research

Meanwhile, the funding and management of strategic research (SBO – *strategisch basisonderzoek*) is developing in parallel, thanks to the expressed political will to favor innovation (the *Innovation Pact* was signed in March 2003 by the Flemish government, industry, higher education institutes and universities), i.e., the production of (strategic) renewal and the successful economic and societal exploitation of new *inventions*. In matters of innovation, incremental improvements in product development, production processes, marketing strategies, design of new services and improved quality of services are considered to be important. But also crucial are the *new* inventions, based on creative, well documented and well structured design methodologies for heterogeneous, complex and distributed systems, an R&D area where universities can play a major role in the context of their policy of developing *strategic research*. Very often, monodisciplinary scientific research skills are insufficient, and multidisciplinary collaboration is required between skilled researchers, developers and end-users from diverse backgrounds, e.g. in the social sciences, legal matters, economics, ethics, science and engineering. The main challenge of many of these kind of projects/programs lies in the *design and organization of complex systems* (e.g. the case-study on the Advanced Media Project, described further in Section 3.3). Essential requirements for ensuring the results have an impact also include the associated aspects of education, training, change management, user acceptance, democratic access and, finally, the availability of risk capital and management of the intellectual property rights. A major role in this area can be reserved for universities, provided they succeed in achieving a change in university policy and management support. A new board, the *IOF Steering Council* (IOF = *Industrieel OnderzoeksFonds*), will therefore be created within the university. The successful operation of the board requires (i) broad autonomy for making thematic choices based on the available background expertise, (ii) fast decision-making for new initiatives, (iii) networking beyond the purely academic spheres, (iv) a system of quality assessment based on output parameters measuring the degree of success and the output of the strategic research (e.g. spin-off creation, patents, volume of industrial projects and technology transfer, etc.). The IOF Steering Council consists of representatives of the university's Research Council (i.e., one for each of the three sub-committees), and diverse (internal/external) experts selected for their particular knowledge of and expertise in various aspects of technology transfer, and affinity with the end-user groups. The working principles of the steering council are quite different from those followed in traditional academic practice, and I anticipate that achieving acceptance within the university community will be quite a challenge for the university's R&D management.

Creating a sustainable environment for excelling research groups, on a program basis rather than at the level of individual projects, is the main task for the university's R&D management. The steering and selection of themes (building on existing strengths and setting out new niches) are mandatory because of the high cost per program. An often-heard criticism on the government's innovation policy is that it tends to support exclusively the economic system while neglecting other spheres in society, such as the social and organizational aspects that can also, indirectly, trigger economic innovation. In this respect, the university's policy on strategic research should be pro-active, by including these aspects too, in the projects it supports, despite the purely economic output parameters imposed by the government on the university's strategic research funded through the IOF.

Steering and selection

A major objective of strategic research is the creation of scientific, domain-specific knowledge pools offering both in-depth and/or interdisciplinary expertise. It is clear that a middle-sized university like the VUB has some difficulty in offering a large set of knowledge pools covering particular scientific domains exhaustively. A challenge for the coming years will be to develop appropriate criteria for decision-making concerning the selection and sustainable (funding) support of certain scientific domains and associated research groups. This process will certainly be driven by the existing, spontaneously developed niches of expertise within the university, and the development of road maps and research visions, as well as world-wide technological prospects (which at present do not necessarily coincide with the centers of gravity of economic activity in Flanders which are responsible for the major part of its gross domestic product). A second type of centers for strategic research will be promoted, namely, those that offer multidisciplinary expertise in certain domains (including, for example, legal, medical, sociological, technical, ethical and other aspects). For setting up this type of strategic research concentrations, maximum participation in the regional *virtual institutes* (see Section 3.1) will be sought.

Input pipeline towards strategic research

To prepare the emergence of these kinds of strategic research centers, the way should be paved for collaboration across the boundaries of individual research domains at the level of fundamental research. With this in mind, the VUB Research Council has recently launched a series of calls for proposals (Horizontal Research Actions, the previously mentioned HOA projects – see Section 3.1) that support excellent research groups willing to develop a transdisciplinary project. Important selection criteria are: the added value obtained through the interdisciplinary collaboration, and the completeness of the expertise created in the selected theme. In the a posteriori and mid-term evaluation criteria, the consortium's capacity to gain financial independence by attracting external funding is rated highly.

One case – The Advanced Media Project

Based on the changes observed in society with respect to content consumption and creation, on the one hand, and the technology push from the ICT industrial sector, on the other, VRT (Vlaamse Radio en Televisie), in collaboration with the government, decided to launch a series of large-scale strategic research projects on the underlying generic technology, the required organizational structure and end-user expectations and behavior, in order to prepare for the well targeted implementation of the required changes.

In the late 1990s, VRT began digitizing its television production platform. Besides conducting field tests with digital television (eVRT), VRT also strengthened its relationship with research institutes in order to prospect for long-term technological decisions. In 2001, this resulted in the first *large-scale strategic research project* in which VRT partnered the VUB and the Interuniversity Centre for Microelectronics (IMEC). The project was baptized the "*MPEG Project*". The starting-point for this project was that content-management systems must be capable of disclosing, in a cost-efficient way, existing and future material over a plethora of channels and platforms. Moreover, existing knowledge and the production/administration system have to be interfaced with such a content-management system. One of the activities therefore focused on the use of ontologies to link existing thesauri with the production/content-management platform.

Ontological approaches were also used at a service level to link together different applications employed at the broadcast station, thereby offering a unified interface between all the components of the system (using J2EE technology). *The complexity of the requirements and the organizational integration of the new technologies were the main bottlenecks in defining a coherent research plan – the approach followed consisted of a mixture of (i) demonstrators illustrating the capabilities of new technologies and triggering the much-needed dialogue for understanding user requirements, and (ii) generic research on standards, technology and design environments.*

The successor to this – the Advanced Media Project – has moved closer to the earlier-described market evolutions and focuses on new methods and tools for designing multiple-channel applications. More specifically, research focuses on distributed architectures for the adaptation of scalable representations, scalable objects, metadata extraction, scalable software and knowledge representations. This collaborative project is driven by the public broadcast station and in collaboration with the recently founded Interdisciplinary Institute for Broadband Technology (IBBT) and the VUB. As IBBT is a *virtual research institute*, researchers from two other institutes are also involved: IMEC and the University of Ghent (UGent). As indicated earlier, this project draws researchers together – 17 in total – in *a multidisciplinary research program on innovative media technologies.*

In such projects, which can be classified as *interdisciplinary strategic research*, it is important that a bottom-up approach is followed in drawing up the research plan. *The management has to set out the application framework in which the team is to operate, but the detailed R&D decisions have to be taken by the joint R&D staff. A mild form of steering is appropriate.* In this particular case, IT specialists and engineers from the broadcast station, typically used to working in a user-driven environment (where the content creators impose the requirements) were mingled – or should we say, confronted – with researchers working in a (semi-) long-term research perspective. Imposing a research program in a purely hierarchical fashion would in this case jeopardize the creative interaction between the project colleagues and impose unrealistically steep learning curves in terms of mutual understanding. Consequently, to ensure a fruitful interaction between knowledge of user needs and long-term insight into technological evolution, a bottom-up approach was selected.

At this stage, the most difficult task for research management is to identify the main research themes and to create small working groups around them. As the project evolves, bigger entities can be created to strengthen the consistency of the project.

Moreover, in order to maximize interaction and knowledge exchange, the team is located at the same physical location at VUB and not – as is usually the case – distributed in interdisciplinary projects. For the collaborators, this is also an enriching experience. On the one hand, the IT specialists and broadcast engineers are decoupled from the immediate pressure of the users at their premises and spend a "sabbatical" period in the center, making it possible for them to broaden their scope and to assess future evolutions. In this way the broadcast station can scale up the intrinsic quality of its personnel. It is important to mention that this is not a sufficient condition for supporting the technology/knowledge transfer. When these employees return to the broadcast station after their "sabbatical", they may be confronted with conservative end-users. *Hence, good communication at this stage of the technology transfer process is necessary as well as training and change management.* On the other hand, researchers are confronted with the specific needs of users and have to question their research goals within this framework, which is also an enriching experience.

It is obvious that, besides a well-organized facility (approx. 150 m^2 research space, a project-specific network infrastructure that interfaces well with the networks of the participating institutes), the above approach requires in particular a local management body with a high emotional intelligence which sees to it that the bottom-up process finally results in an effective research program producing concrete results. In addition, the team is typically composed of a mixture of junior and senior collaborators. Since all collaborators are delocalized, but continue to be employees of their sending institutes to increase cross-fertilization, every junior should have a senior guide on the premises. *It is also crucial that a local identity is created by a mission statement drafted and signed by the group and that, at a practical level, the working environment observes common rules based upon a common understanding* (i.e., the regulations of the researchers' individual employers are overruled).

The above discussion is of course a luxury, since it assumes one has obtained the financial means necessary to support such a collaborative project. *The question remains, of course: how can one manoeuvre a research group into a position where it inspires enough confidence for such an interdisciplinary project? In fact, the term 'interdisciplinary' itself contains part of the answer: research decisions need to be based not solely upon pure academic reasoning, but also to be placed within a broader framework, where their relevance will be questioned with respect to the progress of technology, the consolidation of knowledge (in specific application domains, if they are targeted) and the needs of the end-user community.* Moreover, prospecting is necessary to identify complementary research domains.

3.4. Science communication – actions targeting secondary schools

Science communication has been a well-developed activity within the university for many years. It has been generally accepted as being part of our societal mission. I will not go into a detailed description of all its aspects, but I would like to mention a series of coherent projects that differentiates the VUB from other universities and that may be seen as pilot projects for triggering similar initiatives elsewhere.

- *The ComiX-Files* (http//commix-files.vub.ac.be) is a contest for students aged between 12 and 14, in which they have to discover errors in comic-strips and answer questions. In its third year, 2003-2004, it attracted 3,670 participants. The name is derived from "comics" and *The X-Files*, a popular TV series on science fiction and paranormal phenomena.
- *Stimulus* (http://stimulus.vub.ac.be) is a virtual classroom for pupils aged between 14 and 16 years. It consists of learning packages produced in collaboration with teaching experts so that they can be used as an integral part of the educational program.
- *Virtual Science Museum* (http://virtueelmuseum.vub.ac.be) is a project in which students aged from 16 to 18 years plan, sample and transform information from idea to hypertext content, under the supervision of university experts. It provides an opportunity for the scientific investigation of subjects that directly preoccupy the students themselves, and can be described as goal-oriented and experimental research. Students familiarize themselves with modern web design and get their first glimpse of multimedia technology.

The main challenge for the coming years will be to incorporate the underlying ideas of these pilot projects in the educational programs of secondary schools, in order to give young people an added incentive to pursue studies based on state-of-the-art research in a university or high-school environment.

- *Science Shop*
  Science shops provide scientific knowledge for associations who do not have the resources to conduct research themselves, or to have it done for them. These associ-

ations might be a committee dealing with traffic problems in a local neighborhood, for example, or a group concerned with water quality in a local pond. Thanks to the science shop, a host of societal problems can be addressed and researched (from a variety of viewpoints: physics, sociology, the economy, etc.). Students carry out the research, under the supervision of experienced scientists. In this way, the students get a feeling for social needs and have the opportunity to help solve problems that affect them directly in daily life. Involving citizens in scientific research is the focal point of the science shop.

We performed a needs analysis in Flanders and the Brussels Region to assess whether non-profit organizations felt that they might use a science shop in the future, and for what kind of problems. This allows our science shop to focus on certain domains. We asked some 5,420 organizations for their opinion. Out of 586 responses, 44% in Flanders and 71% in the Brussels Region are struggling with societal issues that could end up as a case for the science shop. This is the case in particular with environmental organizations, associations of elderly people and organizations that group patients with a particular disease. Most of the problems had to do with health, communication or culture.

4. Some challenges for today and the near future

Apart from organizing the structural and operational R&D support described in previous paragraphs, some more conceptual challenges are particularly important for the university's R&D policy. Without attempting to produce an exhaustive list of these challenges, below we briefly discuss some of the main ones.

4.1. Long-term thinking versus short-term results

Maintaining and enhancing the university's *research culture and academic independence*, chiefly by respecting the diversity in problem formulation and in research approaches, as well as individual initiatives and **long-term thinking,** will be the main challenge in the near future, especially given the strong pressure from the political world, government authorities and industry pushing universities, as a primary sources of knowledge, towards **short-term results** with an excessive emphasis on their expectation of direct output and profit. Re-establishing a *long-term career for outstanding scientists* has been an urgent need since the abolition in 2000 of the posts of research leaders and directors at the National Science Foundation. The financial cost of maintaining such a set of top researchers – however limited – is high. A solution that would lower the financial burden could probably be found through the federal government, by the extension of the current framework of tax reductions for the promotion of scientific research.

The *long-term thinking versus short-term expectations of immediate results* polarity is directly reflected in the span covered by fundamental research, strategic research and industrial or societal research.

4.2. Steering versus Supporting

A knowledge enterprise like a university should *support* the three levels of R&D mentioned in Figure 2. This of course does not necessarily imply that every research group should cover all three types of R&D. Intra-university funding (see Figure 2) allows for organizing trajectories covering the chain from "discovery" all the way up to "implementation". Organizing these trajectories and balancing the degree of *steering* and thematic selection is a difficult exercise, in which it is imperative, in my opinion, that there should be no thematic steering whatsoever of the fundamental research. The main challenge is to balance the amount of steering at the strategic research level, since at the industrial R&D level the primary steering comes in any case from the end-users.

4.3. Invest primarily in talent, not technology

A key factor in transferring the benefits of public funding to industry is the encouragement and stimulation of young people to pursue careers in higher education.

VUB contributes to this objective by a full package of *science communication tools* for all age categories in secondary school (12 to 18 years old), so that they "learn by doing", under the supervision of experienced scientists and following a rigorous scientific methodology to solve problems affecting their own world: "Science helps us understand and solve interesting problems".

Continuous support for research in institutes that have educational duties attached to their research mission is the best guarantee for creating a talented and research-minded generation for the future. The notion of a *virtual institute*, as described in Section 3.1, provides an excellent vehicle for achieving the required high-level research combined with relevant education.

4.4. Brain drain, brain gain, shortage of local researchers

To quote Eric Banda, secretary-general of the ESF (European Science Foundation): "*We do want to keep our talent, but we also have to import new talent from other continents*". Improving the mobility of researchers has been a major objective of EU policy (supported by 10% of the research budget of FP6, namely 1.6 billion euro), motivated by the high positive correlation of research excellence and international embedding. *A strong brain drain is perfectly normal*, provided it is offset by brain gain. In my opinion, governments, universities and all socio-economic players should primarily emphasize measures for augmenting the brain gain, although the public opinion usually likes to emphasize the dramatic aspects of brain drain. At the level of the EU, the EURYI awards experiment deserves attention (a competition in which top young researchers can win a sufficiently high award to set up a meaningful research group in the EU university of their choice). Also, at the Belgian level, the federal research agency provides *return grants* for researchers who have worked a minimum of between two and four years in research outside Belgium. At the level of regional policies, several thematic institutes are developing a high visibility that attracts foreign scientists by offering a well-structured and rich research environment. "*It is certainly not the money alone that attracts researchers in the knowledge society*" (Theo Dillissen). At the level of the VUB, we announce our rare vacancies for research professors on the best international websites. The research environment provided by our university is certainly adequate to attract doctoral researchers to compensate for the shortage of local researchers (166 of our 582 scientific researchers are foreigners; out of the 257 PhD grant-holders, 102 are of foreign origin; and despite the language handicap (caused by the government's decree that even at Master's level the educational language should primarily be Flemish), there are 31 foreigners among our 486 professors, while the number of foreigners among the 102 doctoral assistants is 26).

The main overall problem is in attracting top postdoctoral researchers, probably owing to the insufficient attractiveness or visibility of the research environment and infrastructure, the lengthy and tedious administrative procedures, the absence of a university research career structure outside a professorship, lack of job security and the remaining arbitrariness and lack of standards in recruitment, employment conditions and career advancement that still exist, despite many efforts made by individual universities. The plans to draw up a "European Researchers' Charter" are most welcome with respect to these latter shortcomings. The EU delivers more PhDs than the USA, while the number of researchers in the EU is 5.36% of the working population, in Japan 9.72% and in the USA 8.60%. *This prompts the inevitable conclusion that we are the champions at providing research training and preparing postdoctoral researchers to achieve their best performances elsewhere.* The opportunities for long-term research careers, reserved for excellent postdoctoral researchers who remain excellent over time, are too limited even for our own, local, excellent postdoctoral researchers. This is particularly problematic as the number of extra researchers needed in the EU, in order to reach the "3% of GDP" Barcelona norm, is sometimes estimated to be as high as 600,000.

4.5. The researcher-entrepreneur

It is the ambition of more and more scientists to combine aspects of entrepreneurship with their scientific research aspirations. Boundaries between the two are regularly crossed, even by researchers who are world leaders in their own spheres. It is my opinion that universities should at least be supportive towards, and even encourage, this kind of behavior, by providing a professional environment for it. One way to do so, from an early stage on, would be to create a "PhD with industrial affinity", whereby the accompanying PhD program would be oriented towards preparing valorization of the results. I am convinced this formula will attract a new public to PhD programs. Given the growing emphasis on strategic research, a multidisciplinary PhD should also become feasible. A particularly successful example of a high-level researcher-cum-entrepreneur is Leroy Hood (Nobel prizewinner in 1993, and co-founder of 11 companies).

4.6. A close bidirectional link between education and research

The current Bachelor/Master reform in the EU is forcing a closer link between research and education at Master's level. This coupling is bidirectional: (i) the educational mission of universities requires education to be supported by research, which will probably be a major criterion for the Master's accreditation, and (ii) it is difficult to see how university research that is not linked to a Master's educational program will be able to survive, owing to a lack of both financial resources and input of human resources for the research groups. *Lifelong learning*, although not yet fully structured, will gain in importance.

4.7. The university as a catalyst for regional projects and for a region's power of attraction

Despite the globalization of markets, communication and knowledge, the notion of physical proximity continues to play an important role in differentiating one region from another in terms of dynamism, conviviality, welfare and well-being. Even in Belgium, the transition process (overall, slow compared with other developed countries) towards a knowledge society evolves at a different pace dependent on the regional culture. The presence of knowledge centers and their attitude towards creating societal impact, and the responsiveness of local governments, play a major role in this transition process. Location factors that directly enhance the competitive economic position of a region are (i) material in nature, such as the physical infrastructure, the communication infrastructure, the transport network, the existence of marketing networks and (ii) immaterial, such as the availability of technological and management skills, the learning potential and flexibility of the population, the existence of a spirit of entrepreneurship, innovation power, and relations with government authorities. Knowledge centers and universities play an important role in creating the conditions necessary for the development of these immaterial conditions, and nowadays they are called upon more and more to play important roles in regional cultural and development projects. In Flanders, the region of Leuven is a well-known example of success. The Brussels-Capital Region is lagging behind with this respect, primarily owing to political instability. As Martin Hinoul said, in a recent interview: "*We need more than a region of entrepreneurs, we need an entrepreneurial region*". Indeed, entrepreneurs alone are utterly insufficient to achieve the *synergy between well-being, cultural richness, social justice and economic growth that is the key to a region's power of attraction.*

5. University R&D policy-making and management, a balancing act between pro-activeness and reactiveness

In this paper, I have tried to sketch the requirements for R&D management in a university setting. I specified its mission statement, its multiple functions and its duties towards PhD students, researchers and the external environment. I proposed an operational model for a medium-sized university, such as the VUB, and discussed in detail the main bottlenecks, hampering progress, that should be dealt with by such a model. Finally, I tried to sketch some general challenges that are probably preoccupying larger numbers of people in the university world. Here, I would like to come back to what is, in my view, the most difficult balancing act for R&D management in universities.

For their main tasks, universities receive specific government funding that is more and more fragmented and accompanied by rapidly changing and increasingly rigid output constraints, in which there is a tendency to over-emphasize **short-term results**. This forces research management to trigger *flexible reactiveness* within the research community, to avoid the *risk of not being involved* at all. On the other hand, fundamental research at the initiative of the individual researcher and research group is our main added value, and differentiates us in a unique way from other knowledge centers. The **long-term nature** of fundamental research, and also the patience and perseverance needed to find new questions, to solve previously unasked questions, to discover new facts, to set up new theoretical models, to validate them experimentally and to create new knowledge, often conflict with the short-term expectations of the universities' environment (e.g. industry, government, and players in society). Pro-actively organizing support for new domains of research, discovered by researchers long before policy-makers or industry are even aware of them, remains a key responsibility of the university's research management. *In periods of unfavorable economic conditions, keeping the right balance between pro-activeness and reactiveness, and between the production of short-term results and long-term thinking, is a difficult balancing act.*

For some tasks, universities receive no implicit funding from the government, e.g. science communication, networking with industry for knowledge consolidation, lifelong learning. Nevertheless, a modern university should play a role in these domains, which are expected to become important in the future. *Pro-active organization* of support is needed in these cases, requiring support from the *sponsorship program*, usually based on the university's network of alumni, and from the *endowment policy*, both of which have to be organized with increasing professionalism to ensure success.

I agree that we should respond to the requirements of the quantitative R&D output performance indicators imposed by our funding agencies. I also agree that these output performance indicators are playing a more important role in the allocation of research funds, for fundamental, strategic and industrial research. They certainly measure something, but a lot of the value created by research remains intangible and there is a high risk that this value may be destroyed if the importance of quantitative parameters is further increased. It is my opinion that the global performance parameters imposed by the funding agencies and the government should be used with care when applied internally. For internal quality assessment, organized in an eight-year cycle and intended to improve R&D processes within the university, an approach based on peer review by domain experts, who also visit the departments and interview the research groups, has proved to be successful. A recent bibliometric study (carried out for the VUB by CWTS, Universiteit Leiden) points out that although there is a high domain-dependent heterogeneity in bibliometric performance, the overall publication impact of the VUB is higher than that of any other Flemish university. This result emerges naturally from our research culture, without imposed "publish or perish" systems within the university.

Over-emphasizing the measurement of so-called scientific output will ultimately influence research behavior and attitude, and the main goal will become the maximization of output parameters, whereas it should remain:

(i) *The curiosity to discover new things* ("Electricity was not discovered by someone trying to improve the performance of a candle" – Dirk van Dyck).

(ii) *The capacity to develop research results further, up to a level where they can have an impact* ("Engineers may have difficulty in understanding Darwinism and evolution theory, as Richard Dawkins once said, but they make inventions and design new processes rather than explaining existing phenomena").

(iii) *The development of derived implementations that benefit industry, socio-economic life and society* ("A product developer does not bother about the complex fundamentals of the interaction between all of the tens of millions of transistors in a consumer product such as the mobile phone – he cleverly applies development tools that reduce this complexity").

In my view, a modern university should support all three of these phases of research, and their players – which does not necessarily mean that each individual researcher or research group has to be active in all phases.

I am convinced that as our insight into the complexity of nature increases, the complexity of societal organization grows and globalization extends even further, so too should the scale of the research groups studying these phenomena grow, together with the extent of their international networking. Many of the research-management proposals I have made in the paper support a development along these lines. Nevertheless, it is important to preserve creativity and to support research entities whose members can still sit all together around the same table at lunch-time, in a nice restaurant, and talk about fabulous new discoveries and ideas.

Driving home from work through the forest of Zonien and trying to come up with a good conclusion to this paper, the following picture came into my mind. The forest is well known for its high, centuries-old beech trees. In recent times, however, thanks to *short-term* economic and mobility imperatives, the forest has been partitioned by highways circling around the Brussels Region and opening the city up towards Wallonia. While the necessary precautions were taken to preserve the large, old, prestigious beech trees, the highways cut through large areas of the lower bushes. An unexpected *long-term* result is the destruction of whole areas of high trees during stormy weather. This was explained a posteriori as an indirect effect of the removal of the bushes and low trees for the construction of the highway: forest boundary trees and bushes have a higher renewal rate than the trees farther in, and a different root structure, which makes them robust against stormy weather, and by resisting the high winds they form a protective shield for the high trees, allowing them to grow for centuries until they reach full maturity.

If there is one thing that a research manager should aim for first, it is this *respect for diversity*. This is as crucial for sustaining the ecology of research groups at a university as it is for the flora in a wood. Nourishing diversity means, in the first place, fostering a long-term vision and concentrating on sustainability, in opposition to the short term-thinking that is the dominant trend in our society. That is why we have to maintain a variety of research themes, represented by the different research groups and individual researchers. We also need fostering of the *different research types*, ensuring that there is enough institutional flexibility to support them. Academic freedom is crucial for the successful exploration of the unknown, and respect for the individual researcher remains vital for *fundamental research*. The focused and selective support of some upcoming research groups and of existing pools of excellence, without their losing individual depth, is the challenge taken up by the *strategic research-management model* I have presented. Maintaining harmony, balance and cross-fertilization between the different research types ranging from fundamental and strategic to industrial/societal research, and the valorization of R&D results, is the overall challenge for the university's R&D management. It is a task comparable to preserving the biodiversity in a well-tended forest, rather than a well-kept garden center.

6. Acknowledgements

I would like to thank all those who have generously contributed to this paper by creative ideas, pieces of text and improvements made to my writing style. I am particularly grateful to Mieke Gijsemans (Head of the R&D Department), to Sonja Haesen (Coordinator of the Interface Cell) for her input concerning *Interface,* to Marleen Wynants for her suggestions for improving my writing style and her perseverance in going after high quality in all she does. I also received input from Martine Follet, Bruno De Vuyst, Sara Engelen, Bart De Greef, Peter Schelkens (The Advanced Media Project case-study), Wim Van Broeck, Stefanie Goovaerts and Sofie Van Den Bossche. As usual, it was Nadine Rons who provided me with a large quantity of numerical data. In addition, many thanks to Christl Vereecken and Sandra Baeyens, who helped me find numerous documents and pieces of information in my messy files, and who supplied me with excellent coffee and cookies to keep me awake during the writing process.

Luckily, there's a better way to guard against ID theft.

Is Open-Sourced Biotechnology Possible?

Daniel de Beer[1]

When Richard Stallman began writing the free GNU-software operating system with a small group of associates in 1984, little did he imagine what lay in store, or that by 1998 it would have become the "open-source" movement. The movement aims "to develop powerful, reliable software and improved technology by inviting the public to collaborate in software development".[2] These very reasonable words do little to reveal the originality that lies behind the movement's success. Stallman insists that the open-source movement is mainly founded on ideas and logic drawn from the ideals of 1776, the ideas of freedom, of community and voluntary cooperation. Today, the extent and range of those who continue to develop this free software is astonishing: from the individual computer genius who works alone to the research departments of the computer giant IBM – which sees this as part of its commercial battle against Microsoft – and including, along the way, networks of communities caught up in the adventure, all of whom contribute in a non-hierarchical way and without receiving remuneration from the system. Personal motivation is unimportant; what matters is that there are sufficient people who want to be involved in the movement, and that "it works". The free software movement is gaining in notoriety. Munich made the leap in 2003 and by June 2004 the public authorities in Paris were wavering on the brink of migrating from Windows to free software... much to the displeasure of Microsoft, which was only too aware that what was at stake was not simply a market, but a symbol. The company was prepared to agree to a 60 per cent reduction in order not to lose the fight.[3] In June 2004 the Ville de Paris was still wavering. Besides the economic advantages – which may or may not be well-founded, but do not concern us here – the civil service cites, in favour of free software, its independence of a single, ultra-dominant supplier and the fact that it allows the State to adapt the software to meet its own needs, thereby freeing it from dependence on the strategic decisions made by the publisher. As far as Microsoft is concerned, such issues are purely ideological and have no place in the choice of one computer system over another...[4]

While there are those who find the free and open-software movement profoundly irritating, others find it fascinating. The debate on its merits extends beyond information technology and is flourishing in new fields. *Is such a scenario conceivable, for example, in the field of medical research or biotechnology?* Before examining this more closely, we need to investigate the reproducibility of the free and open-source movement.[5]

Technical Environments with Little in Common?

First, to set the scene: technically speaking, the transposition of the open-source model into fields other than that of information technology is not a simple matter. In brief, the information and research equipment used in biotechnology and the pharmaceutical environment are not of the same unequivocal, codified nature as the algorithms used in software. The cartoon image of the computer genius creating new programs using inexpensive equipment stored in his garage has no equivalent in the biotechnology or pharmaceutical industries. Here the knowledge is generally complex and non-adaptable; it may involve a number of disciplines and often requires costly equipment.

The process is also much slower. Moreover, unlike improvements to a computer program which can be given immediate, real-scale testing and find immediate application among the general public, the gap between the discovery or invention of what might become a new biotechnological or pharmaceutical product and its being put on the market is considerable. First it has to undergo technical and regulatory procedures, which are themselves lengthy, complex and expensive. Metaphorically speaking, the image of building a cathedral is better suited to biotechnological research than the image of a bazaar that is associated with the open-source movement.[6]

The Unhelpful Legal Situation

However, it is the legal situation that poses the most difficult problem. Software can usually be protected by copyright, which offers two notable advantages. On the one hand, protection can be acquired without formality or expense. Something created and made public acquires protection. On the other hand, copyright allows for the issuing of a licence which also gives full access to all the information – including the source code – and authorises the modification of this information and the automatic capture of such modifications under the same licence. Again, all this without expense or particular formality.[7] If the information can be found on a website, access can be gained by a simple click of the mouse button to sign up for the licence.

Biotechnology and pharmaceutical research, however, operate under a patent system, which is an entirely different matter. To begin with, the information and research tools on which the research work depends are often subject to patents that have to be negotiated with their patent holders, who are rarely of a philanthropic disposition and can be very reluctant to give broad access to their property. Secondly, it takes considerable time and expense to have a patent granted. The patent system is ill-suited to the simple, flexible management of open licences of the kind that prevail in the open-source domain. The problem therefore lies in the legal status of information and inspiration, and the possibility of escaping the patent system appears in fact to be becoming increasingly remote.

The Patent Empire (I)

One initial problem comes from the continuing growth of what is deemed to be patentable and is therefore patented. In the life sciences, the famous American "Diamond v. Chakrabarty ruling" started the process. Reversing the tradition according to which products of nature were not patented,[8] in 1980 the Supreme Court agreed that the oil-eating bacteria invented by Chakrabarty could be patented.[9] Five years later it was a variety of genetically modified corn that was patented,[10] followed in 1987[11] and 1988[12] by transgenic animals including the famous Harvard oncomouse. Hence, from the smallest to the largest, from the simplest to the most complex, living matter, the basic matter to which research relates has, in less than ten years, become property that can be appropriated. Of course, various conditions have to be met, including that the "invention" should be useful or capable of industrial exploitation: protection is linked to the potential use being claimed. A further condition is that the invention should have been made by a person. It is therefore important to understand the criterion of human intervention as a condition of patentability. Traditionally, human intervention had to be of a creative nature in order to qualify for the right to obtain a patent; it was a matter of invention, not of discovery. Today the boundary between invention and discovery has been eroded. As a result of the rulings given by the relevant institutions, few things now escape the patent trap provided technical process is used to reveal the information, the element of living matter that one intends to appropriate. It is therefore possible to patent an active principle found in nature, including in human beings themselves,[13] without adding anything to it, provided technological means were needed to extract it, to purify it, in short, to bring it to light. In a rather convoluted manner, the European Directive on the legal protection of biological inventions sets the boundaries of what is and what is not patentable.[14] In Europe, at any event, plant and animal varieties shall not be patentable, except if the technical feasibility of the invention is not confined to a particular plant or animal variety.[15] The human body, including the sequence or partial sequence of a gene, cannot constitute patentable inventions, but an element isolated from the human body or otherwise produced by means of technical process, including the sequence of a gene, may constitute a patentable invention, even if the structure of that element is identical to that of a natural element.[16]

So it is that the salmon growth-hormone gene, the gene corresponding to the cold-resistance protein of the ocean pout, a natural colony of marine bacteria extracted from the Sea of Japan, fish genes linked to proteins which have a gelling action, the active principle in yellow yam (West Africa) affecting diabetes, the sweetening element found in the Gabonese plant *Pentadiplandra brazzeana*, the human growth-hormone gene, human insulin, and so on and so forth cannot give rise to, have all been patented. These "inventions" are often used not simply as research material but also as research tools or working tools. For example, a bacterium that is discovered to have the capacity to serve as a vector, a means of transport, that can carry a gene into an environment other than its natural environment, can be patented for this purpose even though it may have been known for decades. Such inventions therefore have a dual potential value: as a direct source of innovation, and as a source of future innovation, as a research tool. Given that one rarely starts from scratch and that research is often cumulative or combinatory, it becomes increasingly difficult to carry out research that does not come up against previous patents. Vitamin A-rich Goldenrice is a well-known example. To exploit this invention would have required the negotiation of licences with a dozen holders of more than seventy patents relating to five fields of technology.[17]

Intellectual property rights continue to nibble away at new domains. Who remembers now that fifty years ago medicines were not normally patentable? Today, even databanks themselves, regardless of their content or originality, can be protected.

The 'No Patent, No Innovation' Argument

The main argument cited in various forms to justify the hegemonic system of intellectual property rights, and in particular patents, is well known: patents are a way of ensuring a return on investment in research; this encourages new products to be researched and developed in the interest of the general public. In other words, market virtues do not provide a solution to the problem of free copying: who would continue to invest in research if the fruits of their efforts could be copied free of charge by competitors?[18]

The Tragedy of the Anticommons

There are those who also maintain that the patent system encourages the rational management of subsequent research. Such research must necessarily go through the patent holder who thus provides a certain coordination which may help prevent wasted energy and encourage useful information transfer.[19] However, this optimistic vision has been strongly challenged. Even the most fervent advocates of the current arrangement have expressed concern. The difficulties and costs associated with the formalities surrounding the use of patented material and the risks associated with the goodwill of existing patent holders have undeniably harmful effects. By dint of patenting, protecting and privatising everything, do we not in fact end up in a situation where research and development are obstructed and innovation is paralysed? It is a system supposed to ensure a movement of continuous innovation, but has it not in fact reached its limits? The problem was illustrated by the metaphor of the tragedy of the anticommons[20] which takes the opposite view of another metaphor, that of the tragedy of the commons.[21] The original story relates to common grazing land that is open to all. If, for example, a hundred animals could be fed on this land without the grazing being destroyed, it will always be in the herdsman's personal interest to add another animal and yet another until disaster finally strikes: the public nature of the resource invites its over-exploitation and this ends in tragedy. Conversely, if too many fences are erected around such resources, this leads to their under-exploitation and, where innovation is concerned, to obstruction; that is the tragedy of the anticommons.

Although it is indisputable that the proliferation of patents has negative effects on research and development, it would nevertheless appear that the expected tragedy has not occurred, at least if one considers that the tragedy in question would be the paralysis of the current system of innovation. Many players are in a good negotiating position, for example because they have built up a solid portfolio of patents as currency. In other cases, the usage value of the patented research tool is considered to be worth the investment in view of the anticipated profits. In still other cases, negotiations lead to an agreement on future profit-sharing. As well as such successful contracting licences, players have developed other working solutions: inventing around patents; going offshore – to areas with more intellectual property freedom; infringement. According to empirical research, one-third of American commercial companies and research institutes more or less regularly disregard patents,[22] or appeal with varying degrees of justification for exemption for research purposes (which allows the use of protected information for the purposes of research but excludes commercial exploitation of any kind). They avoid them because of the development and use of public databases and research tools (to which we shall return later), not to mention court challenges and legal guerrilla warfare.[23] And in certain sectors, such as pharmaceuticals and, in particular, agrobiotechnology, recent years have seen vast mergers and takeovers which, at the end of the day, are another way of solving the problem of access to research tools and putting oneself in a strong negotiating position.[24] The system has therefore been able to adapt – at least in the eyes of its major players.

Sharing of Data and Research Tools

The development and use of public databanks and research tools are among the means available to limit the harmful effects of the tragedy of the anticommons. In fact, simple public disclosure of part of their data, or sharing agreements between players on pre-competitive research tools – on the "I share – you share" principle – are not infrequent. There are cases where commercial firms have invested sizeable amounts of money to create assets that pre-empt intellectual property rights. The decision to engage in such "Property-Pre-Empting Investments"[25] is based on reasons of strategy. Examples can be found in the pharmaceutical industry, despite the fact that it is solidly organised around an aggressive patent policy. Increasingly, gene sequences corresponding to expressed human genes, the genes involved in the production of proteins by the human body, were coming under patent to a large number of independent companies. These miniscule fragments of the human genetic code are essential to medical and biotechnological research. In 1995, the pharmaceuticals giant Merck, in partnership with Washington University in Saint Louis, created the Merck Pharmaceutical Index, a public database of these gene sequences, and it has worked steadily to build up this databank. In 1998 the databank, with more than eight hundred thousand gene sequences, was made freely accessible to the public. After weighing up the advantage of being the patent-holder of a share of these genetic sequences against the usage value associated with access to the whole or the majority of the sequences, the company had come down in favour of the usage value. The viability of the system depended on the a priori knowledge that other players would reach the same conclusion, and that it would not occur to anyone to take out patents on the most interesting sequences. An initiative of this sort therefore forms part of the commercial strategy now available to commercial companies.

Other initiatives relate to working methods and tools rather than to the data itself. One example is that of BioBricks.[26] This research centre, a recipient of public funding at the Massachusetts Institute of Technology, is working on the development of computer programs and standardised procedures for the processing of genetic information, to be made freely available. It is hoped that these programs will make it possible to carry out some of the routine and irksome operations often necessary to biotechnological research quickly, efficiently and without expense. It is noteworthy that here, unlike in the case of Merck, the funding is public. But it is also a question of research tools considered to be precompetitive, of inputs useful or necessary for research but still some way from the actual development of inventions ready to be put on the market. The analogy with the open-source movement is therefore limited to giving free access to the information.

The Patent Empire (II)

In order fully to understand the reproducibility of the open-source movement, it is also important to consider a second fundamental aspect that has turned the economy of knowledge production on its head. This time it relates to universities and research centres which, from the outset, have played an extremely important role in the life sciences and medical research. Again, it occurred in the United States. In 1980, the United States passed a law authorising and encouraging patents to be taken out by universities and research centres on inventions resulting from research financed by public funding as well as from partnerships with the private sector.[27] Although such legislation does not exist at a European level, it is nevertheless an accepted choice. European thinking tirelessly continues to affirm the demand for the tightening of links between research centres and industry in order to improve the integration of research and innovation. The contamination of research by the imperatives associated with the pursuit of profitable innovations is not a consequence of this association, it is its objective. This changes entirely the ecology and economy of research. It is understandable that academic institutions should take offence at being compared with alternative commercial enterprises, but the fact remains that, like it or not, the diffusion and sharing of knowledge, the legal status of this knowledge, the selection of fields of research and the manner in which research is conducted are, to a large extent, affected by the increasing cosiness between academic or similar research and the world of business.

Biotech... Back to Open Source?

It is therefore the case that the specific environment in which biotechnology and the pharmaceutical industry operate – an environment inextricably interwoven with the technical and legal constraints discussed above – makes importation of the open-source model difficult. This model operates under certain principles which, to recap, are the communal development of a technology, complete transparency in how it works, and the ability to use and improve it freely, provided improvements are shared openly.[28] Another important characteristic of the open-source approach is that it does not require major investment in order to function, and this allows complete autonomy for all the institutional and private players involved and enables a multiplicity of players to become part of it.

However, the fact is that in the fields of pharmaceutics and biotechnology there are very few significant, successful examples operating effectively on open-source principles.

The magnificent enterprise that brought together finance and public and private players from different countries to work together on decoding the human genome is often cited as an example of an open-source initiative. There is a good deal of truth in this claim. Serious consideration was also given to protecting the data under an open-source type licence.[29] Tim Hubbard, who headed up the department working on the human genome at the Sanger Institute in Britain, and who was one the promoters of the project, even met with Richard Stallman to get his advice. The question of the legal status to be given to the information was even more critical as the American company Celera Genomics was also in the race and had the firm intention of appropriating its discoveries. However, as it was considered to form part of humankind's common heritage, genomic data had historically been placed in the public domain with unrestricted use. In philosophical, political and symbolic terms, there could be no better decision – at least in my opinion – even if it might entail the risk of all subsequent inventions being patented.

On the other hand, the promoters of the International HapMap Project,[30] in which Tim Hubbard and his institute are again interested parties, have decided on an open-source legal approach. The project deals with research into the genes involved in common diseases such as cancer and diabetes. These diseases are expressed in the genome by the fact that certain elements of the genome implicated in the disease are not in their usual place. The aim of the project is to map these differences, identifying them through comparison between diseased and healthy populations. This mapping would represent a major advance in research into therapies and diagnostic tools. The project involves some thirty Japanese, British, Nigerian, Chinese and American research institutes. If it is successful, the potential commercial value of this data will be enormous. It will require very little for the information to become patentable – the transition from disease marker to patented diagnostic tool is just one small step. To prevent the project from going off-course, the data has been made accessible on the Internet, but an open licence, like open-source licences, is required. Users must undertake not to do anything that might restrict access to the data by other parties, and only to share the data with those who agree to the same licence. Following the open-source example, copyright – in the form of "copyleft" – is being applied to this information. The licence short-circuits any attempts to take out a patent parasite, that is to say, patents taken out on the original material to which just a tiny change has been made. The initial budget is some hundred million dollars, coming mainly from public funding but also from private pharmaceutical firms driven by the same concerns as Merck in the example discussed earlier.

In the field of agrobiotechnology, the so-called MASwheat[31] initiative is interesting because it encourages a participatory approach which, without becoming fully public – given the technical nature of the subject – nevertheless extends beyond the initial project partners. Researchers from a dozen American research institutes have come together in a consortium to try to increase the productivity and disease-resistance of corn. The aim is to identify, through genetic engineering, the genes responsible for high levels of productivity and improved disease-resistance in various types of corn throughout the world. These genes are then transferred from one corn to another by non-genetic techniques, and tested over several generations. The final product will therefore not be a genetically modified organism, and can be grown using traditional farming methods. This project is supported by public funding. The markers – which enable a gene to be identified and tracked – and the research protocols are accessible to all. The promoters of the project hope in this way to encourage a large number of teams to use these resources and make their results known. Those who so wish can have their results protected by a plant-breeder's rights certificate. This confers an intellectual property right specific to plants but allows the knowledge and genetic resources themselves to remain in the public domain. It is significant that this initiative was made possible because the big agrobiotechnology multinationals have little interest in corn. This is partly because of the natural characteristics of corn, which does not easily lend itself to genetic manipulation. However, the main reasons are the numerous patents already obtained on corn, soya, rice and other plant models, the exclusivity contracts binding the university and public laboratories that hold these patents, and the existence of material transfer agreements (whereby the owner of the information required for research to be carried out makes that information available to research centres on condition he or she will have the benefit of an operating licence on the results).[32]

The Field of Medical Research

Initiatives also exist in the field of medical research, but most often when projects have reached a rather advanced stage. Eric von Hippel, a teacher at Massachusetts Institute of Technology's Sloan School of Management, is trying to set up an open network of doctors and patients interested in researching additional uses of drugs.[33] After a long and costly process, drugs are approved for a specific purpose. However, it often happens that new uses are discovered for these molecules that have been put on the market. It would appear that in Europe and the United States almost half the drugs used to treat a specific disease come into this category. It is unusual, however, for the full official approval process to be gone through again for this new use, in particular the costly clinical trials,[34] especially if there is no new patent at the end of it or the market is not a sufficiently profitable one. This situation has a number of disadvantages. The new uses are not officially announced, and therefore patients may not be aware of them. In any event, in the United States insurance companies only cover on-label use. Lastly, the efficacy of these new uses is not formally evaluated. Dr von Hippel's idea is to persuade as many doctors and patients as possible to take part in the evaluation of these new uses and thus establish valuable data. If conclusive, a kind of open-source clinical trial, conducted at minimum expense, would make it possible to obtain official approval for the new use of the drug.

In early June 2004, two lawyers and a computational biologist – Stephen Maurer, Arti Rai and Andrej Sali – argued convincingly at BIO 2004 in San Francisco in favour of "open-source drug discovery" which could galvanise tropical-disease drug research and substantially reduce costs.[35] The idea is to start a website, the Tropical Disease Initiative, fed by voluntary contributions from biologists and chemists working on certain diseases.[36] They would examine and comment on accessible data, which would be made available to all. It is also hoped that they would themselves carry out experiments. The website would facilitate the sharing and discussion of all contributions. The creators believe that the methods used could be purely computational. Once a molecule was identified as being an interesting candidate for drug production, the open-source phase of the process would move aside. In fact, the entire development phase of the drug – following identification of the molecule and prior to its mass production – is ill-suited to the open-source model (with the exception of the case in the preceding example). The final development would be awarded to a laboratory based on a tendering process. Once approved, the drug itself would be put in the public domain for production by generic-drug manufacturers at the lowest price possible.

By Way of Conclusion?

There are other initiatives than those mentioned here, but we do not have the time or space to examine them all. Yet, taken together, they still amount to no more than a tiny drop in the ocean of the Research and Development conducted in what is now the traditional manner for commercial companies and research centres. I am among those who hope that the open-source approach will be long-lived and spawn many offspring, particularly in the fields of pharmaceuticals and biotechnology. Nevertheless, it has been clear throughout this brief article that the technical constraints associated with these technologies and the prevailing legal environment do not favour it. However, the enthusiasm for the open-source movement applied to fields other than information technology raises other questions. In fact the majority of initiatives, if not all, arise from awareness of and in reaction to the shortcomings in – or the downright undesirable effects of – the current intellectual property system. There are ethical considerations, for example, that have resulted in the refusal to allow the human genome to become the property of a handful of companies. There is indignation at the virtual absence of research to combat the tropical diseases that are devastating impoverished populations. There is also the desire to improve agricultural production while respecting farmers' way of life and production methods, the environment and all the living matter in its own right. It is not a question of denying intellectual rights their merits: that would be naive. The belief, however, that intellectual property rights as they exist at present, and are regularly strengthened, are the only way of guaranteeing the research and development of products necessary for the common good, certainly deserves to be questioned.

A gifted student recently championed a report on the uncomfortable coexistence between the right to life and health and intellectual property rights. One of the premises of his work was that patents are unavoidable to ensure research into tropical diseases. He confidently asserted this as a fact that could not reasonably be challenged. The example is trivial, but illustrates just how difficult it is to extricate oneself from the grip of this belief. In fact it is rather like wearing blinkers on one's thinking. It is accepted today that one can and indeed that it is necessary to think about and to modalise the exercise of property rights taking into account such factors as the environment, global warming, sustainable development and the preservation of endangered species. Why then is it so difficult and so marginal when it is a question of intellectual property?

It is understandable that Microsoft should maintain that the not-purely-economic arguments put forward by the Paris authorities are based on ideology. But must the same be true, for example, in academic circles?

Notes

[1] Researcher at *Law, Science, Technology & Society* (LSTS), Vrije Universiteit Brussel, Belgium. This contribution is the result of research carried out under the *Interuniversity Attraction Poles* (V.16) programme *The Loyalties of Knowledge* (info: www.imbroglio.be), financed by the Belgian Federal Science Policy.

[2] Richard M. Stallman, "La licence GNU et l'"American Way'", *Multitudes*, 5, Paris, Ed. Exils, 2001 (http://multitudes.samisdat.net (June 2004) and "The GNU Operating System and the Free Software Movement", *Open Sources: Voices from the Open-Source Revolution*, C. DiBona, S. Ockman & M. Stone (eds) (available at: http:www.oreilly.com/catalog/opensources/book/stallman.html). For an analysis of the foundations of the free software movement, see Yochai Benchler, *Coase's Penguin, or, Linux and the Nature of the Firm*, 112 Yale L.J., 2002 (online at: http://www.law.nyu.edu/benklery/; Eben Moglen, *Anarchism Triumphant: Free Software and the Death of Copyright*, 1999, esp. Ch. III (available at: http://emoglen.law.columbia.edu/my_pubs/anarchism.html).

[3] Florent Latrive, "Chez Microsoft, c'est Paris à tout prix", *Libération*, Paris, 28 June 2004, p. 21.

[4] Florent Latrive, "Les Logiciels gagnent du terrain dans l'administration", *Libération*, Paris, 28 June 2004, p. 21.

[5] The term "open source" does not give a true rendering of the different characteristics of the movement initiated by Richard Stallman. Moreover, the term is semantically inadequate when referring to fields that do not use a "source code" as a term of art. Nevertheless, it is more convenient to continue to talk about "open source" provided it is understood as encompassing all the characteristics of the free software movement.

[6] Eric S. Raymond, *The Cathedral and the Bazaar: Musings on Linux and Open Source by an Accidental Revolutionary*, O'Reilly, 2001 (http://www.catb.org/~esr/writings/cathedral-bazar/cathedral-bazar/ (June 2004).

[7] Dennis Kennedy, *A Primer on the Open-Source Licensing Legal Issue: Copyright, Copyleft and Copyfuture*, 2002, available at: http://www.denniskennedy.com/opensourcelaw.htm. See also the article by Fabienne Brison in this collection.

[8] However, the 1930 Plant Patent Act allowed the patenting of plants that could be reproduced asexually.

[9] *Diamond v. Chakrabarty*, 447 U.S. (*United States Supreme Court Reports*) 303, 100 S. Ct. (*Supreme Court Reporter*) 2204 (1980).

[10] *Ex parte Hibberd* (1985) 227, *United States Patent Quarterly*, 443.

[11] *Ex parte Allen* (1987) 2, *United States Patent Quarterly (2nd Series)*, 1425.

[12] *Leder* et al., *Transgenic Nonhuman Animals*, United States Patent No. 4.736.866, 12 April 1988.

[13] One famous example is the case of "the man with the golden cells". Without informing the patient on whose spleen he had operated, a doctor cultivated his cells and discovered that they produced a special protein. This protein was found to produce a pharmaceutical compound effective against cancer. A patent was taken out on this cellular line in 1984 and sold to the Swiss pharmaceutical giant Sandoz for fifteen million dollars. The patient, John Moore, feeling degraded and exploited, demanded the return of his cells. In July 1988 a Court of Appeal in California ruled that he had no property right

14 over the cellular line of his organs. For further details, see Bernard Edelmann, *La personne en danger*, Paris, Presses Universitaires de France, 1999, pp. 289-304.
14 Directive 98/44/EC of the European Parliament and the Council of 6 July 1998 on the legal protection of biological inventions, O.J.E.C., L. 213, pp. 13-21.
15 Article 4 of Directive 98/44/EC.
16 Article 5 of Directive 98/44/EC.
17 Transformation methods, selection markers, promoters, transit peptides and carotene biosynthesis genes. Cf. David Kryder, Stanley Kowalski & Anatole Krattiger, "The Intellectual and Technical Property Component of Pro-Vitamin A Rice (Goldenrice): a freedom-to-operate review", *ISAAA Briefs*, No. 20, New York, Ithaca, 2000.
18 For an overview of these theories, see Nelson and Mazzoleni 1997, No. 48, XXX.
19 Edmont W. Kitch, "The Nature and Function of the Patent System", 1977, *Journal of Law and Economics*, 20, pp. 265-290; Nancy Gallini and Suzanne Scotchmer, 2002, No. 239, under the heading "IV: Optimal Design: The Case of Cumulative Invention"; online at: http://socrates.berkeley.edu/Xscotch/ip.html.
20 Michael Heller & Rebecca Eisenberg, "Can Patents Deter Innovations? The Anticommons Tragedy in Biomedical Research", *Science*, Vol. 280, No. 5364, May 1, 1998, pp. 698-701.
21 Garett Hardin, "The Tragedy of the Commons", *Science*, Vol. 162, No. 3859, Dec. 13 1968, pp. 1243-1248.
22 John P. Walsh, Ashish Arora & Wensley M. Cohen, "Research Tool Patenting and Licensing and Biomedical Innovation", study paper for US National Academy of Science, Washington, DC., December 2002, online at: http://www.heinz.cmu.edu/wpapers/download.jsp?id=2003-2.
23 For further details on the reality of the "tragedy of the anticommons" and the way in which those involved have limited its effects, see Janet Hope's website "Open-Source Biotechnology Project", Part: Intellectual Property and Biotechnology Industry Structure, available at: http://rsss.anu.edu.au/~janeth/IPIndust.html.
24 It is in the farm-produce industry that the phenomenon is most impressive. For an overview see: http://www.corporatewatch.org.uk.
25 In the words of Robert P. Merges, who examines the example quoted ("A New Dynamism in the Public Domain", *The University of Chicago Law Review*, 71, XXX, 2004, pp. 1-20).
26 http://parts.syntheticbiology.org/
27 Patent and Trademark Law Amendments Act (P.L. 96-517), 12 December 1980, amended in 1984 and 1987, more commonly know as the Bayh-Dole Act. This legislation was supplemented by other laws removing obstacles to partnerships between public research institutes and the private sector.
28 Bruce Perens, "The Open-Source Definition", *Open Sources: Voices from the Open-Source Revolution*, C. DiBona, S. Ockman & M. Stone (eds) (online at: http:www.oreilly.com/catalog/opensources/book/stallman.html).
29 John Solston & Georgina Ferry, *The Common Thread. A Story of Science, Politics, Ethics, and the Human Genome*, London, Bantam Press, 2002; Kenneth N. Cukier, "Open-Source Biotech: Can a non-proprietary approach to intellectual property work in the life sciences?", *The Acumen Journal of Life Sciences*, Vol. I, Issue 3, September/October 2003, 43.

[30] Jennifer Couzin, "Consensus Emerges on HapMap Strategy", *Science*, Vol. 304, Issue 5671, April 30, 2004, pp. 671-672.
[31] http://maswheat.ucdavis.edu.
[32] Pierre-Benoît Joly & Bertrand Hervieu, "La 'marchandisation du vivant'. Pour une mutualisation des recherches en génomique", *Futuribles*, Issue 292, December 2003, pp. 5-29.
[33] "An open-source shot in the arm?", *The Economist (Technology Quarterly)*, June 12, 2004, pp. 15-17, available at: http://www.economist.com.
[34] Clinical safety trials do not have to be re-run. On the other hand, the second and third phases, which relate to efficacy and side-effects must be conducted again based on the hypothesis of the new use of the drug.
[35] Stephen M. Maurer, Arti Rai & Andrej Sali, "Finding cures for tropical diseases: is open source an answer?", online at: http://salilab.org/pdf/136_MaurerBIOESSAYS2004.pdf.
[36] "We see [the Tropical Disease Initiative] as a decentralized, community-wide effort that (a) searches parasite genome for new targets, (b) finds chemicals that bind to known targets, (c) evaluates each candidate drug's chances of success, and (d) selects the most promising candidates for further development".

Biography

Daniel de Beer worked as a lawyer in Brussels for fifteen years. In 1994, he left Belgium and worked for different nongovernmental organisations and the European Commission, mainly in Rwanda, but also in Cambodia, Haiti, Chad and Togo. Between 2000 and 2003 he was the Director of the Belgian NGO *Avocats Sans Frontières*. He is currently preparing a doctoral thesis on intellectual property rights at the Vrije Universiteit Brussel, within the framework of the Interuniversity Attraction Pole project, *The Loyalties of Knowledge*. His research deals in particular with the connection between patents and access to essential drugs and between patents and genetically modified organisms, in the context of food sovereignty.

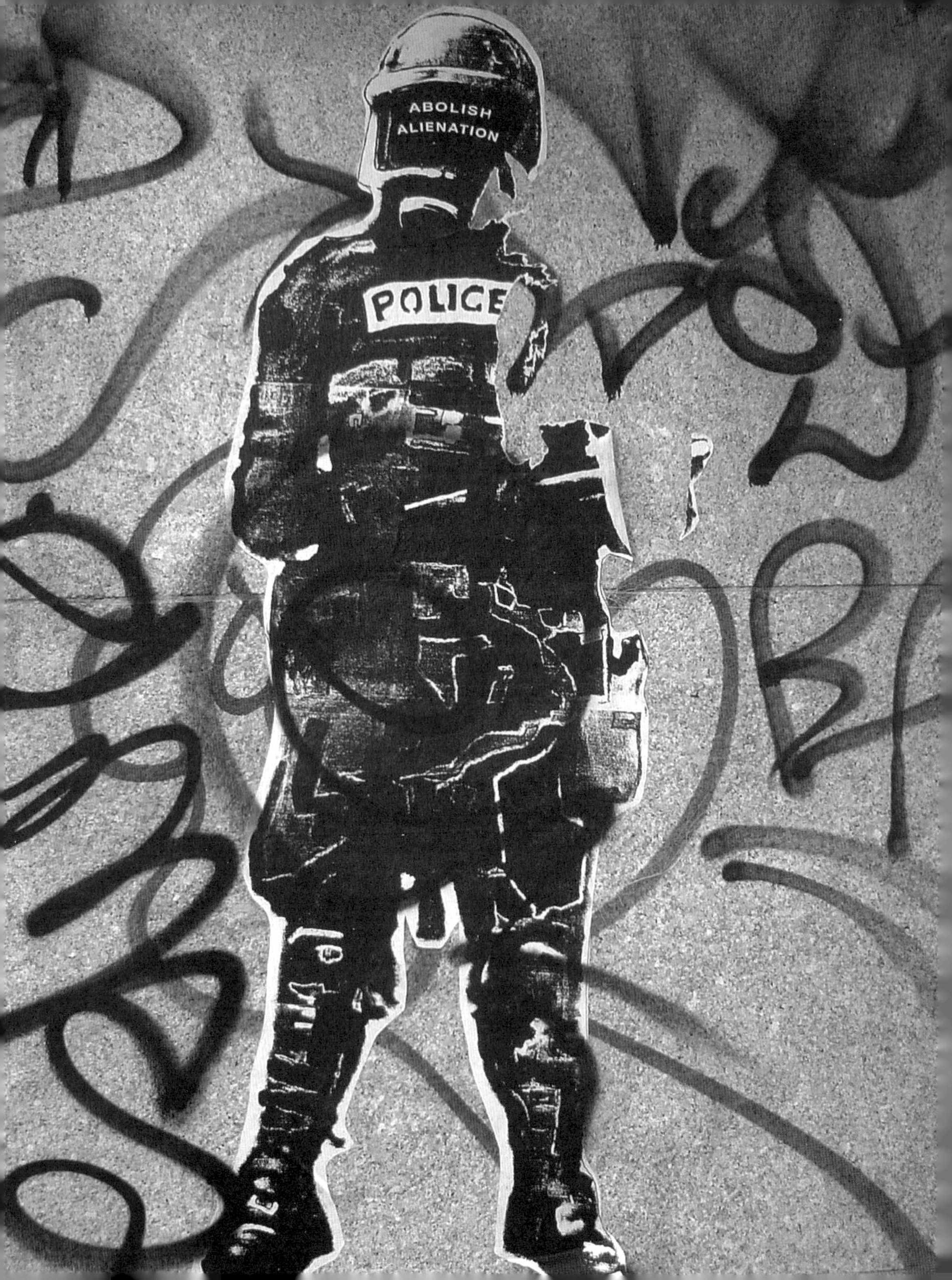
ABOLISH
ALIENATION
POLICE

Legal Aspects of Software Protection through Patents, and the Future of Reverse Engineering

Bruno de Vuyst & Liv Steuts

1. Introduction

Under the Agreement on Trade-Related Aspects of International Property Rights (TRIPS), Annex 1C of the Marrakesh Agreement of 15 April 1994, establishing the World Trade Organization (WTO), software programs are protected by copyright. In this context TRIPS makes an explicit reference to the Berne Convention for the Protection of Literary and Artistic Works (1971). The problem with this protection is that, owing to the dichotomy between idea and expression so typical of copyright protection, the reverse engineering of software is not excluded by this form of protection. This is seen by a number of software makers as economically, and hence legally, unacceptable.

For this reason, U.S. software makers have increasingly – and successfully – turned to patent protection to stop forms of reverse engineering that are not seen as "fair". In Europe, there is an exclusion of patent protection for computer programs in Article 52(2) of the Convention on the granting of European patents (European Patent Convention of 5 October 1973 (EPC)), but this exclusion is being increasingly narrowed and some are calling for it to be abandoned altogether. European case-law uses a technicality as a proxy for allowing computer programs (which have a "technical", "physical" impact) to be patented as a computer-related or -driven invention, hence to a degree excluding reverse engineering. A proposal by the European Commission, put forward in 2002, calls for a directive to allow national patent authorities to have broader scope in patenting software, as a further safeguard against certain forms of reverse engineering, all the while allowing decompilation.

This chapter will show U.S. and emerging European law complementing copyright with patent protection in an attempt to protect valuable investments by innovators, including through the attempted exclusion of certain forms of unfair reverse engineering. Failure to evolve in this direction, the authors argue, would be a disincentive to innovators, particularly those just starting out as entrepreneurs. At the same time, however, patent protection should not be a disincentive to bringing innovation into the world, so certain forms of re-engineering should be allowed. In the authors' view, all of this should be made explicit in TRIPS.

2. Copyright protection of software

A software program is first and foremost a sequence of orders and mathematical algorithms emerging from the mind of the innovator, hence the link with copyright law as the prime source of intellectual property protection.

According to Article 10 of TRIPS, computer programs, whether in source or object code, shall be protected as literary works under the Berne Convention provided that they are (i) original and (ii) tangible. Under Article 9 of TRIPS, which states that copyright protection extends to expressions, but not to ideas, procedures, methods of operation or mathematical concepts as such, copyright protects the actual code of the computer program, and the way the instructions have been drawn up, but not the idea underlying them.[1]

Authors can thus protect their original work against unauthorized copying. Consequently, an independent creation by another person would not automatically be seen as a copyright infringement.[2] With respect to software programs, this could result in other people disassembling – decompiling – an existing software program to determine the underlying idea and then using this idea to "build" their own program ("reverse engineering"). As they only use the idea, which is not copyrightable, no infringement will ever result. This situation may be a definitive disincentive to an innovator, and, hence, further protection is demanded.

3. The protection of software by patent law

Software is a novel form in the technology world, and may make a claim to protection as patents, which require novelty for protection.

The conditions to be met in order to enjoy patent protection are more stringent than those for copyright protection. In Europe,[3] for example, an invention may enjoy protection from patent law provided it (i) is novel,[4] (ii) it is based on inventor activity[5] and (iii) it makes a technical contribution.[6] In the U.S., the patent requirements to be met are (i) novelty, (ii) non-obviousness and (iii) innovation must fall within the statutory class of patentable inventions.

Pursuant to patent law, the underlying technological ideas and principles of a software program can be protected, but not the "original" draft of the software program (i.e., the actual code). A patent-holder can therefore invoke the protection of his or her patent to prevent others from making, using or selling the patented invention. Unlike with copyright protection, the inventor's patent is protected regardless of whether or not the software code of the patented program was copied.

4. Evolution of the legal protection of software

Prior to the 1980s, U.S. courts held that software was not patentable and that its only protection could be found in copyright. Indeed, in two landmark decisions – *Gottschalk v. Benson*[7] and *Parker v. Flook*[8] – the U.S. Supreme Court ruled that software was similar to mathematics and laws of nature (both judicially excluded from being patented) and was, therefore, unpatentable.

In *Gottschalk v. Benson* (1972), a patent application was made for a method of converting binary-coded-decimal (BCD) numerals into pure binary numerals. The claims were not limited to any particular art or technology, to any particular apparatus or machinery, or to any particular end use. Consequently (and in accordance with traditional patent theory), the U.S. Supreme Court stated that this invention was not patentable, as it merely related to a mathematical algorithm.

377

Parker v. Flook (1978) was the second case involving algorithms to reach the U.S. Supreme Court. This case related not to a simple algorithm, but to a complex software control. When the software monitoring the sensors involved in a chemical process recognized trends consistent with a dangerous runaway condition, an alarm was triggered. Despite the unique nature of the algorithm and the fact that the claim only covered petrochemical processing, the Supreme Court again upheld the Patent Office in refusing to patent. The argument was that tying an algorithm to a specific use is not sufficient to make it patentable.

In *Diamond v. Diehr* (1981),[9] however, the court reversed course, deciding that an invention was not necessarily unpatentable simply because it utilised software. The case concerned a method for curing rubber. The process involved a computer which calculated and controlled the level of heat applied to the rubber during the process. The U.S. Supreme Court stated that, in this case, the invention was not merely a mathematical algorithm but a process for moulding rubber, and hence that it was patentable. And this was true even though the only "novel" feature of this invention was the timing process controlled by the computer.

Since the 1981 *Diamond v. Diehr* decision, both the U.S. courts and the U.S. Patent Office have gradually broadened the scope of protection available for software-related inventions,[10] and we now have a situation in which people are plainly expected to obtain a patent for software-related inventions. Since the *State Street Bank and Trust Co. v. Signature Financial Group Inc.* case (1998),[11] even mathematical algorithms and business methods have been found to be patentable (see also the *Amazon One-Click* case).[12] The patent in the *State Street Bank and Trust Co. v. Signature Financial Group Inc.* case covered data-processing systems for implementing an investment structure, developed for use by Signature (the patent owner) as an administrator and accounting agent for mutual funds. When negotiations between Signature and State Street Bank broke down, the latter filed a suit to have the patent declared invalid, unenforceable or not infringing. The district court decided that Signature's system was unpatentable, because it was either a mathematical algorithm or a "method of doing business". However, the U.S. Court of Appeals for the Federal Circuit reversed this decision and held that Signature's system was not an unpatentable mathematical algorithm. Furthermore, they dispensed with the notion that "methods of doing business" could not be patented.

Since this decision, the U.S. focus for patentability has been "utility based", defined as being based on "the essential characteristics of the subject matter", and the key to patentability is the production of a "useful, concrete and tangible result".[13] This development resulted in a rush of patent applications for software-related inventions and business methodologies.

Contrary to the U.S., European states have been unwilling to grant patents for ideas, business processes or software programs. The main reason is their (in)direct exclusion from patent protection, as stated in Article 52 EPC.[14] Nevertheless, the European Patent Office has also changed course. Its view on the patentability of software programs, and more particularly the interpretation of the "as such" limitation (described below), has been under review, in response to pressure especially in the field of computer programs (the so-called computer-implemented inventions).

This evolution within Europe has been marked by three landmark cases: *Vicom/Computer Related Invention*,[15] *Koch & Sterzel/X-ray apparatus*[16] and *SOHEI/General purpose management system*.[17]

In *Vicom/Computer Related Invention (1986)*, the invention consisted of methods for digitally filtering a two-dimensional data array representing a stored image. The European patent application for this invention was refused because (amongst other things) the methods were implemented by a program run on a known computer, which hence could not be regarded as an invention under the terms of Article 52(2)(c) and (3) EPC. However, the Board of Appeals held that "*No direct technical result is produced by the method as such. In contrast thereto, if a mathematical method is used in a technical process, that process is carried out on a physical entity (which may be a material object but equally an image stored as an electric signal) by some technical means implementing the method and provides as its result a certain change in that entity. The technical means might include a computer comprising suitable hardware or an appropriately programmed general purpose computer*".[18] Consequently, the Board decided that "*a claim directed to a technical process, which process is carried out under the control of a program (be this implemented in hardware or in software), cannot be regarded as relating to a computer program as such within the meaning of Article 52(3) EPC, as it is the application of the program for determining the sequence of steps in the process for which in effect protection is sought. Consequently, such a claim is allowable under Article 52(2)(c) and (3) EPC*".[19]

379

The criterion of the patentability of a software-related or -driven invention was refined in *Koch & Sterzel/X-ray apparatus (1978)*, which concerned an X-ray apparatus for radiological imaging that was directed by a software program. The software program allowed the X-ray apparatus to select one of the X-ray tubes, and to set the tube voltage values for the exposure parameters selected, etc. In this case the Board ruled that "*while an ordinary computer program used in a general-purpose computer certainly transforms mathematical values into electric signals with the aid of natural forces, the electric signals concerned amount to no more than a reproduction of information and cannot in themselves be regarded as a technical effect. The computer program used in a general-purpose computer is considered to be a program as such and hence excluded from patentability by Article 52(2)(c) EPC. But if the program controls the operation of a conventional general-purpose computer so as technically to alter its functioning, the unit consisting of program and computer combined may be a patentable invention*".[20]

Furthermore, the *Koch & Sterzel/X-ray apparatus* introduced the "whole content" approach. Following this principle, if it makes use of both technical and non-technical means, an invention must be assessed as a whole. Thus the invention may not be split up into its technical and non-technical aspects.

In 1994, the Board of Appeals once more extended the scope of patentability of software-related or -driven inventions in the *SOHEI/General-purpose management system* case. The invention involved was a computer system for several types of independent management, including at least financial and inventory management, comprising different units (*e.g.*, display, input and output) and a digital processing unit, as well as a method for operating a general-purpose computer management system. Although the hardware elements of the invention were nothing more than already existing parts of an ordinary computer, and the novelty lay in the software elements, the Board was of the opinion that the exclusion contained in Article 52(2) EPC did not apply. Moreover, the Board recognized that "*the non-exclusion from patentability also applies to inventions where technical considerations are to be made concerning the particulars of their implementation. The very need for such technical considerations implies the occurrence of an (at least implicit) technical problem to be solved (Rule 27 EPC) and (at least implicit) technical features (Rule 29 EPC) solving that technical problem*".[21]

To summarize the above-mentioned landmark cases, "*a claim directed to a technical process carried out under the control of a program (whether implemented in hardware or in software) cannot be regarded as relating to a computer program as such within the meaning of Article 52 EPC*" and, as cited above, "*an invention must be assessed as a whole. If it makes use of both technical and non-technical means, the use of non-technical means does not detract from the technical character of the overall teaching*".

Notwithstanding this extension of European patent law by judicial decision, unlike in the U.S., patents have never been granted for software programs "as such" – the main reason being that in Europe an invention has to be technical in nature. This requirement of technicality is not explicitly stated in the EPC, but can be deduced from Article 52 EPC. The provision contains a list of subject matters that are not patentable "as such" (among them programs for computers), which is not meant to be exclusive, as it only gives examples of materials that are non-technical and abstract in nature and, thus, cannot be patented.[22]

In the U.S., on the other hand, a patentable invention must simply be within the technological arts. No specific technical contribution is required. The mere fact that an invention uses a computer or software makes it become part of the technological arts if it also provides a "useful, concrete and tangible result" – and hence makes it patentable.[23]

5. Expected developments in the protection of software in Europe

In Europe too, a number of software innovators would like patent protection to be extended so as to make software programs eligible for patenting, thereby maintaining their financial incentive to create.

One of the main arguments of supporters of the patentability of software is that patent law provides inventors with an exclusive right to a new technology in return for the publication of the technology. Thus patent law rewards innovators for the time and money they have invested, and encourages the continued investment of time and money. Opponents of any extension (indeed, of any protection) through patent law argue that such protection is not needed, and is indeed inappropriate in an industry such as software development, in which innovations occur rapidly, can be made without a substantial capital investment and tend to be creative combinations of previously-known techniques.[24]

The opponents of software patents also point out practical problems in administering the patent system, as software is voluminous and incremental. Indeed, as stated before, an invention can only enjoy patent protection provided it is not part of the prior art. To verify whether or not this condition is met, it is necessary to know the prior art. However, knowledge about software is widespread and unbundled (it is very often either tacit or embedded) and thus may not be sufficiently explicit to enable the patent verification system to work well. In other words, there is too much software, and not enough information about it, and what there is, is hard to find.[25] As transaction costs are high, a patent system will favour only those with enough resources to verify whether their software can be patented and, afterwards, to seek out and deal with possible infringers.

Besides these financial impediments inherent in the patent process, installing a system of software patents entails some theoretical issues. These have to do, first of all, with the basic, global instrument for intellectual property protection, *i.e.* TRIPS, and secondly, with the specific legislation in Europe and the U.S.

TRIPS constitutes an overall – global and uniform – intellectual property framework. Although, according to Article 10 TRIPS, computer programs are protected by copyright, it is the intention of TRIPS not to exclude from patentability any inventions, whether products or processes, in all fields of technology, provided they are new, involve an inventive step and are capable of industrial application (Article 27 TRIPS).[26] TRIPS consequently provides, implicitly, that computer programs may also be the subject of patent protection. It also implies, however, that reverse engineering is allowable (see Section 6 below).

From what has been stated previously (see Section 4 above), it is clear that U.S. legislation allows patenting of software. In Europe, however, Article 52 EPC represents an obstacle to such protection.

In its decision of 4 February 1999, the Board of Appeals of the EPO (hereafter referred to as the "Board") stated:[27] *"The fact that Article 10 is the only provision in TRIPS which expressly mentions programs for computers and that copyright is the means of protection provided for by said provisions, does not give rise to any conflict* between Articles 10 and 27 TRIPS. Copyright and protection by patents constitute two different means of legal protection, which may, however, also cover the same subject matter (e.g. programs for computers), since each of them serves its own purpose. (...) The Board has taken due notice of the developments in the U.S. (and Japanese) patent offices, but wishes to emphasize that the situation under these two legal systems differs greatly from that under the EPC in that it is only the EPC which contains an exclusion such as the one in Article 52(2) and (3). Nevertheless, these developments represent a useful indication of modern trends. In the Board's opinion they may contribute to the further highly desirable (world-wide) harmonization of patent law."

This decision makes it clear that if software "as such" is to be protected on the basis of patents, the exclusion under Article 52 EPC has to be removed. This raises the question of whether this would be desirable in Europe, and whether its consequences would be favourably perceived.

Supporters of software patents would like to win a first battle in the race for software patentability by endorsing the proposal for a Directive on the protection by patents of computer-implemented inventions currently being discussed within the European Union. They are aware that approving this Directive will not immediately result in the patentability of software "as such"; however, as stated by the Board of Appeals of the EPO, it will constitute *"a new development that may contribute to the further highly desirable (world-wide) harmonization of patent law"*, which may result in the removal of the exclusion now contained in Article 52 EPC. Clearly, opponents will do anything to prevent this development from taking place.

6. The future of reverse engineering

Some scholars indicate that an unlimited software patent would result in the exclusion of reverse engineering and, thus, in the creation of monopolies. Indeed, many innovations in software are cumulative or sequential, which means that they build on earlier innovations, thereby giving early innovators greater leverage over later innovators. While it may be possible for innovators to design around individual patents, these could create substantial barriers to obstruct new entrants, especially small ones.[28]

In the U.S., there appear to be conflicting views on decompiling. On the one hand, the Federal Government maintains a protectionist policy, attempting to exclude reverse engineering wherever feasible. On the other, the courts have used the "fair use" concept in U.S. copyright law to allow decompiling.[29]

The protectionist policy of the U.S. Government is reflected in the following examples:

(i) a strong reaction against any proposals (*e.g.*, within the European Union or Japan) to amend laws so as to accept decompiling;

(ii) the Economic Espionage Act of 1996 (EEA), which was adopted in response to an increase in the use of foreign intelligence assets "to steal American business secrets". The EEA criminalizes (i) the theft of trade secrets to benefit foreign powers and (ii) their theft for commercial or economic purposes. Nevertheless, parallel developments of the same information by two or more people are not covered by the statute. Thus reverse engineering appears not to be punishable under the Act. However, as stated in the Manager's Statement, "*the important thing is to focus on whether the accused has committed one of the prohibited acts of this statute rather than whether he or she has done 'reverse engineering'. If someone has lawfully gained access to a trade secret and can replicate it without violating copyright, patent or this law, then that form of reverse engineering should be fine*";[30]

(iii) the Digital Millennium Copyright Act (DMCA),[31] which grants a limited right to reverse-engineer around access controls, but only for legally-obtained software and then only to create a separate, inter-operable and non-infringing program. While this limited right permits the use of circumvention devices to aid such reverse engineering activities, this permission does not affect the ban on circumvention-device distribution for those wishing to undertake permitted reverse engineering. Consequently, to take advantage of this narrow permission one would have to create a proper personal circumvention device from scratch, which is rather unlikely to happen;

(iv) The Uniform Computer Information Transactions Act (UCITA) is a proposed (state) model law for software transactions. UCITA does not mention reverse engineering and, according to some, therefore does not "explicitly" ban it. Most modern software licences do, however, ban reverse engineering. Under UCITA, those licences and their anti-reverse engineering provisions would become law. UCITA could therefore allow software publishers to outlaw, unilaterally, all forms of reverse engineering, even where it is done purely for reasons of inter-operability.[32] Moreover, the states that have so far enacted UCITA have adopted versions differing in significant details from each other and from the model law itself. As a result, UCITA does not promote uniformity and certainty. On the contrary, it guarantees confusion in the rules that apply to software.

Sega Enterprises Ltd v. Accolade, Inc.[33] and *Atari Games Corp. v. Nintendo of America, Inc.*[34] are two examples of the evolution within the U.S. courts that diverges from that within the U.S. Government.

Sega Enterprises Ltd v. Accolade, Inc. (1992) dealt with Accolade's decompilation of Sega's video cartridges to gain an understanding of the lock that was to be placed on a new entertainment system to ensure that only Sega cartridges could work in it. Accolade wanted to determine what the content of this lock was, in order to create software that would be able to interface with the Sega machines. The court stated that if (i) one lacks access to unprotected elements of an original work, such as the ideas behind it, and (ii) one has a "legitimate reason" for accessing those elements, then disassembling the copyrighted work is considered to be a fair use of the Copyright Act. With respect to the first condition, the court held that, because object code can only be understood by decompilation, no other means of access existed. As for the second condition, the court described decompilation for achieving inter-operability (as in the case at hand) as fair use under the Copyright Act. Furthermore, the court stated that to refuse someone the opportunity to create an inter-operable product would be allowing existing manufacturers to monopolize the market, making it impossible for others to compete.

In *Atari Games Corp v. Nintendo of America, Inc.* (1992), similar reasoning was used. Atari tried (unsuccessfully) to decompile Nintendo games in order to make their own software inter-operable with Nintendo. The court came to the same conclusion as in the Sega case.

So decompiling may be regarded as fair use, provided that (i) there is no other means of access to the non-protected elements, and (ii) there is a legitimate reason for gaining access. Nevertheless, in this case, the court held that decompiling should not be used for creating a product that is substantially similar to the original product.

The European Union, unlike the U.S. Government, appears to be aware of the need for a modulated approach, and attempts to respond to this problem in Article 6 of the draft Directive on the protection by patents of computer-implemented inventions by ensuring that (as is already the case with copyright) patents cannot be used to block the inter-operation of complementary programs – thereby falling into line with the attitude of the U.S. courts.

Indeed, the draft Directive makes specific reference, *inter alia*, to the provisions on decompilation and inter-operability contained in Council Directive 91/250/EEC, in such a way that the different scope of the protection granted by patents would not undermine the possibility of carrying out the acts permitted under the existing Directive. Articles 5 and 6 of Directive 91/250/EEC state that copyright in a computer program is not infringed by acts which under certain circumstances would otherwise constitute infringement. These exceptions include acts performed for the purpose of studying the ideas and principles underlying a program, and the reproduction or translation of code if this is necessary to achieve the inter-operability of an independently created computer program.[35]

Such provisions are obviously not favourable to supporters of broad-based software patents, as one of the most important reasons for extending the scope of patent protection appears to be the possibility of excluding reverse engineering and, thus, extending/strengthening the market position of the patent-holder. It is unlikely, however, that the arguments of strict monopolists will prevail, as the European Union appears keen to take into account a general interest – and certain forms of reverse engineering – when dealing with intellectual property protection.

Indeed, the decompilation of software – the first step in reverse engineering – is useful in order to ensure inter-operability. It also has other uses, e.g. in dealing with the "legacy" of software programs no longer maintained by their investors.

From the above, it is clear that TRIPS cannot be left as it is. The differences in opinion between Europe and the U.S. Government are too great to let the matter go unaddressed in TRIPS. The patentability of software needs to be acknowledged explicitly, not only implicitly. At the same time, fair uses of reverse engineering also need to be acknowledged explicitly within TRIPS. Given the U.S. Government position and the legislative action referred to above, obtaining agreement on such an amendment of TRIPS will not be easy. Still, one cannot let reverse engineering escape the rules of software protection, and at the same time one must accord it legitimate protection, where this is fair.

7. Discussion

There is a need to come up with an intellectual property coverage that promotes innovation but at the same time brings investment to society. In this respect, society's general interest can be used to lead towards a balance between different categories of intellectual property, without excluding valorization towards society. The patenting of software benefits innovation, as it offers fuller protection to software creation than reliance on copyright does. Still, reverse engineering's fair-use forms should be allowed.

The more narrow-minded jurists might not comprehend why the scope and protection period of copyright have expanded over time. However, as was recently indicated in the launch, by the European Commission, of the fine-tuning of existing EU legislation on copyright and related rights, the extensions are based on market forces and follow trade needs,[36] once more demonstrating that intellectual property law is an application of political, economic and financial realities or aspirations.[37] This view was confirmed by a recent study on copyright issues and the economics of intellectual property regulation by the Congressional Budget Office in the USA.[38]

As a recent European Commission Working Paper makes clear, the evaluation of computing networks will determine future provisions on decompilation,[39] as will underlying economic interests.

In time, one may perhaps have to admit that software programs are so peculiar that current legal protection models under either copyright or patent law need to be abandoned and further adequate protection developed, e.g. out of non-property-right sources such as contract law (in particular confidentiality clauses and non-competition clauses), trade secrets, or the law of commercial business practices (in particular as regards unfair competition). Nevertheless, if such protection is chosen, criminal law provisions designed to punish theft and outright piracy will also have to be taken into account.[40] Contractual protection will therefore not be a panacea.

A reform of TRIPS – making it explicit that software programs can be protected by patents, but that reverse engineering may be fair, to allow for inter-operability (and legacy) – is needed in order to remove the legal uncertainty that is currently having a negative economic impact on innovation incentives.

Notes

[1] T.F.W. OVERDIJK, "Europees Octrooibureau verruimt mogelijkheden voor octrooiering van computersoftware", *Computerrecht* 1999/3, 158-159.
[2] G.J. KIRSCH, "Software Protection: Patents versus Copyrights", at http://www.gigalaw.com/articles/2000-all/kirsch-2000-03-all.html consulted on February 18, 2004; B. Leijnse, "Softwarepatenten.be", Trends, January 16 2003, at http://www.softwarepatenten.be/pers/trends_20030116.html consulted on February 27 2004.
[3] By Europe, we mean the contracting states whose national patent systems are generally harmonized by the European Patent Convention so that patents can be applied centrally by the European Patent Office (EPO).
[4] *i.e.*, has never been produced before.
[5] *i.e.*, has not been part of prior art.
[6] *i.e.*, contributes to the state of the art.
[7] 409 U.S. 63 at http://digital-law-online.info/cases/175PQ673.htm and http://supct.law.cornell.edu/supct/cases/patent.htm consulted on March 4, 2004.
[8] 437 U.S. 584 at http://digital-law-online.info/cases/198PQ193.htm and http://supct.law.cornell.edu/supct/cases/437us584.htm consulted on March 4, 2004.
[9] 450 U.S. 175 at http://www.gigalaw.com/library/diamond-diehr-1981-03-03-p5.html and http://digital-law-online.info/cases/209PQ1.htm consulted on March 4, 2004.
[10] G. J. KIRSCH, "The Software and E-Commerce Patent Revolution", at http://www.gigalaw.com/articles/2000-all/kirsch-2000-01-all.html consulted on February 18, 2004
[11] 149 F.3d 1368 at http://www.law.cornell.edu/patent/comments/96_1327.htm consulted June 15, 2004.
[12] R.B. BAKELS, "Van software tot erger: op zoek naar de grenzen van het octrooirecht", *IER* 4 augustus 2003, nr. 4, p. 214.
[13] Study Contract ETD/99/B5-3000/E/106: "The Economic Impact of Patentability of Computer Programs" (Report to the European Commission) at http://europa.eu.int/comm/internal_market/en/indprop/comp/study.pdf consulted on February 18, 2004, (p 20-23 of full report).

14 Article 52(2)(c) EPC states that programs for computers shall not be regarded as inventions within the meaning of Article 52(1) EPC and are, therefore, excluded from patentability. Article 52 (3) EPC establishes an important limitation to the scope of this exclusion. According to this provision, the exclusion applies only to the extent to which a European patent application or a European patent relates to programs for computers "as such".
15 T 0208/84 at http://legal.european-patent-office.org/dg3/biblio/t840208ep1.htm consulted on March 10, 2004.
16 T 0026/86 at http://legal.european-patent-office.org/dg3/biblio/t860026ep1.htm#txt consulted on March 10, 2004.
17 T 0769/92) http://legal.european-patent-office.org/dg3/biblio/t920769ep1.htm consulted on March 10, 2004.
18 Point 5 of the decision of TBA.
19 Point 12 of the decision of TBA.
20 Point 3.3 of the decision of TBA.
21 Point 3.3 of the decision of TBA.
22 R. SARVAS and A. SOININEN, "Differences in European and U.S. patent regulation affecting wireless standardization" (p. 8) at http://www.hiit.fi/de/core/PatentsWirelessStandardization.pdf consulted on March 9, 2004.
23 Study Contract ETD/99/B5-3000/E/106: "The Economic Impact of Patentability of Computer Programs" (Report to the European Commission) at
http://europa.eu.int/comm/internal_market/en/indprop/comp/studyintro.htm consulted on February 18, 2004 (summary); and A.P. MEIJBOOM, "Bang voor Software-octrooien", *Computerrecht* 2002/2, 66; and Proposal for a Directive on the patentability of computer-implemented inventions – frequently asked questions at
http://europa.eu.int/comm/internal_market/en/indprop/comp/02-32.htm consulted on March 8, 2004.
24 Quotations on Software Patents at http://swpat.ffii.org/archive/quates/index.en.html consulted on March 3, 2004.
25 B. KAHIN, "Information Process patents in the U.S. and Europe: policy avoidance and policy divergence" *First Monday* March 2003, volume 8, number 3 at http://www.firstmonday.org/issues/issue8_3/kahin/ consulted on March 6, 2004.
26 M.C. JANSSENS, "Bescherming van computerprogramma's: (lang) niet alleen maar auteursrecht", *T.B.H.* 1998, pp. 421-422.
27 Technical Chamber of the Board of Appeals of EPO, February 4, 1999, *Computerrecht* 1999/6, 306-310 with Note by D.J.B. Bosscher, 310-312.
28 B. KAHIN, *op. cit.*
29 R. MISHRA, "Reverse engineering in Japan and the global trend towards inter-operability" in E Law/ Murdoch University Electronic Journal of Law at
http://www.murdoch.edu.au/elaw/issues/v4n2/mishra42.html consulted on May 28, 2004.
30 "The Economic Espionage Act of 1996 – Overview" at
http://www.brinkshofer.com/resources/eea_overview.cfm consulted on June 15, 2004.

31 J. Band, in "The Digital Millennium Copyright Act at http://www.arl.org/info/frn/copy/band.html consulted on June 15, 2004.
32 E. Foster in "InfoWorld commentary on UCITA" at http://archive.infoworld.com/ucita/ consulted on June 15, 2004.
33 977 F.2d 1510 (9th Cir 1992) at http://digital-law-online.info/cases/24PQ2D1561.htm consulted on June 15, 2004.
34 975 F.2d 832 (Fed. Cir 1992) at http://digital-law-online.info/cases/24PQ2D1015.htm consulted on June 15, 2004.
35 M. Flamee and F. Brison, "Auteursrecht toegepast op computerprogrammatuur: een grondslagenprobleem", *T.B.B.R.* 1992, pp. 467-472.
36 IP/04/955, July 19, 2004; statement by Internal Market Commissioner Frits Bolkestein;
37 For a full discussion of the economic forces driving intellectual property changes in particular, see B. de Vuyst, "The Uneasy Case for Intellectual Property Rights", in B. De Schutter and J. Pas (eds), "About Globalisation", pp. 113-135, Brussels, vubpress (2004), and sources cited there, in particular the work of R. Posner.
38 Congressional Budget Office, "Copyright Issues in Digital Media", Washington, D.C., August 2004, http://www.cbo.gov/showdoc.cfm?index=5738&sequence=0, consulted on August 17, 2004.
39 SEC (2004) 995, Commission Staff Working Paper on the review of the EC legal framework in the field of copyright and related rights, July 19, 2004, and sources cited.
40 In this respect, see also the introductory report "Software, business methods & patents" of the international conference "Patents: why and to do what?" prepared by Vincent Casiers, researcher at the Arcelor Chair (UCL) (available at http://www.chaire-arcelor.be/patinovpubint.pdf).

Biographies

Bruno de Vuyst studied law in Antwerp and New York. He was an executive with the World Bank, the United Nations and Citibank NA before becoming an attorney at the Brussels bar and, since 1996, teaching at the VUB's Vesalius College. A former member of the bar association council, he is currently an elected representative on the governing body of the Flemish bar association, while remaining a practising barrister with the firm of Lawfort in Brussels. At the Vrije Universiteit Brussel he is associate professor at Vesalius College and associate researcher at the Institute for European Studies. Furthermore, he is advisor on industrial policy to the Vice-Rector for Research and secretary-general of the BI^3 Fund NV, the VUB's spin-off fund with an equity of six million euro. Bruno de Vuyst publishes and lectures mainly in English, mainly abroad, and mainly in a multidisciplinary context about intellectual property, the Internet and computer law. He is chairman of Raamtheater, a professional theatre company with two platforms in Antwerp, and is also a published novelist and a produced playwright.

Liv Steuts graduated from the law school of the Vrije Universiteit Brussel and received a DES in Droit et Gestion des Technologies de l'Information et de la Communication at Namur. Since this specialization in intellectual property and information technology, Liv Steuts has been member of the Brussels bar (starting in 2002). Since March 2004 she has been working as an assistant at the VUB's Vesalius College.

Part IV

The Future is Open

Everything cometh to he who waiteth, so long as he who waiteth, worketh like hell while he waiteth.

Advancing Economic Research on the Free and Open-Source Software Mode of Production

J.-M. Dalle, P. A. David, Rishab A. Ghosh, and W. E. Steinmueller

1 Re-focusing Research on "Open-Source" Software — as a Paradigm of Collective and Distributed Knowledge Production

What explains the fascination that the "open-source" phenomenon seems to hold for many social scientists? Early contributions to the academic literature on free/libre and open-source software (F/LOSS hereinafter) movements have been directed primarily at identifying the motivations that account for the sustained and, in many instances, intensive involvement of many people in this non-contractual and unremunerated mode of activity.[1] This issue has been particularly prominent in economists' contributions to the literature, and it reflects a view that widespread voluntary participation in the creation of economically valuable goods that is to be distributed without charge constitutes a rather significant behavioral anomaly. Anomalies are intrinsically intriguing, and their identification may serve to alert us to emerging patterns of behavior, or social organization that have considerable economic and social importance. But, while the question of the motivations of F/LOSS developers is one that undoubtedly deserves closer study, the respect(s) in which their behaviors are anomalous should be precisely described by reference to some "normal", or otherwise expected behavioral patterns. The latter exercise is likely to prove valuable in bringing into clearer focus other aspects of the "open-source" phenomenon that, arguably, are even more intriguing and possible far more consequential. This essay describes the re-focusing and re-direction of economic research in order better elucidate those other, less widely discussed features, which concern F/LOSS development as a collective production mode.

As a preamble to that undertaking, however, one should try to understand why the economics literature about open-source software became almost instantly preoccupied with the "puzzle" of the participants' motivations. For many who presuppose economic rationality on the part of individuals engaged in time-consuming pursuits, the fact that there were growing communities of developers who devoted appreciable time to writing and improving code without remuneration presented an aberrant form of behavior, which was difficult to to explain. At least, it was difficult if one resisted the heterodox belief that altruism not only widespread, but had been gaining converts in the population. Such a reading of the facts posed the challenge of how to reconcile participation of F/LOSS activities with the main (ego-regarding) tenets of modern economists' views of the driving motivations of human actions.

A second strand followed in the early economic research literature has been to search for the secret by which the F/LOSS mode of production is able to create information-goods that compete successfully in the market against proprietary software. Moreover, that they do so not simply on the basis of their significantly lower monetary cost, but, as many partisans of F/LOSS allege, on the basis of their superior quality.[2] This framing of the research agenda resembles the first theme in projecting surprise and puzzlement about the apparently greater efficiency that these non-profit, distributed production organizations have been able to achieve in relation to major software companies engaged in "closed" and centrally directed production of the same type of commodity.[3]

It is not uncommon for investigators in a new field to "hype" the mysteries that they are about to dispel, and it is characteristic of such presentations of research that it is rare indeed for their authors to describe the supposedly baffling phenomena and then announce that they remain puzzled. But we would not go so far as to discounting the sense of urgency that has been attached to unraveling the mystery of what is motivating those software developers. We share the view that the F/LOSS movements carry broader economic and social significance, and therefore deserve to be the subject of continuing, systematic, empirical and theoretical study.[4] The fact that much about this particular phenomenon continues to be poorly understood, however, is not unique; the same might well be said about other aspects of the workings of modern economies, which are no less likely to prove important for human well-being.

One might therefore be excused for pointing out that if the research attention that F/LOSS software production attracts from economists is to be rationalized simply on the grounds of the novelty and mysteriousness of the foregoing phenomena, it cannot be very well founded. The emergence of F/LOSS activities on their present scale hardly is so puzzling or aberrant a development as to constitute a rationale for devoting substantial resources to studying it.

The emergence of co-operative modes of knowledge production among members of distributed epistemic communities who do not anticipate receiving direct remuneration for their efforts is not a recent social innovation. Among the numerous historical precursors and precedents for F/LOSS are the "invisible colleges" that appeared in the 17th century and engaged practitioners of the new experimental and mathematical approaches to scientific inquiry in western Europe. The "professionalization" of scientific research, as is well known, was a comparatively late development.[5] Nor is the superior performance of such co-operative forms of organization a novel finding: philosophers of science and epistemologists, as well as work on the economics of knowledge, have noted the superiority of co-operative knowledge-sharing as a mode of generating additions to the stock of reliable empirical propositions.[6]

It is the scale and speed of F/LOSS development work and the geographical dispersion of the participants, rather than the voluntary nature of the latters' contributions, properly should be deemed historically unprecedented. But, the modularity and immateriality that are generic characteristics of software, and the enabling effects of the advances in computer-mediated telecommunications during the past several decades, go a long way towards accounting for those aspects of the phenomenon. Is the open source movement thereby reduced to the status of a mere epiphenomenon, another among many episodes in the unfolding computer revolution? Were that to be seen as the whole of the story, we might simply assimilate F/LOSS into the larger body of "weightless" commodities, intangible information goods whose proliferation characterizes the Age of the Internet.

Yet, in addition to all that, something more seems to be involved. In our view, what warrants the attention that F/LOSS has commanded from social scientists is its connections with three deeper, and interrelated trends that have recently become evident in modern economies. First among these is the movement of information goods to center-stage as drivers of economic growth. Second is the evermore widespread use of peer-to-peer modes of conducting the distribution and utilization of information, including its re-use in creating new information-goods. These two trends are bound together and reinforced by the growing recognition that the "open" (and co-operative) conduct of knowledge production offers economic efficiencies which in general surpass those of other institutional arrangements, namely those that address the resource allocation problems posed by "public goods" by protecting secretive practices, or creating and enforcing intellectual property monopolies.[7] A third trend, which is of obvious practical significance for social scientists and others engaged specifically in empirical studies of the F/LOSS production mode, is the growing abundance and accessibility of quantitative material concerning the internal workings of "open epistemic communities." The kinds of data that are available for extraction and analysis by automated techniques from repositories of open-source code and newsgroup archives, and from the email subscriber lists generated by F/LOSS project members themselves, also offer a rapidly widening window for research on the generic features of processes of collective discovery and invention.

A further source of motivation for undertaking to exploit this opportunity, by systematically examining the micro-economics and micro-sociology of F/LOSS development communities and the "open source way of working", springs from our interest in a conjecture about the longer-term implications of the first two among the trends just described. The open-source software movement may quite possibly have "paradigm-shifting" consequences extending beyond those affecting the organizational evolution of the software industry. The rise of a decentralized and fully networked mode of creating, packaging and distributing software systems, is undoubted a challenge to the dominant organizational model of closed production and a break from the era of marketing "shrink-wrapped" proprietary software packages. Possibly it is also the precursor of a broader transformation of information-goods production and distribution. Software is, after all, but one instance in the universe of information-goods, many of which share the modular and quasi-decomposable architectural features. The latter would tend to facilitate a reorganization of production and the use of advanced computer-mediated telecommunications technologies to mobilize and co-ordinate the work of large "communities of practice" formed by weakly tied and spatially distributed individuals who were able to contribute diverse skills to the collective enterprise.

In this speculative vein, one may wonder whether the principles of organization employed by open-source software projects could not also be applied to integrate existing knowledge concerning the functioning of living systems (such as the human body) by creating a computer simulation structure that would have general utility in medical education, in the design of medical devices and even – if implemented at the molecular level – in the design of pharmaceutical therapies. Might such methods prove relevant for international partnerships aimed at education and development, the exchange of cultural information such as compilations of folklore and culinary encyclopedias, or the construction of repositories of knowledge on the world's flora and fauna? If software production is simply the first manifestation of an emerging pattern of division of labor that has not been effectively organized (and perhaps cannot be effectively organized) using traditional employment and wage relationships, it seems well worth trying to understand better the opportunities arising from, and the limits to, the innovation that the "open source way of working" represents in the organization of human cultural endeavors.

Those opportunities and constraints must surely be linked to the specific problems of forming and sustaining these largely voluntary producer-associations, a consideration that leads one back to the focal point of the early literature on the motives of the people who participate F/LOSS development work, albeit with a different research agenda in mind. Motivation, recruitment and retention of developers' efforts are likely to be affected by perceptions of the utility of a project's code to a wider population of users, and hence by the performance of the development process in dimensions such as modularity, robustness, security, frequency and persistence of bug, etc. By examining those dimensions of quality, it would be possible in principle to characterize levels of project "output" performance (i.e., for software that is sufficiently "completed" to have been released for public use). Further, even in the absence of normal market indicators, it may be feasible also to gauge end-user relative "valuation" of various "products, by observing the comparative measure value extent and speed of adoption of software belonging to broadly similar open source offerings. Such objective and behavioral measures of the relative "utility" of F/LOSS products might provide a useful starting point for assessments of their contributions to improving economic welfare and human well being in society at large.[8]

The trajectory of our ongoing program research into the organizational features of the F/LOSS phenomenon has been guided by the preceding, "formative" considerations. Its main elements and their interrelationships are described in the following part of this essay, which begins by taking up issues of resource mobilization and resource allocation in the highly decentralized, non-market-directed system of F/LOSS production. The discussion proceeds next to examine questions concerning the match between the motivating interests of developer communities, on the one hand, and, on the other hand, the needs of the final users of the software systems that are being created. Then the essay's third part looks toward the future directions that research in this area may usefully pursue, considering the way that agenda may be shaped by the trajectory of technological developments and the related social organization of open source communities. The fourth and concluding discussion therefore focuses on the significance of questions concerning the social dynamics of the movement, and returns to examine further the implications of interactions between the generic features of this mode of producing digital information goods and newly emerging advanced network infrastructures and the networked computer applications they will be able to support.

II An Agenda for Research on the Economics of F/LOSS Production

Proceeding from the conceptual framing of the phenomenon that has been sketched above, we have taken a rather different conceptual approach from that which has hitherto dominated the recent economics literature concerning F/LOSS. A correspondingly distinctive research strategy is being pursued at Stanford University and its academic partners in France, the Netherlands and Britain by the project on *The Economic Organization, Performance and Viability of Free and Open Source Software*.[9]

Many of the researchers associated with our project come to this particular subject-matter from the perspective formed by previous and on-going work in "the new economics of science". Their research in that connection has been directed to questions about the organization of collaborative inquiry in the "open-science" mode, the behavioral norms and reinforcing reward systems that structure the allocation of resources, and the relationships of these self-organizing and relatively autonomous epistemic communities with their patrons and sponsors in the public and private sectors.[10] As economists looking at F/LOSS communities, the interrelated central pair of questions that remain of prime interest for us are both simple and predictably familiar. First, how do F/LOSS projects mobilize the resources, allocate the expertise and retain the commitment of their members? Secondly, how fully do the products of these essentially self-directed efforts meet the long-term needs of software users in the wider society, rather than simply providing satisfaction of various kinds for the developers?

In other words, we have begun by setting ourselves research tasks in regard to F/LOSS that address the classic economic questions of whether and how it is possible for a decentralized system of decision-making concerning resource allocation to achieve coherent and socially efficient outcomes. What makes the problem especially interesting in this case is the possibility that the institutions developed by the F/LOSS movements enable them to accomplish that outcome without help either from the "invisible hand" of the market mechanism by price signals/incentives, or from the "visible hands" of centralized managerial hierarchies. To respond to this challenge the analysis must be directed towards providing a basis for evaluating the social optimality properties of the way "open science", "open source" and kindred co-operative communities organize the production and regulate the quality of the "information tools" and "information goods" that will be used not only for their own, internal purposes, but also by others with quite different purposes in society at large.

The parallels with the phenomenon of "open science" suggests a need for a framework that is capable of integrating theories of the micro-level incentives and social norms that structure the allocation of developers' efforts within particular projects and that govern the publication of the resulting outputs as periodic "releases" of code. Theories about why researchers choose to focus on particular lines of research, and why they publish their results, provide a starting-point for examining which open source projects receive developers' attention and how these communities of developers reach decisions about the publication (i.e., release) of their work. The recognition that all systems, even very large ones are bounded also suggests a system-wide analysis. For example, general equilibrium economics tells us that we should be asking how efforts within projects are related to the mechanisms that allocate the total (even if expanding) resources of the larger community among different concurrent projects, and directing the attention of individuals to successive projects, including investment in the formation of particular capabilities and sub-specialties by members of those communities. Obviously, those capabilities provide "spill-overs" to other areas of endeavor – including the production of software goods and services by commercial suppliers. It follows that to fully understand the dynamics of the F/LOSS mode, and its interactions with the rest of the information technology sector, one cannot treat the expertise of the software development community as a given, an exogenously determined resource.

Implementing the Organizational Economics Approach

In implementing the approach just outlined, four lines of complementary investigation are being undertaken by our collective research effort, three of them directed to expanding the empirical base for the analysis of distinct aspects of the micro- and meso-level workings of F/LOSS communities. The fourth is integrative and more speculative, as it is organized around the development of a stochastic simulation structure designed to show the connections between the micro- and macro-level performance properties of the larger system of software production. The three areas of empirical study, along with findings from other such inquiries, are expected to provide distributions of observations which a properly specified and parameterized simulation model should be capable of simulating; whereas, reciprocally, the simulation model is intended to provide insights into the processes that may be responsible for generating patterns of the kind that are observed, and to allow an investigation into the counterfactual conditions that various policy actions would create. Thus, although these lines of inquiry can advance in parallel, their interactions are iterative: the empirical studies guide the specification of the simulation structure that is to be used to investigate their broader, systemic implications. The initial thrust of these four complementary research "salients" can be briefly described, taking each in turn:

Distribution of developer efforts within software projects:

The information extracted from code repositories should eventually provide robust answers to the following array of questions, which give the flavor of a major group of micro-level allocation issues that this line of inquiry is designed to address. Is the leftwards skew in the frequency distribution of contributions to the Linux kernel (i.e., the fact that relatively few contributors are responsible for a disproportionately large share of all contributions) also a feature of the distributions found to hold for the modules within the kernel? Does this hold equally for other large and complex projects?. Or, putting that question another way, is the pattern of concentration in self-identified F/LOSS "authorship" one that arises from a general "power law" distribution? Alternatively, is the concentration significantly greater for some components than for others – raising questions about how efforts are directed or re-directed to achieve a higher or lower intensity of contribution? Are these distributions stationary throughout the life of the project, or does concentration grow (or diminish) over time (the former having been found to be the case for the distribution of scientific authorship in specific fields over the lives of cohorts of researchers publishing in that field)?

Micro-level resource allocation processes governing the allocation of developer efforts within software projects can be studied quantitatively by tracking the authorship distributions found in specific projects over time. A start is being made by examining an atypical yet very important and emblematic F/LOSS product: the Linux Kernel, the successive releases of which constitute a very large database containing over 3 billion lines of code. The data production work – referred to by the acronym LICKS (Linux: Chronology of the Kernel Sources) is being conducted by Rishab A. Ghosh and his colleagues at MERIT/Infonomics. It has significantly advanced the state of basic data: first, by identifying the distinctive packages of code (or "modules") within the evolving Linux kernel, and secondly, by extracting the code for successive versions and linking the dated code (contributed by each identified author, along with the components to which it relates), so that dynamic analyses of code evolution become feasible. The resulting dataset is providing a basis both for subsequent studies of the dynamics of the participation of the population of all contributors to the Linux kernel, and their patterns of co-participation across the modules, as well as the chronology of the development of the major components of the code for the operating system. In addition, this line of research is providing measures of evolving structure and the degree of technical dependence among the "modules" that form the Linux kernel.[11]

Using data on the technical features (e.g., size, technical dependency structure) of the modules forming the Linux kernel and the distributions of authorship credits, measured by the fraction of signed "commits" in each of the modules in a given release (version) of the kernel, it is possible to estimate the equations of an econometric model of code-signing and participation behaviours and draw statistical inferences from the results about the factors that influence the distribution of developers' code-writing efforts within this large, emblematic project.[12]

In addition, it has been found to be quite feasible to identify clusters of authors who work together within and across different components of the Linux kernel project; to trace whether these "clusters" grow by accretion of individuals or coalesce through mergers; and to learn whether, if they do not grow, they contract or remain constant. Further, by correlating the clusters of authors with the data on the dependence of code sections, it may be possible to obtain characterizations of the nature of "knowledge flows" between identified groups.

An important methodological issue in this line of research is to ascertain whether or not there are significant biases in the ability of the extraction algorithm to identify the distribution of authorship in this particular dataset, for which the algorithm was designed. Inasmuch as one cannot treat the Linux Kernel as a "representative" F/LOSS project, other projects, which may differ in their conventions with regard to the self-identification of contributions in the code itself, are likely to require extensions or modification of the foregoing technique of data extraction and analysis. Tools to permit the study of archival repositories of the open source codes created by concurrent version systems (e.g., CVS, Bit-Keeper), and kindred dynamic database management and annotation systems, are being developed and tested by an emerging community of "open source/libre source" software engineers with whom we have been engaged in active trans-disciplinary collaboration.[13]

Allocation of developer communities' efforts among projects:

The SourceForge site[14] contains data on a vast number of ongoing projects, including both successful and failing ones.[15] Taking the project as the unit of observation, this data provides an evidentiary basis for seeking to establish statistically the set of characteristics that are particularly influential in determining whether or not a project meets one or more of the criteria that are taken to define "success". The latter can be measured in terms of the delivery of versions of the software at various stages of completion, continued participation by players, or the citation of the project's outputs in various F/LOSS forums. Taking it as our hypothesis that software projects are most likely to achieve a number of these objectives when they are able to align a "critical mass" of adherents and develop a self-reinforcing momentum of growth, the empirical challenge is to identify the combinations of early characteristics that statistically predict the attainment of "critical mass". A supply-driven approach to the question would interpret the "community alignment" problem as one of recruiting individuals who share a belief in the efficacy of the F/LOSS mode of developing software, the diversity of their own particular interests and motives for joining the project notwithstanding; and who collectively possess the mix of differentiated skills that are needed for the work of rapidly designing, programming, debugging and upgrading early releases of the code.

Both large- and small-scale analysis seem feasible as a way of pinpointing the characteristics that enable (or fail to enable) the creation of "burgeoning" communities that propel the growth of open source projects towards critical mass and into the phase of self-catalyzing dynamics. SourceForge itself provides sufficient information about the initial features of projects to make it possible to analyze the influence of factors such as technical nature, intended users/audiences, internal project organization, release policies, and legal aspects (e.g., projected form of licensing).

Timing and path-dependencies may be hypothesized to affect the success or failure of F/LOSS projects, and it may be important to recognize that success or failure is not determined in isolation from the characteristics of other projects that may be competing for developers' attention. A population ecology perspective therefore may be fruitful in this connection, and for that reason interactions between the characteristics of the project and the features of the "niche" into which it is launched are being empirically investigated. Given that "developer mind-share" is limited, we may suppose that older projects are entrenched through technological lock-in processes that make it more difficult to engage the community in competing/similar ones.[16] Developers will tend to increase their co-operative activities in these older projects as they gain in experience and knowledge about them (these individuals are moving up project-specific learning curves, as well as acquiring generic and more transferable skills). Their attention to, and willingness to co-operate in other/new projects would therefore tend to decline.[17]

This kind of externality effect, through which accidents of timing and initial momentum may serve to "lock in" some projects, while locking-out others that are technically or socially more promising if considered on their intrinsic merits, has been identified in studies of the (competitive) commercial development and distribution of other technological artefacts. It would therefore be of considerable interest to establish whether or not dynamics of this kind can be observed in the non-market allocation of developmental resources among software systems products. The fact that SourceForge makes it possible to filter projects according to the tools (such as programming languages and techniques) used in their development, and that the differences between these tools may be an important factor in lock-in, makes the analysis of this kind of processes easier. The possibility of tracking down the history of individuals' co-operative activities may also make it feasible to study their involvement, entry and exit patterns in different projects. Mathematical methods used to identify the presence or absence of path dependence, including an analysis of Markov chains in the attainment of successive "states" of project growth, may be employed in this analysis.

Sponsorship support and relations between individual developers and commercial sponsors:

This component of our research program is concerned with understanding the formation of the variety of complementary software products and services that commercial ventures have developed around the software-system code created by the larger "open-source" projects. These activities are a source of direct support for some F/LOSS projects, and a beacon that may affect the launching of new programs, stimulate individuals to enter the community (which may result in their eventual participation in other projects that have no commercial ties), or signal which project is likely to achieve a critical mass of adopters. The degree to which such related, profit-oriented activities develop symbiotic connections with an open-source project, rather than being essentially parasitic, can be investigated. But to do this would necessitate gathering evidence of individuals' overlapping participation in F/LOSS projects and commercial ventures based upon either proprietary or F/LOSS projects of both kinds; and by examining the formal commitments that are entered into in relation to existing projects.

A two-pronged approach to studying the issues this raises has therefore been pursued.[18] A web-based survey of developers, the NSF-supported FLOSS-US Survey for 2003, has been conducted by the research group led by Paul David at Stanford University's Institute for Economic Policy Research. This survey replicated a number of the questions answered on the European Commission-sponsored FLOSS (2002) survey carried out under the leadership of Rishab Ghosh at the International Infonomics Institute at the University of Maastricht, but it elicited more detailed information from developers about their contacts with, and possible involvements in complementary/collateral commercial enterprises.[19] Although there are some significant demographic and regional variations in the responses to the FLOSS-US, the following general picture emerges from a preliminary analysis of this data:[20]

a) F/LOSS developers tend to be highly educated and employed, with ambitions of future career advancement. Contradicting the impression of the open-source community as being made up largely by students and otherwise unemployed "hackers," more than two thirds report themselves to be in paid employments. Regardless of whether they started writing "open-source" code in the 1970's, 1980's or more recently, their mean age at the time was 26-27. The median of their starting ages, however, is closer to 22.

b) Contributing to the community of developers, promoting the F/LOSS movement, and improving software's functionality all figure frequently among the reasons that respondents list as having motivated them to become involved in F/LOSS development activities. Most respondents support the use of the GNU GPL and similar "open-source" licenses as a means of protecting software users' general freedom, and ensuring that credit is given for their work. F/LOSS developers tend to believe their way of working can supplant much of proprietary software development.

c) Most developers report working on F/LOSS mainly on weekends and after the end of their employed workdays, although many work on F/LOSS in connection with their employment or studies. They spend the greatest amounts of this time coding, debugging, and testing software, rather than in other project activities (e.g., distribution support, administration, etc.).

d) As their careers in F/LOSS development progress, developers describe themselves as typically taking more influential roles in their projects; they also tend to work more hours per week and in more intense stints.
e) Approximately 50% of the respondents report having earned money directly or indirectly through their work on F/LOSS. Support for F/LOSS projects from external businesses and organizations has increased significantly since a decade ago, particularly since 2000. Over half of the survey sample population worked on F/LOSS projects that were being supported by external sources (including those being supported in higher education institutions).
f) Approximately 50% of developers launched their own projects, or were the "project maintainer" for their current project; the latter are typically small, and so correspond roughly with the "I-mode" (independent developer) type of project, rather than to the class of larger, "C-mode" (community) project organizations.
g) While most of the respondents report having contributed to only a few projects – a generalization that holds even when one excludes those who only recently became engaged in F/LOSS activities, there a small fraction (some 7-8 percent) of very active "core" developers who participated in many projects (the mean and median number of their projects being 5.5 and 6, respectively - approximately half of the developers say they wrote almost all of their most recent project's code, and an equal proportion rate their contribution to their current (and often their sole) project as "very important". Approximately one-third of developers say they contributed only incrementally to their most recent project.

By asking respondents to identify the first F/LOSS project on which they worked, and the two projects in which they deemed their participation to have been the most significant/important (for reasons given), the survey design has made it possible to link responses with the project characteristics information available from SourceForge and other open source project platforms, such as FreshMeat, and Savannah. The second related line of inquiry also connects with the work on the determinants of project "success", previously described: data available at SourceForge is being used to investigate whether there are significant statistical relationships between the specifics of the licensing arrangements adopted when projects are launched and the subsequent development of derivative commercial enterprises around those projects that eventually do release code.[21]

Using Simulation Modeling as an Integrative Device

The fourth strand of the project is the development of a simulation model of the F/LOSS production system. This model-building activity aims eventually to provide more specific insights into the workings of F/LOSS communities. It seeks to articulate the interdependence between distinct sub-components of the resource allocation system, and to absorb and integrate empirical findings about the micro-level mobilization and allocation of individual developer efforts, both among projects and within them. Stochastic process representations of these interactions are a major tool in identifying critical structural relationships and parameters that affect the emergent properties of the macro system. Among the latter properties, the global performance of the F/LOSS mode in matching the functional distribution and characteristics of the software systems produced to meet the evolving needs of users in the economy at large is an issue that it is obviously important for our analysis to tackle.[22]

To characterize the structure of the relative rewards associated with the adoption of various roles and participation in projects of different types, our initial approach has been to implement a sub-set of the "ethnographic" observations describing the norms of F/LOSS hacker/developer communities, notably following Eric S. Raymond's insights in the well-known essay "Homesteading the Noosphere".[23] The core of this is a variant of the collegiate reputational reward system: the more significance attached to a project, the agent's role, and the extent or critical importance of the contribution, the greater the anticipated "reward" in terms of peer regard, professional reputation and whatever psychological satisfactions and/or material benefits may be derived therefrom. Caricaturing Raymond's more nuanced discussion, we stipulate that launching a new project is as a rule more rewarding than contributing to an existing one, especially when several contributions have already been made; typically, early releases are more rewarding than later versions of project code; there are some rewarding "project-modules" that are systematically accorded more "importance" than others, and these are ordered in a way that reflects meso-level technical dependencies.

One way to express this is to posit that there is a hierarchy within a family of projects, such that contributing to, say, one or another of the many modules (or "packages") of code making up the Linux kernel is deemed to be a potentially more rewarding activity than providing a Linux implementation of an existing and widely used applications program; and, correspondingly, a contribution to the latter would take precedence over writing an obscure Linux driver for a newly-marketed printer. In other words, we postulate that there is a lexicographic ordering of rewards following a discrete, technically-based "ladder" of project types. Lastly, new projects are always created in relation to existing ones, and here we consider that it is always possible to add a new module to an existing one, thereby adding new functionality, and we assume that this new module will be located one level higher up on the ladder.

As a consequence, all the modules of the project, taken together, are organized as in a tree which grows as new contributions are added, and which can grow in various ways depending on which part of it (upstream or downstream modules, notably) a developer selects. We further conjecture that the architecture of this notional "tree" will be to some extent correlated with both the project's actual directory tree and with the topology of technical interdependencies among the modules – although this correlation will probably be especially imperfect in the case of our initial specifications of the simulation model. A typical example of a simulated software tree is shown in Figure 1 below, where the numbers associated with each module represent versions, considering further that versioning accounts for performance.

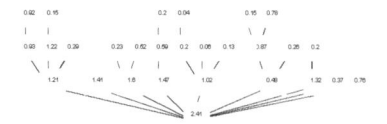

Figure 1: A F/LOSS Simulation-Generated Software System

With the help of such a simulation tool, we are then able to study social-utility measurements according to two basic ideas: (1) downstream modules are more valuable than upstream ones because of the range of applications that can eventually be built upon them, and (2) a greater diversity of functionalities (breadth of the tree at the upstream layers) is valuable because it provides software solutions to fit a wider array of user needs. In this regard, preliminary results indicate the social efficiency of developer community "norms" that bestow significantly greater reputational rewards for contributing and adding to the releases of downstream modules.

Further, these preliminary explorations of the model suggest that policies of releasing code *early* tend to generate tree shapes with higher social-efficiency scores. The intuitively plausible interpretation of this latter, interesting, finding is that early releases are especially important (adding larger increments to social utility) in the case of downstream modules, because they create *bases* for further applications development, and the reputational reward structure posited in the model encourages this "roundabout" (generic infrastructure) process of development by inducing individual efforts to share the recognition for contributing to downstream code.

The work described here is only a start on the integrative task of simulation modeling, and the agenda of work that lies ahead is consequently a long one. The behavior of developers (contributors) thus far is caricatured as myopic and, more seriously, it still lacks several important dynamic dimensions. Learned behaviors on the part of the developers, for instance, has not been allowed for in the pilot simulation model – a step that will make it necessary to keep track of the individual histories of the agents' participation activities. Acquiring the skills relative to a particular module is not without cost, and the model does not make any allowance for these "start-up" costs, which would also affect decisions to shift attention to a new package of code in the project. Further, and perhaps most obtrusively limiting, the first state of the model abstracts from heterogeneity in the behavior of the developers (in respects other than that arising from the endogenous formation of individual effort endowments); such differences could derive from the variety of motivations affecting the amount of effort that developers are willing to devote to the different modules, or to different projects. In particular, users are likely to have preferences for modules and projects that they will be able to use directly. To capture an effect of that kind will necessitate representing functional differences among software projects, and relating those characteristics to developers' "use-interests". We envisage such a simulation being employed to evaluate the influence of "user-innovators" – the importance of whose role in open source communities (as in other spheres of technological development) has been stressed in the work of Eric von Hippel.[24]

The personal rewards associated with contributing to the development of a project (whether psychological or material) will be most fully obtained only when the "maintainer" of the module or project accepts the code or "patches" that the individual in question has submitted. Rather than treating maintainers' decisions as following simple "gate-keeping" (and "bit-keeping") rules that are neutral in regard to the identities and characteristics of the individual contributors, it may be important to model the acceptance rate as variable and "discriminating" on the basis of the contributing individuals' "experience" or "track records". This would enable the model to capture some features of the process of "legitimate peripheral participation" through which developers are recruited. Contributions made to modules situated in the upper levels of the project "tree" (where comparatively fewer modules "call" them in relation to the modules on which they depend) might be supposed to require less developer experience and expertise for all significant likelihoods of being accepted by the project's maintainers. Comparative neophytes to the F/LOSS community ("newbies") would thus have incentives to start new modules or contribute to existing ones at those upper levels, but over time, with the accumulation of a track record of successful submissions, they would tend to migrate to work at lower branches of the trees.[25]

All of the foregoing complicating features of resource allocation within and among F/LOSS development projects are more or less interdependent, and this short list is not exhaustive. There is therefore a great deal of challenging model-building work to be done, and further empirical research absolutely must be devoted to shedding light on these conjectures, and ultimately to permit approximate parameterizations of the most plausible versions of the simulation model. We believe that a modeling and simulation effort of this kind is a worthwhile undertaking because it can provide an integrative framework, assisting the synthesis and evaluation of the rapidly growing theoretical and empirical research literature on many distinct aspect of F/LOSS development. The results of the studies by "libre software engineers" and the findings of social scientists should be brought together to orient future model-building and -specification work, and should in turn be confronted with simulation findings obtained by exercising the model. It is important, too, that economic theorists become regularly engaged in dialog with empirical researchers, and so it is hoped that – uncommon as that seems to be in many fields of economics – the necessary forum and language for maintaining such exchanges will be provided by the availability of a flexible and "open" simulation structure. By pursuing this approach, it is to be hoped, it will prove eventually to bring social science research on the free and open-source model of software development to bear, in a reliably informative way, upon issues of public and private policy for a sector of the global economy that is, manifestly, of rapidly increasing importance.

III Envisaging the Future Trajectory of Research on Open-Source Software

To envisage the future trajectory of useful research concerned with open source software development, one has to begin by thinking about the likely trajectory of the phenomenon itself. To know where this dynamic process is heading, it helps to have a broader sense of "where it's coming from".[26]

The open-source software movement is a "paradigm-shifting" development in the organizational history of the software industry. Software production has evolved through a succession of paradigmatic modes – originating in the vertical integration of hardware and software, achieving a measure of autonomy through the emergence of an industrial sector comprised of independent software vendors, gathering momentum through the general separation of hardware production from the software-systems development that marked the ascent of the mass-produced personal computer "platform".[27] The most recent production mode in the software industry, the open-source mode, is closely connected with the continuing evolution of the personal computer platform into an information and communication appliance, a vehicle for network exchanges of digital data that is supplanting postal telecommunication for interpersonal communication and actively challenging the position of voice telephony.

"Communicating information appliances" must be enabled by software that provides for a far greater measure of technical compatibility and inter-operability than was the case when the dominant paradigm was the "stand-alone" personal computer. By the same token, the new paradigm has opened up the possibility of an entirely networked mode of creating, packaging, and distributing software systems – thereby marking a break with the era of "shrink-wrapped" software packages.

J.-M. Dalle, Paul A. David, Rishab A. Ghosh, W.E. Steinmueller

Emerging challenges in the software industry

In view of the disruptive character of the developments just described, it is not surprising that the dominant mode of economic organization and the dominant incumbent firms that had emerged from the personal-computer revolution are now finding themselves challenged. Indeed, quite a number of distinct challengers have emerged in the areas of software production, packaging and distribution – object-oriented mini-universes such as the JAVA world, the ongoing development of UNIX-based workstation environments, the new application platforms of mobile telephones with graphic displays, DVD-based games machines, and digital television. The distinguishing feature of the open-source movement is that it is attempting to insert itself into the heretofore rigid link between a personal computer "desk-top" and the underlying operating system/application program environment, and, by so doing, to create an entirely different model for software acquisition, which would supplant packaged, shrink-wrapped software.

Open-source software also is distinctive in discarding the industry's previously dominant business model: it contests the proprietary and quasi-proprietary systems based on the presupposition that software development costs must be recouped from the sale of individual "units" of software, integrated hardware and software systems, or service charges for using such integrated services (e.g. by playing digital-television games). This aspect of free and open-source software is seen by some observers as defining the movement as a radical rejection of dependence upon the conventional intellectual property rights regime, and seeking to replace that mechanism for stimulating innovative activity with a voluntary "communal ethos" for the creation of intangible goods (in this case code) that possess the properties of "public goods".

Understandably, there is a good deal of skepticism about the realism of expecting the enthusiasm and energy that often attends the launching of collective undertakings to be sustained, and therefore to go on supporting and elaborating the highly durable artefacts to which their early efforts give rise.[28] For quite some time even sympathetic observers have been noticing that delivery has not been made on the promises that a new, viable business model would appear "real soon now", providing an alternative to the conventional business model based upon private appropriation of the benefits of invention and cultural creativity by means of legal intellectual property rights monopolies. Those who have been waiting for a new and economically viable *free-standing* business model for free and open-source software, one uncoupled to any complementary commercial activity, may justifiably wonder whether they, too, are "waiting for Godot" But, instead any such miraculous business plan — permitting the recouping of initial, fixed costs of open source code which is distributed at its marginal cost, along with all of the other elements of sunk costs associated with sustainable maintenance bug-tracking and patching activities, something else has emerged: the apparent willingness of profit-seeking producers of complementary goods and services to subsidize the production and distribution of free and open-source software.

But, in addition to that somewhat surprising development, there are two potent forces that have continued to impart considerable momentum to the open source software movement. The first of these can best be described as a perfectionist impulse, charismatically projected by community leaders such as Richard Stallman, reinforcing the conviction that the evident virtues of voluntary co-operation will suffice to expand the availability of these software systems to the point where they will pose a full-scale challenge to the viability of the dominant commercial software firms. This can remain a potent force if it succeeds in bringing new members into the movement. The other driver of the movement is more of market "pull-force" than a social "push-force": the practical, purely instrumental need for a robust and "open standard" software environment to support the continuous availability of networked information resources. The attractive technological goal, then, is to fill the vacuum that has been left by the absence of any apparent winner among the available commercial offerings in the movement of local area network software products to the Internet and World Wide Web environment.

The dynamics of "open source" as a socio-political movement

The former of these two drivers may well succumb eventually to the dynamics typical of other charismatic movements: having thrust a few leading developers into international prominence, their followers gradually allow their own energy and attention to dissipate. The status gap separating leaders from followers widens, and low odds of replicating the spectacular reputational triumphs of members of the movement's vanguard slowly become more apparent (both factors taxing the abilities of even the most charismatic figures to animate the community as a whole); the day-to-day requirements of ordinary life, and the exigencies of earning a living overtake the idealist commitment that motivated many among the multitude of obscure followers. Yet, it is on precisely that (now flagging) enthusiasm that the demonstrated efficacy of this mode of production depended, and the load shed by the many among the disaffected must therefore fall more heavily, and eventually intolerably, upon the shoulders of the few who remain most committed. This is the skeptical, pessimistic sociological scenario depicting the fate of idealistic communalism in economic affairs.[29]

The optimistic scenario, on the other hand, highlights the possibility that the potency of the demand-pull force may well survive to become a sustaining factor, because in essence it involves a re-integration and viable reconfiguration of numerous constituencies that share an interest in information technology and that also possess the skills and have the personal commitments necessary to impel them to continue working that field. A division of labor between the large population of individuals who have secured employment in managing the new infrastructure of what is referred to (in Europe) as "the Information Society", and the hardware companies that are responsible for the physical artefacts of that infrastructure, may suffice to maintain this mode of software production. But it would have to do so in an environment in which access to the Internet markedly lowers the costs and organizational challenges of promoting and distributing innovative software solutions.

To date, such social science research attention as has been devoted to the open source software movement has focused (understandably) upon the role of leaders, and the interpretation of the variety of tracts emanating from the most charismatic branch of the movement. This line of inquiry is topical, as well as intellectually engaging: it provides the basis for understanding the conditions on which individuals are recruited into the movement, and how their interest and commitment are maintained throughout the arduous process of creating useful and reliable software. It also provides an observational field for the systematic re-examination of the sociology and economics of voluntary association, the organizational processes governing the definition of goals and the achievement of "closure" in reaching goals, and the formation and functioning of an interface between open source and commercial efforts. In particular, it offers an illuminating set of comparisons with the governance norms and organizational structures of co-operation found in other universalistic, distributed, epistemic communities that have created their own, collegiate, reputational reward systems – such as the research communities working in academic "open-science" institutions. The latter, similarly, exist only through patronage, or the formation of other symbiotic relationships with agencies that furnish the participants with material support for their creative endeavors.

All of the immediately foregoing lines of inquiry are, in one way or another, and in varying degree, threaded through the agendas of social science research projects already underway throughout the world, including the one we have described in the preceding pages. It should be rewarding, and it may be possible, to venture still farther afield by beginning to think about research agendas that would direct attention to the second "branch" or "force" that may well continue to sustain the growth of the open-source software movement. That, at least, is our purpose in the following paragraphs.

Implications of prospective advances in information technology

It is important, first, to consider the significance of the next important development in information exchange standards, XML, which transcends the powerful but limited capabilities of the HTML standard that (with extensions) has to date been driving World Wide Web developments. XML provides a much broader base for creating complex informational artefacts and, correspondingly, has an enhanced capacity for the development of proprietary tools to exploit these capabilities. In the later stages of HTML, technical compatibility issues in maintaining web sites have favored the growth of proprietary tools – i.e., sites are increasingly created and maintained using a single-platform design package. This development can be empirically detected by the automated methods emerging from the Internet research field.

How the community responsible for creating and maintaining the information infrastructure will respond to this development is not at all clear. On the one hand, its members may refuse to be tied to proprietary platforms for content creation because of the inevitable cost of such systems. If such is the case, a focus for future open source activity may become the building of the tools used to create HTML/XML content. On the other hand, that community may embrace commercial packages, creating a major division within the open-source community between those concerned with "lower layer" connectivity and those concerned with "higher level" content.

Second, the relationship between open-source software and peer-to-peer networking movements warrants closer scrutiny. On the one hand, peer-to-peer has been a major instrument in what is described in some circles as "direct action against usurious copyright fees", and in other circles as "large-scale piracy". On the other hand, peer-to-peer extends the Internet's function as a publishing engine, thereby providing the basis for a new exchange economy. Systematic research into the nature of the assets being created and exchanged within this economy, and the response of the developer communities involved to sustained efforts to suppress the abridgment of intellectual property rights, would provide an early indicator of the new patterns of information production and exchange that are likely to emerge towards the end of this decade and during the next one.

Third, a basic characteristic of open-source software communities that has also been undergoing development and elaboration in other contexts, such as computer gaming, is the systematic and explicit assignment of "status" to community participants by their peers. Systems such as that developed by Advogato involve interesting voting rules and procedures for determining user valuation, and these are worth analyzing in the light of the theoretical and empirical social science literature on "demand revelation" and "preference aggregation" mechanisms. Further research may well need to be focused on the technical and social factors involved in deliberately constructing peer-based "status systems," including the creation of a capacity for codified, formalized and automatically generated reputational hierarchies to motivate and direct the efforts of individual participants, and mechanisms for reducing the "voting costs" of generating the information that such systems require. Research findings in this area could serve a variety of practitioner and policy communities alike, by indicating how best to create complex goods under conditions of asymmetric information and high monitoring costs.

Fourth, the interface between open-source-type distribution and other forms of publication and distribution deserves greater attention. A variety of new intermediaries have emerged in the industry publishing e-books, music, and other information commodities. Some of these are operating within a full commercial model, while others (such as the long-established Xanadu project) utilize a variety of public information models. The relative performance of these different communities in achieving goals of distribution and access provides important information about the long-term viability of public information creation and distribution systems, as well as quasi-public good-production modes such as clubs and voluntary consortia.

Consider how best to proceed along the last-mentioned line inquiry immediately raises the more difficult and longer-term challenge of envisaging the future structure of processes of information creation and exchange, and the problems of devising incentive systems that will be compatible with the future production and distribution of information, including scientific information. The sense of enjoyment derived from being attached to (embedded in) a community engaged in some higher, trans-individual (tribal?) purpose is a source of satisfaction that many reasonably well-paid professionals seemingly find hard to obtain in their work as members of hierarchically managed profit-seeking organizations. The Internet would appear to have addressed that need, at least in part. On the evidence of both the tenor of survey responses from a substantial proportion of the developer community, and the impressively complex and reliable software products created by the large open source projects, the formation and support of "virtual communities" of co-operating software developers serve to mobilize participants and satisfy their (otherwise unfulfilled) need to enjoy the exercise of their skills. Moreover, the Internet allows them to enjoy the exercise that skill at convenient times and at pecuniary costs that are low in comparison to those entailed by other, more conventional modes of production.

In this regard, the Internet obviously has great advantages of size and speed of communication over the means that enabled the formation of networks of correspondence and association among the amateur gentlemen scientists of the early 19th century. Is the voluntaristic impulse to create and share knowledge – now manifesting itself in a great variety of virtual communities on the Internet, one of them being the open-source community – likely to increase in scale and scope with the growth of real income and the liberation of larger proportions of the world's population from physical work? This is a question that economists can usefully tackle, even if certainty in prediction remains elusive. At the very least, it appears that they may in that way make considerable progress towards identifying the "boundary conditions" within which such voluntary productive entities can expand and be maintained. Other social- and behavioral-science disciplines may then be left to seek the sources of individual psychological motives and social cohesion that occasion the emergence of such movements and energize their members.

IV Summing Up

Every one of the subjects that have here been identified as warranting further investigation takes as its point of departure the existence of a community (usually a virtual community) striving to assemble the tools and organizational resources necessary to accomplish some purpose. The open-source mode of software development may constitute a paradigmatic framework for collective creative activities whose scope extends far beyond the writing and debugging of computer code. To develop the means of assessing how, where, and why this and other related frameworks succeed in supporting other specific objectives – and where they are likely to fail – is both a challenge and an opportunity to contribute significantly the advancement of the social sciences, but also, and even more significantly, to effective human social organization. Indeed, in this exciting and important research area, there is ample work to engage for many hands and many minds.

Notes

[1] J. LERNER and J. TIROLE, "The Simple Economics of Open Source", Cambridge, MA, National Bureau of Economic Research, Working Paper 7600, 2000, and Eric von Hippel, "Horizontal innovation networks – by and for users", Cambridge, MA, MIT Sloan School of Management, Working Paper No. 4366-02. June, 2002.

[2] J.-M. DALLE and Nicolas JULLIEN, "'Libre' software: turning fads into institutions?", Research Policy 32, 2003, pp. 1-11; D. NICHOLS and M. TWIDALE, "The Usability of Open sourceOpen source Software", *First Monday* (http://firstmonday.org/issues/issue8_1/nichols/index.html), 2003, last accessed 5 February 2003, and Eric S. RAYMOND, *The Cathedral and the Bazaar: Musings on Linux and Open Source by an Accidental Revolutionary*. Sebastopol, CA, O'Reilly and Associates, Inc., 1999.

[3] See Steven WEBER, *The Success of Open Source*, Cambridge, MA, Harvard University Press, 2004, which justifies its examination of the open sourceopen source phenomenon by emphasizing the posing of "a

significant challenge to Microsoft in the marketplace". On the relationship between the development of Microsoft Corporation's business strategy and its software process and product characteristics in the era preceding the U.S. government anti-trust suits of the late 1990s, see Michael A. CUSUMANO and Richard W. SELBY, *Microsoft Secrets*, New York, The Free Press, 1995.

4   This and the following part draw upon material from J.-M. DALLE, P.A. DAVID, and W.E. STEINMUELLER, "Integrated research on the Economic Organization, Performance and Viability of OS/FS Software Development," a statement prepared for the Workshop on Advancing the Research Agenda on Free/Open sourceOpen source Software, held in Brussels on 14 October 2002 under the sponsorship of the EC IST Program and NSF/CISE & DTS.

5   For accounts of the historical conditions under which "open science" developed, see P.A. DAVID, "Common agency contracting and the emergence of open-science institutions," *American Economic Review* 88(2), 1998, pp. 15-21; P.A. DAVID, "Understanding the emergence of 'open-science' institutions: functionalist economics in historical context," *Industrial and Corporate Change*, 13(4), 2004, pp. 571-590; Joseph BEN-DAVID, *Scientific Growth: Essays on the Social Organization and Ethos of Science*, edited by G. FREUDENTHAL, Berkeley, CA, University of California Press, 1991, esp. Part II, pp. 125-210.

6   See John M. ZIMAN, Reliable Knowledge, Cambridge, Cambridge University Press, 1978; Philip Kitcher, *The Advancement of Science: Science without Legend, Objectivity with Illusions*, New York, Oxford U.P., 1993; P. DASGUPTA and P.A. DAVID, "Towards a new economics of science," *Research Policy*, 23, 1994, pp.487-521.

7   See, e.g., P. A. DAVID, "The Economic Logic of 'Open Science' and the Balance between Private Property Rights and the Public Domain in Scientific Data and Information: A Primer," in National Research Council, *The Role of the Public Domain in Scientific Data and Information*, Washington, D.C.: National Academy Press, 2003.

8   The results of the approach suggested here might be compared with those of the an alternative procedure that our project currently is exploring, which is to measure the "commercial replacement cost" of software, using industry cost models based on empirical data for closed, proprietary production of code packages of specified size, language and reliability (as measured by post beta-test bug report frequencies).

9   This project has been supported by NSF Grants (IIS-0112962 and IIS-032959) to the Stanford Institute for Economic Policy Research's "Knowledge Networks and Institutions for Innovation Program," led by Paul DAVID. The three associated groups in Europe are led, respectively, by Jean-Michel DALLE (University of Paris VI), Rishab Ghosh (University of Maastricht-MERIT/Infonomics Institute), and W. Edward STEINMUELLER (SPRU-University of Sussex). Further details and working papers from this project are available at: http://siepr.stanford.edu/programs/OpenSoftware_David/OS_Project_Funded_Announcmt.htm.
This collaboration sometimes refers to itself as the Network on Software Technology Research Advances (NOSTRA). A wit, remarking on the fact that Project NOSTRA appears to be the creation of a "community of open science analysts," has asked whether the authors and their research colleagues will soon be adding "COSA" as part of their collective acronymic identity.

10 For an introduction to research on the economics of "open science" see, e.g., P. DASGUPTA and P.A. DAVID, "Towards a new economics of science," *Research Policy*, 23, 1994, pp. 487-521; P.A. DAVID, "The Economic Logic of 'Open Science' and the Balance between Private Property Rights and the Public Domain

in Scientific Data and Information: A Primer," Ch. 4, in *The Role of Scientific and Technical Data in Information in the Public Domain: Proceedings of a Symposium*, J.M. ESANU and P.F. UHLIR (eds), Washington, D.C., The National Academies Press, 2003. [Available at: http://www.nap.edu.]

11 For the methodology developed for this investigation, see R. A. GHOSH, Clustering and Dependencies in Free/Open Software Development: Methodology and Preliminary Analysis, *SIEPR-Project Nostra Working Paper*, February 2003 [available at: http://siepr.stanford.edu/programs/Opensoftware_David/Clustering and Dependencies.html]; R. A. GHOSH and P. A. DAVID, The Nature and Composition of the Linux Developer Community: A Dynamic Analysis, SIEPR-Project Nostra Working Paper, March 2003 [available at: http://siepr.stanford.edu/programs/OpenSoftware_David/NSFOSF_Publications.html].

12 This approach has been pursued as a first step towards more complex quantitative analyses that will exploit the self-revealing ontological features of open source software, and the array of new tools for machine extraction of data from code repositories. See J.-M. DALLE, P. A. DAVID, R. A. GHOSH, & F. A. WOLAK, "Free & Open Source Software Developers and 'the Economy of Regard': Participation and Code-Signing in the Modules of the Linux Kernel," *SIEPR-Nostra Working Paper*, June 2004, [available at: http://siepr.stanford.edu/programs/OpenSoftware_David/the_Economy_of_Regard.html].

13 See Jesus GONZALEZ-BARAHONA and Gregorio ROBLES, "Free Software Engineering: A Field to Explore," *Upgrade*, IV(4), August 2003; Gregorio ROBLES, Stefan KOCH and Jesus GONZALEZ-BARAHONA, "Remote Analysis and Measurement by Means of the CVSAnalY Tool", Working Paper, Informatics Department, Universidad Rey Juan CARLOS, (June) 2004 [available at: http://opensource.mit.edu/papers/robles-koch-barahona_cvsanaly.pdf; Jesus GONZALEZ-BARAHONA and Gregorio ROBLES, "Getting the Global Picture", a presentation at the Oxford Workshop on Libre Software (OWLS), Oxford Internet Institute, 25-26 June 2004. [Available at: http://www.oii.ox.ac.uk/fiveowlsgohoot/postevent/Barahona&Robles_OWLS-slides.pdf].

14 The SourceForge.net website contains data on 33,814 open source projects, including their technical nature, intended audiences and stage of development. Records of their past history and the involvement of members of the F/LOSS community in their initiation, growth and improvement, also are available.

15 The success/failure of a project can be defined in terms of its rate of development and the involvement (or lack of it) by the community of developers in its improvement/growth.

16 J. MATEOS-GARCIA and W.E. STEINMUELLER, "The Open Source Way of Working: A New Paradigm for the Division of Labour in Software Development?", Falmer, UK, SPRU – Science and Technology Policy Research, INK Open Source Working Paper No. 1, January, 2003 [available at: http://siepr.stanford.edu/programs/OpenSoftware_David/The%20Open%20Source%20Way%20of%20Working.html]; J. MATEOS-GARCIA and W. E. STEINMUELLER, "Population Dynamics of Free & Open Source Software: A Research Roadmap," Presented at the OWLS Conference, Oxford Internet Institute, 25-26th June 2004 [available at: http://www.oii.ox.ac.uk/fiveowlsgohoot/postevent/Mateos-GarciaOWLS.pdf].

17 In contraposition to this tendency, there will be developers who are abandoning old projects as these reach their end, or because their interest waned. Individuals seeking to increase their status within the community may have incentives to terminate their roles as collaborators on existing projects in order to start new ones (a possibility will be considered later). If individuals derive utility from the excite-

18 ment associated with "new hacks", persisting attachments to projects – of the sort described in the text — would be less likely to be formed; indeed, were the typical exit/entry rates of developers participating in open source projects to remain high, that would suffice to mitigate the problems of secularly rising resource immobility within the community as a whole.

[18] A third approach is under consideration: automated web-crawling searches to capture email addresses from proprietary software project sites and re-capture those addresses at open source software project sites may be feasible. Variations in an individual's email identities, however, would in all likelihood result in this method providing only lower-bound estimates of the extent of overlapping participation.

[19] The survey questions, and "The FLOSS-US Survey (2003) Report: A preliminary analysis" by P. A. DAVID, A. H. WATERMAN and S. ARORA may be obtained at: http://www.stanford.edu/group/floss-us/; simple tabulations of the results for each question are posted on the Web at: http://www.stanford.edu/group/floss-us/stats/. These are based on the 1,494 usable responses, out of a total of 1588 that had been received by the time the survey was closed (on 17 June 2003). Links to the FLOSS Survey Report (2002) are given at the former website. As well as increasing the sample density on particular questions, the replication of many of the questions has made it possible to establish the relationship between the two sample populations.

[20] For further details one should consult P. A. DAVID, A. H. WATERMAN and S. ARORA, "FLOSS-US: The Free/Libre/Open Source Survey for 2003," SIEPR-Nostra Project Working Paper, September 2003, [available at: http://www.stanford.edu/group/floss-us/report/FLOSS-US-Report.pdf].

[21] See J. MATEOS-GARCIA, "Factors in the success and failure of free and open sourceopen source software projects: design of a study based on the SourceForge archives", June 2004. Available at: http://www.sussex.ac.uk/spru/publications/mateos_garcia.pdf.

[22] See J. M. DALLE and P.A. DAVID, "The Allocation of Software Development Resources in 'Open Source' Production Mode", in *Making Sense of the Bazaar: Perspectives on Open Source and Free Software*, J. FELLER, et al. (eds), Cambridge, MA, MIT Press, forthcoming in Winter, 2004.

[23] See Eric S. RAYMOND, *The Cathedral and the Bazaar: Musings on Linux and Open Source by an Accidental Revolutionary*, Sebastopol CA, O'Reilly, 2001, pp. 65-112.

[24] See, e.g., E. VON HIPPEL, "Horizontal innovation networks – by and for users," Massachusetts Institute of Technology, Sloan School of Management, Working Paper No. 4366-02, June 2002 [available at: http://web.mit.edu/evhippel/www/UserInnovNetworksMgtSci.pdf]; K. LAKHANI and E. VON HIPPEL, "How open source software works: 'free' user-to-user assistance," *Massachusetts Institute of Technology, Sloan School of Management, Working Paper No. 4117*, May 2000 [available at: http://web.mit.edu/evhippel/www/opensource.PDF].

[25] The complex interplay of factors of learning and trust, and the ways in which they may shape the path-dependent career trajectories of members of the F/LOSS developer communities, have been carefully discussed in Juan MATEOS-GARCIA and W. Edward STEINMUELLER, "The Open Source Way of Working: A New Paradigm for the Division of Labour in Software Development?", INK Open Source Working Paper 2, SPRU University of Sussex, 2003. The abstract and text of this paper is available at: http://siepr.stanford.edu/programs/OpenSoftware_David/OSR01_abstract.html.

[26] The following paragraphs draw upon the statement presented by DAVID and STEINMUELLER to the workshop convened at the National Science Foundation, Arlington, VA, 28 January 2002, on: "Advancing the Research Agenda on Open Source".

[27] W. Edward STEINMUELLER, "The U.S. Software Industry: An Analysis and Interpretive History", in David C. MOWERY (ed.), *The International Computer Software Industry*, Oxford, Oxford University Press, 1996, pp. 15-52.

[28] See, e.g., the strongly skeptical (but not entirely well-informed) opinions expressed by a highly regarded legal scholar at the University of Chicago: Richard Epstein, "Why open source is unsustainable," *Financial Times - Comments and Analysis*, 21 October 2004 [available at: http://news.ft.com/cms/s/78d9812a-2386-11d9-aee5-00000e2511c8.html]. James Boyle's critique of Epstein's article the in FT.com ("Give me liberty and give me death?") is available from the same URL.

[29] It is quite possible, however, that before dissipating the movement would have become strong enough and sufficiently sustained to thoroughly disrupt and even displace the once dominant proprietary sector of the software industry. Consequently, the survival of the conventional commercial model is not implied by a prediction of the *eventual* decay of the free and open source software movement. History is usually messy. From the envisaged "crisis" that would overtake the commercial software industry, one socio-political solution that could well emerge might be something akin to the Tennessee Valley Authority program of rural electrification — massive public subsidization and regulation of the production and distribution software, seen as the critical technological infrastructure for the knowledge economy.

Biographies

Jean-Michel Dalle is an Associate Professor at the Pierre-et-Marie-Curie University and an associate researcher with IMRI-Dauphine (both in Paris, France) whose general interest lies in the economics of innovation. Dr Dalle has worked on technological competition, standardization processes and interaction models, focusing from 1998 on the economics of open-source – "libre" – software. He has had research articles published in various international peer-reviewed journals and conference proceedings, and he is a regular speaker at international conferences. Dr Dalle is an alumnus of the École Polytechnique and ENSAE, and holds a PhD in economics. Apart from his academic activities, he is also the director of Agoranov, a public incubator co-founded by several prestigious academic institutions in Paris to help create new business ventures based upon scientific discoveries.

Rishab Aiyer Ghosh is Founding International and Managing Editor of *First Monday*, perhaps the most widely read peer-reviewed academic journal on the Internet. He is Programme Leader at MERIT/International Institute of Infonomics at the University of Maastricht, Netherlands. He writes and speaks frequently on the socio-economics of the Internet and free/open-source software. He coordinated the European Union-funded FLOSS project, one of the most comprehensive studies of free/libre/open-source users and developers. He is actively involved in initiatives related to government policy on open source, and is currently taking part in research projects on related topics funded by the European Union, the Dutch government and the US National Science Foundation.

Paul A. David is known internationally for his contributions to economic history, economic and historical demography, and the economics of science and technology. A pioneering practitioner of the so-called "new" economic history, his research has illuminated the phenomenon of path dependence in economic processes. Two strands of David's research – one focusing on the ways in which "history matters" in the evolution of network technology standards, the other on the organization of scientific research communities (including the impact of IPR policies on "open science") – have recently coalesced in his undertaking of an extensive international collaborative program of research on free/libre and open-source software development. During the past decade David has divided his time between Stanford University, where he is Professor of Economics and a Senior Fellow of the Stanford Institute for Economic Policy Research (SIEPR), and the University of Oxford, where he is a Senior Fellow of the Oxford Internet Institute and an Emeritus Fellow of All Souls College.

W. Edward Steinmueller studied computer science, mathematics, economics, and Chinese language and history at the University or Oregon and Stanford University. He was engaged in teaching, research, consulting and university administration at Stanford University's Center for Economic Policy Research and its Department of Economics for twenty years before accepting a professorial chair at the University of Maastricht, in the Netherlands. He has been Professorial Fellow at SPRU since 1997. Steinmueller has published widely on the industrial economics of the information and communication technology industries, including on integrated circuits, computers, telecommunications and software, and on the economic and social policy issues of the Information Society. Steinmueller has been an advisor to the European Commission, the National Academies of Science and Engineering (US), the Ministry of Economic Affairs (the Netherlands), the Department of Trade and Industry and Office of Telecommunications (UK), and the United Nations University Institute for New Technologies (UNU-INTECH).

BICYCLES
SKATEBOARDS
ROLLER BLADERS ON
LOWER LEVEL ONLY

★ ★ ★ ★ ★

RESPECT OTHERS
GO SLOW

The Future of Open Source

Ilkka Tuomi

Introduction

Open source has seen phenomenal interest and growth in recent years. In many ways, it has been a great success story. Clearly, it is no longer just hype, or a temporary fad. Yet it is interesting to think about the conditions that would enable the open-source movement to remain viable, and thrive. This chapter explores the driving forces behind this model, and the constraints on it, discussing both the factors likely to promote the continuous growth of the open-source movement and those that could lead to its downfall.

The sustainability of the open-source model depends on several factors. Some of these are internal to the model itself, including the economic viability of the model, the availability of competent contributors, and the extensibility and flexibility of the model. Other factors are external, including the potential reactions of proprietary-software developers and policymakers, as well as technological developments leading to evolutionary paths that are fundamentally incompatible with the model. Below I will discuss these factors, in an attempt to locate potential discontinuities that require new approaches from the open-source model if it is to maintain its vitality.

The history of open source

In the age of the Internet, new empires are rapidly built and lost. Successes quickly sow the seeds of their own destruction. The Internet, however, has proven to be extraordinarily flexible and capable of overcoming many of its inherent technical limitations, constraints and bottlenecks. This ability to innovate around emerging obstacles has been based on the distributed social model that underlies the evolution of the Internet and its key technologies. This distributed innovation model, in turn, is closely related to the phenomenon that we now know as the open-source development model. One might therefore expect that open-source software projects – and the open-source approach itself – would show similar viability and robustness when the time comes for them to reap the successes that they have sown.

The open-source software development model has been used since the first multi-user computers became available in the early 1960s. Robert Fano, one of the key architects of the first time-sharing system at MIT, described the phenomenon in the following words:

> "Some of the most interesting, yet imponderable, results of current experimentation with time-sharing systems concern their interaction with the community of users. There is little doubt that this interaction is strong, but its character and the underlying reasons are still poorly understood.
>
> The most striking evidence is the growing extent to which system users build upon each other's work. Specifically, as mentioned before, more than half of the current system commands in the Compatible Time-Sharing System at MIT were developed by system users rather than by the system programmers responsible for the development and maintenance of the system. Furthermore, as also mentioned before, the mechanism for linking to programs owned by other people is very widely used. This is surprising since the tradition in the computer field is that programs developed by one person are seldom used by anybody else... The opposite phenomenon seems to be occurring with time-sharing systems. It is so easy to exchange programs that many people do indeed invest the additional effort required to make their work usable by others." (Fano, 1967)

Fano further argued that a time-sharing system can quickly become a major community resource, and that its evolution and growth depend on the inherent capabilities of the system as well as on the interests and goals of the members of the community.

A system without a display, for example, could discourage the development of graphical applications, or if it were difficult for several people to interact with the same application this could discourage some educational uses. Moreover, Fano noted that after a system starts to develop in a particular direction, work in this direction is preferred and it accelerates the development in this direction. As a result, "the inherent characteristics of a time-sharing system may well have long-lasting effects on the character, composition, and intellectual life of a community" (cf. Tuomi, 2002: 86).

The modern concept of proprietary software emerged in the 1970s, when the computer-equipment industry began to unbundle software from hardware, and independent software firms started to produce software for industry-standard computer platforms. Over the decade, this development led to the realization that software was associated with important intellectual capital which could provide its owners with revenue streams. In 1983, AT&T was freed from the constraints of its earlier antitrust agreement, which had restricted its ability to commercialize software, and it started to enforce its copyrights in the popular Unix operating system. The growing restrictions on access to source code also started to make it difficult to integrate peripheral equipment, such as printers, into the developed systems. This frustrated many software developers, and led Richard Stallman to launch the GNU project in 1983 and the Free Software Foundation in 1985. Stallman's pioneering idea was to use copyrights in a way that guaranteed that the source code would remain available for further development and that it could not be captured by commercial interests. For that purpose, Stallman produced a standard license, the GNU General Public License, or GPL, and set up to develop an alternative operating system that would eventually be able to replace proprietary operating systems.

Although the GNU Alix/Hurd operating-system kernel never really materialized, the GNU project became a critical foundation for the open-source movement. The tools developed in the GNU project, including the GNU C-language compiler GCC, the C-language runtime libraries, and the extendable Emacs program editor, paved the way for the launching of other open-source projects. The most important of these became the Linux project, partly because it was the last critical piece missing from the full GNU operating-system environment. Eventually, the core Linux operating system became combined with a large set of open-source tools and applications, many of which relied on the GNU program libraries and used the GPL.

The first version of the Linux operating system was released on the Internet in mid-September 1991. The amount of code in the first Linux release was quite modest. The smallest file consisted of a single line and the longest was 678 lines, or 612 lines without comments. The average size of the files in the first Linux package was 37 lines without comments. In total, the system consisted of 88 files, with 231 kilobytes of code and comments. The program was written in the C programming language, which the creator of Linux, Linus Torvalds, had started to study in 1990 (Tuomi, 2004).

During the 1990s, the Linux operating system kernel grew at a rapid pace. The overall growth of the system can be seen in Figure 1. The accumulated number of key contributors recorded in the Credits file of the Linux system increased from 80 in March 1994, when they were first recorded, to 418 in July 2002, and 450 by the end of 2003. The developers were widely distributed geographically from the beginning of the project. In July 2002, there were 28 countries with ten or fewer developers and seven countries with more than ten developers. At the end of 2003, the Credits file recorded contributors from 35 countries (Tuomi, 2004).

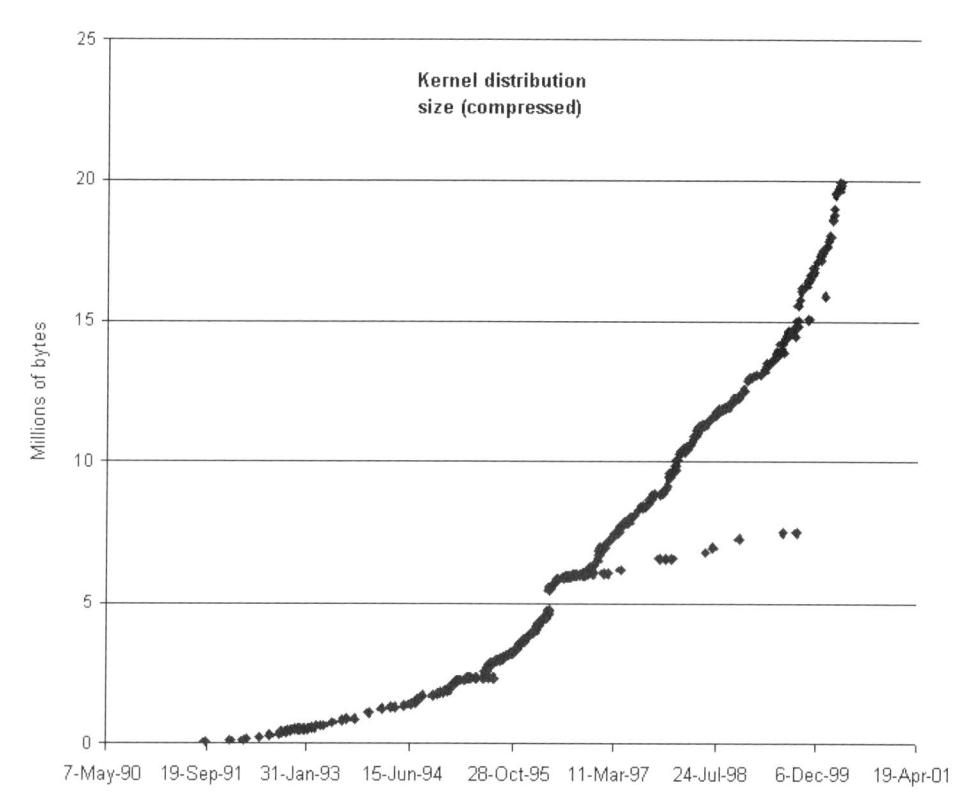

Figure 1 – Growth of Linux kernel, 1991-2000 (source: Tuomi, 2001).

Linux has become a particularly visible example of open-source software, as it has often been perceived as a challenger to Microsoft's dominance in personal-computer operating systems. Other important open-source projects, such as Apache, Perl, MySQL, PHP, Sendmail and BitTorrent, have also considerably shaped the modern computing landscape. In fact, the global Internet now operates to a large extent on open-source software. Commercial concerns, such as IBM, Sun Microsystems, Oracle, SAP, Motorola and Intel, have become important players in the open-source field. Policymakers from South America to Europe, China, Republic of Korea, and Japan have become involved in open-source initiatives.

This widespread interest in open source, however, dates back only a few years. The breakthrough of open source to public consciousness occurred only after the turn of the decade. Although the first explorations of the open-source phenomenon appeared already in 1998, the first empirical articles started to become available in 2000.[1] The first policy-oriented studies began to emerge in 2001, when the public authorities in many European countries also became interested in open source.[2]

Driving forces behind the open-source phenomenon

There have been at least five major reasons for the growth of interest in open source. The first has been the cost. Open-source systems typically do not involve license fees, and users can download them from the Internet without paying for them.[3] Second, the open-source model has been claimed to produce better software than the proprietary closed-source model. The argument has been that the open-source development model allows multiple participants to peer-review effectively code developed by others. This has been claimed to lead to the fast development of high-quality systems. Third, open-source licenses and the availability of source code make it possible for users to modify the system to the specific needs of the user. Thus, if someone has particular, idiosyncratic requirements that will not be addressed by the producers of commercial software, the open-source model allows this end-user to extend the system so that it meets all his or her major needs. Fourth, the open-source development model has been claimed to lead to the faster incorporation of innovative ideas and new useful functionality than proprietary systems. This is because the distributed development model allows all the developers to contribute to the development of the system and, for example, to feed useful extensions to the system back to the developer community. Fifth, the availability of the source code enables users to check the functionality. This is expected to reduce the likelihood that the code may contain security vulnerabilities, such as back doors or malicious code.

In fact, these rationales for open source have rarely been carefully justified or studied. Proprietary-software developers have thus been able to make the counter-argument that, when the total lifetime costs for installing, operating and maintaining software are taken into account, the low cost of open source becomes questionable. In this argument, license costs are in any case a minor part of total costs.

The claims that open-source code is of better quality than proprietary code have also been mainly anecdotal, partly because very little has been known about the quality of individual open-source systems, or the open-source approach in general. Although its proponents have argued that the open-source development model leads to high-quality software, a quick glance at historical open-source releases typically reveals major quality problems even in the most successful of these systems.[4]

The argument that open source has more value for users than a closed system because open-source code can be modified does seem to have some historical justification. Successful open-source projects have grown because the end-users have been able to solve problems that they know well, and which are important to them. This, however, has typically meant that in successful open-source projects the "end-users" are themselves competent software developers. Successful open-source projects have an underlying social structure in which technology-producing communities substantially overlap with technology-using communities.

This, indeed, is the main difference between the proprietary commercial model and the open-source model. In the commercial model, users and developers typically form independent communities that are only indirectly connected through economic transactions. In the open-source model, by contrast, the development dynamic crucially depends on users who are also the developers of the technical system. Although there may be hundreds and even thousands of peripheral members in this community, the core community typically consists of a relatively small group of people. If these core developers stop the development, and no other developers take up their tasks, the system quickly dies away.

In this regard, many popular accounts of the amazing number of people involved in open-source projects have clearly exaggerated the size of open-source communities. It has often been argued that the success of the open-source model depends on thousands and even hundreds of thousands of community members. A more careful study of the nature of open-source communities, however, shows that, sociologically speaking, there is no such thing as "the open-source community", that almost all contributions to open-source projects come from a very small group of developers, and that hardly any open-source projects ever succeed in attracting the interest of more than a couple of developers or users.[5] In fact, a back-of-envelope calculation of the total resources used to develop Linux – the flagship of the open-source movement – indicates that, on average, it has been developed by the equivalent of perhaps a couple of dozen developers per year.[6] This is by no means a trivial software development project, but it could hardly be called an extraordinarily large development effort.

The argument that the open-source model would lead to more innovative systems, and the faster incorporation of new technological ideas, is an interesting one. It also leads, however, to the difficult and important question of what, exactly, we mean by innovation. At first sight, there is nothing particularly innovative in projects such as Linux, which basically re-implements commercially available operating-system functionality. Software engineering, in general, is engineering: the implementation of a specific, given functionality using commonly accepted tools and methods. Innovative operating-system architectures exist, including the Unix system architecture, on which Linux is based, was innovative in the early 1970s, when it was first developed. Instead of characterizing the Linux project as an innovation project, one might therefore be justified in arguing that it is more accurate to view it as an engineering and implementation project.

If, however, by innovation we mean all kinds of technology development, a detailed study of the evolution of open-source projects shows that they structure innovation processes in very specific ways. In the case of Linux, for example, the social control of technology development has become tightly aligned with the modularity of the technical system architecture. Some parts of the system were frozen and excluded from modifications in the very early stages of the development. These stable, core elements of the system have, in turn, allowed the rapid expansion of the system in the more peripheral areas. Indeed, almost all of the growth seen in Figure 1 results from code that has been added to link the core operating system with new hardware and peripherals. This can se seen in Figure 2, which shows the incremental code changes in one of the core modules of the Linux operating system – the kernel module – and one directory path consisting of code that includes some of the main extensible parts of the system.

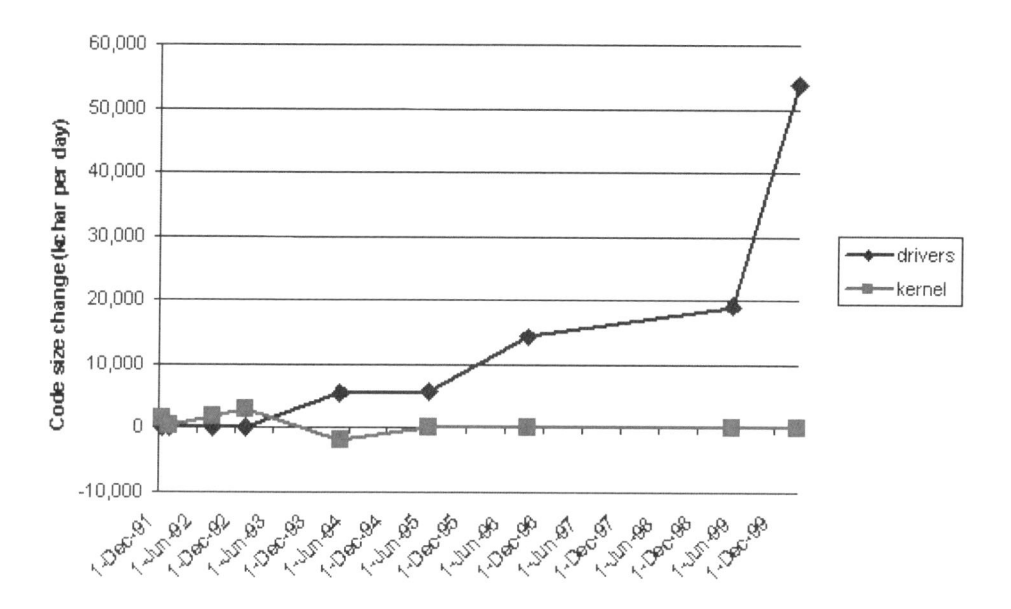

Figure 2. Growth of source code in two main Linux code directories (data from Tuomi, 2002).

This model of development has the social advantage that the developer community can absorb enthusiastic new developers without any great difficulty. The new developers can learn their skills and work practices by developing code that extends the system's functionality but does not interfere with its core functionality. Gradually, the novices can then earn a reputation as reliable developers, and become masters and gurus in the project community.

This process of social integration and skills development is closely related to the architecture of the technical system that is being developed. Not all systems can be built in a modular and incremental fashion that simultaneously supports skills development, the socialization of community members and the development of a functional technological artifact.

The roots of Linux's success can be found in the architectural features of Unix. The main architectural insight contributed by the Unix system was its modular structure, which allowed new functionality to be added to the system simply by adding on new program modules which used the existing resources to get the job done. Historically, the GNU project relied on the fact that a full replacement for the commercial Unix operating system could be built piecemeal, by using the existing Unix platform as the development platform. The GNU project, therefore, could start to replace the proprietary components of the Unix system one by one, and test the functionality of the newly developed open-source modules in the context of the existing system. In this sense, the GNU project tried to keep the functionality of the GNU system compatible with the existing Unix, while incrementally reworking the commercial Unix in the direction of an open-source version. Indeed, the GNU project gradually built almost a complete system, which finally became a full operating system when the Linux developers plugged in the missing piece, the operating-system kernel.

The skills development model in GNU/Linux closely resembles the social learning processes that underlie the dynamic in communities of practice. Such social learning processes have already been studied for a long time outside the software-development domain. Lave and Wenger (1991) proposed a model in which communities of practice form the social entities that maintain particular social practices and stocks of knowledge, and Brown and Duguid (1991) extended this model to organizational innovation models. Historically, these models were based on ideas developed as part of the cultural-historical activity theory, which emphasized the development of skills and cognition as a process in the "zone of proximal development" where the performer was able to show competent behavior when supported by others, but where autonomous performance was still lacking.[7] By borrowing skills and knowledge from others, the learner was able to do things that still remained outside his or her current capabilities and, through such socially supported action, learn them. In this model, parents, for example, built mental and practical "scaffolds" that allowed their children to climb to new levels of performance, where these new, advanced forms of cultural and cognitive behavior could be experienced and learned, and eventually performed without support. In technology-development communities, a similar process of skills development leads to social structures that consist of "novices", "old-timers" and "gurus", and which center around community-specific knowledge and artifacts (Tuomi, 1999).

The problem inherent in this model is that it is fundamentally a conservative one. A commercial Unix system can be transformed into an open-source version piece by piece only if most pieces are kept stable at every point in time. As depicted by Lave and Wenger, the "community of practice" model was focused on the transfer of existing social practices and traditions. The power structure was concentrated in the "center", with the members of the core community defining what counted as knowledge and development in the community in question. The novices could enter the community gradually, by first gaining access to the community, then internalizing its values and world-views, and eventually becoming full, competent members.

This community-centric developmental model, therefore, could be expected to be particularly suitable for incremental innovations and extensions that enforce the basic values of the community. In this model, it would be quite difficult to introduce radical innovations that shake the current power structure or contradict the core values of the community. For example, if the basic hardware architecture of personal computers were to change radically, such a change might require extensive changes to the structure of the Linux developer community, possibly leading to the end of Linux.

The fifth reason for the increasing visibility of open source – better security through the availability of the source code for inspection – has gained some importance in recent years. In general, computer viruses, daily announcements of security problems in commercial software and frequent hijackings of network-connected computers in order to relay spam have pushed security to the forefront of users' concerns.[8] Computer users have realized that their broadband-connected computers are accessible across the globe, and policymakers have become worried that unauthorized access could lead to problems with national security and computer crime. Well-publicized US initiatives on monitoring and tracking electronic communications and the lack of transparency of government efforts to fight terrorism have also increased the perceived possibility that commercial software vendors may be required to incorporate unpublicized back doors to their systems to permit and facilitate the monitoring of computer-based activities around the world.

If the commercial software producers cannot be trusted, or held liable for damages, the only alternative is to establish an independent control process that guarantees that problems do not exist. At first, it might perhaps look as if the availability of the source code would solve this problem. If the code can be inspected, then in theory the inspectors can easily see a code that implements back doors or other unacceptable functions. In practice, this is more difficult, as can be seen from the constant flow of security-related updates for both closed-source and open-source software. The inspection of software code is relatively easy for the people who have been involved in the development of the system, but it is difficult for people who are given source code that represents perhaps years of accumulated work.

More fundamentally, however, the source code does not itself reveal all security problems. When the system is compiled into a working binary code, the compiler decides how the transformation of the source program code is done. If the compiler, for example, instructs the programmed system to use code that includes a back door, all systems compiled with this compiler will include the back door. Similarly, if the microprocessor microcode, which the program eventually mobilizes to do its tasks, includes undocumented instructions, no amount of inspection of the program source code will reveal the related security problems. Such microcode instructions could be used to bypass security mechanisms implemented in the open-source program.[9]

Although it is clear that the availability of source code does not completely solve the problem of security or lack of trust, it does, however, considerably limit the types of problems. Only microprocessor manufacturers can implement microcode on their chips, and only compiler-developers can change the basic functionality of compilers. The question still remains, however, whether the open-source approach leads to better security than closed source. The argument for closed source has been that keeping the source code unavailable makes it more difficult for hackers and computer criminals around the world to develop malicious code. This "security through obscurity" argument, however, has been discredited by most security experts.

The proper argument would be that the developmental path of open-source leads to systems that have different security characteristics than closed source systems. This could happen, for example, because security problems were detected faster in the open-source model, as more people were able to study the code, or because the availability of source code enabled the developers to build mental models of the system architecture, system functionality and accepted development styles that facilitated the detection of anomalies. It could also happen because existing security problems were widely publicized within the development community, thus enabling its members to learn faster how to develop code without security problems. The open-source model could also lead to better security simply because the transparent development model makes the individual developers personally and socially liable for the quality of code.

All these reasons, of course, depend on the poor quality of commercial-software development processes. In principle, one could invest in improvements of commercial software development processes to make them start to produce software as good as the open-source model. In theory, however, one might also argue that the open-source model is inherently better than any closed-source models in addressing security problems. Such a claim could be based on two separate points. The first is that the open-source model allows users to organize independent quality-control mechanisms. The second is that distributed development is inherently better, and that it requires open access to the source code.

Independent quality controls and the possibility of inspecting code are important if the quality-control mechanisms of commercial software developers cannot be trusted. Normally, in such a situation, commercial partners try to manage the risks by agreeing on liability and remedies in case damage occurs. In practice, however, this is an option only when the risks are relatively small or controllable, for example by insuring against them. In reality, many producers of prepackaged software and operating systems would probably go bankrupt if they had to cover all the damage and loss generated by quality problems with their products. For this reason, software vendors typically only license the right to use their products under conditions where they are not liable for any damage caused by such use. In this situation, the possibility of reviewing vulnerabilities and defects independently, and reacting to them, does have some value for users.

The second argument for the inherent security of open source would be that distributed and self-organized development processes always win in the end, even over the best-organized development processes. This argument would be akin to the Hayekian view that market-based economies are always better than command economies because they allocate resources more effectively and process information better than any hierarchical decision-maker. One could argue, for example, that detecting and solving security problems requires local, context-specific knowledge that always remains inaccessible to central decision-makers, who can therefore never make optimal choices.

This Hayekian story, of course, would not be the full story. Taken to its extreme, it would leave open the question of why organizations exist. Indeed, this question is also central to the future of open source.

The economic organization of open source

From the point of view of economic theory, the open-source development model is a challenge. Much of the literature on economics starts out from the assumption that economic players need to appropriate the returns of their investments. In this theoretical world, economic players produce new technology only if they can make a profit. Furthermore, if the developers are unable to perceive and appropriate all the benefits of their development, investment may remain below the social optimum. As complex production requires the division of labor and capital, entrepreneurs set up business companies. Business organizations, therefore, emerge as the principal actors on the stage of modern economy, and, in this theoretical framework, need to become owners of the products they produce.

The concept of ownership is a central one in modern society. It translates the social phenomenon of power into the domain of ethics, rights, and legal institutions. In practice, the concept of ownership makes it possible for people to exchange valuable things and services in an orderly and predictable way, without relying on pure and random violence. We can always take the goods we need if we are powerful enough, but if the power is physical instead of social, the behavior can appropriately be called asocial. Ownership stops us acting purely individually, as we cannot fulfill our own needs without asking who the others are who control goods and resources, and what they want. In this sense, the concept of ownership is the foundation of social worlds and ethical behavior. The acceptance of ownership structures means that we have tamed our nature as beasts, and accepted the structures of society.

In open-source communities, however, the concept of ownership becomes redefined. Instead of controlling a given good, open-source communities control the developmental dynamic of an evolving good. The "openness" of open source, therefore, is more about open future than about access to currently existing source-code text.

Simple extensions of conventional economic concepts, such as ownership and intellectual property, are therefore bound to create confusion when applied in the context of open-source development.

In economic discussions on open source it has frequently been argued that open source may be understood as a public good. In economic theory, public goods are goods that are non-exclusive and in joint supply. A feature of non-exclusive goods is that if they are available, they are available to all. Public goods that are in joint supply, in turn, are goods that do not lose value when someone benefits from them. Open source fulfills both conditions: when it is made available, it can be downloaded by anyone, and when someone downloads the system, its value for other users does not decrease.[10]

Von Hippel and von Krogh (2003) have argued that the open-source model works well because the developers have sufficient private benefits to keep the development going. The traditional theoretical problem with the production of public goods is that when the good is available to everyone, those who have not contributed to its production can also benefit from it. This leads to free-riding and less-than-optimal investment in development. For this reason, economists often believe that in well-operating markets all production should be private production where the producer is fully entitled to maximize the profits from his or her investment. The von Hippel and von Krogh argument was that free-riding does not necessarily have to be destructive. The developers may gain access to valuable learning and system functionality that is tailored to their specific needs, whereas the free-riders can only benefit from the system itself. If the private benefits to developers are sufficient, the open-source model can produce public goods without the risk that all developers may end up free-riding on the work of others. The apparent miracle of open source can therefore be compatible with the established beliefs of economic theory. More specifically, the miracle is shown to be an illusion, which reveals its true nature when the private benefits of the benefit-maximizing individual developers are taken fully into account.

O'Mahony (2003) pointed out that although open source may be a privately produced public good, one still has to consider the conditions that make it difficult to steal this good. In particular, she highlighted the different tactics that open-source communities have used to keep the system they have produced a public good. These include the open-source licensing terms and branding that restrict the possibility for commercial players to extend the code to make it, effectively, proprietary.

O'Mahony also noted that open-source software could be described as a common-pool resource. In economic theory, common pools have been used to analyze tragedies of commons, where individual players maximize their benefits to the eventual loss of everyone. Traditional discussions on common pools and tragedies of commons assumed that economic players are norm-free maximizers of their immediate individual benefits, without the capacity to cooperate. Empirically, these assumptions are obviously wrong when applied to open-source communities. Since the foundation of the GNU project, the explicit goal of many open-source projects has been to collaborate in the production of common goods, and history shows that they have successfully done exactly that.

A feature of common-pool resources is that they are subtractable. In other words, when someone uses the pool, its value diminishes. This, in fact, is a common feature in real life if resources are not renewable or if their renewal occurs more slowly than their depletion. From this point of view, open source is an interesting resource. As the future value of the system depends on the amount of developers and the availability of complementary products, the open-source pool may in fact become more valuable the more people use it. In this sense, open source could be described as a fountain of goods. Traditional economic theories have difficulty modeling such phenomena, as they are built on the assumption that resources are scarce. In "fountains of goods" models, the limiting factor for growth is not the decreasing marginal benefit and increasing cost; instead, it is to be found in the dynamic of social change and the development of the skills needed to seize the emerging opportunities. In other words, such models require that we move beyond traditional economic theory.

Economists have typically tried to show that existing theoretical models can be compatible with the open-source model when purely economic transactions are complemented with concepts such as investment in reputation and network effects. Lerner and Tirole (2000) highlighted the potential importance of delayed payoffs, such as enhanced career opportunities and ego gratification generated by peer recognition. Johnson (2001) showed that open-source development may be modeled as a simple, game-theoretic model of the private production of a public good, where the developers optimize their benefits under the conditions of perfect knowledge about the preferences of others. Dalle and Jullien (2001), in turn, showed that network externalities could make software users switch from proprietary systems to open systems, modeling Linux users essentially as a magnetic material which jumps from one organized state to another depending on external forces and the interactions between its nearest neighbors.

In fact, many early models were quite independent of the empirics of open source, simply because relatively little was known about open source. The models could easily have been generalized to fit practically any economic activity where network effects, interdependent investments, or delayed benefits would have been relevant. Economic theory, however, has usefully highlighted the essential economic characteristics of open source. It can be understood as a privately produced good, in the sense that individual developers create contributions to the system that creates public benefits. The developers make decisions about joining development projects based on their perceived benefits and costs. The benefits may include enhancement of reputation, the value of developed functionality to the developer, peer recognition, and other short-term or long-term benefits. When the individuals are working for commercial firms and paid for their work, they may also develop the system because they are paid for it. Although it is not clear whether the developers maximize their benefits in any systematic sense, it is clear that they do take them into account. In addition to straightforward economic benefits, however, open-source developers consider a broad set of possible benefits, including the excitement of being part of a meaningful social project that can potentially change the world.

In other words, open-source developers are motivated and incentivized in many ways and for many different reasons. The particular strength of the open-source model is that it allows multiple motivational systems to co-exist and to be aligned so that the system development goes on. In open-source development, in particular, it is not only money that counts. In this economy, sellers, buyers, and producers may market things for example because they like being on the market, and because the game of social interaction is fun and socially meaningful.

Conventional economic thinking has had conceptual difficulty in dealing with open source because economic theory has historically centered on scarce resources. The basic historical problem for classical economists has been how to maximize the consumption of scarce goods. This was a relevant question in a world where the lack of consumption possibilities was a daily challenge and where people lived in poverty and hunger. Open-source development, in contrast, is a social process that creates goods where they did not exist before. The concept of scarcity cannot easily be applied when the economy becomes creative. The open-source development model, therefore, shakes one of the core building blocks of the modern economic worldview.

In fact, some of the excitement in open-source communities seems to result from the realization that open source stands the basic principles of the modern global economy on their heads. In open-source projects, consumers become producers. Instead of becoming alienated from the results of their work, open-source developers engage in individually and socially meaningful production, and retain the moral authorship of their work. In this sense, the social currents that express themselves in open-source projects can also be viewed as a positive and productive version of anti-globalization critiques, for example.

Perhaps the most obvious – if somewhat controversial – reason for the inability of conventional economic theories to describe the open-source phenomenon is that economic transactions and economic rationality operate only in limited social domains. A modern economy has a very particular way of organizing social interactions. In its present form, its history in industrialized countries goes back only a couple of centuries. Many areas of social life, therefore, remain outside the sphere of economic models and conventional economic theorizing.

Most fundamentally, perhaps, the concept of rational choice that underlies microeconomics does not work well in innovative worlds. In practice, people are able to revise their priorities and perceptions rapidly, and in the modern world, where new social and technical opportunities emerge frequently, such revisions are common. In effect, this means that people change the reasoning behind their actions and their preferences in ways that make traditional economic models unable to predict social behavior, except when social change is of minor importance. In new technology development this is rarely a good approximation. The conceptual structure of traditional economic models requires that the rules of the game remain essentially constant and that the world of preferences is closed. In technology development, however, innovation produces essentially novel social phenomena, opens up new worlds for social action, and constantly changes the rules of the game. This makes it necessary for individuals and other economic decision-makers to re-evaluate and reinvent their value systems continuously.

Economic theories normally cannot handle such situations, as, methodologically speaking, they rely on an implicit empiristic and positivistic epistemology. In other words, they assume that stable value systems exist, and that economic behavior consists of expressions of individual preferences within objective value systems. The lack of stable, objective value systems in society means that conventional economic theories do not, in general, converge towards any social reality. Economic explanations of technology-creation activities, such as open-source development, therefore remain abstractions lacking predictive power.

This theoretical challenge, of course, does not mean that concrete economic factors are irrelevant to the future of open source. In fact, both the sustainable evolution of community-specific value systems and the accumulation of traditional economic resources are critical for the success of open-source projects. These projects are interesting for economic theory, as they highlight the importance of community-based value systems and social structures at the foundation of an economy. The substructure of a modern economy is revealed in these technology-development projects, which organize themselves for the purpose of collective production and social exchange. The particular characteristics of modern, monetarized economic transactions, in turn, become visible when open-source projects need to interface their activities with the rest of the modern economy.

The basic challenge for sustainable social activities is that they need to generate and accumulate sufficient resources to maintain themselves. In conventional economics, this requirement has often been understood as the need to generate profit. Businesses are viable if they can pay for their activities and investments and pay their investors.

In the case of open-source development, early descriptions of the phenomenon often argued that the developers worked completely outside the economic sphere. This, of course, was never the case. Richard Stallman, for example, explicitly pointed out in the 1980s that he generates income for the GNU project by charging for the distributions of the system, that he makes the work on the project possible by commercial consultancy and teaching, and that the continuity of the project depends on donations of money and equipment. Open-source developers have used technology developed by commercial firms and computer networks funded by universities and governments, and they have often had to pay for their pizzas in real currency. In this sense, open-source development can also be understood as a parasitic activity that has been free-riding slack resources and activities within the sphere of economic transactions. In fact, the tradition known in French as *la perruque*, whereby workers skillfully transfer their employer's resources into gifts or meaningful and unintended productive activities, could easily be used to explain some characteristics of the open-source economy (Tuomi, 2002:28).

A more careful look at the parasitic nature of open source, however, reveals that it is not obvious who the parasite is and who is the host. All economic players – including commercial software vendors – free-ride extensively. For example, they rely on skills development processes that are paid for by others, often by the workers, competing firms, or the public schooling system. Public and private investment in the Indian university system, for example, allow many commercial software firms to lower their expenditure. Non-commercial software activities, such as hobbyist development, computer gaming, demo development, and various other forms of computer hacking have provided critical sources of skills for commercial vendors at least since the 1970s. Innovative commercial activities paid for by competitors have also been important. The history of Microsoft is an illustrative example here.

It may therefore be claimed that open-source developer communities have been possible because they have successfully appropriated resources without paying for them. It may also be said, however, that commercial software vendors have been possible for the same reason. Instead of one or the other being a parasite, these two modes of software production have been living in symbiosis for a long time. The question for the viability of the open-source model, then, is whether the growth of the open-source movement disturbs this symbiosis in major ways, or whether open-source communities may, for example, jump to a new symbiotic relationship where commercial software vendors are no longer needed for open-source development.

Recent developments have shown that both commercial vendors and open-source communities are transforming themselves in order to address this challenge. New hybrid models are emerging in which open-source communities and commercial profit-making firms redefine their relations and explore mutually viable models. MySQL, for example, has successfully developed a Janus-like model where it shows one face to the open-source community at large and has a different, commercial interface available for profit-making players. Several Linux distributors have developed business models that combine value-added services with open-source community models. IBM and other profit-making firms have internalized some open-source activities with the aim of developing a competitive advantage over closed-source competitors.

The politics of open source

Experiments with hybrid models that combine community-based open-source development with profit-making organizations will show what types of symbiosis are possible. For the open-source community, however, there is also another alternative. If open source is, indeed, a public good or a public fountain of goods, it could also legitimately be supported through public policy.

The challenge of public policy, in general, is that if it is effective it changes the world. Successful policy, therefore, by definition, cannot be neutral. In particular, if public policy supported open-source activities, it would implicitly reorganize the field in which software producers operate. When the assumption is – as it commonly is – that policy should not interfere with market forces, all policy changes that have a market impact appear problematic. For example, if public resources were used to fund open-source software production, the producers of closed systems could claim that such behavior threatened free competition. More importantly, if public authorities required open-source licenses for publicly procured systems, they could easily be viewed as interfering with competition.

The European Union has a particular challenge in this regard. National policies can often override or balance competition concerns when other policy objectives – such as wars against terror, national security, or industrial and economic development – are involved. In the European Union, however, the legal basis for action is to a large extent built on the assumption that competition in a free market is a priority. This apparently neutral approach is not as neutral as it may seem at first sight. Free competition is not something abstract or absolute: it can only exist within given institutional structures. Any change in these institutional structures, therefore, necessarily interferes with the current state of competition. In this sense, the idea of free competition is inherently conservative, and it often quite strongly influences existing and established interests.

Policy intervention with a clear market impact has, therefore, often focused on the particular cases where theoretically accepted reasons allow policymakers to claim that markets have failed to operate as they should. As a consequence, much of the competition policy in free-market societies has centered on antitrust issues and monopolies.

The open-source phenomenon opens up new challenges for policy. For example, it is possible to argue that a feature peculiar to the dynamic of the software industry is that, in this domain, positive returns, first-mover advantages, and scale-effects of production generate an industry structure that is socially and economically not optimal. New software is often adopted in environments where interoperability is important. After new systems have been integrated into existing environments, switching costs may become very high, and in practice users may therefore be stuck with the choices they have made in the past. Producers of new, improved software may therefore find it impossible to survive in this competitive landscape, where entry-points are tightly controlled by existing players. The end result might be, for example, that the structure of the software industry will evolve rapidly into one where those first in are the dominant players, and where small newcomers have great difficulty in growing. From a policy point of view, this could mean, for example, that fewer jobs and services are produced than would be the case if the rules of competition were balanced by policies that mitigated the excessive impact of network effects and first-movers' historical advantages.

One could also argue, for example, that wider use of open-source software would make it easier to find socially beneficial uses for new technology. When a society becomes increasingly computerized and many of its systems depend on software, the transparency of these systems can give entrepreneurs and innovators the chance to see where their contributions might create value. This, essentially, is how the existing open-source projects have become successes. When competent developers can access the source code and see what functionality could best extend the capabilities of current systems, they can maximize the impact of their work. One might expect that the benefactors of such improvements would often be happy to reward this development work, thereby also providing commercial opportunities for software developers. In policy terms, therefore, open source could lead to demand creation, economic growth, and jobs.

These simple examples highlight the point that policies relating to software access and openness may have serious social and economic consequences. Software is becoming one of the main economic factors in society. Software-related policy issues are therefore bound to become increasingly important. In the future, we may, for example, need a better understanding of the development dynamic in software industries, as well as new concepts of system innovation and interoperability that will allow policymakers accurately to define policy issues. Research on open-source projects will provide useful insights on these challenges.

The future

The history of open source indicates some factors that will also be important for its future. As was noted above, a critical characteristic of the open-source model has been the ability to integrate new community members and to support them effectively with social learning models. The access to competent community members, community discussions and historical records has played an important role here.

This collaborative learning model could potentially be extended beyond software development projects. For example, it could provide a foundation for community-centered social innovation projects, where simultaneous knowledge creation and skills development are important (Tuomi, 2003). This, in itself, could generate global demand for open-source tools that support such processes.

A unique characteristic of software is that the description of the system is also the system that is developed. In this domain, the technical artifact and its specification coalesce into one. When developers have access to the source code, their technical skills and knowledge about the functionality of the system can therefore be developed with great effectiveness. For example, when the developers talk about specific problems within the current system, they refer not to abstract descriptions of the system but to the system itself. Alternative solutions to problems can simply be compiled into binary code and run on computer hardware to resolve different opinions about the functioning of code.

This also makes open-source software development different from science. In the empiristic scientific tradition, the idea was that abstract theories could be tested by comparing their predictions with observable natural phenomena. Given an objective, observer- and theory-independent reality, theories were expected to converge eventually towards an accurate description of this reality. As philosophers of science have pointed out, this project was, in itself, unrealistic. The relevance of observations depends on the theories used, and theories depend on historically accumulated conceptual systems. In open-source projects, the dream of objectivistic knowledge, however, is approximately true. As long as the underlying technical architecture stays unchanged, it works as an objective, external world, against which different theoretical models and abstractions can be tested.

When the underlying technical architecture changes, the impact of this depends on the nature of the change. If it affects only minor features, many of the previous abstractions remain valid. If the changes are radical, the abstractions may need to change radically.

In the world of open source, radical changes could be generated, for example, by innovative new hardware architectures that require completely new approaches to design. For example, if Intel suddenly switched its microprocessor architectures to support parallel message-passing, quantum computing, or new adaptive information-processing approaches, the Linux operating system community might have great difficulty in adjusting its designs and its internal social structures.

The history of open source also highlights the importance of developer motivation and needs. Open-source development has often met the needs of the developer, and addressed the frustrations generated by constraints generated by others. If, for example, Xerox had given access to the source code of its printer drivers, and if AT&T had not restricted the sharing of Unix among universities, it is quite possible that the GNU project would never have been launched. When commercial software vendors increasingly make their source code available, therefore, some of the motivation for launching open-source projects disappear. Indeed, this "embrace of death" strategy is probably part of what underlies some current commercial open-source initiatives.

Open-source developers have also often pointed out that they develop software because it is fun. If software development were no longer fun, open-source projects would look less attractive. For example, if programming tools become so advanced that useful applications could easily be developed by anyone, many of the low-hanging fruits of software development could be picked by people who are not particularly interested in technical challenges.

Some technical and policy changes could also lead to dead ends in open-source development. One widely discussed issue has been the conflict between open-source licenses and legal restrictions to reverse-engineer or publish code and algorithms that implement security or digital rights management. Open-source licenses require code to be distributed in a form that allows its modification. If the system, for example, interfaces with commercial products that protect against unauthorized copying, the copy protection algorithms may need to be published whenever the system or its modifications are distributed. Or if the system has encryption or privacy characteristics that cannot be exported without government permission, the system may be incompatible with open-source principles. Similarly, in the future some governments might require all operating system to include back doors for crime enforcement. Such requirements could make open source impossible or illegal in its present form.

The ingenuity of the original GNU license was that it applied recursively a very generic constraint that guaranteed the growth of the system. The name GNU itself was a play on the principle of recursion, an acronym coming from "GNU is Not Unix." The C language that was used to program Unix is often used in this recursive way, where program subroutines or functions iteratively use themselves to compute complex programs in a simple and compact way. The GPL is a similarly recursive program. It keeps the constraints of development constant for all unforeseeable situations, as long as the development goes on. In this sense, the GPL license was a nice, clean example of good programming. This time, however, it was social engineering: it programmed social behavior, instead of computers.

Many modified open-source licenses lose this basic characteristic of the GPL. At the same time, they allow a partially recursive process of open-source development to go on as one specific developmental branch. The growth constraints and viability of this open-source branch, however, are no longer defined from the start. Instead of having only the choice between growing and dying, the more restricted forms of open-source licenses can also lead to privatized developmental paths and the withering of the original open-source project. This is exactly the reason why additional social procedures, such as those discussed by O'Mahony, become necessary. If open-source pools can be converted into private wells or private fountains, branding and social sanctions such as excommunication from the programmer community may become necessary. Such social strategies, however, are rarely foolproof. If pool conversion is possible in principle, in practice it may crucially depend on incentives and on the possibility of offsetting the immediate damage generated during the conversion. If the price is high enough, open-source developers may happily sell their fountains, even though they might afterwards find themselves running out of water. A similar issue underlies much of European thinking of privacy regulations and consumer protection, which often starts from the assumption that individual bargaining power may sometimes need policy support, and that some types of economic transactions should not be allowed on free markets.

One interesting challenge for future open-source development is also the issue of liability. Commercial software vendors are able to make contracts that free them of all liability. As open-source developers typically form open and undefined communities, usually there are no institutionalized agents that could make contracts for open-source systems. Modern legal systems simply do not acknowledge the existence of such open, productive communities. Furthermore, the success of open source greatly depends on the fact that its users and developers do not have to sign contracts with all the people who have contributed to the code.

This opens up a loophole for competitive strategies that use the historical institutions of the law as a weapon against new forms of organizing and acting. Relying on the institutional blindness of justice, closed-source software vendors can make open-source systems unattractive to established institutions. This, of course, is exactly what has happened recently with Linux and its competitors, such as SCO. As another example, in mid-2004 a think-tank from Washington, D.C., published a report alleging that the Linux kernel code was probably borrowed or stolen from an earlier Minix system. The fact that there was no systematic documentation on the history of Linux code, and no simple way to trace the sources of all the various contributions, made it possible to argue that someone might eventually sue Linux users for damages.[11] As under the legal system in the US it is possible to claim very large punitive damages, this risk could obviously be a problem for Linux users operating there. Similar approaches, where existing legal systems are used as competitive weapons, could potentially slow down or kill open-source projects in the future. For the viability of the open-source model, it might, therefore, be necessary to develop liability rules that limit the possibility of misusing such competitive approaches.

The final challenge for the open-source model is its ultimate success. Many open-source developers have built their identities around a project that has been designed to resist the hegemony of the dominant software giant, Microsoft. If Linux one day succeeds in conquering servers and desktops around the world, this basis for resistance will evaporate.

In the Hegelian explanation of world dynamics, development is driven by contradictions. Success sows the seeds of its own destruction, and revolutions eat their children. Before this happens it, however, open source may become normal. Revolution may turn into evolution. Open-source communities may traverse the historical phases of social development in Internet time, finding again the traditional forms and problems of community, organization, economy; and eventually moving beyond them. Commercial developers may perhaps become open-source developers, as the software industry finds new forms of synthesis, reconciliation, and symbiosis. This, exactly, is why open source can survive: the future is open.

Notes

[*] The views expressed in this chapter do not represent the views of the Joint Research Centre, the Institute for Prospective Technological Studies, or the European Commission.

[1] The early papers included several papers published in First Monday including Ghosh, 1998; Bezroukov, 1999; Kuwabara, 2000; Ghosh & Prakash, 2000; Edwards, 2000; Moon & Sproull, 2000; and other important contributions such as Kollock, 1999; Dempsey, Weiss, Jones, & Greenberg, 1999 Mockus, Fielding, & Herbsleb, 2000; Koch & Schneider, 2000; Feller & Fizgerald, 2000; Ljungberg, 2000; and Yamauchi, Yokozawa, Shinohara, & Ishida, 2000. The research on open source got a boost when the MIT Open-source repository was launched in the summer of 2000, distributing working papers such as Lerner & Tirole, 2000; Lakhani & Von Hippel, 2000; Tuomi, 2000; and Weber, 2000. Many of the early papers were inspired by the descriptions of open-source development models in Raymond, 1998 and DiBona, Ockman, & Stone, 1999.

2. A good early, policy-oriented study was Peeling & Satchell, 2001.
3. Some open-source systems, such as MySQL, use dual licensing, which requires license fees for commercial use.
4. Some empirical and consultant studies, however, lend support to the claim that at least some parts of the Linux system have smaller error ratios than closed-source code. Some survey-based studies have also shown that the speed at which errors are corrected may be faster in open-source than in closed-source projects. In general, comparative research between open- and closed-source projects has so far been rare, however.
5. The distribution of effort among developers has been studied, for example, by Mockus, Fielding, & Herbsleb, 2002, who found that only a few programmers contribute almost all code. The size distribution of open-source projects has been studied by Krishnamurthy, 2002, who found that half of the hundred projects studied had fewer than four developers, with an average of 6.7 developers.
6. Using data from González-Barahona, Ortuño Pérez, et al., 2002, one may estimate that during the first decade of Linux development the effort that went into developing the system was roughly equal to 500 person-years of commercial development. It is difficult to translate this number into actual work hours or developer-community size, as it is difficult to estimate the productivity of Linux-kernel developers without further study. In general, individual programmer productivity differences are often found to vary more than an order of magnitude, and one may assume that, on average, the core Linux programmers have worked with relatively good programming productivity. One might also expect that in recent years the programming effort has increased, partly because many commercial firms are now involved in Linux development.
7. The cultural-historical school was developed by Lev Vygotsky and his colleagues in the 1920s in the Soviet Union. For a historical review of the Vygotskian school and its central ideas, see e.g. Kozulin, 1990 and Wertsch, 1991.
8. In the first half of 2004, an average of 48 new vulnerabilities a week were reported for Windows-based PCs. The total number of reported security vulnerabilities for Windows software reached 10,000 by mid-2004 according to Symantec's Internet Security Threat Report.
9. Historically, microprocessors have included undocumented microcode instructions, for example for testing and because the processor developers have left some options open for the final specification of the processor.
10. Strictly speaking, it is possible that the value of an open-source system may decrease as more people use it. As long as only a few users have found the system, it may have some temporary scarcity value, for example because the early users may benefit from cost advantages that have not yet been appropriated by competitors. An innovative open-source user could even maintain such a competitive advantage by continually adopting state-of-the-art open-source systems. Such situations, of course, can not be described using economic theories that start out from the assumption that economic players operate in an equilibrium.
11. The report, released by the Alexis de Tocqueville Institution in May 2004, was widely discredited by the people quoted in it, but it created an avalanche of commentary in the public press and on the Internet. In Europe, the report's author interviewed Andrew Tanenbaum, the creator of the Minix system, and the

author of the present chapter. After extensive discussions about Microsoft's role in the production and funding of the report, Microsoft eventually repudiated it, commenting that it was an unhelpful distraction.

References

BEZROUKOV, N. (1999). "A second look at the Cathedral and the Bazaar." *First Monday,* 4 *(12)* http:// firstmonday.org/issues/issue4_12/bezroukov/

BROWN, J.S., & DUGUID, P. (1991). "Organizational learning and communities of practice: toward a unified view of working, learning, and innovation." *Organization Science,* 2, pp. 40-57.

DALLE, J.M., & JULLIEN, N. (2001). "Open-source vs. proprietary software." Guest lecture at ESSID Summer School, Cargèse.

DEMPSEY, B.J., WEISS, D., JONES, P., & GREENBERG, J. (1999). "A quantitative profile of a community of open-source Linux developers." School of Information and Library Science, University of North Carolina at Chapel Hill. Technical Report TR-1999-05.

DIBONA, C., S. OCKMAN, & STONE, M. (1999). *Open Sources: Voices from the Open-Source Revolution.* Sebastopol, CA: O'Reilly & Associates, Inc.

EDWARDS, K. (2000). "When beggars become choosers." *First Monday,* 5 *(10)* http://firstmonday.org/issues/issue5_10/edwards/index.html.

FANO, R. M. (1967). "The computer utility and the community." IEEE International Convention Record, 30-34. Excerpts reprinted in *IEEE Annals of the History of Computing,* 14 (2), pp. 39-41.

FELLER, J. and FITZGERALD, B. (2000). "A framework analysis of the open-source software development paradigm." The 21st International Conference in Information Systems (ICIS 2000), pp. 55-69.

GHOSH, R.A. (1998). "Cooking-pot markets: an economic model for the trade in free goods and services on the internet." *First Monday,* 3 *(3)* http://firstmonday.org/issues/issue3_3/ghosh/index.html.

GHOSH, R.A., & PRAKASH, V.V. (2000). "The Orbiten Free-Software Survey." *First Monday,* 5 *(7)* http://firstmonday.org/issues/issue5_7/ghosh/index.html.

GONZÁLEZ-BARAHONA, J.M., ORTUÑO PÉREZ, M.A., HERAS QUIRÓS, P., CENTENO-GONZÁLEZ, J., & MATELLÁN-OLIVERA, V. (2002). "Counting potatoes: the size of Debian 2.2." http://people.debian.org/~jgb/debian-counting/counting-potatoes/.

JOHNSON, J.P. (2001). "Economics of Open Source." Available at http://opensource.mit.edu/papers/johnsonopensource.pdf.

KOCH, S., & SCHNEIDER, G. (2000). "Results from software engineering research into open-source development projects using public data." *Diskussionspapiere zum Tätigkeitsfeld Informationsverarbeitung und Informationswirtschaft,* p. 22.

KOLLOCK, P. (1999). "The economies of online cooperation: gifts and public goods in cyberspace." In M.A. SMITH & P. KOLLOCK (eds), *Communities in Cyberspace.* London: Routledge, pp. 220-239.

KOZULIN, A. (1990). *Vygotsky's Psychology: A Biography of Ideas.* Cambridge, MA: Harvard University Press.

KRISHNAMURTHY, S. (2002). "Cave or Community?: An Empirical Examination of 100 Mature Open-Source Projects." *First Monday,* 7 *(6)* http://firstmonday.org/issues/issue7_6/krishnamurthy/index.html.

Kuwabara, K. (2000). "Linux: a bazaar at the edge of chaos." *First Monday*, 5 *(3)* http:// firstmonday.org/issues/issue5_3/kuwabara/.

Lakhani, K., & Von Hippel, E. (2000). "How open-source software works: 'Free' user-to-user assistance." MIT Sloan School of Management Working Paper, 4117.

Lave, J., & Wenger, E. (1991). *Situated Learning: Legitimate Peripheral Participation.* Cambridge: Cambridge University Press.

Lerner, J., & Tirole, J. (2000). "The simple economics of open source." National Bureau of Economic Research. NBER Working Paper No. 7600.

Ljungberg, J. (2000). "Open-source movements as a model for organizing." *European Journal of Information Systems*, 9 *(4)*, pp. 208-216.

Mockus, A., Fielding, R., and Herbsleb, J. (2000). "A case-study of open-source software development: the Apache server." *Proceedings of the 22nd International Conference on Software Engineering*, pp. 263-272.

Mockus, A., Fielding, R., & Herbsleb, J. (2002). "Two case-studies on open-source software development: Apache and Mozilla." *ACM Transactions on Software Engineering and Methodology*, 11 *(3)*, pp. 309-46.

Moon, J.Y., & Sproull, L. (2000). "Essence of distributed work: the case of the Linux kernel." *First Monday*, 5 *(11)* http://firstmonday.org/issues/issue5_11/moon/index.html.

O'Mahony, S. (2003). "Guarding the commons: how community-managed software projects protect their work." *Research Policy*, 32 *(7)*, pp. 1179-98.

Peeling, N., & Satchell, J. (2001). "Analysis of the Impact of Open-Source Software." QinetiQ Ltd. QINETIQ/KI/SEB/CR010223. Available at http://www.govtalk.gov.uk/interoperability/egif_document.asp?docnum=430.

Raymond, E.S. (1998). "The Cathedral and the Bazaar." *First Monday*, 3 *(3)* http:// firstmonday.org/issues/issue3_3/raymond/index.html.

Tuomi, I. (1999). *Corporate Knowledge: Theory and Practice of Intelligent Organizations.* Helsinki: Metaxis.

Tuomi, I. (2000). "Learning from Linux: Internet, Innovation and the New Economy. Part 1: Empirical and Descriptive Analysis of the Open-Source Model." SITRA Working Paper, Berkeley, 15 April 2000.

Tuomi, I. (2001). "Internet, innovation, and open source: actors in the network." *First Monday*, 6 *(1)* http://firstmonday.org/issues/issue6_1/tuomi/index.html.

Tuomi, I. (2002). *Networks of Innovation: Change and Meaning in the Age of the Internet.* Oxford: Oxford University Press.

Tuomi, I. (2003) "Open source for human development." Paper presented at the EU-US Workshop on Advancing the Research Agenda on Free/Open-Source Software. Brussels, 14 October 2002. Available at http://www.infonomics.nl/FLOSS/workshop/papers/tuomi.htm.

Tuomi, I. (2004). "Evolution of the Linux Credits file: methodological challenges and reference data for open-source research." *First Monday*, 9 *(6)* http://firstmonday.org/issues/issue9_6/tuomi/index.html

Von Hippel, E., & von Krogh, G. (2003). "Open-source software and the 'private-collective' innovation model: issues for organization science." *Organization Science*, 14 *(2)*, pp. 209-223.

WEBER, S. (2000). "The political economy of open-source software." BRIE Working Paper 140. http://brie.berkeley.edu/~briewww/pubs/wp/wp140.pdf.

WERTSCH, J.V. (1991). *Voices of the Mind: A Sociocultural Approach to Mediated Action*. Cambridge, MA: Harvard University Press.

YAMAUCHI, Y., YOKOZAWA, M., SHINOHARA, T., AND ISHIDA, T. (2000). "Collaboration with lean media: how open-source software succeeds." CSCW '00, Philadelphia: ACM. pp. 329-338.

Biography

Ilkka Tuomi is currently working with the European Commission's Joint Research Centre, Institute for Prospective Technological Studies, Seville, Spain. He graduated in theoretical physics at the University of Helsinki, and has a PhD on Adult Education from the same university. His recent research has focused on innovation, open source, information society technologies, and the knowledge society. Before joining the IPTS in 2002 he was a visiting scholar at the University of California, Berkeley, where he conducted research on the new dynamics of innovation networks, working with Manuel Castells. From 1987 to 2001 he worked at the Nokia Research Center, most recently as Principal Scientist, Information Society and Knowledge Management. His most recent book, Networks of Innovation (Oxford University Press, 2002), studies Internet-related innovations and the history of computer networking, the World Wide Web, and Linux.

67

The Future of Software: Enabling the Marketplace to Decide

Bradford L. Smith*

For well over two decades, people have debated the merits of developing and distributing software under what has become known as the "open-source" model. As the name implies, the defining feature of this model is that it allows users to review and in many cases modify and redistribute the human-readable form of software known as source code. Supporters sometimes claim that the open-source model produces software that is technically equal or even superior to programs developed under the "commercial" model pursued by most software firms.

At times, however, the open-source debate goes beyond a comparison of technical merits. When comparing commercial to open-source software, some advocates claim that the open-source model generates a higher level of innovation than the commercial model, can deliver better economic benefits for local economies, and is even ethically superior to commercial software because it does a better job of promoting freedom.[1] According to this line of reasoning, open source is not merely a valid or even better model, it is the *right* model. For some, this conclusion also justifies the enactment of laws and regulations that favor open-source software.

This paper offers an alternative perspective on the open-source debate, one grounded in three central claims. The first is that *both* open source and commercial software are integral parts of the broader software ecosystem. The open-source and commercial models have co-existed within the software ecosystem for decades, and both have played important roles in its evolution. Moreover, recent actions by several leading software firms suggest that elements of these two models are beginning to overlap in important ways. Notably, this process is occurring solely in response to market forces and is not the result of law or regulation.

Second, this paper posits that the best catalyst for software innovation and industry growth is the marketplace. Only the marketplace, founded on a robust regime of property rights, can provide the combination of incentives and flexibility that will ensure not only that innovation occurs, but also that it proceeds in directions that satisfy actual market needs. Forecasting the twists and turns of this marketplace is notoriously difficult and beyond the predictive capability of any regulatory regime. While government intervention into the software marketplace may at times be necessary to correct specific instances of market failure, there is currently no such market failure that would justify regulatory preferences for open-source software.

Third, governments can help promote software innovation and broader economic growth by supporting basic research. Such research generates the raw material that information technology (IT) industries utilize in creating new products, and many important software innovations are the product of private-sector commercialization of publicly funded research. Governments can support this process by enacting policies that promote basic research by both the public and the private sectors. Governments should also ensure that the results of publicly funded research are not subject to licensing restrictions – such as those set out in the GNU General Public License (GPL)[2] or similar "free" licenses – that would prevent industry from utilizing this research in commercial products.[3]

Part I of this paper briefly compares the open-source and commercial software models and describes certain respects in which these two models are beginning to overlap. Part II then describes benefits of the commercial model that might be sacrificed by regulatory biases favoring open-source software and examines steps governments can take to promote software innovation in a neutral, non-biased manner. Part III offers some concluding thoughts on the future of the software industry.

I. A Comparison of the Open-Source and Commercial Models

Participants in the open-source debate tend to use the terms "open-source" and "commercial" (or "proprietary") to refer to three distinct categories of models – development models, licensing models, and business models. Analyzing each category separately helps illuminate key differences between the open-source and commercial software models, as well as the ways in which software firms are beginning to adopt elements of both models within their broader strategies.

A. Development models

Commercial software is typically created by a clearly defined group of developers who are paid for their work by a single firm. The firm, which normally owns the results of the developers' efforts, defines the scope and goals of the project, allocates work, and acts as a single point of accountability for the program vis-à-vis the outside world. In these respects, commercial software development is relatively structured.

The commercial development model is also customer focused in the following sense. Because commercial firms ordinarily generate revenue by selling or licensing their software, they have a financial incentive to identify – in advance and as precisely as possible – the needs of the market (which may include other developers, end-users, or others) and to design their software to meet those needs as effectively as possible. Thus, commercial firms have an economic incentive to link product development closely to market demand, and firms whose products most effectively and efficiently satisfy these market needs are the ones most likely to succeed.

open-source software, by contrast, is often developed by a relatively fluid group of volunteer programmers. The process of defining the project's goals and allocating work may be directed by a single person or group, or may be determined by rough consensus. Similarly, ownership of the final product may be concentrated in one individual or dispersed among many hundreds or thousands of contributors. In these and other respects, open-source development is less structured than typical commercial software development.

In contrast to the commercial model's customer focus, open-source development may be characterized as developer focused. Because open source developers usually volunteer their time, they are relatively more likely to work on problems that they find personally challenging or rewarding and tend to be less concerned about whether these challenges respond to actual market demand. And, as most open-source projects do not generate significant revenue, these projects seldom have the resources to undertake market research or otherwise determine customer needs. Instead, open-source projects often rely on releasing test, or "beta," versions of software to gauge market reaction before arriving at a final version of the software.

B. Licensing models

Although there are many differences between commercial and open-source licenses (and between various types of open source licenses), the most salient distinctions relate to the terms governing: (i) access to source code; (ii) the right to modify the software; and (iii) the right to re-distribute the software, whether in modified or unmodified form.

Commercial software developers typically generate revenue and fund future research and development (R&D) by exploiting the economic value of their software (specifically, the intellectual property (IP) embodied in the software) in the marketplace. While many commercial developers accomplish this by selling their software outright to customers, others – particularly those who distribute their software to multiple customers – do so by means of commercial software licenses. These licenses typically restrict the licensee's right to copy, re-distribute, or modify the software and normally do not grant access to the software's source code. These restrictions help to protect the developer's investment in the software by preventing third parties from expropriating the software's economic value without the developer's authorization.

While the past decade has seen an explosion in the number and variety of open source licenses, most licenses fall into one of two categories. The first category includes what might be called "permissive" licenses.[4] Permissive open-source licenses allow licensees to copy, re-distribute, and modify the software at no charge, whether in source code or object code, and do not seek to restrict these rights in any meaningful way. Thus, licensees are free, if they wish, to modify and redistribute the software as part of a commercial product subject to standard commercial licensing terms. The Berkeley Software Distribution license, or "BSD," is a commonly used permissive open source license. Apache, a well-known Web server software package, is distributed under a variant of the BSD license.

A second type of open-source license might be called a "restrictive" license.[5] Like permissive licenses, restrictive licenses permit licensees to copy, re-distribute, and modify the software in either source code or object code. Unlike permissive licenses, however, restrictive open-source licenses prohibit users from distributing both the code and any derivative of the code under terms that do not also permit licensees to copy, re-distribute, or modify the program. Thus, restrictive licenses prohibit licensees from modifying and distributing the code under commercial terms – or indeed under *any* terms that are not essentially identical to the original license. Because this restriction has the effect of replicating itself through all subsequent iterations of the software, these licenses are often referred to as "viral."[6] The GPL is one of the most widely used restrictive open-source licenses, but there are many others.

C. Business models

Open-source and commercial software are also generally identified with distinct business models. As noted above, commercial software firms typically generate revenue by exploiting the IP embodied in their software in the marketplace. In the case of pre-packaged software, because most of the costs associated with the software are the up-front, fixed costs related to developing the product, vendors of packaged software typically pursue a mass-market strategy in which growth in unit sales brings down per-unit costs by spreading the developer's fixed costs over a larger number of units.

This business model has generated dramatic gains in the performance and functionality of commercial software products even as the price of these products has remained stable or even fallen.[7] The success of this business model has also fueled remarkable economic growth. For instance, from 1990 to 1998, the packaged software industry experienced average annual market growth of over 15 percent, making it one of the fastest growing segments of the U.S. economy.[8] The broader software industry employed over 800,000 workers in 1998, and the average annual wage in the core software industry in 1997 was $66,500, over double the wage average for all private industry excluding the software industry.[9] The packaged software industry alone generated over $7.2 billion in U.S. federal and state corporate income taxes in 1997, a figure that is expected to rise to $25 billion by 2005.[10]

open-source software presents a more challenging business model. Although the lack of licensing fees has enabled some open-source software programs to achieve significant market share in a relatively short period of time, the basic economics of the industry still require open source firms to generate sufficient revenue to recoup their costs and earn at least some profit. Because open source licenses allow third parties freely to copy and distribute open-source software, however, open-source firms often find it difficult to capture the economic value of their software in the marketplace. For instance, Red Hat, one of the leading distributors of the Linux operating system, recently estimated that, of the 15 million to 20 million copies of its Linux software package that had been distributed in the marketplace, only about 1.5 million had actually been purchased from the company.[11]

Red Hat's experience is not unique. Countless open-source firms launched during the "dot.com" boom of the late 1990s have since been forced to downsize or even close their doors for good. Of those firms that remain, almost all are searching for new ways to generate revenue. These methods are often variations of a "loss-leader" business strategy, which involves distributing at a loss one thing of value (open-source software) in the hopes that customers will purchase something else that will generate a profit (such as hardware, services or even proprietary software).

D. Movement toward the middle?

While the philosophical differences between the open-source and commercial models are substantial, in practice, software developers of all types are beginning to pursue development, licensing, and business strategies that reflect elements of both models. Among commercial firms, two trends seem to be emerging. The first is to incorporate open-source code into otherwise proprietary systems. Apple Computer's use of the FreeBSD UNIX kernel within the company's recently launched OS X operating system is one such example. Another is the decision by IBM to use elements of the Linux operating system as a platform for some of its commercial hardware and software offerings.

The second trend among commercial firms is to adopt attributes of the open-source model into a broader commercial strategy. For instance, Microsoft's Shared Source initiative seeks to emulate the benefits of source code access associated with the open-source model by giving licensees the right to review – and in some cases modify –

the source code for several Microsoft platform products. Among other things, these Shared Source licenses enhance the transparency of the Windows platform and make it easier – at least for sophisticated customers – to debug applications and protect applications against viruses. The Shared Source initiative likewise fosters the growth of a strong community of software developers and IT professionals while promoting broad-based collaboration in the development of IT industry standards.[12] Shared Source licenses are proving particularly attractive to academic institutions, where access to source code is helping to foster a deeper understanding of Microsoft products among educators and future software developers.

On the other side of the spectrum, a growing number of firms traditionally identified with open-source software are beginning to adopt aspects of the commercial model. For instance, several open-source firms are developing and selling closed-source software to complement their open-source offerings. In addition, many open-source companies have begun modifying standard open-source programs in-house in order to meet the needs of specific customers or market segments. In essence, these companies are working to adopt what they perceive to be the best elements of commercial software industry's development, licensing, and business models within a basic open source framework.

This phenomenon of software firms adopting elements of both the open-source and commercial models is noteworthy in at least three respects. First, this process is taking place purely as a result of the market. Software firms are facing classic market pressures – from customers, from shareholders, even from industry partners – and are working to respond to these pressures within their broader business strategies by seeking to take advantage of what they perceive to be the best elements of both the commercial and the open-source software models. Significantly, this process is taking place absent of any form of government intervention.

Second, the ways in which software firms are responding to these market pressures vary tremendously. Whether this variety reflects a unique, short-term period of experimentation, or represents a more fundamental shift in the software industry's development, licensing, and business models, remains (at least at this stage) unclear. What is clear, however, is that consumers are benefiting from these industry efforts in the form of increased choices and greater competition. In short, this entire process bears all of the hallmarks of a well-functioning market.

Finally, it is worth noting that this process is making it increasingly difficult to classify any specific firm as pursuing *either* an open-source *or* a commercial model. While this does not mean that the terms "open-source" or "commercial" are no longer useful, it does suggest that merely applying these labels may reveal relatively little about how a particular firm actually develops and licenses its products or generates revenue. It also suggests that lawmakers should proceed carefully before enacting measures designed to influence the shape of the software industry based on a simplistic distinction between "open-source" and "commercial."

II. Strengths of the Commercial Software Model

Among the claims often made in support of the open-source model are that it promotes innovation, promotes domestic IT industry growth, fosters interoperability, and provides a more cost effective IT solution than commercial software. In reality, the commercial software model has a strong track record on each of these issues. The following sections explore these issues in more detail and examine their relevance to governmental policies affecting the software industry.

A. Innovation

While quantifying innovation is notoriously difficult, two useful proxies for measuring innovation are investments in R&D and the impact of new products on users. By either measure, the commercial software industry is highly innovative. For instance, in 1998, the U.S. software and computer services industries invested an estimated $14.3 billion in R&D, which exceeded the level of R&D spending by the U.S. motor vehicles, pharmaceuticals, and aerospace industries.[13] Furthermore, innovations in software have enabled businesses across the economy to become more productive. As a recent study by the U.S. Department of Commerce concluded, innovative new software programs have enabled firms "to create extraordinary efficiencies and improve decision making within their own operations and supply networks."[14]

The primary stimulus for innovation under the commercial software model is intellectual property protection. Property rights in software give developers the certainty of knowing that, for a limited period of time, they and no one else will have the right to exploit the economic value of their software in the marketplace. By establishing this possibility of financial reward, intellectual property rights give software developers an economic incentive to develop innovative, useful products. IP protection also helps to resolve the free rider problem that would arise if second-comers were free to copy and sell software programs without the original developer's consent.

Whether the open-source model can match the commercial software industry's record of innovation is uncertain. The revenue challenges confronting open-source firms make it unlikely that an open source industry could rival the level of R&D spending by the commercial software industry. And, while open source's unstructured development model arguably provides an avenue for the airing of unorthodox ideas that might not be available in some commercial contexts, translating even the best of these ideas into commercially viable products will often require resources that the open-source model simply cannot provide.

This does not mean, of course, that the open-source model is not an important contributor to software innovation. Indeed, many significant strides in software technology have their roots in universities or other publicly funded research labs, which are primarily based on the open-source development model. In most cases, however, this research results in viable products only through the efforts of the private sector, whose incentive to commercialize this research depends on its ability to recoup R&D costs through IP protection. This complex process of interaction and collaboration between the public and private sectors – which itself constitutes an important part of the broader software ecosystem – should be nurtured, for it improves consumer welfare through useful new products while also fueling economic growth.

Governments have an important role to play in fostering such innovation. Because basic research constitutes an important resource for further IT industry innovation, governments can promote private-sector innovation by expanding funding for university science departments and federal research labs, and by extending tax credits and similar incentives for privately funded research. At the same time, governments should support policies that facilitate the commercialization of the resulting research by industry.

For these reasons, governments should carefully consider the policy implications of using public funds to sponsor research that is licensed under the GPL or similarly restrictive licenses. As already discussed, the GPL forbids the commercial licensing of software that includes or is derived from GPL-covered code. Thus, if code developed in a government-funded lab is derived from or licensed under the GPL, the private sector would be foreclosed from using or building upon this code to develop commercial products. In short, use of the GPL in publicly funded research projects would drive an impenetrable wedge between the public and private sectors, thereby undermining the innovation and economic growth that has resulted from such public-private collaboration in the past.[15]

B. Local IT industry growth

Open-source advocates sometimes portray the commercial software model as one that tends to favor entrenched players and leave few opportunities for newcomers. In fact, however, the commercial software industry includes thousands of profitable and innovative firms located all over the world. These firms have generated jobs, tax revenues, and economic growth in dozens of nations – including many in the developing world.

Over the past twenty-five years, the commercial software industry has evolved from a niche sector catering primarily to large enterprises into an exceptionally diverse industry serving customers across the economic spectrum. This process has created opportunities for existing IT firms and entrepreneurs to share expertise, create new products, and exploit new markets. Microsoft, for example, partners with over 750,000 hardware manufacturers, software developers, service providers and channel companies, including 350,000 firms located outside the United States.[16] Total IT revenues based on Microsoft products reached over $200 billion in 2001, meaning that every $1 earned by Microsoft generated $8 in additional revenue for firms offering complementary products and services.[17]

Among the beneficiaries of this IT industry diversification have been developing nations. A recent IDC study commissioned by Microsoft found that the IT industries in Argentina, Brazil, Chile, China, Columbia, Costa Rica, Czech Republic, India, Malaysia, Mexico, South Africa, and Venezuela experienced compound annual growth rates of anywhere from 6.8 percent to 43.7 percent between 1995 and 2001, and are projected to realize compound annual growth of between 6.3 percent and 26.8 percent through 2005.[18] The number of IT industry jobs in these countries grew by at least 35 percent between 1995 and 2001, while eight of these countries – Chile, China, Costa Rica, India, Malaysia, Mexico, South Africa, and Venezuela – experienced IT industry job growth of 75 percent or more during this period.[19]

Commercial software firms have been important drivers of this broader IT industry growth.[20] The software industry is expected to grow ten percent annually in 82 percent of the countries examined by IDC (which included all of the developing countries listed above).[21] In a separate study commissioned by the Business Software Alliance, PricewaterhouseCoopers calculated that the packaged software industry alone generated an estimated $21 billion in annual tax revenues during 1996/97 for non-U.S. governments, a figure that was projected to reach $34 billion in 2001.[22]

India's IT industry illustrates the benefits that developing nations can realize from the commercial software model. Between 1994-95 and 2000-01, gross earnings from the Indian software industry grew from $835 million to $8.2 billion, while the value of software exports grew from $485 million to $6.2 billion.[23] India had over 16,000 IT firms in 2001 (double the number of firms just six years earlier), which employed over 561,000 workers.[24] Overall IT spending in India grew an average of 20.6 percent annually from 1995 to 2001 and is expected to increase to 26 percent annually from 2001 to 2005.[25]

Whether the open-source model can provide similar economic opportunities for nations working to develop domestic IT industries remains to be seen. Given the significant revenue challenges currently facing open-source firms, however, it seems at best premature to suggest that the open-source model provides a more certain path to economic growth than the commercial model.

C. Interoperability

The commercial software model is also an important driver of interoperability. Commercial developers promote interoperability through industry-wide standardization efforts and through their support of market-based standards. Indeed, there are reasons to believe that the commercial software model may do a better job of promoting interoperability than the open-source model.

Commercial software firms have historically been active contributors to broad-based IT standards bodies, and Microsoft's efforts in this area are no exception. Microsoft participates in every leading IT standards body, including the Internet Engineering Task Force (IETF), the World Wide Web Consortium (W3C), the European Computer Manufacturers Association (ECMA), the Web Services Interoperability Organization (WS-I), and many others. Microsoft also encourages its researchers to publish the results of their work and in this way to contribute to the knowledge "commons" from which broad-based IT standards are often born.[26] The commercial software model has also promoted interoperability through the creation of market-based standards and through the popularization of computing platforms like UNIX and Windows.

The result of these various efforts is that literally thousands of off-the-shelf hardware and software products on the market today can communicate and exchange data. Further evidence of these efforts can be seen in the IT systems of large enterprises, which often include a range of hardware, software, and platform products from several different vendors. Whereas sharing data between the disparate elements of these systems typically would have been difficult or impossible only seven or eight years ago, industry efforts since then to promote open standards – including support for the Internet as a common communications layer – have helped to create an environment today in which data can be shared among most elements of these IT systems with much greater ease.

The most significant recent example of the commercial software model's promotion of IT interoperability is embodied in a group of standards based on the Internet format XML, which stands for "eXtensible Markup Language." XML is an open standard maintained by the W3C that is available to all on a royalty-free basis.[27] Although the technologies that support XML are sophisticated, the XML vision is simple: Use open, industry-wide standards to enable applications running on any platform and written in almost any programming language to interoperate with one another.

Microsoft, together with several other leading commercial software vendors, has contributed millions of dollars to help develop the basic XML architecture. Microsoft has also submitted key elements of its implementation of XML – known as the Microsoft .NET framework – to ECMA, Europe's leading IT standards body, for standardization. ECMA members recently adopted and published as open standards two Microsoft technologies – its Common Language Infrastructure and its C# programming language – which means that these technologies are now freely available for use by anyone. In addition, Microsoft has worked closely with the non-profit MONO project to develop open source implementations of the basic .NET infrastructure.

The IT industry's recent history demonstrates that the commercial software industry thrives when IT interoperability flourishes. By working closely with IT standards bodies and other IT firms, commercial software vendors have helped drive significant improvements in IT interoperability in recent years and are likely to continue to do so for the foreseeable future.

D. Cost effectiveness

Another claim often made in support of the open-source model is that open-source software is more cost-effective than commercial software. Because (the argument goes) users can freely load open-source programs (depending on how they are licensed) on as many computers as they like without incurring additional license fees, they can channel resources that would otherwise have been spent on such fees to more productive uses. In fact, however, many factors besides software license fees contribute to the overall cost-effectiveness of an IT system — factors that can make systems based on open-source software *less* cost-effective in the long run than those based on commercial software.

First, software licenses normally comprise a minor component of the purchase price of a complete IT system. Moreover, an IT system's purchase price usually forms only a small portion of its total cost of ownership (TCO), which is typically dominated by post-purchase costs such as customizing the system to the user's specific needs, maintaining and servicing the system, and training costs. In fact, software acquisition costs are often less than 5% of the overall cost of an enterprise system. An accurate assessment of cost must also take into account a system's return on investment. For instance, if a system with a higher purchase price enables an organization's workers to be more productive than one with a lower purchase price, the higher-priced system may provide a quicker return on investment – and thus be more cost effective – than the lower-priced alternative.

Although few independent analysts have examined rigorously the relative TCO of IT systems based on open-source software as compared to those based on commercial software, there is relatively broad consensus that software license fees have relatively little impact on a system's TCO. As one open-source commentator recently observed, "Every analyst has a proprietary total-cost-of-ownership model, and everyone's equation is slightly different. But they all show that the low cost of acquiring free software is not a significant benefit when amortized over the lifetime costs of the system."[28]

In addition, several analysts that have examined the issue have noted that, because open-source solutions tend to be more customized than their commercial counterparts, open-source solutions will often require more sophisticated (and thus more expensive) support and maintenance. Moreover, IT services often prove quite difficult to scale in a cost-effective manner. For these reasons, IT systems using commercial software may, in many cases, prove more cost-effective to operate in the long run than similar systems based on open source software.[29] As analysts at the independent IT research firm META Group concluded, "Linux is typically not a low-cost alternative [as compared to Microsoft Windows] when viewed from a total-cost-of-ownership perspective, because it costs more for organizations to support it."[30]

More fundamentally, it remains open to question whether the open-source model will be able to replicate several key efficiencies that are now commonplace in the commercial software industry. As already discussed, the emergence of standardized platforms and interfaces has made it possible for many commercial vendors to pursue mass-market business strategies and thereby to realize significant economies of scale. The absence of constraints on modifying software under the open-source model, by contrast, suggests that open-source vendors may find it significantly more difficult to achieve similar economies of scale.

III. The Future of Software

The open-source and commercial software models have been critical elements of the software ecosystem for decades, and both are likely to continue to play important roles in the years ahead. Recent events suggest that firms across the industry are now working to incorporate what they perceive to be the best elements of both models in their broader strategies. While predicting the final result of this process is difficult, much easier to predict is that the principal beneficiaries of this process will be consumers in the form of more choices and lower prices.

This prediction, however, rests on two assumptions. The first is that the marketplace will determine the path along which the software industry evolves. Only the marketplace – comprised of thousands of developers and firms reacting to millions of customer decisions every day – offers both the flexibility and incentives necessary to ensure that software innovation proceeds in a direction that satisfies actual consumer needs. And, the marketplace can function effectively only if it is based upon a clear regime of property rights, and where government intervention is limited to addressing specific instances of market failure.

The second assumption is that governments will continue to invest in basic IT research. Publicly funded research has played a critical factor in the success of the U.S. IT industry by helping to create a bedrock of technical knowledge that industry can then develop into commercially useful products. So long as such research is made available under terms that do not limit its utilization in commercial products, this research will be an extremely important resource for continued innovation in the software industry. This combination of a robust, open marketplace and public support for IT research will provide the groundwork for a diverse, competitive and innovative software ecosystem.

Notes

[*] The views expressed herein are solely those of the author and do not necessarily represent the position of Microsoft Corporation.
[1] Although these views are often associated with the Free Software Foundation and its founder, Richard Stallman, strands of this thinking can be found throughout the open-source community.
[2] "GNU" is a recursive acronym that stands for "GNU's Not UNIX." The acronym reflects the original purpose of the GNU Project, which was to develop a "free" alternative to the UNIX operating system. See Richard Stallman, *The GNU Project* (2001).
[3] This topic is discussed in more detail in Part II.A, *infra*.
[4] See, e.g., Sean Doherty, *The Law and Open Source Software*, NETWORK COMPUTING (Oct. 29, 2001) (describing BSD license and similar licenses as "permissive").

⁵ *See id.* (describing GPL and similar licenses as "more restrictive" than BSD license).
⁶ As Brian Behlendorf, a leading open-source developer, has noted, "[The GPL's] 'viral' behavior has been trumpeted widely by open-source advocates as a way to ensure that code that begins free remains free – that there is no chance of a commercial interest forking their own development version from the available code and committing resources that are not made public." Brian Behlendorf, *Open Source as a Business Strategy,* in OPEN SOURCES: VOICES FROM THE OPEN SOURCE REVOLUTION (1999), at 167.
⁷ *ee, e.g.,* Bureau of Economic Analysis, U.S. Department of Commerce, *Recognition of Business and Government Expenditures for Software As Investment: Methodology and Quantitative Impacts, 1959-98* (2000), at 28, 32-36. This report concludes that, for the period 1959 through 1998, "prices for prepackaged software have fallen sharply." *Id.* at 6.
⁸ *See* Business Software Alliance, *Opportunities and Growth: A Vision for the Future, 2001-2005* (2000), at 6.
⁹ *Id.* at 8-9.
¹⁰ *See* PricewaterhouseCoopers, *Contributions of the Packaged Software Industry to the Global Economy* (1999), at 10.
¹¹ *See* Tim Reason, *Linux: When Free Isn't,* CFO.COM (Sept. 13, 2001).
¹² *See* Microsoft Corporation, *The Microsoft Shared Source Philosophy* (2002).
¹³ *See* U.S. Department of Commerce, *Digital Economy 2000* (2000), at 31.
¹⁴ *See id.* at 3, n.5.
¹⁵ Some open-source advocates also argue that innovation might better be served by curtailing or even eliminating IP rights in software. *See, e.g.,* Lawrence Lessig, THE FUTURE OF IDEAS: THE FATE OF THE COMMONS IN A CONNECTED WORLD (2001), at 250-53, 255-59 (arguing, among other things, for shorter and less robust copyright protection for software). Yet, just as legal protection for real and personal property is a necessary prerequisite for a market in land and goods, legal protection for intellectual property is a necessary precondition for a market in intangible goods. The marketplace is the single most important driver of software innovation. The primary impact of curtailing IP rights in software would be to distort or even destroy this marketplace, neither of which would promote innovation or consumer welfare.
¹⁶ *See* Microsoft Corporation, *Creating a Vibrant Information Technology Sector: Growth, Opportunity and Partnership* (2002), at 12.
¹⁷ *Id.* at 13.
¹⁸ *Id.* at 16-20 (summarizing IDC data).
¹⁹ *Id.* at 16, 20-21.
²⁰ None of the studies cited in this section distinguish in their analyses between commercial and open-source software firms. However, given that open-source firms represent a relatively small share of revenue and employment in the software sector, and that most open-source firms are located in developed nations, the present economic impact of the open-source software industry on developing nations is presumably negligible.
²¹ Microsoft Corporation, *supra* note 16, at 16.
²² *See* PricewaterhouseCoopers, *Contributions of the Packaged Software Industry to the Global Economy* (1999), at 10.
²³ *See* Oxford Analytica, *India: National IT Development: Explaining Success* (2002) at 1, at

http://www.microsoft.com/presspass/events/glc02/docs/IndiaCS.doc (downloaded Apr. 25, 2002).
24 *See* Microsoft Corporation, *supra* note 16, at 21.
25 *Id.*, at 17, 19.
26 *See, e.g.*, Marco Iansiti and Josh Lerner, *Evidence Regarding Microsoft and Innovation* (2002), at 9 (finding that, "[c]ompared to articles published by other institutions in 1996, a higher percentage of Microsoft publications were cited by other academic works, Microsoft publications had the highest average number of citations per cited paper, and they had the highest maximum number of citations per paper.").
27 In the past four years, Microsoft has made 19 submissions to the W3C, sixteen of which were contributed under royalty free terms.
28 J.D. Hildebrand, *Open Source Watch: Does Open Source Still Matter?*, SD TIMES.COM (March 1, 2001).
29 *See, e.g.*, J.D. Hildebrand, *Open Source Watch: Proving Open Source Still Matters*, SD TIMES.COM (Apr. 1, 2001) ("[T]here is evidence to support the notion that Windows-based systems enjoy a lower TCO [than Linux-based systems]. User, administrator and developer training are plentiful and cheap for Windows. Device support is much better, so Windows users have a wider range of hardware and peripherals from which to choose. Initial setup is simpler and less expensive. All of these factors... could make an investment in Windows more cost-effective than an investment in Linux.").
30 META Group, *Commentary: Making the Move to Linux*, CNET NEWS.COM (Aug. 31, 2001).

Biography

Bradford L Smith is Microsoft's Senior Vice-President, General Counsel, and Corporate Secretary. He leads the company's Department of Law and Corporate Affairs, which is responsible for all legal work and for government, industry and community-affairs activities.

Smith graduated *summa cum laude* from Princeton University, where he received the Class of 1901 Medal, the Dewitt Clinton Poole Memorial Prize, and the Harold Willis Dodds Achievement Award, the highest award given to a graduating senior at commencement. He was a Harlan Fiske Stone Scholar at the Columbia University School of Law, where he received the David M. Berger Memorial Award. He also studied international law and economics at the Graduate Institute of International Studies in Geneva, Switzerland. He has written numerous articles regarding international intellectual property and electronic commerce issues, and has served as a lecturer at the Hague Academy of International Law.

WOOLWORTH BUILDING

Tourists
Are Not Permitted Beyond This Point

Thank You-Building Management

Dual Licensing
A Business Model from the Second Generation of Open-Source Companies

Kaj Arnö

Can you do business with open source? And if you do, will you be limited to delivering services only? In this short essay, I will formulate answers to these questions. The first will be answered with a resounding "yes": you *can* do business with open source. The answer to the second one is an equally resounding "no": in addition to services, you can also live comfortably on licence revenues, thank you very much.

However, if one attempts to build up such a business, the right decisions have to be made from the outset. Most importantly of all, ownership of the copyright on the product has to reside fully in-house. Hijacking existing open-source software projects and making them "dual licensing" will not work, unless every single contributor to the project agrees to set up a joint company to sign the copyright over to.

Having gained most of my open-source experience from my career at MySQL, I will take the liberty of using MySQL as an example for most of this essay.

First-Generation Open Source

When first attempting to create a business based on open source, companies concentrated on delivering services on top of open-source products. "Lack of professional support" is often quoted as a common worry on the part of enterprise users contemplating a more widespread use of open-source software, especially in studies financed by closed-source providers. No wonder the first successful open-source companies recognised the opportunity, and started providing professional services for widely-used open-source software, such as Linux and Apache.

Today, providing professional services for users of open-source software is still an increasingly profitable business. Technical support is usually the biggest revenue-earner. Training and consulting are other major business opportunities, while smaller possibilities exist in publishing and certification.

Second-Generation Open Source

Companies like MySQL AB, Trolltech and Sleepycat can offer something besides services: the right to use and distribute their software within commercial, closed-source software.

The short sentence above calls for an explanation. First, the expression "their software" requires some attention since, unlike projects like Linux and PHP, second-generation open-source companies are real companies. Just like any software company, they have some basic characteristics. One of them is ownership of their own software.

Open-source software that is wholly developed by the community has no single owner (or, to be more specific, no single copyright-holder).

Open-source software developed by a company has the company as its single owner and copyright-holder.

Secondly, full ownership of the copyright (and, usually, the trademarks) related to a particular open-source product gives second-generation open-source companies considerable freedom. They can do whatever they wish with their software, including selling commercial licences that relieve their customers of the limitations of the GPL.

Of course, second-generation open-source companies cannot simply revoke licences already issued. Hence, their open-source users do not need to rely upon the goodwill and good intentions of the company. A piece of software already released under the GPL will remain so forever. Only extensions can even theoretically be offered under more restrictive (or commercial) licences.

Dual licensing

The practice of offering the same software under both an open-source licence (usually GPL) and a commercial licence (usually similar to those of closed-source vendors) has become known as "dual licensing".

Dual licensing means providing the very same piece of software under two parallel licences. This is in contrast to handing out a "light" or "crippled" version of a product at no cost and selling the full version for money.

So why do some users turn into customers, handing out cash for the very same product that others use at zero cost?

The answer lies in the limitations imposed on the user by the licence. Software based on GPL software (linked to it for example in the way that database software is linked to MySQL client software) can be distributed to others only if it is itself licensed under the GPL.

By building a bridge between free/open-source software and commercial/closed-source software, second-generation open-source companies make it possible for these two worlds to become fully integrated.

Consequences for the development model

Copyright signover is required from community contributors to second-generation open-source companies. Otherwise, the companies would no longer be the sole copyright-holders of their software. By extension, this would mean that they could no longer offer commercial licences in parallel to the GPL versions.

Is the need for copyright signovers not a big drawback, and quite in conflict with how open source is expected to work? The answer is "no", it is not a big drawback.

First, anyone who contributes to software developed by the Free Software Foundation will have to sign a similar copyright handover. Thus, the practice is known.

Secondly, second-generation open-source companies tend to get very few contributions in the form of usable extensions to the core product.

481

Thirdly, the main advantage of open-source development stays intact: the ecosystem. Even if the ecosystem of a product like MySQL does not produce many extensions to the MySQL Server, it does produce extensions on the client side, it does provide a lot of testing and it does provide a lot of recognition for the product.

Client-side extensions allow a wider spread of MySQL. But they do not poke holes in the copyright ownership that allows for the sale of commercial licences, which focuses on the MySQL Server and the core MySQL Client Library written in C.

Testing provides MySQL AB with quality assurance equivalent to that of a huge department of tens, if not hundreds, of well-orchestrated QA engineers. MySQL AB gets reports or reproducible bugs from the most varied types of usage of MySQL, stressing the size of the database, the number of transactions per second, the lesser-used operating systems, the freshest features just introduced into MySQL, and the combination of all of the above, to an extent that an in-house QA department cannot mimic.

Credibility and recognition of the MySQL brand name helps MySQL AB open doors that would otherwise have remained closed. MySQL AB has been able to enter commercial partnerships from which companies of equivalent size would have been excluded. This is because MySQL is so well known, thanks to its large user-base.

MySQL AB is deeply grateful to its ecosystem for the value provided by the client-side extensions, the testing and the product recognition. In keeping with its "quid pro quo" philosophy, MySQL AB provides something valuable in return: a high-performance, stable, easy-to-use database.

In summary, the development of open-source software by a team internal to the company makes the development model hybrid. It is a combination of the virtues of a central development model, with one "cathedral" giving product direction and possessing expertise, and a big "bazaar" of developers contributing to auxiliary products, and in the form of QA. Additionally, many of the community contributors to MySQL have ended up on the MySQL AB payroll.

The impact and relevance of dual licensing can be considered from different perspectives: that of the customer, the analyst and society at large.

Dual licensing from the customer's perspective

From the perspective of customer, dual licensing addresses three of their biggest concerns with respect to open-source software:
- availability of support
- vendor accountability, and
- vendor viability.

Second-generation open-source companies combine the powerful development model of open source with full legal protection for the end customer. Vendors become viable in the long term, and they can offer their customers product warranties and indemnifications.

Dual licensing from the analyst's perspective

Analysts pay special attention to dual licensing. Forrester Research[1] named dual licensing as the software business model that is most "commerce-friendly" and also "strongest", in terms of keeping the software code and community together. META Group[2] comments in their report on MySQL that the dual licensing model "is becoming a blueprint for a successful open-source business".

Consequences from the perspective of society at large

Dual licensing has proven itself successful as a way of developing and marketing software, while at the same time preserving licensing as a source of revenue. One might therefore ask whether dual licensing is generally applicable, or whether it applies only to a limited set of software projects.

The simple answer is that the licensing model has to provide benefits for both the vendor and the customer. No software can remain free of cost indefinitely, unless there is some kind of self-interest on the part of the vendor.

Consequently, the more users the software has, the more it makes sense to provide it under open source. And the more specialised the need, the less likely it is that the software can successfully be open-sourced.

The incentive to open-source software is at its greatest when the need for it is shared by a wide community. The existence of an industry standard (such as SQL in the case of database software) further increases the mutual client/vendor benefit of open-source software.

To conclude this article, I would like to dispel some of the mystery surrounding open-source companies and prejudices against proprietary or closed-software companies, as these are fundamental to people's perception of existing and future business models.

Similarities with closed-source companies

Second-generation open-source software companies (here abbreviated to 2GOSS companies) share many traits with established closed-source software companies (here abbreviated to CSS companies):

Just like traditional CSS companies, 2GOSS companies strive for profit. The more, the better. Shareholder interest directs actions. This does not constitute a conflict of interests for 2GOSS companies: as non-paying customers are significant contributors to the value of a 2GOSS company, self interest dictates that, for success, high ethical standards should be built into it.

Just like traditional CSS companies, 2GOSS companies earn a significant part of their revenue from licensing. In the case of MySQL AB, licence fees constitute over half of its revenue. This is similar to what happens in large industrial players using CSS.

Just like traditional CSS companies, 2GOSS companies own the rights to their source code. Consequently, both respect intellectual property in the form of copyright and trademarks.

Just like traditional CSS companies, 2GOSS companies value technology, expertise and know-how. Both appreciate the value of the community or ecosystem around the product. Both agree that even though the community provides great value, vendor accountability through commercial support by the vendor is necessary for most customers.

Just like traditional CSS companies, 2GOSS companies know that program licences constitute only a small portion (4-10%) of the total cost of ownership, with personnel costs having the highest share (over 60%). At least in principle, CSS and 2GOSS companies agree that the best way for a customer to decide which software is best is to study and estimate the total cost of ownership. Ironically, both CSS and 2GOSS companies claim that honour for themselves.

Differences between open- and closed-source companies

A detailed comparison between 2GOSS and CSS companies will of necessity involve some simplification. When it comes to examining the differences between them, I have therefore deliberately picked MySQL as a 2GOSS company, and I compare MySQL with my impression of the dominant industry player in operating systems and office applications.

First of all, MySQL believes in open source. It gives better quality, and better community support, and is completely reliable. It is better for customer and vendor alike. I do not see the dominant industry player sharing this value.

Secondly, MySQL believes in the Occam's Razor maxim of "no complexity beyond necessity". It avoids features that benefit few but confuse many. I confess to having been confused by the new features of the dominant word-processing and spreadsheet programs, to the point of actually having lower productivity than I did ten years ago.

Thirdly, MySQL puts stability and performance first. MySQL sacrifices features for bug-freedom and speed. It is known for releasing software when it is ready, having actively chosen to slip release deadlines rather than ship buggy software. I do not see this set of priorities being shared by all CSS providers.

Fourthly, MySQL believes in freedom and openness. Of course, no company in its right mind would claim *not* to believe in such values, but the content they give these words may differ. In the case of MySQL, we try to make it easy to migrate to *and from* MySQL. We keep internal formats unchanged as far as possible, and so far a conversion has been necessary only once in the entire history of MySQL. By contrast, I have many times had compatibility problems between different versions of the dominant word-processing software. Over and over again, I have been unable to open files sent to me by other users of the same word-processing software that I use, forcing me to upgrade without having any actual need for new features.

Conclusion

Open-sourcing software is good for entrepreneurs and venture capitalists. It creates value for customers and personnel alike. Dual licensing is good for society at large, since it creates employment and constitutes healthy competition for closed-source software companies.

In short, with dual licensing, a better method for producing and marketing software products has been born. It cuts development costs for the vendor by reducing expenditure on quality assurance and accelerating the development cycle. It saves on marketing costs for the vendor by making the product well known without a huge marketing budget. It increases revenue beyond services, into licensing revenue. For the customer, this translates into lower cost, greater reliability, and a more viable relationship with the vendor.

Notes

[1] T. Schadler, et al. (Forrester WholeView TechStrategy Research), Your Open-Source Strategy (September 2003), Forrester Research, Cambridge (Massachusetts, USA), 2003, S. 12.
[2] META Group report, "Open Source and the Commodity Effect", http://www.mysql.com/news-and-events/news/article_314.html, 4 April 2003.

Biography

Kaj Arnö has trained more than 2,000 IT users and developers in about 200 training classes across Europe, the US and Asia. With a successful track record in consulting assignments, often serving customers in their respective native languages, Arnö leads the localization efforts of MySQL AB. Prior to joining MySQL AB in June 2001, Kaj Arnö was founder and CEO of the Finnish solution provider Polycon Ab. At present, he is the Vice-President of MySQL and the creator and designer of the MySQL training programme.

CAUTION
SHARED PATH
BICYCLISTS WATCH FOR PEDESTRIANS

Towards an EU Policy for Open-Source Software

Simon Forge*

The importance of open-source software arises from its role in preserving choice in a market characterised by growing monopolisation in key areas. It may also offer cost savings for public bodies, in terms of both the initial outlay and total cost of ownership. Fostering an environment in which open-source software can flourish could encourage innovation and a more pluralistic software market at a time when software has become a critical factor in the economy and in society as a whole.

Introduction[1]

Open-source software (OSS) is considered by many to be now a stable and sustainable model of software development and distribution, making the trend towards its use almost inevitable. OSS has been recognised officially and developed since 1984, but its basic development model predates this. Its origins include the development in the 1960s of ARPANET (a precursor of today's Internet) which gave rise to the first *ad hoc* development community. The open-source movement is therefore expected to continue to mature as a model for innovation in the knowledge economy. Here we wish to explore the implications of this technology and its development for policy at a European level.

To date the European Commission's approach to the OSS debate has largely been passive, although some attention has been given to tacit support for OSS, especially in information and communication technology (ICT) research projects and policy within the Framework Programmes.

In contrast, the European Parliament has already taken an active stance on certain freedoms in software, specifically with the vote against software patents of 24 September 2003. The essential question that needs to be addressed is whether the EU should merely lend passive support (i.e. take a laissez-faire approach), or whether it should be more proactive in its promotion of OSS.

Reasons for taking a proactive approach include the dependence of the EU's economic development on quality software at the right price, available under non-limiting conditions – interoperability and the advantages of public standards. A further reason is the need for creativity and openness in software, in order to develop a more advanced form of economy, an information society, which will be based on very large-scale, open and secure platforms at low cost, that is, the information society's infrastructure. Effectively, a proactive policy approach to open-source software could bring benefits such as encouraging competition and a flourishing European software industry.

A pro-active OSS policy initiative could be beneficial by protecting strong competition in the software sector, as our economic dependence on it increases each year. It would also ensure that the real benefits of products deriving from the software industry are passed on to users – and this may well require a rebalancing of market power. Moreover, the encouragement of education and training in OSS can help the advance of a flourishing European software industry.

These would all require some form of explicit support for OSS in EU policy. First, however, it is necessary to define the aims of policy in this area.

The goals of OSS support

The debate on the importance of open-source software has so far focused on the need to prevent monopolisation in the software market and enable cost reductions, particularly in the public sector. The debate has highlighted three main areas in which OSS is important: first, in preserving an open choice in software against a growing monopolisation of the market in crucial segments, and so winning power back for the users, while giving more freedom of development. Second, the potential savings in government expenditure if OSS is admitted as a contender for public procurement. Finally, there are the benefits promised in by reducing the total cost of ownership, by eliminating the commercial software industry's externalities from its practices.

It may be useful for policy to go further. At the most general level, the goal is to support a better business model for software creation, as our dependence on software is already high and will continue to increase. OSS will have an increasingly important role in this new model of software creation, and so will play an increasingly crucial part in our economic destiny over the next 50 years.

So the EU policy for OSS can be viewed as having two main goals – primarily that of ensuring the freedom for OSS to prosper and be successful, by protecting competition. This in turn will imply the second goal – that of positively supporting OSS development and take-up with active measures to encourage new avenues while creating employment inside the EU, and possibly elsewhere.

The strategy for OSS: competition *vs* regulation

To take the first goal, policy instruments will be necessary to restore real competition in software, for a society ever more dependent on it, and with a market situation of polarising oligopoly. Until recently, software was not perceived as being important enough to deserve such attention.

But this attitude is now changing. As we become increasingly dependent on it, there is an argument that the economic consequences of the commercial software industry's failures and inefficiencies are so serious that we should regulate it closely, to protect its users. And far more closely than the considerable efforts that go into protecting the intellectual property rights (IPRs) of its publishers – because software is now as fundamental in our hierarchy of dependence as food, energy, transport and telecommunications.

It is notable that in these other essential areas anti-trust measures have been applied and regulation continues to be strong. Possible areas for regulation in the software market include mandating backward compatibility, open access to program interfaces, and separation between operating systems and applications.

Regulation could be mooted for software for reasons similar to those that prompted regulation in other areas where it has been introduced. Several key factors need to be covered, especially in cases where one software publisher dominates the market to the point of having market power.

A prime candidate here is backward compatibility legislation – making backward compatibility mandatory so that the new and old versions of an application dominating more than 30% of its market continue to work with earlier versions of software and document and data formats. (The exact market share at which this mechanism should be triggered needs to be decided, but at the lower end of the scale for the threshold might be a market share of around 30%). If the product itself cannot be made backward compatible, then filters and adaptors should be provided by the supplier for agreed, common, open formats. Following this is the requirement for open access – the software package or module's interfaces, especially application program interfaces (APIs), should be made freely public, for any product with more than 30% of its market.

Finally, we come to the issue of market control for basic platforms, such as operating systems and utilities of the level of browsers and databases, when they dominate more than 30% of their market.

Here, stricter controls should apply, to avoid abuse of the dominant position. Legal measures might well apply at thresholds of market share, with the intention of controlling the use of the network effect to squeeze out competitors. Such measures might include provisions such that if applications are produced by the same software publisher as the platform, they may only be released one year after all competitors have received the same information and support material as the internal division (documentation and test software) and this transfer must be audited as to time and content.

As part of this, applications supplied by the company that developed the operating system could not exploit special (secret) platform features not open to all competitors, in order to ensure a level playing field in software competition. Also, rulings would ensure that operating systems, or added basic utilities such as browsers, could never treat rival utilities covering the same functions in a degraded fashion, nor act maliciously or confusingly, or reject inputs or accesses from rival suppliers. Otherwise, the dominant supplier could, for instance, place software updates or news from rivals in junk mail, or produce error messages during normal operations to deliberately sow uncertainty in the minds of customers as to the reliability of rival software.

But can a policy do all this? A good example of how policy was able to protect and encourage growth despite resistance from incumbent players (telecommunications operators in this case) is the Internet. Consequently, a possible alternative to the above examples of specific legislation would be to follow what the US FCC chose in the case of the Internet, encouraging and protecting its growth, between 1970 and 1995, against the incumbent telecommunications operators – a policy of defending competition. In the case with which we are concerned here, competition in software would come from OSS, as real competition will ensure that the dependence on software is a healthy relationship, thus enabling our economy to thrive.

At this point in the discussion on policy, we come to the question of software patents. A public debate has recently arisen over the legality of the 30,000 software patents issued by the European Patent Office (Roffel, 2004). Patents are monopoly rights granted by the state. Their overall effect on software is a tendency to inhibit rather than encourage innovation and they also tend to result in legal uncertainties that could endanger OSS (Perchaud, 2003; Probst, 2001; Commissariat Général, 2002; Bessen, 2003; Hall, 2001). Commercial practices such as a nebulous description and a tactic of "patent thicketing" can delay innovation for the lifetime of the patent.

Consequently, for software, they tend to reduce competition, raise prices, slow down innovation, and encourage cartel behaviour (for example, patent pools), so that even if the licensing periods are relatively short (three years, for example), the idea of a software licence is untenable. As well as there being a risk that the negative aspects of proprietary software patent rights might spill over into OSS, there is a risk to commercial software companies if it is shown that their code contains OSS concepts (inadvertently or otherwise) and that the copyleft principle in the open-source licence is being infringed.

Allowing software patents raises a number of issues for open-source software, particularly as regards the risk of OSS being strangled by patent infringement litigation. In the event of an infringement, software patent law would provide the instrument for punishing the company concerned, not at all the intention of OSS licences. Refusal to endorse software patents is one key to open-source expansion of creativity and widespread OSS usage, as the fears of patent misuse are avoided. The EU should perhaps avoid going down the same road as the US, where many now regret that software patents were permitted and acknowledge that this move might have been a mistake.

Far more is at stake than the fate of particular software publishers, and their attendant semiconductor manufacturers and PC vendors. The risk, if competition in software is not preserved, is that the continuing evolution of the information society might be jeopardised.

We should maintain the opportunity for users, interested industry groups and individuals to contribute to OSS works in open communities of development. That is, open access to source code should be assured in a key part of the software industry, as the resulting products are often so superior in many ways.

Would active EU support for freely distributed open-source software be justified?

Is there an economic justification for providing financial support to OSS projects in certain areas, not just creating a level playing field by suitable legislation to protect competition? Does it make economic sense for governments to subsidise work that becomes publicly accessible and which may be diverted into proprietary software?

Some economists have tried to show that government subsidies are at best an inefficient use of public funds. But do these calculations take into account the benefits of giving access to OSS as a result of subsidies, rather than leaving the initiative to chance in the hands of a commercial concern? These benefits are particularly marked given the unique character of OSS development – which can lead to products that may never be produced in a purely commercial software model. For instance, without OSS, we would have no large-scale shared environments at all, as no single commercial concern has sufficient interest in a shared resource or could foresee the results and predict success, or create sound business models for profits. The commercial risk of such an enterprise, dependent on a wide public take-up, is too high.

However, it is quite possible, within the bounds of commercial risk, for a software company to take what is already an OSS success, such as Linux, and create a sustainable business by supporting a packaged version of that OSS or commercialising an application for it. In this way OSS has the capability to generate a new software model, as technical risk for the publisher and support-service provider is reduced.

If there is a policy to support OSS, what should its key aims be?

Taking OSS as analogous to free speech – as a way of communicating software freely – sets the scene for an OSS policy to drive European excellence in software while creating wealth and employment. The policy's key aims are to produce major programmes with a perspective over at least 20 - 30 years.

The first plank in the policy would be to ensure that dependence on software occurs in a way that is safe and sustainable for the economy, through general policy initiatives across all actions the EU takes. This will demand support for forming a large, stable OSS community which could then facilitate employment creation through OSS while protecting competition and the use of open standards for inter-operability.

Such an initiative calls for support for advancing the research into OSS and creating OSS applications that can be harnessed widely by business, and by the EU software industry in its support and systems-integration roles. EU policy should also ensure competition between a number of business models – exploiting synergies between OSS and other models on the basis of "co-opetition" (i.e. combining features of both competition and cooperation) to provide more choice.

A key policy area is to support new software usage directions which are simply not possible under the commercial banner. We may need to establish large-scale shared 'commons' projects at the level of the Internet – cross-industry and cross-society infrastructures. For instance, a strong contender for an OSS demonstrator project would be the next generation of the Internet, one which is secure and rejects malicious software and criminal exploitation.

Any OSS policy would ensure that the provision of the software, data repositories and document formats needed in the public sector is made in an open, unfettered manner, with long-term support.

Policy should also be driving towards a mixed software-industry model, based on a combination of OSS and commercial enterprise, through the positive encouragement of OSS and its open design methods in several aspects. This would include encouraging the development of self-organising creative communities for OSS, involving the users as much as the developers. Furthermore, OSS provides an innovation model for other fields of high technology, where a shared approach may yield common benefits. OSS will flourish with support for education from an early stage on OSS utilities and products, to raise knowledge levels in all types of software, via OSS itself. OSS also opens the door to creating employment in software. It requires vocational training and university-level courses, and a move to an inclusive mode of software employment. Retraining could help mop up unemployment and increase the knowledge value of work in the EU.

A further policy goal is to stimulate the private sector. The overall aim would be to drive an SME-based software industry comprising system integrators – with a new set of common platforms, which come with more robustness and experience of interfacing with alien applications and environments. This would be supported by a value-added resellers (VARs) market, bringing a source of functional modules at low cost plus an educated market. Support and maintenance companies, representing a whole new source of revenues and employment, may thrive on the long-term support of these common platforms. Independent software vendors (ISVs) can flower, having the chance to extend the OSS basic platform, wherever the OSS licence allows it, adding high functionality at low cost. Also, they can build products designed specifically for the OSS operating systems and database markets, in the knowledge that these are market leaders with an educated customer base.

Possible policy approaches

Several options can be entertained, but each requires some deliberation. Certain policies may be rejected as possibly doing more harm than good, and a balanced approach to support is needed. Industrial research, encouraging shared business platforms, and education and training are all areas where policy could possibly play a useful role in promoting OSS.

Towards an EU Policy for Open-Source Software

One support approach could be to mandate OSS in all software open to government influence. This range would cover public-sector or private finance initiatives (PFI) for government projects, or for those private-sector projects receiving public funds, including corporate venture support. However, this could undermine the idea that policy should support *competition* in software – not replace one monopoly by another.

Another approach might be strong official support for the OSS movement in the form of large, closely managed, OSS projects. Again this may well be undesirable, as the close management would destroy the *ad hoc* creative community approach, the key ingredient for success and sustainability, especially with commercial participants. A series of measures that are too heavy and monolithic could kill off spontaneous fast reaction, motivation and creativity by a bureaucratic stranglehold with its overheads of inefficiency.

The way forward must give a *balanced support* that preserves the creative spirit of OSS, that makes real progress in encouraging its use. It should also provide *effective* support to its development and create opportunities for innovation in discontinuities in technology and business models.

Concrete measures for policy

First, concrete measures should focus on competition – the intention of basic policy should be to foster competition through open applications access and an open architecture, with published document formats and interfaces such as APIs. Policy should preclude closed access – which would limit competition, experimentation, and innovation. Policy should also clarify the legal status of OSS, so that users and participating developer companies know where they stand. A selection of carefully constructed conditions for driving open competition will be needed.

Perhaps it is most important not to endorse software patents, for the reasons stated above. The EU should maintain its position, and refuse software patents. Going further, support for OSS in public procurement policy might be pursued by requiring proposals for mixed solutions, as well as pure OSS and pure proprietary environments.

Responding to the need for a public proofing process is also a necessity, to ensure that the OSS source is not contaminated by lines of commercial source code, perhaps with a public certification of "cleanliness". This rights area could also be advanced with a re-examination of the role of trade-related IPR for software in the WTO agreements (TRIPs), and of the place of OSS, to encourage free interchange so that the developing countries may participate in global software markets, joining in the OSS community.

As part of these measures on IPR, it is worth examining the potential role for a body that would hold OSS IPR in a commons at EU level, so that any subsequent recourse is to that body. The body might be financed by the software industry itself, and its associated partners, such as the embedded systems suppliers. This measure would be advanced by an OSS source-code and documentation repository for the whole of the EU, with a set of template OSS licences, acceptable in courts across the EU.

Secondly, concrete measures should encompass support for a range of funded programmes (or simple policy support). Five potential key areas are considered here:

Shared business platforms – The application of OSS to engender the sector and cross-sector *use* of software for shared business activities such as trading, open innovation, and in embedded software within products. The policy must ensure that the commons model really delivers what the commercial model can never provide – additional wealth and employment across many sectors from a common platform without commercial property restrictions, specifically from being *one open* platform. Applications for such common generic platforms and their basic utilities might be:
- trading networks and secure financial transactions, both business and retail;
- health systems and networks for the operation and management of health services;
- education from pre-school – primary, secondary and tertiary, including academic research;
- mobile communications for secure, ubiquitous environments;
- embedded systems for consumer appliances and industrial controls;
- vertical shared innovation environments – pharmaceuticals, oil and gas, central banking and insurance;
- energy management and distribution;
- grid computing and e-Science platforms and databases.

Industrial OSS research – Create an industrial research programme of ten projects per year for *ad hoc* development communities, which can be seeded by the EC. Three examples showing the levels of subjects for these projects are:
- IT security and commercial transactions, including personal privacy, and protection of identity;
- robust, networked, open architectures for mobile and mesh (*ad hoc*) networking for pervasive and ambient computing, for the next generation of mobile multimedia Web;
- middleware for distributed applications, including grid computing.

Education and training – Encouragement of education and vocational training in OSS should be considered at all levels, to form a new generation of students well versed in OSS and to harness their creativity and ideas for the EU community. OSS technology is particularly apt here in its culture, working practices and appeal. The programme of vocational training would help to tackle unemployment among the under 25s, and to quickly create an energetic, well-educated pool of OSS programmers throughout the EU. The educational policy should promote learning programmes at all levels of the education system:
- for schools – distribution of OSS environments and applications as the basis of educational infrastructure within the school;
- in university courses – where OSS can play an important role in computer-science courses;
- in vocational software apprenticeship courses – for vertical markets and for support technicians, to create youth employment.

A further initiative would be to form an open university of OSS – a "Web university" (there will be a need to pay attention to culture) with course materials published electronically, openly, at no charge. It may be spread across many existing universities as a virtual department that collectively works together, over the net across Europe and the world. It could provide formal undergraduate studies in software with degree qualifications, including OSS software development management (software engineering) and legal aspects of OSS, with narrowcast Web conferencing tutorials. A post-graduate research faculty, including testing labs and licence approvals for close industrial collaboration on joint European projects, would continue education. Most importantly it would offer through-life education, with *ad hoc* courses to be taken at will and informally – for example, in a specific (e.g. Linux) or a more generic subject (middleware and application servers), full-time or part-time or on demand, with Web tutorials.

Support the EU software industry in using and participating in OSS – Form a new European software industry segment around OSS and ensure long-term employment opportunities. This would be closely linked to the previous education initiative. It would be based on funded support for two key activities.

The first is to clarify the legal status of OSS licences, via the creation of a holding body for OSS licences, in concert with the main European software publishers and the embedded systems suppliers in Europe. This would contrast with the current situation, of a series of not-for-profit companies.

The second is to engage initiatives for large systems-integration projects using OSS platforms, probably in the (secure) government and military segments, and also for the generic vertical platforms mentioned above, in health, mobile multimedia and so on.

Leverage public procurement – Endorse the use of OSS in the public sector, with support in key areas such as document processing, for formats which must last over 50 years.

Choices for implementing the measures

Each policy area requires the right choice for implementation. A selection of the possible tools that may be used to implement policy, and the application of each, is given in Table 1:

Table 1 – Choices for the implementation of policy measures	
Policy tool	Application
1. Legislation – areas for legislative tools are those concerned with the protection of competition and with restrictive practices, which could include the refusal and reversal of software patents	• Mandate open document formats for public records and documents • Inclusion of OSS in public tenders, in competition with commercial software packages • International trade – protection of OSS in TRIPS-related discussions to ensure the TRIPS agreements are not used as a weapon • Control of monopoly in software markets with anti-trust law • Force interfaces to be revealed, where they harm competition and act as a restrictive practice under EU law • Ban software patents and reverse those given already
2. Supporting funds – a suitable tool for furthering OSS technology and encouraging vocational and general education in OSS, hand in hand with funded R&D	• Software infrastructure, as development and implementation projects • Programmes of innovation – research, development and implementation • Education, at all levels of schooling, plus an OSS administrative environment, university courses, and also an open Web university of OSS, with course materials published electronically, at no charge • Vocational training in the technical and legal aspects • A centre for OSS: an institute for encouraging and co-ordinating OSS, centrally holding licences and the OSS source-code repository
3. Directives – require common agreement across all EU members on aims and content. OSS is likely to be more acceptable as it offers direct cost savings	• Inclusion of OSS in public tenders, in competition with commercial software packages • Legal status of OSS and acceptance of its 'template' licences within local courts
4. Recommendations – show local and central government how and where to use OSS	• Guidelines for procurement of OSS in public-sector tenders • Recommendations to local and central government on where, when and how to use OSS and the various licences
5. Information campaigns	• Promote OSS in all sectors • Promote education in OSS

In conclusion

Open-source software offers us a way to level the playing field in an area where competition is easily stifled due to the nature of the product and its technology. More generally, it also offers a useful model for innovation. But its importance lies in being a significant direction for economic expansion in its take-up in Europe.

On the latter point, OSS may be expected to become a significant factor in strengthening the European software industry and to contribute to the EU's future competitiveness in Information Society technologies. In this regard, it will have a positive influence on the development of two areas in particular: packaged applications – a market currently dominated by overseas software vendors – and the systems-integration business, a European strength. Moreover, OSS could create new opportunities for business development and employment in the knowledge industries. With support and encouragement, its positive impact could be felt across the EU's economy.

Notes

* The views expressed in this chapter do not represent the views of the Joint Research Centre, the Institute for Prospective Technological Studies, or the European Commission.

1 This paper is based on a position paper prepared for IPTS/JRC, delivered January 2004, *'Open-Source Software: Importance for Europe'*.

References

ROFFEL, W., *'What software patents'*, letter to *Business Week*, 12 Jan. 2004.

PERCHAUD, S., 'Software Patents and Innovation', *The Journal of Information, Law and Technology (JILT)*, 4 July 2003. Online at:
http://elj.warwick.ac.uk/jilt/03-1/perchaud.html and elj.warwick.ac.uk/jilt/03-1/rtfs/perchaud.rtf

PROBST, D. (Mannheim University), 'Software-Patentierbarkeit aus wirtschaftswissenschaftlicher Sicht', paper for the German Federal Parliament, Bundestag, 21 June 2001.
http://swpat.ffii.org/events/2001/bundestag/probst/index.de.html

Commissariat Général du Plan 2002/10/17: *Rapport sur l'Économie du Logiciel*, published in France, 17 October 2002.

BESSEN, J. 2003. 'Patent Thickets: Strategic Patenting of Complex Technologies', ROI Working Paper, MIT, 2003.

HALL, B. H. and HAM ZIEDONIS, R., 'The Patent Paradox Revisited: An Empirical Study of Patenting in the US Semiconductor Industry,1979-1995', *RAND Journal of Economics,* vol. 32, 2001, pp. 101-128.

Biography

Simon Forge has Bachelor's, Master's and PhD degrees in engineering from the University of Sussex, UK, and is a Chartered Engineer.

Forge has worked for over 20 years in the information industries, managing a range of assignments in strategy, futures, marketing and business planning in telecommunications, software and computer systems in various countries. He works on strategy formulation, marketing and business planning, by assessing the impacts of technology, regulatory policy and commercial issues. Forge also has hands-on experience of delivering software and systems, most recently in multi-media mobile applications, creating the first multimedia consumer and business services for 3G mobile and in security platforms for mobile.

Annexes

Appendix I

The GNU General Public License (GPL)

Version 2, June 1991

Copyright © 1989, 1991 Free Software Foundation, Inc.
59 Temple Place, Suite 330, Boston, MA 02111-1307 USA

Everyone is permitted to copy and distribute verbatim copies of this license document, but changing it is not allowed.

Preamble

The licenses for most software are designed to take away your freedom to share and change it. By contrast, the GNU General Public License is intended to guarantee your freedom to share and change free software – to make sure the software is free for all its users. This General Public License applies to most of the Free Software Foundation's software and to any other program whose authors commit to using it. (Some other Free Software Foundation software is covered by the GNU Library General Public License instead.) You can apply it to your programs, too.

When we speak of free software, we are referring to freedom, not price. Our General Public Licenses are designed to make sure that you have the freedom to distribute copies of free software (and charge for this service if you wish), that you receive source code or can get it if you want it, that you can change the software or use pieces of it in new free programs; and that you know you can do these things.

To protect your rights, we need to make restrictions that forbid anyone to deny you these rights or to ask you to surrender the rights. These restrictions translate to certain responsibilities for you if you distribute copies of the software, or if you modify it.

For example, if you distribute copies of such a program, whether gratis or for a fee, you must give the recipients all the rights that you have. You must make sure that they, too, receive or can get the source code. And you must show them these terms so they know their rights.

We protect your rights with two steps: (1) copyright the software, and (2) offer you this license which gives you legal permission to copy, distribute and/or modify the software.

Also, for each author's protection and ours, we want to make certain that everyone understands that there is no warranty for this free software. If the software is modified by someone else and passed on, we want its recipients to know that what they have is not the original, so that any problems introduced by others will not reflect on the original authors' reputations.

Finally, any free program is threatened constantly by software patents. We wish to avoid the danger that redistributors of a free program will individually obtain patent licenses, in effect making the program proprietary. To prevent this, we have made it clear that any patent must be licensed for everyone's free use or not licensed at all.

The precise terms and conditions for copying, distribution and modification follow.

Terms and Conditions for Copying, Distribution and Modification

0. This License applies to any program or other work which contains a notice placed by the copyright holder saying it may be distributed under the terms of this General Public License. The "Program", below, refers to any such program or work, and a "work based on the Program" means either the Program or any derivative work under copyright law: that is to say, a work containing the Program or a portion of it, either verbatim or with modifications and/or translated into another language. (Hereinafter, translation is included without limitation in the term "modification".) Each licensee is addressed as "you".

   Activities other than copying, distribution and modification are not covered by this License; they are outside its scope. The act of running the Program is not restricted, and the output from the Program is covered only if its contents constitute a work based on the Program (independent of having been made by running the Program). Whether that is true depends on what the Program does.

1. You may copy and distribute verbatim copies of the Program's source code as you receive it, in any medium, provided that you conspicuously and appropriately publish on each copy an appropriate copyright notice and disclaimer of warranty; keep intact all the notices that refer to this License and to the absence of any warranty; and give any other recipients of the Program a copy of this License along with the Program.

   You may charge a fee for the physical act of transferring a copy, and you may at your option offer warranty protection in exchange for a fee.

2. You may modify your copy or copies of the Program or any portion of it, thus forming a work based on the Program, and copy and distribute such modifications or work under the terms of Section 1 above, provided that you also meet all of these conditions:

   a) You must cause the modified files to carry prominent notices stating that you changed the files and the date of any change.

   b) You must cause any work that you distribute or publish, that in whole or in part contains or is derived from the Program or any part thereof, to be licensed as a whole at no charge to all third parties under the terms of this License.

   c) If the modified program normally reads commands interactively when run, you must cause it, when started running for such interactive use in the most ordinary way, to print or display an announcement including an appropriate copyright notice and a notice that there is no warranty (or else, saying that you provide a warranty) and that users may redistribute the program under these conditions, and telling the user how to view a copy of this License. (Exception: if the Program itself is interactive but does not normally print such an announcement, your work based on the Program is not required to print an announcement.)

   These requirements apply to the modified work as a whole. If identifiable sections of that work are not derived from the Program, and can be reasonably considered independent and separate works in themselves, then this License, and its terms, do not apply to those sections when you distribute them as separate works. But when you distribute the same sections as part of a whole which is a work based on the Program, the distribution of the whole must be on the terms of this License, whose permissions for other licensees extend to the entire whole, and thus to each and every part regardless of who wrote it.

Thus, it is not the intent of this section to claim rights or contest your rights to work written entirely by you; rather, the intent is to exercise the right to control the distribution of derivative or collective works based on the Program.

In addition, mere aggregation of another work not based on the Program with the Program (or with a work based on the Program) on a volume of a storage or distribution medium does not bring the other work under the scope of this License.

3. You may copy and distribute the Program (or a work based on it, under Section 2) in object code or executable form under the terms of Sections 1 and 2 above provided that you also do one of the following:
    a) Accompany it with the complete corresponding machine-readable source code, which must be distributed under the terms of Sections 1 and 2 above on a medium customarily used for software interchange; or,
    b) Accompany it with a written offer, valid for at least three years, to give any third party, for a charge no more than your cost of physically performing source distribution, a complete machine-readable copy of the corresponding source code, to be distributed under the terms of Sections 1 and 2 above on a medium customarily used for software interchange; or,
    c) Accompany it with the information you received as to the offer to distribute corresponding source code. (This alternative is allowed only for noncommercial distribution and only if you received the program in object code or executable form with such an offer, in accord with Subsection b above.)

The source code for a work means the preferred form of the work for making modifications to it. For an executable work, complete source code means all the source code for all modules it contains, plus any associated interface definition files, plus the scripts used to control compilation and installation of the executable. However, as a special exception, the source code distributed need not include anything that is normally distributed (in either source or binary form) with the major com-

ponents (compiler, kernel, and so on) of the operating system on which the executable runs, unless that component itself accompanies the executable.
If distribution of executable or object code is made by offering access to copy from a designated place, then offering equivalent access to copy the source code from the same place counts as distribution of the source code, even though third parties are not compelled to copy the source along with the object code.

4. You may not copy, modify, sublicense, or distribute the Program except as expressly provided under this License. Any attempt otherwise to copy, modify, sublicense or distribute the Program is void, and will automatically terminate your rights under this License. However, parties who have received copies, or rights, from you under this License will not have their licenses terminated so long as such parties remain in full compliance.

5. You are not required to accept this License, since you have not signed it. However, nothing else grants you permission to modify or distribute the Program or its derivative works. These actions are prohibited by law if you do not accept this License. Therefore, by modifying or distributing the Program (or any work based on the Program), you indicate your acceptance of this License to do so, and all its terms and conditions for copying, distributing or modifying the Program or works based on it.

6. Each time you redistribute the Program (or any work based on the Program), the recipient automatically receives a license from the original licensor to copy, distribute or modify the Program subject to these terms and conditions. You may not impose any further restrictions on the recipients' exercise of the rights granted herein. You are not responsible for enforcing compliance by third parties to this License.

7. If, as a consequence of a court judgment or allegation of patent infringement or for any other reason (not limited to patent issues), conditions are imposed on you (whether by court order, agreement or otherwise) that contradict the conditions of this License, they do not excuse you from the conditions of this License. If you cannot distribute so as to satisfy simultaneously your obligations under this License and any other pertinent obligations, then as a consequence you may not distribute the Program at all. For example, if a patent license would not permit royalty-free redistribution of the Program by all those who receive copies directly or indirectly

Appendix I

through you, then the only way you could satisfy both it and this License would be to refrain entirely from distribution of the Program.

If any portion of this section is held invalid or unenforceable under any particular circumstance, the balance of the section is intended to apply and the section as a whole is intended to apply in other circumstances.

It is not the purpose of this section to induce you to infringe any patents or other property right claims or to contest validity of any such claims; this section has the sole purpose of protecting the integrity of the free software distribution system, which is implemented by public license practices. Many people have made generous contributions to the wide range of software distributed through that system in reliance on consistent application of that system; it is up to the author/donor to decide if he or she is willing to distribute software through any other system and a licensee cannot impose that choice.

This section is intended to make thoroughly clear what is believed to be a consequence of the rest of this License.

8. If the distribution and/or use of the Program is restricted in certain countries either by patents or by copyrighted interfaces, the original copyright holder who places the Program under this License may add an explicit geographical distribution limitation excluding those countries, so that distribution is permitted only in or among countries not thus excluded. In such case, this License incorporates the limitation as if written in the body of this License.

9. The Free Software Foundation may publish revised and/or new versions of the General Public License from time to time. Such new versions will be similar in spirit to the present version, but may differ in detail to address new problems or concerns.

   Each version is given a distinguishing version number. If the Program specifies a version number of this License which applies to it and "any later version", you have the option of following the terms and conditions either of that version or of any later version published by the Free Software Foundation. If the Program does not specify a version number of this License, you may choose any version ever published by the Free Software Foundation.

10. If you wish to incorporate parts of the Program into other free programs whose distribution conditions are different, write to the author to ask for permission. For

software which is copyrighted by the Free Software Foundation, write to the Free Software Foundation; we sometimes make exceptions for this. Our decision will be guided by the two goals of preserving the free status of all derivatives of our free software and of promoting the sharing and reuse of software generally.

No Warranty

11. BECAUSE THE PROGRAM IS LICENSED FREE OF CHARGE, THERE IS NO WARRANTY FOR THE PROGRAM, TO THE EXTENT PERMITTED BY APPLICABLE LAW. EXCEPT WHEN OTHERWISE STATED IN WRITING THE COPYRIGHT HOLDERS AND/OR OTHER PARTIES PROVIDE THE PROGRAM "AS IS" WITHOUT WARRANTY OF ANY KIND, EITHER EXPRESSED OR IMPLIED, INCLUDING, BUT NOT LIMITED TO, THE IMPLIED WARRANTIES OF MERCHANTABILITY AND FITNESS FOR A PARTICULAR PURPOSE. THE ENTIRE RISK AS TO THE QUALITY AND PERFORMANCE OF THE PROGRAM IS WITH YOU. SHOULD THE PROGRAM PROVE DEFECTIVE, YOU ASSUME THE COST OF ALL NECESSARY SERVICING, REPAIR OR CORRECTION.
12. IN NO EVENT UNLESS REQUIRED BY APPLICABLE LAW OR AGREED TO IN WRITING WILL ANY COPYRIGHT HOLDER, OR ANY OTHER PARTY WHO MAY MODIFY AND/OR REDISTRIBUTE THE PROGRAM AS PERMITTED ABOVE, BE LIABLE TO YOU FOR DAMAGES, INCLUDING ANY GENERAL, SPECIAL, INCIDENTAL OR CONSEQUENTIAL DAMAGES ARISING OUT OF THE USE OR INABILITY TO USE THE PROGRAM (INCLUDING BUT NOT LIMITED TO LOSS OF DATA OR DATA BEING RENDERED INACCURATE OR LOSSES SUSTAINED BY YOU OR THIRD PARTIES OR A FAILURE OF THE PROGRAM TO OPERATE WITH ANY OTHER PROGRAMS), EVEN IF SUCH HOLDER OR OTHER PARTY HAS BEEN ADVISED OF THE POSSIBILITY OF SUCH DAMAGES.

END OF TERMS AND CONDITIONS

How to Apply these Terms to Your New Programs

If you develop a new program, and you want it to be of the greatest possible use to the public, the best way to achieve this is to make it free software which everyone can redistribute and change under these terms.

To do so, attach the following notices to the program. It is safest to attach them to the start of each source file to most effectively convey the exclusion of warranty; and each file should have at least the "copyright" line and a pointer to where the full notice is found.

Appendix I

one line to give the program's name and a brief idea of what it does.

Copyright (C)

This program is free software; you can redistribute it and/or modify it under the terms of the GNU General Public License as published by the Free Software Foundation; either version 2 of the License, or (at your option) any later version.

This program is distributed in the hope that it will be useful, but WITHOUT ANY WARRANTY; without even the implied warranty of MERCHANTABILITY or FITNESS FOR A PARTICULAR PURPOSE. See the GNU General Public License for more details.

You should have received a copy of the GNU General Public License along with this program; if not, write to the Free Software Foundation, Inc., 59 Temple Place, Suite 330, Boston, MA 02111-1307 USA
    Also add information on how to contact you by electronic and paper mail.

If the program is interactive, make it output a short notice like this when it starts in an interactive mode:
    Gnomovision version 69, Copyright © year name of author Gnomovision comes with ABSOLUTELY NO WARRANTY; for details type 'show w'. This is free software, and you are welcome to redistribute it under certain conditions; type 'show c' for details.

The hypothetical commands 'show w' and 'show c' should show the appropriate parts of the General Public License. Of course, the commands you use may be called something other than 'show w' and 'show c'; they could even be mouse-clicks or menu items – whatever suits your program.

You should also get your employer (if you work as a programmer) or your school, if any, to sign a "copyright disclaimer" for the program, if necessary. Here is a sample; alter the names:

Yoyodyne, Inc., hereby disclaims all copyright interest in the program 'Gnomovision' (which makes passes at compilers) written by James Hacker.

signature of Ty Coon, 1 April 1989
Ty Coon, President of Vice

This General Public License does not permit incorporating your program into proprietary programs. If your program is a subroutine library, you may consider it more useful to permit linking proprietary applications with the library. If this is what you want to do, use the GNU Library General Public License instead of this License.

Appendix II

Building Innovation through Integration

A Microsoft White Paper

July 2000

Integration - A Brief Introduction

One of the hallmarks of human creativity is synthesis – the ability to improve and innovate by making new connections between existing objects and knowledge. Without synthesis, there could be no improvisation, no jazz, no science fiction, no haute couture, and no trendy restaurants serving fusion cuisine. There also could not have been an industrial revolution – or more recently an information revolution – since innovation in industry, as in art, depends on the ability to integrate new ideas into existing systems.

Research and development statistics confirm that the vast majority of industrial innovation relies on existing knowledge. In the United States, for example, more than $169 billion of public and private money was devoted to industrial research and development in 1998. Ninety-two percent of that money was spent in search of ways to apply existing knowledge either to improve existing products or processes (74 percent), or to create a new product or process (18 percent). Only 8 percent of R&D expenditures went toward discovering something completely novel.[1]

Integration is one of the chief methods of creating new applications for existing knowledge. This process of incorporating different functions into a single system in new and better ways is commonplace – so much so that we often hardly notice its importance. In fact, integration has played a behind-the-scenes role in many of the "technological revolutions" that we commonly think of as having been inspired by novel inventions.

Appendix II

The revolutionary expansion of agriculture from mere subsistence into a society-supporting industry rested, in large measure, on the development of a complex instrument for plowing hard soils. The heavy plow was much more a product of centuries of integration than of fresh invention. Early farmers integrated technologies from the fields of metallurgy and engineering, among others. These included the addition of iron blades and a shovel-like moldboard to turn back furrows (credited to the ancient Chinese and later Europeans) and the addition (by the Romans as well as others) of wheels.

Johannes Gutenberg's printing press has long been thought of as a pathbreaking innovation in the history of information distribution. There is no doubt that Gutenberg's innovations in metal casting, alloying, and other areas were essential to the development of movable type. But true mass production of books required more than just Gutenberg's contribution. Only the later integration of movable type with other printing process innovations, including refinements in the manufacture of ink, new and cheaper forms of paper, and later the mechanization of the typesetting process, allowed production of printed material on a massive scale. This in turn opened the way for modern automated printing, in which the imaging, ink and paper are all part of an integrated, computer-controlled process.

Robert Fulton's 1807 steamboat opened a new era in the history of transportation. But its important components, including its basic hull design, the paddle wheel, and the steam engine, had already existed in some form for many years. Indeed, modern steam engines date back as far as the 18th century (when they were used to power sump pumps in flood-prone mines) and the idea of steam power dates back even farther, to the ancient Greeks. Fulton's genius lay in his ability to integrate steam power into a marine propulsion system – a feat that many others were attempting in his time, but with much less success.

Introduced in 1979, the Sony Walkman portable cassette player, which was conceived by company co-founder Akio Morita, ushered in a modern revolution in portable consumer electronics. The novelty of the Walkman lay not in its technology, almost all of which existed in some other form prior to the Walkman. Rather, its novelty came from the way in which Morita and the engineers at Sony combined these existing technologies to create a totally new product and, with it, a new market. Indeed, the "microcassette" had already been around for several years, as had portable transistor radios and earphones. Meanwhile, another technology that would later be integrated into portable electronics – the microprocessor – was emerging as a force in the field of computing by the time the Walkman was introduced.

Integration and the Growth of Computing

Integration has driven the personal computer ("PC") revolution at every level of PC architecture – from the tiny microprocessors at the heart of every individual machine all the way up through the Internet that connects computers around the world. The microprocessor itself began with the integration on a single chip of transistors, resistors, capacitors and connecting wiring. As microprocessors were made more powerful, manufacturers like Intel also integrated on a single chip functions like math processing and digital signal processing that formerly were performed by separate microprocessors.

At the same time, the rapid improvement of microprocessors enabled operating system software developers to make the leap from DOS to an increasingly sophisticated graphical user interface. Further integration multiplied the capabilities of that interface, and thereby multiplied the opportunities for applications that run on top of them. And, of course, one of those opportunities – the capability to connect PCs to the Internet and the World Wide Web – established once and for all that the PC was not just a glorified calculator or typewriter, but an information tool with incredibly broad capabilities for communications, media, commerce, and so on. All of this breadth of capability that we take for granted today was the product of integration.

A.   Integration from Mainframes to Early PCs

In fact, the history of integration in computing goes well beyond the PC. As far back as the mammoth IBM mainframes of the early 1960s, functions like disk control and memory were not integral to the computer's central processing unit, as they are today. They were completely separate – even housed in separate units. Integration of these functions enhanced the interoperability of systems, made them less cumbersome and more user-friendly, and paved the way for modern PCs.

Appendix II

A similar trend emerged on the software side of mainframe computing. Early programs for mainframe computers were purpose-built to suit the customer's specific data processing needs. If the user wanted to perform a task, the user hired programmers to tell the computer how to do it. Programmers quickly realized that this was duplicative, and that by integrating components of past programs they could create general-purpose applications capable of handling different kinds of data that needed to be processed in a variety of ways. This form of integration led to the modern packaged software industry.

With the emergence of the PC in the 1970s, a new wave of hardware integration began that extended well beyond innovation in microprocessors themselves. The very first PCs had no keyboard, no monitor, and no memory that survived after the machine was turned off. Turning the PC into a consumer product required linking the microprocessor with technologies for display, storage, input, and other functions. Most of those technologies already existed in some form, but in other contexts. The disk drive, for example, was developed by IBM for use with mainframe computers and only later integrated into the PC.

B.   Integration in PC Software

The real untold story of the PC era, however, is the importance of integration in the development of PC software. Time and again, software developers have created new, more powerful and more useful products by integrating functions that were once regarded as separate.

Word and Spell

Back in the era of monochromatic screens, Microsoft Spell originated as a separate program used to analyze documents created in Microsoft Word and to notify the user of possible spelling errors. Users lived with the constant hassle of switching from the word processing program to the spell checking program to identify and correct errors. The program switch had to be repeated every time the document was modified, wasting time and potentially taxing the very limited computer memories of the day.

Nonetheless, there was a certain functional logic in the separation. Microsoft Word performed a document creation function, and Microsoft Spell performed a document analysis function. Different functions, different programs.

Responding to consumer demand and their own increasing technical sophistication, the software developers at Microsoft, as well as at WordPerfect Corporation and other makers of word processing software, decided to bridge the functional barrier between the two programs and incorporate spellers into later versions of their word processing programs. In Microsoft's experience, integration of this analytical function into Word itself initially had a very simple benefit: It eliminated the need to switch programs. This spared users considerable hassle and made the speller itself more efficient, since it no longer needed to duplicate all the infrastructure of a stand-alone program.

By marrying two conceptually distinct functions – document creation and document analysis – the word processor developers, probably without realizing the full implications, also created the potential for further expansion of a new hybrid functionality that combined document creation and document analysis. For example, developers quickly recognized its potential for allowing users to customize the spelling dictionary, and its potential for allowing users to pause in midsentence to check the spelling of a particular word.

As the spell feature evolved through later versions it became more active and offered more sophisticated analysis. In the case of Word, users could identify a misspelled word the moment it was typed by setting the program to underline it in red. A user's most common typographical errors could be corrected automatically by comparing them with an AutoCorrect list maintained by the user. Later versions of Word analyzed grammar and syntax on the fly, identifying everything from subject-verb agreement to excessive wordiness. And the most recent versions of Word incorporate an active Thesaurus with which a user can identify possible synonyms for a word simply by right-clicking on it with the mouse.

The incorporation of active language analysis into word processors has proven invaluable in other ways as well. With this feature built in to the program, newer versions can tell what language the writer is using and adjust the spelling and grammar rules accordingly. Word processing programs for pictographic languages like Chinese, which require numerous keystrokes for a single character, have been made vastly less difficult to use by enabling the computer to anticipate a small selection of possible characters based on the first few strokes. The same ability to analyze language is proving crucial in the development of voice recognition software that can distinguish similar or identical vocalizations – like "two," "to" and "too" – based on their context.

All these benefits have come as a direct outgrowth of the integration of document creation and document analysis. They would not have happened without it.

The Arrow Button and Windows

Integration has also influenced the development of Microsoft operating systems. For example, arrow buttons in software programs began outside the operating system as a response to the navigational challenges of the Internet environment. To enable users to "browse" the Web, developers had to come up with an easy way to retrace and re-retrace steps without constantly reentering long Internet addresses. Arrow keys provided an intuitive solution to this navigational challenge. The user who wants to revisit briefly information visited five pages earlier simply clicks the "back" arrow five times. To return again, the user clicks "forward" five times.

Developers immediately recognized that the same navigational device could work in other content-rich environments, such as in Microsoft Encarta and other electronic encyclopedias, or even in navigating through the many files and subfiles on a user's hard drive. As soon as it became clear that more than one program could use arrows, incorporating the code that makes arrows into the Windows operating system made sense as a simple memory-saving measure. Serving many programs with one set of code is more efficient than having many sets of code performing the same function simultaneously.

But the integration of arrows into the operating system also made it easy for software developers to add arrows in any other context where navigation was required. Once the facility for incorporating arrows became readily available, they began to crop up in a wide range of programs where users were confronted with the need to navigate through a large amount of information. Using arrow keys was second nature – like turning the pages in a book – and consumers showed their willingness to embrace the new interface even outside the Internet and reference contexts. Indeed, the ability to navigate through a single arrow-equipped window rather than across multiple separate windows became a feature of Windows itself. In this way, the benefits of a good idea born in one context quickly enriched many others.

The Toolbar and Windows

Toolbars are yet another example of the benefits of operating system integration. Spreadsheet programs were among the most powerful early applications for the PC, allowing users to record and analyze different kinds of data in a complex variety of ways. But the same sophistication that made spreadsheets powerful also made them relatively difficult to use. Struggling for a way to make these programs more accessible, the developers of Microsoft Excel 3.0 for Windows settled on the concept of a "toolbar" – a graphic representation of key functions like "open" and "save" that could be invoked at the click of a mouse. Creating the toolbar was a difficult and time consuming programming task, but one that has produced great benefits for users.

Although Microsoft Excel was the first Windows-based application to include a toolbar, the possibilities that the idea held for other programs were obvious. Other software makers also expended a great deal of effort creating their own versions of the same concept. This was inefficient in three respects: First, developers were wasting time reinventing the wheel rather than working on new ideas. Second, users were confronted with variations in toolbar design that made the user experience less fluid. Third, having multiple toolbars that served the same basic purpose, each running off different source code at the same time, unnecessarily taxed the computer's memory.

The efficient solution to this problem was to expand the operating system platform to provide a single set of code that would support many toolbars simultaneously. Thus, when Microsoft released Windows 95, it included a new toolbar system service available to all software developers. Availability of toolbars as a system service does not, of course, preclude any software maker from creating its own toolbar. It simply takes a function that is inevitably present in some programs and makes it available to many other programs.

The initial benefit of this act of integration was simply that it addressed the inefficiencies of the old design: Developers could spend less time writing the code to support their toolbars and more time concentrating on more important functions. Users working with new programs found familiar toolbars that worked in familiar ways. And multiple toolbars could simultaneously rely on the same basic code, saving memory.

Over the longer term, however, an extremely important additional benefit was that toolbars began to appear in more and more programs. The ready availability of the toolbar code encouraged developers to look for ways to expand the universe of tasks that a toolbar could help to perform. As with arrow button navigation, integration of toolbar support helped developers take a useful idea developed in one context and spread its benefits to many others. And, of course, consumers were the ultimate beneficiaries.

HTML Integration

A more recent innovation came in the mid 1990s, when software developers began to apply the lessons of past integration efforts to the technologies that drive the Internet. One of the fundamental technologies of the Internet was (and continues to be, at least for the moment) the programming tool known as Hypertext Markup Language, or "HTML." At its simplest level, HTML allows web developers to link one set of information to another, thus enabling users to surf from one site to another by clicking on underlined links.

As with past innovations, developers began to realize that HTML offered potential applications beyond its original field. In addition to Internet browsing, HTML could be used to imbed and link information in other, non-Internet applications. For example, most help files for common software applications are now written in HTML, because that format best enables users to find the information they need within a large volume of text. HTML can also be used to help readers navigate within large documents created in Microsoft Word, or among the files on a computer's hard drive. To support these functions, the basic HTML code has to be available to all programs. Integrating HTML code into the Windows operating system made that possible.

C. Lessons of Integration

In a world without integration, ideas developed in one context would never wander far from home. If that were the case, it would place severe constraints on technological innovation. A lot of time and energy would be wasted in coming up with new solutions to address the same basic problems in many different contexts. Also, the number and variety of solutions would produce a great deal of unnecessary complexity, placing a heavy burden on engineers and users alike.

In our world today, of course, integration is virtually inseparable from technological innovation. As we have seen, integration in the field of computers – and computer software in particular – has enabled developers to expand the benefits of particular innovations beyond the boundaries of a single application, creating new possibilities for innovation in other areas. Without integration, we simply would not have achieved the extraordinary advances in computing that we have seen in recent decades.

Integration and the Future of Computing

As they create new frameworks for the future of Internet computing, major software companies are again viewing integration as a crucial element of innovation. Oracle Corporation, for example, recently released its new E-Business Suite 11i, which it touts as "the industry's first fully-integrated e-Business applications suite." The 11i suite integrates functions like web selling and supply chain management, which are now normally managed with separate software applications, into a single set of software tools. Oracle Vice President Ron Wohl argues that "[w]hen given the choice, any business would prefer e-Business applications that are already integrated rather than undertake the custom integration effort themselves."

The newer and smaller dotcom companies are also using integration to drive innovation. RealNetworks, Inc., for example, is less than five years old, but nonetheless a prominent practitioner of software integration. Products like Real Player, Real Jukebox, and Real Download have made the company a leader in the field of online music and video through tools that help Web users discover, acquire, manage, and play audio and

Appendix II

video content. Recently, the company announced that it would for the first time offer these functions, previously relegated to different programs, within a single, integrated suite – the Real Entertainment Center.

The integration of new features into operating systems continues as well. We have seen how the addition of new features and functions has contributed to the development of Microsoft software into a broad, rich platform. The same approach has been reflected in other OS products. Notable among them is Apple's new OS X, which provides an operating system with integrated web browser, media player, address book, e-mail, and other features. In the near future, both OS and application products will undoubtedly integrate additional features that are now being developed separately, including speech recognition, handwriting recognition, and protocols for consistent handling and display of data across many different formats and devices.

Note

[1] National Science Foundation, *Research and Development in Industry: 1998 [Early Release Tables]* at tbl. E-9 (2000).

Index

A

academic freedom, 331, 353
agrobiotechnology, 362, 366-367
Apache, 15, 53, 89-90, 96-97, 102, 109, 152, 433, 464, 480
ARPAnet, 16, 489
ASCAP (American Society of Composers, Authors and Publishers), 234-235

B

Babbage Charles, 105
backward compatibility, 239, 492
Bell Labs, 95, 275
Berne Convention, 113, 116, 131, 375-376
Berners-Lee Tim, 102
biotechnology, 22-23, 295-297, 306-307, 330, 357-359, 361, 363, 365, 367-369, 371
BitTorrent, 218, 433
black box, 43, 280
BRCA (BReast CAncer), 297, 301, 304
Bruns Axel, 267, 272
BSD (Berkeley Software Distribution), 95, 120, 138, 258, 464, 475-476
Burroughs William, 237

C

C programming language, 276, 432
Cage John, 238
Celera Genomics, 365
Christensen, 91-92, 94, 96
C language, 453
closed-source, 57, 434, 440-441, 449, 454, 456, 467, 480-481, 484-486
co-ownership, 288
copyleft, 14, 17, 45, 51, 60, 69, 71-72, 119-121, 143, 150, 162, 256-258, 366, 493
copyright, 19, 24, 26, 34, 40, 45, 51, 53, 60, 70-72, 78, 111-123, 125-126, 129-131, 146-147, 200-201, 206, 226-228, 232, 234, 237, 240-247, 249, 251, 255-257, 261, 265-266, 359, 366, 375-377, 382-387, 390, 418, 476, 479-482, 484, 508-509, 512-515
Creative Commons, 13, 71, 81, 121-122, 125-126, 129, 201, 208, 210-211, 227, 256-257, 268
Creative Commons Licence, 5, 51, 111-112, 122, 130, 208, 210, 212
CROSSTALKS, 5-6, 17-18, 27, 70, 81, 85, 197, 272, 310, 324, 335-337
CSS companies (closed-source software companies), 484-485

Index

D

da Vinci Leonardo, 11-12
Debian, 94, 192, 197, 206-207, 457
digital commons, 51, 69, 314
digital democratization, 184
Digital Literacy Plan, 178, 184, 188
Digital Rights Management, 111, 115, 132, 205, 453
DMCA (Digital Millennium Copyright Act), 242-243, 261-262, 384
Dot.com, 466
dual licensing, 26, 456, 479, 481-483, 486
dub, 148-150, 158
Dyne:bolic, 154-155, 161

E

eBay, 91, 99-100, 103-105, 214
ECMA (European Computer Manufacturers Association), 472-473
EcoScene, 219, 223
ecosystem, 25, 94, 199-200, 205-206, 209, 215, 219, 223, 461, 469, 474-475, 482, 484
Edison Thomas, 203, 233
e-government, 22, 286
Einstürzende Neubauten, 217, 228
ElectronicScene, 200, 213
Emacs, 71, 83, 431
EPC (European Patent Convention), 375, 379-383, 389
EU Copyright Directive of 2001, 113, 117
European Commission, 26, 34, 36, 40, 60, 132, 169, 258, 321-322, 372, 375, 387-389, 407, 426, 455, 459, 490, 502

F

Fanning Shawn, 241
Fano Robert, 430-431, 457

file-sharing networks, 139, 218, 233, 249, 253
first Copyright Act, 112
Fofito, 219, 221-222
Forrester Research, 57
Fortress Europe, 297, 301
FOSDEM, 70-71
FOSS (Free/Open Source Software), 12, 20, 24, 36, 168-169, 182, 186-188, 192, 196, 206-213, 215-219, 224-226
Fountains of goods, 444
free culture, 37, 51, 233, 242
free inquiry, 23, 312-313
free licences, 112, 119-121, 126, 130
free rider, 469
free software, 14-16, 18-20, 36, 41, 44-48, 50-52, 63, 69-76, 78-82, 88, 92, 95-97, 106, 109, 111, 120-121, 126, 135, 137, 139-141, 143, 145, 147, 149-151, 153, 155-159, 161-162, 167-169, 171, 173, 175, 177, 179, 181, 183, 185, 187, 189, 191, 193, 195, 197, 202, 206, 226, 255, 258, 265, 280-281, 312, 357-358, 422-423, 431, 474, 507-508, 512-514
Free Software Foundation, 45, 47, 50-51, 61, 70, 120, 226, 228-229, 431, 475, 481, 507, 512-514
Free Software Movement, 14, 18, 63, 69-74, 76, 81, 232, 251, 312-313, 357, 370
FreshMeat, 121, 408
fundamental research, 23, 296, 309, 311, 315-317, 319-320, 323, 325, 340, 346, 351, 353

G

Garageband, 236, 239, 255, 257, 268
Gardner Joy, 152, 161
gatekeepers, 213, 255
Gates Bill, 11, 37, 54, 98
General Public License (GPL), 13, 33, 41, 45, 120, 140, 431, 462, 507-508, 512, 514-515
GIMP, 154, 161

GNU, 14-15, 44-45, 67, 69-73, 83, 97, 120-122, 127, 135, 140, 154, 187, 192, 194, 206, 229, 258, 276-279, 357, 407, 431-432, 438, 444, 447, 452-453, 462, 475, 507, 509, 511, 513-515
GNU C compiler, 97, 276
GNU Free Documentation License, 121, 127
GNU/Linux, 15, 45, 70-73, 121, 135, 140, 154, 187, 192, 194, 206, 258, 438
gnuLinEx, 169, 185, 187-188, 192, 194-195, 197
Gnutella, 227, 232, 244
Google, 88, 91-92, 100, 104-105, 147
Grateful Dead, 236
Gutenberg project, 16

H

hacker culture, 32, 36, 44, 48, 51-52, 63, 136, 139
Hacker Survey, 208, 212, 228
HapMap Project, 366
Hardin Garrett, 13-14, 371
Harraway Donna, 141, 146, 159
Harwood Graham, 151, 154, 159, 161
Hippel von Eric, 367-368, 411, 420, 423, 443, 455, 458
HTML, 89, 102, 152, 209, 216, 222, 285, 333, 417, 524
Hubbard Tim, 365-366
Human Genome project, 16, 302

I

IBM, 18, 65, 85-87, 91, 93, 105, 140, 226, 252, 357, 433, 449, 466, 519-520
Icotec, 199-200, 211, 213, 225
IETF (Internet Engineering Task Force), 101-102, 472
I-mode, 408

intellectual property rights, 24, 111, 113-114, 116, 119, 132, 333, 339, 361, 363, 369, 372, 390, 414, 418, 469, 491
IP, 93, 96, 143, 332, 464-465, 469, 476
iPod, 106, 249-250
iTunes Music store, 226, 250

K

Kay Alan, 107, 109, 180-181, 195-197, 216
KaZaA, 232, 244, 249
Kepler Johannes, 187
Kuhn Thomas, 86, 107-109, 146, 160

L

Latour Bruno, 42, 54, 64-66
Lessig Lawrence, 37, 51-52, 66, 101, 215, 228, 233, 242, 256, 266, 268-269, 272, 476
Lin Nan, 202, 214, 227-228
Linux, 15, 17, 32-37, 39-41, 45-46, 48-50, 53-54, 56-61, 65-66, 70-73, 88-89, 91-92, 94-95, 101, 103, 109, 121, 135, 140, 152, 154, 187, 192, 194, 206, 213, 248, 250, 258, 276-280, 337, 403-404, 410, 420, 422-423, 431-433, 436-439, 445, 449, 452, 454-459, 466, 474, 480, 495, 500
Lions John, 280, 282

M

Magnatune, 200, 208, 211
Maurer Stephen, 368, 372
McLuhan Marshall, 54, 66, 231, 267
memetic engineering, 48
MERIT/Infonomics, 403, 421
Merlot, 126
Microsoft, 32-36, 39, 48-49, 53-61, 65, 85-87, 89-91, 94, 98, 102, 105-106, 140, 154, 252, 357-

529

358, 369, 421, 433, 448, 455, 457, 466-467, 470, 472-477, 517, 520-524, 526
Microsoft's Shared Source initiative, 58, 466
MINIX, 15, 280, 454, 456
MIT OpenCourseWare, 125-126
Moglen Eben, 34, 51-52, 62, 65-66, 140, 370
Mongrel, 151-153, 155
MP3, 123, 200, 211, 215, 223, 240-243, 249-251, 257-258, 268-269
MPEG (Motion Picture Experts Group), 216, 341
MUDDA (Magnificent Union of Digitally Downloading Artists), 253, 270
MySQL, 25, 152, 226, 433, 449, 456, 479-486

N

Napster, 78, 97, 103, 105, 232, 241-248, 254, 267, 269-270
Netscape, 48-49, 89, 102
Newton Isaac, 141, 187, 296
Nine9, 153-154, 161

O

O'Mahony, 443-444, 454, 458
O'Reilly Media, 37
O'Reilly Tim, 5, 18, 85, 97, 109, 248, 253, 268
OAL (Open Audio License), 256
Occam's razor, 485
open content, 125-126, 129-130, 132
open courseware, 19, 111-113, 115, 117, 119, 121, 123, 125, 127, 129, 131
open ecosystems, 20, 199-201, 203, 205, 207, 209-211, 213, 215, 217-219, 221, 223, 225, 227, 229
open epistemic communities, 398
open source, 13, 16-17, 19-21, 25, 31-42, 46, 49, 51, 57-59, 61-62, 65, 76, 85, 88, 90-91, 93, 95-98, 100-103, 105-108, 140, 143, 168, 187-188, 215, 229, 250, 265, 275, 279, 281, 302, 337, 365, 397-401, 404-405, 408, 411, 413, 415-417, 419, 422-425, 429, 434-435, 439, 441-449, 451-455, 461, 463-464, 466-467, 469, 473-474, 479-480, 483, 485
open standards, 22, 62, 90, 102, 143, 281, 285, 287-289, 313-314, 472-473, 495
open university, 499
open-source movement, 12-13, 15, 18, 25, 33, 43, 56, 58, 62, 71, 76, 106, 254, 267, 310, 357-358, 364, 369, 414, 429, 431, 436, 448, 489
open-source software, 12, 14, 18, 20, 24-26, 33-34, 36-39, 41, 52-53, 57-59, 61, 63, 70, 81, 87, 90, 92-93, 97, 109, 119, 140, 143, 153, 187, 201-202, 206, 226, 233, 251, 257-258, 264, 270, 281-282, 286, 288, 302, 310, 313-314, 337, 395-399, 401, 403, 405, 407, 409, 411, 413-415, 417-419, 421, 423, 425, 430, 433, 440, 444, 449-450, 452, 457-459, 461-463, 466-467, 473-474, 476, 479-484, 489-491, 493-495, 497, 499, 501-503

P

P2P, 103, 244-247, 253-254, 262, 267
paradigm shift, 18, 85-89, 91, 93, 95, 97, 99, 101, 103, 105, 107-109, 337
patent, 11, 22-24, 40, 60-61, 74-75, 77, 90, 131, 266, 295-304, 306, 318-319, 331-333, 359-364, 366-367, 375-379, 381-384, 386-389, 493-494, 503, 508, 511
patent system, 75, 77, 359, 361, 371, 382
patents, 11, 24, 34-35, 40, 51, 60-62, 71, 73-77, 147, 281, 295-304, 306, 332, 339, 359, 361-364, 366-367, 369, 372, 375, 377, 379, 381-383, 385-391, 490, 493-494, 497, 508, 512
peer-to-peer networking, 231, 267, 418
Perl, 15, 96-97, 102-104, 109, 433
piracy, 161-162, 237, 239-242, 245-249, 251, 255, 388, 418
Presley Elvis, 235, 239

proprietary, 12-13, 18, 25-26, 42, 44-45, 47, 53, 58, 69, 71, 73-75, 81-82, 87-93, 95-96, 98-99, 102, 108, 120-121, 125, 132, 155, 186-188, 226, 238, 252, 257-258, 280-282, 288-289, 310, 313-314, 326, 396, 398, 407, 414, 417, 421, 423-424, 429, 431, 434-435, 438, 444-445, 457, 462, 466, 474, 484, 493-494, 497, 508, 515
protecting versus sharing, 304
protection of databases, 116
Public Library of Science (PLoS), 128-129
Pure Data, 157, 161, 258, 268, 271

R

Rai Arti, 368, 372
Rand, 141
Rastafari, 136-137, 139, 148, 151, 158
Raymond Eric, 34, 43, 46-50, 62, 65-66, 89, 93, 100, 106, 109, 140, 229, 233, 250, 370, 409, 420, 423, 455, 458
Reboot.fm, 233, 263-266, 268, 271-272
Red Hat, 33, 35, 53, 85, 90-91, 94, 194, 466
research management, 309, 311-313, 315, 317-319, 327, 342, 350-351
RIAA (Recording Industry of America Association), 116, 226, 229, 232, 237-238, 242-245, 247, 253-255
Rifkin Jeremy, 215, 224-225, 229
Roche, 298, 303
Rojo Dennis (aka jaromil), 154, 161

S

Salk Jonas, 295
Savannah, 408
2GOSS companies (second-generation open-source software companies), 484-485
Sendmail, 15, 89, 96, 102, 109, 433
Seti@home, 98, 105

Slashdot, 38, 61, 71
Sleepycat, 480
social learning, 438, 451
software patents, 34-35, 40, 60-61, 71, 73-76, 281, 382-383, 386, 389, 490, 493-494, 497, 502, 508
sound systems, 149-150
SourceForge, 37, 58, 121, 206, 211, 257, 404-406, 408, 422-423
spin-offs, 303-304, 332-333
Stallman Richard, 5, 13-14, 16, 18, 43-47, 49-50, 58, 69-73, 75, 77, 79, 81, 83, 95, 97, 120, 135, 138, 140, 155, 229, 232, 248, 256, 312, 357, 365, 370, 415, 431, 447, 475
Steiner Rudolf, 13
strategic research, 23, 311, 313, 316, 319-320, 322-323, 328-329, 338-342, 346, 349, 353
Stutz David, 89-90, 106, 108
SuSe, 94, 108
Symbolics, 69

T

Tanenbaum Andrew, 280, 282, 456
Torvalds Linus, 15, 33-34, 36-37, 44-45, 47, 49-50, 57, 62, 83, 101, 213, 227, 229, 248, 432
trademarks, 71, 74, 116, 131, 480, 484
tragedy of the anti-commons, 300
Tragedy of the Commons, 13-14, 362, 371
Tramiel Jack, 175, 196
TRIPS, 24, 113, 375-376, 382-383, 386-388, 498
Tropical Disease Initiative, 368, 372

U

UCITA (Uniform Computer Information Transactions Act), 384-385, 390
Unix, 14-15, 44-45, 47, 70, 85, 89, 95-96, 101, 135, 154, 275-276, 278, 280, 414, 431, 436-438, 452-453, 466, 472, 475

531

V

Vicom, 379
ViverNet, 189-190, 195

W

Web Consortium, 216
Weber Steven, 38, 209, 229, 420, 455, 459
weblog, 38
Wi-Fi, 262-263

Wikipedia, 16-17, 81, 103, 112, 127, 130, 195, 227
Windows, 5, 32-33, 35, 39, 54, 59, 90, 101, 105, 154, 265, 276-279, 337, 357, 456, 467, 472, 474, 477, 522-524
WTO (World Trade Organization), 302, 375, 498
W3C (World Wide Web Consortium), 90, 472, 477

X

XML, 98, 285, 417, 472

List of Pictures

p. 10   No Trespassing – Copyright 2002 Daniel J. Williams, Glennmoore, Pennsylvania.
p. 134   Hasciicam - jaromil, dyne.org rasta coder, http://rastasoft.org

All other pictures by Marleen Wynants:

PART I

p. 30   Make Art, Not War – Chambers Street, New York, 2004
p. 68   Emack & Bolio's Icecream Parlour - 54 Cooper Square, New York, 2004
p. 84   Halp! Earthquake - Chambers Street, New York, 2004
p. 110   Fix your own bike – Animation stand Battery Park, New York, 2004

PART II

p. 166   Noseman – near Warren St, New York, 2004
p. 198   Put things back, you're not alone – AI Lab VUB Brussels, 2004
p. 230   Piper drummer, Bridge Of Allan, Highland Games, Scotland, 2004
p. 274   Cycling, Walking, Skating, Running – West Street, New York, 2004
p. 284   Pourquoi les Bruxellois, Rue de Noyer, Brussels, 1983

How Open is the Future?

PART III

p. 294   No Standing Anytime – Battery Park City, New York, 2004
p. 308   Rector St – New York, 2004
p. 356   Luckily, there is a better way - Citibank Building, Broadway at Chambers St, New York, 2004
p. 374   Abolish Alienation – near Murray St, New York, 2004

PART IV

p. 394   Everything cometh... citation by Charlie Chan – near West Broadway, New York, 2004
p. 428   Bicycles Skateboards Roller Bladers – Liberty St, World Financial Center, New York, 2004
p. 460   Soho door, New York, 2004
p. 478   No tourists beyond this point – Woolworth Building, Broadway at Barclay St, New York, 2004
p. 488   Caution Shared Path – South End Avenue, New York, 2004